U

(

THE DESIGN AND UNDERSTANDING OF SURVEY QUESTIONS

The Design and Understanding of Survey Questions

WILLIAM A. BELSON

North East London Polytechnic

Gower

Published by Gower Publishing Co. Ltd., Gower House, Croft Road, Aldershot, Hants, England.

Reprinted 1982.

Printed and bound in Great Britain by
Robert Hartnoll Ltd, Bodmin, Cornwall.

British Library Cataloguing in Publication Data

Belson, William Albert
 The design and understanding of survey questions

 1 Social surveys
 2 Interviewing
 3 Questionnaires
 I Title
 309'.07'23

ISBN 0-566-00420-8

Contents

PART II: Appendix
(Presented through sheets of microfiche inside the back cover)

Foreword

This enquiry was one of a series of studies of problems in question design carried out by the Survey Research Centre under the direction of Dr William Belson. The total series was financed by grants from a large number of organisations with a working interest in the conduct of survey research and in the application of research findings.

Anglia Television Ltd
Ashridge Management College
Aspro-Nicholas Ltd (Nicholas Products Ltd)
Attwood Statistics Ltd
Audience Studies Ltd (later Market
  Decisions Ltd)
Audits of Great Britain Holdings Ltd
Audits & Surveys, Inc. USA
Australian Broadcasting Commission
Australian Broadcasting Control Board
Bass Charrington Ltd
Beecham Products (UK)
Benton & Bowles Ltd
Birkbeck College, Department of
  Occupational Psychology
Boots Pure Drug Company Ltd
Bovril Ltd
British-American Tobacco Co. Ltd
British Broadcasting Corporation
British Market Research Bureau Ltd &
  J. Walter Thompson Ltd
British Petroleum Ltd
Brown & Polson Ltd
Bureau of Commercial Research and
  Wasey Quadrant Ltd
Bureau of the Census (US Dept. of
  Commerce)
Bureau of Social Science Research, Inc.,
  USA
Cadbury Schweppes Ltd
California State College
Chesebrough-Pond's Ltd
Colgate Palmolive Ltd
Columbia Broadcasting System Inc.
Communications Research Ltd
Doyle, Dane, Bernbach Ltd
Doyle, Dane, Bernbach Inc. Advertising, USA

The Economist and the Economist
  Intelligence Unit Ltd
The Electricity Council
Enskilder Utrednings Institutet AB (Consul-
  tants on Survey Research Methods)
Esso Petroleum Company Ltd
Fisons Pharmaceuticals Ltd
Ford Motor Co. Ltd
The Gas Council
Gillette Safety Razor Company
The Health Education Council Ltd
H. J. Heinz Company Ltd
Hobson Bates & Partners Ltd
Universidad Iberoamericana, Mexico
Imperial Chemical Industries Ltd (Paints
  Division)
Imperial Tobacco Co. Ltd
Independent Television Authority
Independent Television Companies Association
  Ltd
Institute of Statistics, University of Stockholm
I.P.C. (Group Management) Ltd
Intercontinental Medical Statistics Ltd
Jours de France
KBMS Limited
The University of Kent at Canterbury
Kimberley-Clark Ltd.
Kodak Ltd
University of Lancaster
University of Technology, Loughborough
J. Lyons Ltd (Tea Division)
Market Analysis (Australasia) Pty. Ltd
Makrotest Ltd
Market Facts of Canada Ltd
Market Information Services Ltd
MIL Research Ltd
Marketing Advisory Services Ltd

Marketing and Economic Research Ltd
Marplan Ltd
Mars Ltd
Masius, Wynne-Williams Ltd
Mass-Observation Ltd
Merck Sharp & Dohme Ltd
National Central Bureau of Statistics, Sweden
National Criminal Justice Statistics Center, USA
National Opinion Polls Ltd
National Opinion Research Center, USA
Newcastle upon Tyne Polytechnic
The University of New South Wales
Norman Craig & Kummel Ltd
North East London Polytechnic
ODEC, Spain (Consultants on Survey Research Methods)
Office of Economic Opportunity, USA
Ogilvy, Benson & Mather Ltd
The Open University
Petfoods Ltd
Philips Electrical Ltd
Portsmouth Polytechnic, Applied Linguistics Research Unit
The Post Office
Proctor & Gamble Ltd
The Rank Organisation
Reader's Digest Association Ltd
Reckitt & Sons Ltd
Research Services Ltd
Response Analysis Corporation, USA
Roche Products Ltd

Rowntree Mackintosh Ltd
Sales Research Services Ltd
Sandoz Products Ltd
University of Saskatchewan Regina Campus, Communications Programme
Schweppes (Home) Ltd
The Scott & Turner Company and Phillips Laboratories Ltd
G. D. Searle & Co. Ltd
Shell International Petroleum Co Ltd
Shell-Mex & BP Ltd
Smith Kline & French Laboratories Ltd
Social Science Research Council, Survey Unit
Southern Television Ltd
Spillers Ltd
Swedish Broadcasting Corporation
Tate & Lyle Refineries Ltd
The Tavistock Institute of Human Relations
Tilastointi, Finland (Consultants on Survey Research Methods)
Henry Telfer Ltd
The Thompson Organisation Ltd
The Toni Company
Transmark (British Rail)
Unilever Ltd
United States Information Agency
Wasey, Prichard Wood & Quandrant Ltd
The University of York

The author wishes to express his deep appreciation to these organisations for their generous and unconditional support of the series, which included the present enquiry.

Research staff who worked on this project were:

W. A. Belson, BA, PhD, (design and direction);
B. M. Speak, BSc, PhD, Dip.Psych.;
V. R. Yule, BA.

PART I

AIMS, METHODS, FINDINGS AND RECOMMENDATIONS

1 Introduction

On just about every day of the year, survey interviews are being conducted all over the United Kingdom. So too in many other countries. Social and business researchers alike are having questions delivered, by interviewers, to people in all walks of life. On the bases of such investigations, decisions of many different kinds are being made. Some of these decisions relate to social or to political matters. Others relate to business in all its diverse forms. Provided the information produced by these enquiries is accurate, research can have a very constructive part to play in our social and business affairs. Certainly social and business research is widely used. Moreover it is my view, based upon years of professional study and checking of research methodology, that the *competent* and *rigorous* researcher will in general produce findings that are sufficiently accurate for the decisions that have to be made. Indeed, the potential of research as an aid to the decision maker is enormous. I ask my readers to keep this view of the matter firmly in mind as they read what follows in this introductory section and as they work through the report itself.

Confidence in research and in its potential are very important to any society in which it is usual to base major decisions on evidence rather than on someone's unchecked hunch or unchallenged policy or fixation. But that confidence will not go on developing—indeed will not endure—if research findings are from time to time found to be in serious error. Experience with demonstratively inaccurate opinion polls has made this abundantly clear to the research profession and to those who make use of the profession's findings. Untrained or careless or corner-cutting individuals, whether they be in the academic, the social or the business sectors, can produce misleading findings. The methods and tactics of some of them are certain to do this on at least some occasions. For such people, there are many pitfalls. Let me list a few of the more common of them: generalising with confidence from very small samples; generalising from the responses of volunteers; the use of the results from a postal survey for which the percentage returning completed questionnaires is low; generalising to the population from the evidence of discussion groups; asking questions which have not been tested to see if they are understood as intended; asking for sensitive and memory-dependent information through naive questions designed more or less in the armchair; the use of untrained and ill-supervised interviewers; the over-clever interpretation of numerical findings. At the more detailed level, there are many

3

more pitfalls for the untrained, the incompetent and the careless.

The experienced and rigorous researcher who understands both research methodology and scientific method will not fall into the known traps, possibly dragging the decision maker in with him. But even this class of researcher faces problems. Social and business research is still very young as a science and because of this some of its methods and measures are as yet less reliable than they need to be. But their development is an on-going process and it is against this background that the present methodological investigation was undertaken.

The enquiry reported in this book had its initial stimulus in a by-product of a study by the Survey Research Centre of the accuracy of the National Readership Survey of the United Kingdom.[1] This by-product was evidence of considerable misunderstanding, by respondents, of the central question of the research procedure of the National Readership Survey. The salient features of that evidence are given in the 'Review of research reports' on pages 15, 16. That evidence helped to sharpen the interest of Survey Research Centre staff in the general issue of question understanding.

An examination of the available literature on the matter[2-7] provided further evidence of respondent misunderstanding of survey questions. However, those studies, along with that reported by the Survey Research Centre, did no more than open up this important issue: they indicate that misunderstanding was often to be expected, but they did not provide insight into how the misunderstanding occurred.

What seemed necessary as a next step was a broadly based exploratory study of a kind that would provide leads or pointers to the types of misunderstandings that could occur and to the principles that lie behind such misunderstandings. It was expected that such leads and pointers would allow the development of hypotheses about the principles in operation and that in due course (i.e. through subsequent research) these hypotheses would come in for testing through controlled experimentation. There was considerable support amongst research practitioners for such a project.

This broadly based exploratory enquiry consisted of a study of respondent understanding of some 29 survey questions. Into many of these questions had been built, quite deliberately, the kinds of difficulties most frequently found to occur in questions designed for use in social and business investigations.* This seemed to be a realistic approach for identifying the kinds of question misunderstanding that tend most to occur and for a well-grounded consideration of what lies behind such misunderstandings. Such an approach automatically means that the levels of understanding exhibited by the survey respondents in this case cannot

---

*As indicated by a content analysis of over 2000 survey questions drawn from social and market research questionnaires (see details later).

be regarded as fully typical of understanding levels of the general run of survey questions. In fact, the results have not been used in that manner. At the same time, it must be noted that the built-in difficulties are the more commonly occurring kinds. Moreover, many of the question misunderstandings actually found to have occurred sprang out of question features that are very common indeed. Accordingly it would be a form of 'head in the sand' behaviour were the question designer to put aside the findings of this enquiry on the grounds that they could not apply to his own practices.

One feature of this enquiry is that the experimental questions were first delivered as they would have been in a standard pilot interview before any testing was begun. During this initial administration of them, a watch was kept for any expression of difficulty or uncertainty on the part of the respondent. There was virtually no such evidence. *On the other hand, the subsequent testing of the 29 questions provided abundant evidence that each had in fact been subject to a great deal of misunderstanding.*

This finding is totally in line with subsequent experience and it is of considerable significance and importance. Standard piloting is widely used as the sole system for checking the adequacy of questionnaires and their constituent questions. Standard piloting involves having interviewers deliver questionnaires in the usual way, looking for difficulties for either respondents or themselves. Whereas there seems little doubt that piloting is a very useful way of detecting the difficulties which a questionnaire raises for the *interviewers,* its power to reveal *respondent*-centred difficulties is another matter altogether. That is abundantly clear from the results of this enquiry: major misunderstanding of questions occurred without the interviewer being aware of this in a normal administration of the questionnaire. It thus appears that survey researchers who rely upon piloting alone are failing to detect even substantial misunderstanding of their questions by their respondents. Because of this, the technique developed through this enquiry for testing respondent understanding of questions has been described in full and a shortened working version of this testing procedure has also been presented. The *piloting* of a questionnaire is needed for detecting interviewer difficulties—but genuine question *testing* is essential for identifying *respondent misunderstanding* of questions.

An important part of the report described in this book is the Appendix, in which are presented all the different ways in which the 29 test questions were understood by the respondents. With this Appendix the student interested in further analyses of response data will be in a position to carry out such analyses. However, for economy reasons, this Appendix is presented only in microfiche form (inside the back cover). A limited number of full printed copies of the Appendix is available through the author, but a well-equipped library should allow students to get enlargements of the microfiches of any required section of the Appendix.

The findings of this enquiry have implications that go well beyond the boundaries of survey research. They have a strong bearing upon the efficiency of mass communication, whether by radio or television or press or film. If statements being made by the would-be mass communicator are being misunderstood, then he is not succeeding as far as those parts of his message are concerned. In fact, research into the comprehensibility of mass media output has brought out very clearly indeed the failure of many members of the audience to understand what is being said to them.[9-12] Interestingly, these failures are not limited to the intellectually dull. Those in the upper sector also misunderstand. Not as much as those in the duller sector, but they misunderstand nonetheless. In broadcasting, the reasons for the failure are not hard to find. In the first place, broadcasters do not always talk in the language of their audiences—some seem particularly averse even to *trying* to do so. But there are other reasons as well—the same kinds of reasons as produce misunderstanding of survey questions.

Perhaps the biggest offender amongst the mass media is the official 'form', where an obsession with complicated expression can defeat all but those who are very determined to understand. Even these are frequently defeated because they don't have the language or the legalistic skills necessary for decoding the message on the form. Consider taxation forms, various employee forms, social security forms, legal aid forms, and so on. The financial and social waste produced by the basic incomprehensibility of many such forms is well known to society and particularly to those who are defeated by them. But those forms go on being printed with their incomprehensible questions and with equally incomprehensible explanations about some of the terms in them. What is needed is the systematic testing of forms for the detection of any sources of misunderstanding or incomprehensibility within them. The methods described in Chapter 9 can be used directly for such a testing programme.

But let me return to the testing of *survey* questions. By and large it is not being done, most research agencies being content to stop at the level of piloting—a procedure quite unsuited to the detection of respondent misunderstanding of questions. Part of the reason for this situation is that researchers and those who pay for research are not aware of what they are omitting to do—of the real need to go beyond piloting. But there is another reason. Question testing costs money and it eats up a little time. However, the extra time and the extra money are both of a minor order and many research organisations could afford question testing if they really cared enough. My own view is that change will occur when the *client* demands it. And I think it much more likely that his demand will be met if he also makes available the relatively small amount of extra money that is needed to pay for question testing. As in most other fields, progress in question design depends upon a combination of caring and of the means to do something about one's caring.

William Belson, 1980

2 Brief guide to aims, methods, findings and recommendations

Aims

This was an exploratory study designed to investigate respondent misunderstanding of survey questions and to provide insights into the processes and the principles involved in such misunderstandings.

Methods used

Twenty-nine experimental questions were spread between four carrier questionnaires. Each questionnaire was first delivered in the ordinary way to a sample of adult respondents. Following, this these respondents were asked for a second interview. This was a long intensive interview designed to reveal how the seven or so experimental questions included in their particular carrier questionnaire had been understood in the first interview. Between the four carrier questionnaires, a total of 265 persons went through both interviews. In the process all 29 questions were tested for respondent understanding. The intensive interview was fully tape-recorded.

Findings

Findings for each of the 29 questions tested are presented in detail on page 49– 349 and are brought together on pages 350–389 under appropriate headings:

1 The proportion of respondents who understood the test questions as intended (pages 350– 351).

2 The relationship between respondent characteristics and tendency to understand the questions as intended (pages 351– 355).

3 The interpretation of a number of commonly used words and some other indications (pages 352– 370).

4 Fifteen sets of hypotheses about the nature and the causes of respondent misunderstanding of survey questions (pages 370– 389).

Recommendations

Recommendations stemming from this enquiry are set out on pages 390–397 and are as follows:

1 There should be regular use of the shortened question testing technique described in this enquiry for detecting misunderstanding of survey questions.

2 Steps should be taken to investigate further the 15 sets of hypotheses that emerged from the enquiry. This work should be undertaken as a means of extending reliable knowledge about the nature and the causes of misunderstanding of survey questions.

3 Aims and origins

Aims

The enquiry had four principal aims:

1 To investigate the particular ways in which survey respondents understand/misunderstand a wide range of questions put to them in a survey interview.

2 To determine the level of understanding of each of a number of experimental questions and to establish the relationship between question understanding and various characteristics of respondents.

3 To provide an empirical basis for the formulation of hypotheses about the principles and processes involved in such misunderstanding as occurred.

4 To formulate an easy-to-use system for general use in testing survey questions.

The investigation of misunderstanding was necessarily exploratory in character, being designed mainly to indicate where, in this broad area of enquiry, detailed and controlled studies might most usefully be concentrated.

Origins

The origins of this enquiry have already been described in the Introduction. They are, briefly, evidence of major misunderstanding by respondents of a central question in the National Readership Survey of 1959,[1] the findings of research published up to that time[2-7] and the support for the enquiry by members of the market and social research professions. The indications of the published research findings available at the time the present study was originated and planned are presented in Chapter 4, which is a review of that research.

4 Review of published research on the understanding of survey questions

At the time this study was designed, relatively few reports of empirically based research into the understanding of survey questions had been published. Since the appearance of the present report in mimeographed form, very little else has appeared. It is to nobody's credit that anything so important to survey research should have been so neglected.

Section 4.1 is concerned solely with relevant research published (or then available to the writer) up to the time the present enquiry was being designed. Studies that have become available since its completion are referred to in Section 4.2 (later reports of research).

4.1 EARLIER RESEARCH

In what follows immediately, a distinction is made between reports bearing directly upon the understanding of survey questions and reports about the understanding of other material.

Understanding of survey questions

In 1944 Hadley Cantril and Edrita Fried[2] published a paper based on a small-scale (40 cases) but intensive study of the understanding by respondents of survey questions.

The researchers set up a number of situations or difficulties which they expected to produce question failure of some hypothesised kind, for example: questions that are too vague to permit precise answers; questions that are obscure in meaning; questions that are misunderstood because they involve technical or unfamiliar words. Cantril and Fried chose a series of opinion poll questions that they considered characterised these situations or difficulties. They proceeded to deliver these poll (experimental in this situation) questions to a set of 40 respondents, and to follow up each experimental question with a testing sequence intended to reveal how that experimental opinion poll question had been understood. The methods and the results of doing this are of considerable relevance to the present enquiry. Hence for several of the experimental questions, the methods and the results have been presented here fairly fully.

1 *A question thought to contain terms too vague to permit precise answers*

(a) *The question to be tested.* 'After the war is over, do you think people will have to work harder, about the same, or not so hard as before?'

(b) *Finding out how the experimental question was understood.*

(i) *The term 'people'.* The respondent was asked: 'When you said that people would have to work (harder, about the same, or not so hard), were you thinking of people everywhere and in all walks of life—labourers, white-collar workers, farmers and business men—or did you have in mind one class or group of people in particular?' If the respondent said that by 'people' he meant one class or group, he was asked to say not only which class or group he meant but also how other groups will fare in this respect.

(ii) *The term 'harder'.* The respondent was asked: 'When you said before that people would have to work harder, did you think then that they would have to work longer hours, that there would be more competition, or that in general a higher quality of work would be demanded?

(iii) *The term 'as before'.* The respondent was asked: 'And when you said that people would have to work _____, did you mean to say that they would have to work _____ than/as now in these war times, or _____ than/as in the old days of peace?'

(c) *Some findings.* The researchers concluded as follows for some of their findings. To slightly more than half the group of 40 respondents, the word 'people' meant 'everybody'; to a third of them it meant 'a particular class'; about one in ten did not know what it referred to. The word 'harder' meant 'higher quality' to some, 'more competition' to others, and 'longer hours' to the rest. The phrase 'as before' meant 'before the war started' to half the group, and 'after the war started' to the rest.

2 *A question thought to be obscure in meaning*

(a) *The question to be tested.* 'If the German army overthrew Hitler and then offered to stop the war and discuss peace terms with the Allies, would you favour or oppose accepting the offer of the German army?'

(b) *Finding out how the experimental question was understood.* The interviewer said: 'We are wondering whether the question I just read to you means the same thing to everybody who answers it. Would you mind telling me in your own words what you understood it to mean?'

(c) *Some findings.* The authors concluded as follows: only 11 of the 40 respondents could be said to have understood by the question what was intended; 7 could not say precisely what the question meant to them. The meaning most commonly accepted by the others revealed what the authors describe as an 'obvious confusion'—they identified the German people with the German army.

The Cantril/Fried enquiry yielded numerous other findings of a similar kind.

Obviously the Cantril/Fried enquiry has weaknesses: the number of respondents was small and their origin and character were not given; some of the test questions imposed rather arbitrary choices upon respondents; some of the checking questions were themselves quite difficult. Nonetheless the results do strongly indicate that serious misunderstanding occurred with the types of questions that were studied—types that the authors regarded as not uncommon. In addition, the checking procedures used by Cantril and Fried offer a clear line of advance for the systematic testing of questions—a line of advance that appears to have been almost completely lost to researchers during the next decade or so and which is likely to be much more effective than the simple-minded piloting procedure that is still in general use today.

Angus Campbell[3] in his 1946 paper raised again the issue of question understanding, also in the context of an opinion poll. He referred to a check made by the Division of Program Surveys of the US Department of Agriculture, upon a wartime opinion poll question* dealing with the 'loyalty' of German aliens living in the USA during the 1939—1946 war. In the checking study, this poll question was asked of a small Philadelphia sample, but its delivery was followed up by a non-directive probe to find out the meaning the poll question had for the respondents. Approximately the same proportion (percentage not given) endorsed the answer (only a few are loyal', as did in the original opinion poll. But according to the checking study, people saying that these aliens were disloyal did not necessarily mean that they would do or say things harmful to the USA. Many meant something quite different. The Campbell paper gives too little information for a critical appraisal of the

---

*I am going to ask you about several groups of people in this country. First, let's take Germans who are not citizens—that is, German aliens. Do you think most of them are loyal to the United States, about half are loyal, or only a few are loyal?'

of the checking study or of its findings, but it does indicate a possibly serious source of trouble.

Using a different methodological approach, Terris[4] in 1949 presented a paper under the title 'Are opinion poll questions too difficult?' She had 144 opinion poll questions rated for 'readability' in terms of both the Flesch and the Dale and Chall readability indices.[5] From these ratings she arrived at a pair of 'reading ages' for each of the 144 poll questions, that is, the average educational age of those able to read the questions concerned. She linked those reading age ratings to available normative data about the educational levels attained by the population of the USA. On the basis of this evidence she concluded that:

132 of the questions were too difficult for 12 per cent of the
    US population
106 of the questions were too difficult for 23 per cent of the
    US population
14 of the questions were too difficult for 73 per cent of the
    US population

For a number of reasons, we should be very careful in interpreting these results. The Flesch and the Dale and Chall indices are based upon the *reading* process—and not on 'called out' material as in survey interviewing. The Flesch and the Dale and Chall ratings for specific poll questions were by no means the same. In the circumstances, perhaps we should limit our interpretation of the Terris[4] findings to saying that they provide grounds for concern about the understandability of opinion poll questions.

Nuckols[6] in 1949 reported on a study in which 315 opinion poll questions were rated in terms of the Flesch 'yardstick'[5] (an earlier version than that used by Terris). Its application yielded 'estimated reading age' for each poll question. Nuckols reported that: 'Many questions are framed and presented to the general population that are either too abstract or too wordy' [these terms being references to the indicators making up the Flesch index] 'for people with little or no formal schooling to understand'. He qualified this conclusion by explaining, 'for the majority of questions the readability level is satisfactorily low. It is the occasional flight into verbosity that the pollsters should attempt to reduce'. Here too, because of the methodology used, the findings should be interpreted with wariness.

In a later study by Nuckols[7] (1953), different elements of methodology were introduced. He checked on 9 opinion poll questions through 48 middle-income respondents. In this checking system, each of the 9 questions was delivered to the respondent and immediately after this the respondent was asked to 'repeat in his own words the meaning of the question as nearly as he could'. Nuckols reports that of the 430 verbatim replies so gathered, 17 per cent were either wholly or partly wrong and he added 'In no instance did a respondent say that he did not hear a question or that he misunderstood it'.*

Of the methodology used by Nuckols, we should note that the respondent who repeats back the question with its various concepts seemingly intact may yet have interpreted those concepts in a highly individualistic way. On the other hand, repeating a question back 'in your own words' is, in the writer's experience of that process, a very difficult and chancy task for the survey respondent, and one that may produce a false impression of failure to understand—especially for the respondent who lacks verbal skills. So here too, some wariness in interpreting the findings is necessary.

In a 1962 publication[1] Belson reported on the results of a study of the validity of the National Readership Survey of the United Kingdom. One part of this study involved assessing the degree to which the key question in the procedure was understood as intended:

> 'I want you to go through this booklet with me, and tell me,
> for each paper, whether you happen to have looked at any
> copy of it in the past 3 months, it doesn't matter where."

> NOW EXPLAIN
> 'looked at', 'any copy',
> 'past 3 months (i.e. since ...)'
> 'doesn't matter where'.

Normal practice in the National Readership Survey was that the interviewer was required to deliver this question in conjunction with a booklet of the mastheads or logos of about 90 publications. For each publication named as 'looked at in the past 3 months', a second question was asked with the purpose of finding out when was the *last time* that publication was 'looked at'.

In the special check made on the accuracy of the results of the NRS survey, a normally conducted NRS interview was followed by an extended intensive interview focused upon 4 of the 90 or so claims made by the respondent in the NRS interview. The purpose of the extended intensive interview was to secure a fresh and heavily challenged estimate of when those four publications were last looked at. When this had been done, the results for the original NRS survey and the intensive interview were compared (for the four publications under scrutiny). If a difference was found to exist for any one of the four, then the respondent was put through a confrontation process intended to illuminate how the differ-

---

*This particular study also introduces Flesch ratings again, but these are not of much relevance to the main thrust of the enquiry or its findings.

ence had occurred.

In the course of the confrontation, a lot of evidence emerged about how the NRS question had been interpreted by the respondent. This evidence indicated that considerable misunderstanding had taken place. Confrontation was of course limited to those estimates for which there was a difference in the readership results from the two interviews, namely from 557 of the 3515 first interview claims that were checked. From those 557 confrontations, there emerged considerable evidence of misunderstanding of at least one of the two questions. The principal forms of misunderstanding of the first question are set out below.

> The expression 'in the past 3 months' was sometimes interpreted as one of the following: usually; regularly; ever; recently.

> The expression 'any copy' was sometimes interpreted as 'your own copy'.

> The expression 'and tell me, for each paper, whether you have looked at ... ' was frequently interpreted as ' ... and call out only the ones you have looked at'.

> The expression 'you' was sometimes interpreted as 'you or your spouse'; 'you and your spouse'.

> The qualifying terms 'any copy' and 'doesn't matter where' were often overlooked.

This particular study was not designed to yield quantitative evidence about each type of misunderstanding of the NRS questions. Rather it was meant to determine the extent of error in the NRS results and to provide evidence about the *kinds* of difficulties and events that lay behind such errors. Nonetheless it was clear that question misunderstanding was a major source of trouble*—and that there existed a strong

---

*It is noteworthy that the NRS questions have changed but little since the Belson enquiry, the present form of the key question being:

> "I want you to go through this booklet with me, and tell me
> for each paper, roughly how many issues you have read or
> looked at recently—it doesn't matter where.
> As you look at each card, will you tell me which of the
> statements applies?"
> > NOW EXPLAIN
> > 'read or looked at'
> > 'it doesn't matter where'
> > 'any copy'

case for launching a special investigation into that source of trouble.

Another line of thought on question misunderstanding was presented in Klare's[8] paper of 1950. Klare referred to earlier findings of a negative association between educational level of respondents and the percentage of them giving indefinite replies to poll questions. He regarded this evidence as strengthening his hypothesis that the percentage of indefinite responses to a poll question could be used as an index of understandability. He presented results from several analyses.

1 For 7 pairs of questions which had been delivered in split run surveys by a research organisation, he had each question rated on the Flesch index of readability. For each pair, the Flesch index was different. For 6 of the pairs he found that the question with the lower readability index got the higher level of indefinite responses. For the seventh pair, there was no difference in percentage of indefinite answers in spite of the difference in the Flesch indices.

2 In a second study he linked a Flesch rating and the percentage of indefinite responses for each of 138 poll questions. He reported a correlation of +0.25 between difficulty level of questions as indicated by the Flesch index and the number of respondents giving an indefinite answer.

Nuckols[6] (1949), carrying out a similar type of comparison, found no meaningful correlation. Unfortunately there is insufficient information in the Nuckols article for speculative comment about the reasons for the different findings. At the same time, the Klare correlation is really only very small (0.25).

Research bearing indirectly upon the issue of question understanding

At the time the present study was planned, there were available for study several reports dealing with the comprehensibility of radio talks. It seemed to the research team that these enquiries were of relevance to the problem under consideration, both with respect to their findings and to the methods used to assess level of understanding.

Vernon[9] reported in 1950 on an investigation into the intelligibility of Forces Educational Broadcast talks. He based his studies on members of the Forces and on the listening public. For each of a number of talks, a group of Army personnel, widely varied in terms of intelligence, listened to a recording of the talk, rated it for interest and for apparent difficulty and then were asked to make a written reproduction of the main points presented in it. These 'essays' were then marked by examiners and a score was allocated to each. Adults from the BBC's listening panel also took part and were processed in the same way. In addition, the script of each talk was analysed in order to relate the characteristics of talks to the degree to which the talks were understood.

Results indicated that little of the average broadcast was taken in except by those with secondary school education and above average intelligence and even for these there was a considerable degree of failure. Comprehension varied substantially between talks and in this study it was quite highly related to interest in the talk. The analysis of scripts indicated that the talks which were best understood tended to be those featured by simplicity of language and style, concreteness of content, short sentences, simple words and low density of prepositions.

The methods used by Vernon for measuring and grading a listener's understanding of a talk leave much to be desired. With the essay method there is no guaranteeing that the evidence that a particular major point has been understood will be presented in the written reproduction. Further, anyone judging the essay output of the average listener (for understanding of a major point or points) will rapidly become aware of the unreliability and the general chanciness of the marking process.

Some years later, Belson[10] tested the comprehensibility, for members of the general radio public, of short talks designed for them by journalists who were each keyed to the purpose of getting a number of principal ideas across to that public. These were ten-minute talks in the series 'Topic for tonight'. About 1,100 adults, representative of the listening public in terms of age, sex and occupational level, came in groups of about fifteen at a time to a meeting room in central London. There they were asked to listen carefully to a record of a single talk, knowing that they would then be asked questions about it. After the playing of the record, they wrote down, under examination-type conditions, brief answers to questions each of which had been designed to test understanding of a specific point in the talk. This is the specific question method—a development intended to overcome some of the weaknesses of the essay method and extending an approach used by Cantril and Fried.[2] Personal details about each respondent were also gathered and an intelligence test was delivered. The 26 talks tested in this way were content analysed to provide a basis for identifying those of their features which were positively or negatively correlated with understanding.

The results indicated a considerable failure to grasp either major or minor points in these talks, the average score for the 26 talks being 27 per cent. Major points were no better grasped than minor points. There was considerable variation in score between individuals and it was also found that comprehension was higher for men than for women, for the better educated and the more skilled, for the more intelligent, and for those aged under 35 years. The results also showed that three major sources of comprehension failure in these talks were: the over-estimating by the broadcaster, of the extent of the listener's background knowledge of the subject matter of the talk; the use of too many words that were unfamiliar to the respondent; the presentation of a talk in a poorly organised and unsystematic way. It was also reported that comprehensibility of these talks was *positively* associated with the frequency of numerical references and with density of active verbs, of adverbs, of personal pronouns; that it was *negatively* associated with density of abstract nouns and of adjectives.

Both the Vernon and the Belson studies provide evidence of considerable communication failure—where such failures were unexpected and had been guarded against by the broadcasters. Moreover, intelligence in the respondent was not sufficient to overcome the failure to understand. And the extent of the failure to understand was associated with certain characteristics of the spoken output.

Knowledge of words, concepts and facts relevant to the understanding of survey questions

Finally, it is worth considering the findings of several enquiries which dealt with certain of the public's basic equipment for understanding things that have been said to them, namely their knowledge of words, concepts, facts.

Mass Observation Limited published a report in 1947[11] of a check on reader understanding of words in a government White Paper of which the then British Prime Minister had said: 'The White Paper is written in simple language, and I am sure the bulk of the people can read it and understand it'. The check was limited to men drawn from the lower middle, the artisan and the unskilled working class sections of a population. The words so tested were of varying difficulty and they were all tested in the context of the White Paper itself. The test results showed that although words such as 'flexible', 'deprive', 'preceding', 'attainment', and 'assess' were reasonably well understood (actual figures were not given in the report), words like 'ultimately', 'resources' and 'subordinates' were understood by only about half the respondents and very few people understood 'formulate' or 'conception'. When two difficult words were used together, understanding was further reduced and only a third of the respondents understood phrases such as 'rigid application'.

In a BBC enquiry reported in 1954,[12] Belson tested viewers to determine their knowledge of words and concepts which were to be used in a television series, this series being designed to inform the general public about current economic facts and figures.

Tests were delivered to 300 persons representative, in terms of age, sex and occupational level, of the projected audience of the series, namely the general public less (only) the lower 20 per cent in terms of occupational level. The results indicated that there was a great deal of variation in terms of the percentage of people knowing the words tested. Thus while the words 'exports', 'imports', 'overtime' were known by about 8 in 10, less than 1 in 10 knew the meaning of terms like 'primary producers', 'terms of trade', 'commodity prices'. Between these extremes, some of the findings were as follows: between 4 and 5 in 10 knew the meanings of 'dollar reserves', 'devaluation', 'wage rates'; about 7 in 10 knew terms such as 'retail prices', 'volume', 'stable', 'manufactured goods'.

Obviously there are major gaps in the word knowledge of the general public and this bodes ill for any broadcaster who ventures beyond simple language. It constitutes another sharp warning to the question designer who cannot express his questions in the language of the people he wishes to have interviewed.

Summing up on the literature of research

The research that had been published by the time the present study was being planned left little doubt that misunderstanding of messages and of survey questions is likely to occur and does occur. At the same time, the research bearing directly on the understanding of survey questions does little more than open up the issue. It tells us that failures occur and it indicates a range of methodological approaches for conducting studies of question understanding. But it does not tell us much about the processes and the principles that are involved in the misunderstanding phenomenon and it is far from providing the question designer with guide lines—even vague indicators—for the construction of his survey questions. The present enquiry was to be an exploratory beginning intended to make advances in that direction.

4.2 LATER REPORTS OF RESEARCH

Since the planning of the research reported in this book, the main published contribution to the study of respondent understanding of survey questions is a report by W. D. Gordon[13] (1963), under the title *Double Interview*.

Gordon set out to test question understanding through a two step process in a single interview. In a first step, the informants were taken through a questionnaire in the usual way. In a second step, each question in turn was repeated to the respondent with the request to tell the interviewer: what exactly he thought the question had asked for; and why he thought the question had been asked of him. Gordon reported on the results coming from a test he made with 30 men and teenage boys.

Case 1, involving the question 'Which of these shops are near enough for you to buy a suit from if you wanted to?' Some of the interpretations reported by Gordon were as follows: the term 'shops' was interpreted as 'local shops I can reach without public transport'; the total question was interpreted as 'Which particular one of the shops on the list is the nearest I could get to?'/'Which shop is the nearest to my style'/'Which is the most popular tailor in my district—the one I prefer?'

Case 2, involving the question 'How many suits do you have at present— that is, suits you are still wearing for some occasion or other?' Some respondents replied in terms of respectable suits (i.e. excluding ones worn only 'round the house').

Case 3, involving the question 'Have you ever bought any other clothing apart from suits at the last shop?' Some said they had thought of sports jackets as opposed to underwear and others understood they should exclude overcoats and raincoats.

Case 4, involving the question 'Which of these tailors have you heard of?' The expression 'have you heard of' was sometimes interpreted as 'Which of those on your list have you seen *personally?*'/'Have you actually come in contact with them?'

Gordon enquired also into *why the respondent thought the questions had been asked of him*. He concluded that there was a lot of misunderstanding of a defensive kind about why the questions were being asked ('you wanted to grade me'/'you wondered if I was just looking for the cheapest thing'/'did I feel out of place in the shop?') Gordon suggests that this reaction is 'likely to produce unreliable answers and may well play havoc with research findings'. He points out that the double interview allowed him to recognise ambiguities that may not have come to light in a less intensive testing operation.

Gordon's findings contribute to the strong case for acting on the results from the present enquiry. Question testing must be seen as an integral part of the development of survey questions.

5 Methods of research used: summary

Some 29 questions were tested to determine the degree to which survey respondents understood them. Most of these questions were designed to incorporate difficulties of the kinds quite frequently found in survey research questionnaires. The test questions were spread fairly evenly among four (carrier) questionnaires (i.e. 7 or 8 to each). Apart from the test questions, the four carrier questionnaires were much the same. The 29 test questions and their carrier questionnaires dealt with the public's use of and reactions to television.

For each of the four carrier questionnaires, the testing procedure was as follows. The questionnaire, with its 7 or 8 test questions, was delivered to a sample of survey respondents in the usual way by ordinary market research interviewers. Next day this interview was followed by a second interview conducted by a different person, namely an intensive interviewer. The latter spent an hour or more attempting to find out how well or badly the respondent understood the test questions which had been included in her/his particular questionnaire and the nature of such misunderstanding as occurred.

In all, 265 respondents went through the double interview (i.e. first plus intensive interview), 57-64 on each of the four versions of the questionnaire. The four samples of 57-64 were approximately equal in terms of age, sex and occupational background. The whole enquiry was regarded as exploratory in character in that it was meant to provide grounds for formulating hypotheses about the principles and processes of respondent misunderstanding of survey questions; and to identify the different kinds of misunderstanding that occurred with enough frequency to warrant further enquiry.

6 Methods of research used: details

THE QUESTIONS TO BE TESTED

Establishing the categories of questions which it would be relevant to test

For the proposed work to be of value to research practitioners, it was necessary that the forms of the questions studied should be similar to the forms used in general practice. Thus if questions with double negatives in them were *not* being used in questionnaires, there would be little practical value in featuring such questions in the enquiry. On the other hand, if it was common for single questions to have in them three or four separate ideas or elements of meaning, then there would be a strong case for including examples of such questions in the enquiry.

In line with this sort of reasoning, an analysis was made of a wide range of questionnaires for general guidance as to the relative frequencies with which different forms of questions were asked by research practitioners. The questions so analysed were provided by research organisations whose representatives made available questionnaires which they had used over the past two years. Between them, these questionnaires carried approximately 2,180 questions, designed by over 24 different research workers.

The basic point of reference in this analysis was the occurrence in a question of any element or characteristic which it was expected might reduce or impair *easy understanding*—that is, to at least some degree: these different forms, characteristics, etc. were classified into relatively homogeneous categories. These categories or types of question are set in Table 6.1, with examples, in order of frequency of occurrence. Over 10 per cent of 2,180 questions were primarily examples of category 1 and less than 1 per cent were primarily examples of category 13. For obvious reasons, the examples given have been modified with respect either to product group or to brand name. In the present state of knowledge, this classification had to be subjective in character and this means that its results must be treated warily. Nor can the sample of 2,180 questions be regarded as representative of all market research questions asked, so that on this ground too we must be wary about the classification. However, all that the classification was meant to do was to help the research team to focus effort upon possible difficulties of the more recurrent kind rather than upon the kinds that occur but rarely.

Table 6.1
Categories of question difficulty, arranged in
order according to frequency of occurrence
(Category 1 occurred most frequently and
category 13 least frequently)

1 Instances of two questions presented as one (e.g. questions offering two long and rather cumbersome alternatives which could be difficult for a respondent to hold in mind while making a decision between them; questions in which there is overlap between the alternatives offered; questions in which the alternatives, separated by the word 'or', do not cover all the possibilities).

Examples:

(a) 'Did you, personally, get our letter of invitation to come here tonight or did you come as a guest of someone else who got our letter of invitation?'

(b) 'Do you think there are enough job opportunities for a person like you in this district or do you think there are better jobs elsewhere?'

(c) 'Do you usually get it from the shop or do you usually have it delivered?'

(d) 'Which brand do you use or do you change brands frequently?'

2 Questions which contain a lot of meaningful words (possibly quite simple ones) in a short space and where each contributes an element of meaning necessary to the question.

Examples:

(a) 'Can you estimate the proportion of your sales accounted for by this brand?'

(b) 'How many of each sized packet have you bought?'

(c) 'How many hours do you usually watch TV on a weekday?'

(d) 'Did you buy any ..... in the last 7 days?'

3 Questions which conclude with a qualifying clause or phrase.

Examples:

24

(a) 'Have you bought any chocolates in the last 7 days, not counting today?'

(b) 'Do you ever buy something other than X because X is not available?'

(c) 'Have you ever bought any paint to use for home decorating?'

4 Questions which contain multiple ideas or subjects.

Examples:

(a) 'Can you give me some idea of the number, makes and sizes of each that you have sold to date or have in stock at the moment?'

(b) 'Amongst the different brands of cigarettes that you know well, which ones do you like?'

(c) 'Which of these have you heard of or shopped at?'

5 Questions which contain difficult or unfamiliar words.

Examples:

Informal/constituency/excluding/merit/to-date/vary/ antiseptic/failure/availability/experimenting/non-frozen/ impartial/periodical/proportion/associate/property/estimate/ impressions/appropriate/consider/solvent.

6 Questions which contain one or more insturctions to the informant.

Examples:

(a) 'Have you bought any chocolates in the last 7 days? Do not include today's buying in your answer.'

(b) 'Which of these words applies to .....'s toothpaste? Look at the words in the list and choose the ones that apply. It doesn't matter how many you choose.'

7 Questions which start with words meant to soften the question's impact or its seeming harshness or directness.

Examples:

(a) 'Would you mind telling me how old you are?'

(b) 'Do you happen to know the names of any brands of X?'

(c) 'Can you give me some idea of when you last bought X?'

8 Difficult phrases in questions.

Examples:

Is there any advantage in having ..... /brand name associations/ taking everything into consideration/display material/would you be inclined to ... /of these same qualities/which classes of people/what is the appropriate alternative to ...

9 Questions which contain conditional or hypothetical clauses.

Examples:

(a) 'Supposing I were to take you into a shop and show you a television set and say 'That's what I call a really good-looking TV set—what would it look like?'

(b) 'If you were buying a refrigerator, what would be the qualities you would most want it to have?'

10 Questions which are dependent in character in that they are linked to a master question without which they would not make sense.

Examples:

(a) 'Have you seen any booklets on safety in the home? ..... *Which were they?* ..... *Where did you get them?'*.....

(b) 'Was last week's copy of ..... delivered to your home? *Where is it now?'*.....

(c) 'During the last week did you buy any ..... chocolates? *How much did you get then?* ..... *On the last occasion, where did you do your buying?'*

11 Questions which have a negative element in them.

Examples:

'Is there any particular reason why you do not use coal?'

(b) 'Why have you not bought X since then?'

12 Sentences which are inverted.

Examples:

(a) 'The ones you bought last time, what were they?'

(b) 'The car you have now, did you buy it new or second hand?'

13 Questions which have in them the term 'if any', or 'if at all'.

Examples:

    (a) 'Which of these, if any, have you ever bought?'

    (b) 'How much, if at all, do you think that the brand of your petrol matters?'

14   *Other types of difficulty*

    (a) Questions which are very long.

    (b) Questions in which the present and the past tense are used.

    (c) Questions in which both the singular and the plural are used.

The categories and the number of questions chosen for testing

On the basis of the argument presented on page 23, the present enquiry was concentrated upon questions classifiable under one or another of the six more recurrent categories in the list (i.e. upon the first six in the list).

Within each of these six categories, four questions were developed for testing. Each of the four involved the same broad kind of difficulty, but they differed in terms of question content (i.e. topic) and in terms of expected level of difficulty. The reason for this arrangement was that variability of this kind seemed likely to increase the chances of discovering processes relevant to respondent grasp of questions.

The resulting 24 questions were fed into four (similar) questionnaires, six to each questionnaire, the six being composed of one example of each of the first six categories defined in Table 6.1. The four sets of six questions were meant to be roughly equivalent to each other in terms of expected level of difficulty, though this was not an essential feature of the research design.

The four (similar) questionnaires are referred to here as 'carriers', in the sense that their only purpose was to carry the test questions. Each carrier had in it about 25 ordinary questions (i.e. of normal form and complexity) in addition to the six test questions. To provide contrast and to give greater breadth to the enquiry, *one* of the 25 other questions was selected for study as well. As this was done for a different question in each of the four carrier questionnaires, the number of questions to be tested rose to 28, made up of 24 questions from the six test categories and four more which had been selected as quite ordinary questions. One other question was later added for testing, making 29 in all.

There were two reasons for limiting the number of questions to be tested to seven per questionnaire. The main reason was that preliminary work had indicated that many respondents could not 'take' more than an hour of intensive interviewing—even when paid for it and when it was done by appointment—and that it took all of an hour for the intensive interviewer to deal with seven different questions with the necessary thoroughness. This hour was also the limit to the period during which an intensive interviewer could function at top level. Second, it was considered undesirable to load any single carrier questionnaire with more than about this number of questions specially designed for testing, for it would be all too easy to overload the carrier and so make it seem odd or unrealistic to the survey respondent. It is true of course that all the questions specially designed for test were of a kind that frequently occurred; but to bring them all together in a really big bunch might have been too much.

Thus a single survey respondent was to be put through a carrier questionnaire in which were seven test questions and the whole point of this was to allow a second interviewer subsequently to test the respondent's understanding of each of those seven test questions.

THE CONTEXT IN WHICH QUESTIONS WERE TESTED

Each of the questionnaires dealt with the public's ideas about and reactions to television. More specifically, they had in them questions about the use made of the television service; how programmes are selected; satisfaction with the television service and programmes; television as an influence on young people; attitudes towards advertising; personal details of the informant. The test questions were also focused on such issues and each was meant to form an integral part of the questionnaire in which it was placed. The four versions of the questionnaire are given in the Appendix (Part II, pages 173–193). The 29 test questions are also presented in Table 6.2 below, grouped together within the different categories they were meant to represent.

Television was chosen as a topic because most people were viewers and because the subject of television was sufficiently broad in character to allow the asking of a wide range of questions. Obviously the wider the range of matters about which questions were asked, the greater was the possibility of reaching a broadly based conclusion. On the other hand (and although it was difficult to see what the alternative might be), it must be recognised that a possible disadvantage of choosing television as a topic was that the average respondent might give somewhat more attention to questions about television than he would give to questions about a specific commercial product.

28

Table 6.2

The 29 questions developed or selected for testing

1 *Instances of two questions presented as one*

(a) *Questionnaire I, Q9.* 'When you turn on your television set in the evening, do you generally go on viewing till the *end* of the evening or do you just watch one or two programmes?'

(b) *Questionnaire II, Q20.* 'Do you think that people who plan the advertising in programmes are using the advertising time properly, or do you think that this time is being used badly?'

(c) *Questionnaire III, Q21.* 'Do you go on watching the screen when the television advertisements come on, or do you do something else at that time?'

(d) *Questionnaire IV, Q14.* 'Thinking about television over the last few years, do you think that programmes are better nowadays or do you think that they are worse than they were?'

2 *Questions which present a lot of meaningful words in a short space*

(a) *Questionnaire I, Q20.* 'Is television advertising time used properly?'

(b) *Questionnaire II, Q10.* 'On an average evening, how often do you switch from one station to the other?'

(c) *Questionnaire III, Q16.* 'Do you think any programmes have bad effects on young people's morals?'

(d) *Questionnaire IV, Q8.* 'Do you use weekly printed pro-grammes regularly when deciding what to view?'

3 *Questions which conclude with a qualifying clause or phrase*

(a) *Questionnaire I, Q16.* 'Do any programmes have a bad effect upon young people, by setting them poor moral standards?'

(b) *Questionnaire II, Q15.* 'Do you think that children suffer any ill effects from watching programmes with violence in them, other than ordinary westerns?'

(c) *Questionnaire III, Q10.* 'How many times do you usually switch from one station to the other, when viewing on a week-

(Table 6.2 continued)
day evening?'

(d) *Questionnaire IV, Q18.* 'Do you think any programmes have a bad effect on young people, by teaching them slang?'

4   *Questions which contain multiple ideas or subjects*

(a) *Questionnaire I, Q19.* 'Remembering that advertisements pay for ITV programmes, do you think that there *should* be advertising on television?'

(b) *Questionnaire II, Q11b.* 'Amongst the programmes you watch at weekends, which ONE do you find the most interesting?'

(c) *Questionnaire III, Q20.* 'On ITV, a certain amount of time is spent showing cartoon advertisements. Do you think that this sort of advertising is done properly?'

(d) *Questionnaire IV, Q21.* 'When the advertisements come on *between* two television programmes on a weekday evening, do you usually watch them?'

5   *Questions which contain difficult or unfamiliar words*

(a) *Questionnaire I, Q13b* 'Do you think that the television news programmes are impartial about politics?'

(b) *Questionnaire II, Q14b.* 'Do you think that television programmes seen by children are appropriate for them?'

(c) *Questionnaire II, Q21b.* 'What is your general impression of television advertising?'

(d) *Questionnaire III, Q14b.* 'What proportion of your evening viewing time do you spend watching news programmes?'

(e) *Questionnaire IV, Q20.* 'Is television advertising time being used efficiently?'

6   *Questions which include one or more instruction to the informant*

(a) *Questionnaire I, Q4.* 'How many days of the week do you usually watch television? I mean weekdays and Saturdays and Sundays of course, and daytime viewing as well as evening viewing.'

(b) *Questionnaire II, Q21.* 'When the advertisements come on between *two* programmes, what do you usually do when you stay in the room with the television set?'

(c) *Questionnaire III, Q5.* 'For how many hours do you usually watch television on a weekday? This means Monday to

(Table 6.2 continued)
Friday but not Saturday or Sunday, and includes daytime
viewing as well as evening viewing?'

(d) *Questionnaire IV, Q3 of personal details.* 'How many
people are there in your household? Do not include yourself.'

7   *Questions drawn from other parts of the questionnaire but
not designed as examples of any particular type of difficulty*

(a) *Questionnaire I, Q21.* 'What do you usually do when the
television advertisements come on?'

(b) *Questionnaire II, Q5.* 'For how many hours do you usually
watch television on a weekday? This includes evening viewing.'

(c) *Questionnaire III, Q12.* 'What are the things you *dislike*
about programmes on television?'

(d) *Questionnaire IV, Q4.* 'How many days of the week do
you usually watch television?' (Let them answer, then say)
'I'm including Saturday and Sunday, of course—does that
make any difference?'

A special feature of the carrier questionnaire

In the carrier questionnaire, most test questions were followed by a
check question, for example: 'Why do you say that?' This was done
(i) to help the respondent to think back to the original question when
next day the *intensive* interviewer raised it with her again; (ii) to give
the *intensive* interviewer something to work on in starting up her
special interview; (iii) to make it more difficult for the respondent to
claim, *wrongly,* that the first interviewer had made a mistake in recording his 'yes' or 'no'. It was expected, too, that this check question alone
would help provide evidence of at least some of the respondent's misunderstandings (if there were any).

THE DELIVERY OF THE 'CARRIER' QUESTIONNAIRES

It was important that the carrier questionnaires should be delivered
normally and by ordinary market research interviewers.

The choice of interviewers

Six different market research organisations were each asked to provide experienced interviewers whom they considered to be of an average standard (i.e. not poor interviewers; not the best they had; about average, not newcomers). In fact, four of the six organisations co-operated, to provide six different teams of three to four interviewers each. These interviewers were not told the true purpose of their work. Any one team of interviewers (all from one organisation) worked for only one week, being replaced in the following week by another team, so that in the course of the six weeks of the project a total of 19 different market research interviewers took part. The reason for doing this was twofold. One reason was to introduce into the project a large number of different interviewing talents and tendencies so that the results would not be dependent upon the personal oddities or excellencies of a few (possibly atypical) interviewers. The use of a number of different research organisations had a similar purpose. The second reason was that the constant change of interviewers delivering the carrier questionnaires reduced the likelihood that any one of them would become aware of the true purpose of her interview and so deliver it in some atypical way.

Briefing of market research interviewers concerning the delivery of the questionnaires

There was a two-hour briefing each Monday morning. The enquiry was presented to the market research interviewers as dealing with the public's attitudes towards television. The interviewers were taken through each of the four carrier questionnaires, with the explanation that they would be using these in rotation on their respondents. There was nothing on or in the carrier questionnaire to reveal the true purpose of the operation.

The following rules were set up about the delivery of a questionnaire to a respondent.

1 Interviewers were not to alter the wording of questions.

2 Interviewers were not to offer explanations of the meaning of questions or of parts of questions, or to offer help to respondents in formulating answers.

3 If respondents commented on questions or asked anything about them, the interviewer was to record what the respondent said (as in standard piloting).

4 Interviewers were instructed to record *all* that respondents said in reply whether the question asked was open or structured in form.

Briefing in relation to getting appointments for the intensive interviewers

A vital step in this project was the making of an appointment for a second interviewer to call on the respondent next day. This had to be done by the first interviewer at the *end* of her interview and it was this which made it necessary to take special steps to prevent the first interview from becoming atypical. Thus the market research interviewer delivering the carrier questionnaire was told that the purpose of the appointment was simply to allow a second interviewer to gather additional and detailed information about people's reactions to certain television programmes.

There were certain requirements and rules concerning the making of appointments. One of these was that the interviewer must not refer in any way to the appointment or the second interview till she had finished her own interview. Only then could she seek the appointment for the second interviewer. Another requirement was that appointments be sought with all respondents interviewed. The respondent was to be told that the second interviewer would be paying a small fee for the time given to her and that the second interviewer would be somebody from the university who would be coming out specially to keep the appointment. The market research interviewer was to leave with the respondent a card stating the time of the appointment and a letter introducing the second interview (i.e. explaining that it was part of an important enquiry by the university). No fee was to be paid for the first interview and no suggestions of any kind were to be made to this effect. The appointments were to be sought for particular times which were in fact geared to the working schedules of the intensive interviewers. The number of appointments required of a market research interviewer was three or four (for the next day), and she was told that so many of them had to be with men and so many had to be with women.

The market research interviewers worked from Monday to Friday inclusive, passing in their questionnaires and appointment arrangements at a local centre (see later) at the end of each interviewing day.

THE INTENSIVE INTERVIEW

The purpose of the intensive interview was to find out how the respondent had understood the seven questions assigned for test, with special reference to any misunderstandings, omissions, distortions, etc. For this there was a clearly specified procedure which was administered by interviewers selected and trained for the job (see later for details of their selection and training).

33

The intensive interview itself was in principle a detection process in which were incorporated: the use of memory aids, considerable probing after details, a form of challenging and quite a lot of cross-checking of the avaialble evidence. It was fully tape recorded. The intensive interviewer was given the first interviewer's completed questionnaire when she went out to do the intensive interview.

The several steps in the intensive interview are given below.

1 The intensive interview started with informal conversation about television and then about the first interview in order to relax the respondent. The purpose of the *present* interview was then explained quite frankly. Thus the respondent was told that the research was being done to find out the best way of asking questions—so that people had a fair chance of answering them. After all (they were told) questions can be worded badly or can be asked too quickly, and it is always possible for the person answering to be distracted, or a bit deaf, or in a hurry. What we were doing therefore (the respondent was told) was asking people lots of things about some of the questions they had answered in 'yesterday's' interview, about what they had thought the questions meant, and so on. We hoped they would not mind all our questioning to find out about this and we hoped that they would be completely frank in all that they told us.

This introduction was meant to get the respondent thinking helpfully *with* the intensive interviewer, rather than wondering what all the questions were leading to. In most cases, this explanation appeared to have the desired effect, with respondents entering into the 'game'.

2 The intensive interviewer dealt *fully* with the first of her (seven) test questions before going on to the next one. For each test question the procedure was in five parts, (a), (b), (c), (d) and (e). Parts (a) and (b) together constituted an open, probing and interrogating process, focused progressively upon different points, and designed to find out just how the respondent understood the test question when it was delivered in the first interview. Part (c) was a set of quite specific questions designed to augment the information gathered through (a) and (b). Details of all parts of the intensive interview are given below and the instructions to the intensive interviewers are given in full in Appendix 3 (Part II, pages 194—197).

(a)   After preparation of the kind indicated in (1) above, the intensive interviewer opened the first part of the procedure with the request to the respondent to think back to the interview she gave 'yesterday', and she was reminded of the test question by the interviewer who read it out slowly. She was also reminded (by a further slow reading) of her *reply* 'yesterday', including the full statement given in the 'check question', and including anything

34

else she had said to the first interviewer in relation to it.

This information had been written on the intensive interviewer's report form by the survey administrators working at the local office (see later). The respondent was asked if she remembered giving that particular reply 'yesterday', the term 'yesterday' being heavily stressed and repeated. After this 'setting of the scene', the respondent was asked: 'When you were asked that question *yesterday,* exactly what did you think it meant?' The respondent's reply was written down in full (and also tape recorded).

Experience had shown that this question would not necessarily give the intensive interviewer the information she wanted, respondents sometimes thinking that the intensive interviewer wanted to know 'what *lay behind* the question'. Accordingly, the intensive interviewer had been given auxiliary probes and questions to help the respondent to grasp what was in fact wanted (e.g. 'What was it she wanted to know yesterday when she asked that question?' 'In your own words, what was it the interviewer was asking you?') It was up to the intensive interviewer to get the respondent thinking on the required lines and to rephrase the question about what she thought the first interviewer meant if the respondent seemed (from her replies) still to be missing the point.

The intensive interviewer was responsible also for getting *all* the respondent's ideas out of her (e.g. 'Is that *everything* you thought she was asking you in that question yesterday?' 'Was there anything more you thought she was asking through that question yesterday?') The intensive interviewer was required also to probe any obscurities in the respondent's (present) replies (e.g. 'How do you mean?' 'I don't quite understand'). If the respondent's answers were not in line with the reply she gave 'yesterday' to the 'check' question, this inconsistency was to be put before the respondent and pursued to some satisfactory conclusion. The intensive interviewer was directed to watch for any relevant leads at all times and to follow these, either straight away, or at the first opportunity.

(h) Next, the intensive interviewer was required to reapproach, from a different direction, the basic problem of what question the respondent had actually answered (yesterday). The respondent was reminded (slowly) of the original question and of her answer 'yesterday'. The intensive interviewer then said 'Now tell me how you worked out your answer from that question. Think it out for me just as you did yesterday. Only this time, say it aloud for me'. Here again, the intensive interviewer was responsible for getting the respondent to do as required, and to rephrase the probe if necessary (e.g. 'What went on in your mind when you were asked that question yesterday?' 'You answered ... You must have got your answer somehow ... You must have worked it out somehow ... How did you work it out?'). The intensive interviewer was responsible also for probing for a *full* reconstruction, for challenging inconsistencies between the indications of the present evidence and the answer actually given 'yesterday', and for keeping the respondent thinking of how she answered the question *yesterday* as distinct from her interpretation of it *now*.

(c)   After this, the respondent was asked a number of quite specific things about 'yesterday's' questions. Take for example the test question: 'Do you think that any programmes have a bad effect on young people, by teaching them slang?'
Of this question, respondents were asked:

  (i) (To find out the ages of the people referred to.)

'When you answered that question yesterday, what did you think were the ages of the people she was asking about?'

 (ii) (To find out, amongst other things, what sort of programmes the respondent was thinking of.)

'What sort of programme was it you thought had this effect on young people?' (She had answered 'yes' to that question yesterday.)

'Do these programmes have any slang in them?'

'Do you think that any of these programmes would teach young people to talk slang?'

(iii) (To find out what sort of 'bad effect' respondent had in mind.)

'What sort of effect was it you were thinking about when you gave your answer?'

Batteries of such questions were asked for each of the seven test questions and those relating to the total 29 test questions are given in the Appendix Part II.

(d)   After this, the respondent was asked to listen carefully to the question once more, and then to answer it as she *now* thought it should be answered. If the new answer was different from that given to the first interviewer, and if there were no obvious omissions or distortions in the respondent's apparent understanding of it (as indicated by the interrogation described above), then the respondent was asked to explain how it was that his/her answer *now* differed from the answer of *yesterday*. This additional step was intended to provide a further chance of the intensive interviewer to pick up evidence of any misunderstandings.

(e)   As preparation for a similar treatment of the next question amongst the seven allocated for test, the intensive interviewer was required to summarise, for the respondent, the latter's interpretation of the question just dealt with (i.e. what she thought it meant and, if this was in error, the question that the respondent actually answered). After summing up in this way, the intensive interviewer was to thank the respondent for her efforts on the test just completed, praise her if she had worked hard at the job *and tell her that the next one was to be done in just the same way.* As planned, this summing up process appeared to sharpen the respondent's learning (from the first test) of what was wanted of her and it made the remaining tests easier and quicker to deliver.

The total time for dealing with the seven test questions in the way indicated above was a little in excess of an hour.

THE SELECTION, TRAINING AND CONTROL OF INTENSIVE INTERVIEWERS

Selection of intensive interviewers

It was necessary that the interviewers doing this work should be well above average intelligence, well educated, acceptable to respondents of all classes and that they should have the outlook necessary for what was, in fact, a form of detective work. Of the 130 people who applied for the advertised positions, 22 were given a personal interview and of these, 15 were asked to conduct a short (tape recorded) trial interview of the intensive kind. These recorded interviews were then rated for interviewing manner, apparent ability to establish satisfactory rapport, detective ability and adherence to instructions. As a result, six people were asked to attend a fortnight's training course on the intensive interviewing method.

Training and control

Although a fortnight was allocated for initial training, training went on throughout the survey. In the initial fortnight, the trainees were introduced to the purpose of the enquiry, to the four carrier questionnaires to be delivered by first interviewers, and then to the intensive interview on which most of the training period was spent. The method of training was to have trainees (after verbal instruction in the technique, and after classroom practice in its administration) administer the intensive interview to ordinary members of the public in their homes. The trainee tape recorded each interview, passing the recordings to the person in charge of training. These practice interviews were done each morning (up till midday). Each afternoon various of the tape recordings were played to the whole group of trainees and to the person training them. The trainees were required to ask for a stoppage of the playback each time they thought the interviewer concerned had gone wrong and each time they thought she had missed a promising lead. This apparent failure was then discussed by the trainees under the guidance of their trainer. If the trainees did not notice a particular failure in the recorded interview, the trainer stopped the playback and focused the attention of the trainees on the failure, saying what should have been done. After this, another recording (by a different trainee) was played back and criticised in the same way. In the course of a fortnight, all the different trainees had about the same number of their interviews criticised in this way. One of the things the trainer tried to develop in the trainees was a willingness to accept criticism and trainees were encouraged to join in with criticisms of their own work. Ordinarily, people unwilling to accept criticism are dropped from the team.

This process of critical discussion was continued throughout the 6-week survey period. It took place each Monday, all day. The use of Monday in this way fitted in with the total operation because on Monday the market research interviewers were conducting the first interview and making appointments for the intensive interviewers to call on Tuesday.

In addition, a quality controller was appointed to listen to the tape recordings of a proportion of the intensive interviews conducted each day. In fact, he listened to about half of them. He had then to take up failures with the interviewers concerned, telling them what was wrong and suggesting ways of correcting the failure. In the process it was necessary for them to listen to some of the weak parts of their own (tape recorded) interviews. Where difficulties of a recurrent kind showed up, or where methods for dealing with recurrent difficulties were developed, instructions for procedure were marked up on the notice board at the local centre from which the intensive interviewers were operating (see later deatails of local centres).

THE USE OF LOCAL CENTRES AS OPERATIONAL HEADQUARTERS

For a number of reasons which will be explained shortly, the conduct of this testing operation necessitated the use of a local office in each of the polling districts in which the team worked.

The ordinary interviewers' use of the local centre

At the end of each working day and sometimes during it, the ordinary 'interviewers' reported to the local centre in order to pass in their completed questionnaires, on which were recorded the details of appointments made for the calls of intensive interviewers next day. At the same time they reported any failures to contact respondents or to secure appointments. These ordinary interviewers were also free to come to the local centre to have their lunch or for a cup of tea or coffee or to pick up fresh questionnaires and letters. Ordinarily, they were not there long and their contact at the centre was always with the local centre manager or her assistant.

The intensive interviewers' use of the local centre

The intensive interviewers were based at the local centre. They returned to it after each intensive interview. There, each of them was allocated a next appointment and finalised the report on the interview just made (working from basic notes made during that interview and from the tape recording of it). During this short stay at the centre, intensive interviewers had to check with the quality controller for any of his comments about the quality of their work. They had to look at the daily notice board for any special instructions (e.g. how to cope with some new difficulty experienced by one of the intensive interviewers; a reminder to do something which intensive interviewers generally seemed to be forgetting to do). They had also to test battery strength and reload tape recorders with fresh batteries if necessary. The intensive interviewer had to collect the appropriate report form for the next appointment (there was a different one for each of the four carrier questionnaires). The intensive interviewers worked in a separate room at the centre—a room to which the ordinary interviewers did not come, the point of this being to keep the two teams of interviewers quite separate.

The quality controller also worked at the local centre, in the same room as that to which the intensive interviewers returned between interviews. All tape recorders could be fitted with earphones so that their use at the centre did not disturb others.

The office manager's role at the centre

The office manager and her assistant were responsible for the general running of the local centres. The office manager briefed the ordinary interviewers for their week's assignment. This was done each Monday morning (at the local centre). When (each day) ordinary interviewers passed in their questionnaires and appointments, the office manager selected the appropriate set of intensive interview report forms and on these made certain entries. Thus for carrier questionnaire III, she took out the seven intensive interview report forms geared to the seven test questions of this particular carrier questionnaire. If one of these test questions was question 16, then on the report form prepared for this test question she entered the full answer to question 16 as given by the respondent in the first interview, including the respondent's answer to the 'check' question. The same thing was done separately for each of the other six test questions to be dealt with by the intensive interviewer. The pack of seven intensive interview report forms was then clipped to the original carrier questionnaire (on which the time of the appointment and the respondent's name and address were written) and was put ready for allocation to one of the intensive interviewers.

The office manager saw all the ordinary interviewers as they reported in, checking on their failures and difficulties and seeing that they were using the four carrier questionnaires in rotation, as required. She kept a progressive tally of appointments for intensive interviews, saw that the ordinary interviewers and the intensive interviewers did not come into conversational contact, looked after the petty cash assigned for the pay-payment of a small fee to respondents (by the intensive interviewer for the intensive interview) and generally kept things running and in order.

The local office itself

The local office consisted of two rooms, one for the intensive interviewers (and the quality controller) and the other for the office manager, her assistant, and the ordinary interviewers when they called. The local office had to be situated in the centre of the polling district in which the team was currently working; otherwise intensive interviewers would have had to spend too much of their time travelling to and from respondents' homes.

Each week, the team worked in a fresh polling district and this meant that a new local centre had to be opened up each week, the move being made early each Monday morning. Such centres were not easy to get and those used in the enquiry included two community centres, rooms at a public baths, rooms in a town hall, a civil defence training centre and a church crypt! The centres were occupied from 9.45 am till 10.30 pm six days a week.

SAMPLING DETAILS

Selection of interviewing areas

The requirement that a centre be used in each survey area put a sharp limit upon the number of these areas that could be used in the total enquiry. In fact, the number used was six and each of these was a polling district within London.* The reason for using polling districts instead of the larger wards was that a ward was so large that the intensive interviewers would spend too much of their time going to and from interviews within it. The six polling districts were selected using the random principle, but with a control over economic level (as indicated by the percentage of electors with juror status) and geographical location.* The point of using these controls was to increase the likelihood that the small sample of six polling districts would yield a sample of people not unduly atypical of Londoners.

First interviewers' success in securing interviews

For each polling district, 90 names were drawn from electoral registers (equal interval selection), and these were split equally amongst the three market research interviewers who were to work in any one polling district. Thus they had 30 each. Since there were 19 market research interviewers operating in the course of the whole enquiry, the total number of names allocated in this way for interview was 570 (= 19 x 30). Interviewers were told to make three calls before abandoning a respondent. When an interviewer reported that she had exhausted her list of potential contacts, she was given a supplementary list of 12 names, also drawn at equal intervals throughout the electoral register for the polling district.

If this list, too, was reported as exhausted, a further list of 12 names was given to the interviewer. A total of 460 extra names was given out in this way to the 19 interviewers in the course of the six-week enquiry. There were thus 570 persons named in the original lists and 460 in the supplementary lists. The total number of successful contacts was 465

---

*The six selected polling districts were as follows, the juror percentage figure appearing in brackets after each one: Bermondsey, South (M) [[0.68] ; Hammersmith, Wormholt (C) [1.25] ; Wandsworth, Tooting (M) [1.57] ; Islington, E, Canonbury (G) [3.48] ; Camberwell, Peckham, St. Giles (W) [3.51] ; Greenwich, S.E. (Fb and Fc) [7.25] .

This low response figure stems from the urban character of the survey area, and from the special recruitment objectives imposed upon this part of the interviewing operation (i.e. to obtain a follow-up intensive interview next day). See footnotes 1 and 2 for elaboration.* In a sense, what was done here was to use the survey method for setting up a controlled experiment. The persons going through both interviews were in fact fairly closely representative of the London adult population in terms of age, sex and occupational level. See page 43 for details.

---

*Non-responses

Refused to undergo first interview	53	Abandoned as 'not at home'	
Moved	70	After 1 call*	208
On holiday	50	After 2 calls	71
Incapable, ill, deceased	44	After 3 calls	69
	217		348

(Contacted: 465)

The 465 contacted were 45 per cent of the 1,030 names given out. The reasons for this low figure appear to be as follows:

1 The sub-areas surveyed were all within 10 miles of the centre of London, where non-response loses are relatively high.

2 The first interviewers had not only to contact respondents and conduct interviews with them in the normal way, but they had also to secure appointments for second interviews the next day, with a specified number of men and with a specified number of women. In effect this meant that when an interviewer had fixed all her tomorrow's appointments for men (and she could not make appointments for more than one day ahead), she did not pursue more of her interviews that day with men but concentrated her efforts instead upon the interviewing of women. Also, when towards the end of the day or evening she had failed to find many of her listed contacts at home (and hence had few of her quota of appointments made), she was permitted to ask at the local office for more names rather than pursuing (through second and third calls) people she had not expected to find at home that day or later that evening. What this situation means is that many members of the original sample and many of the substitutes could not be pursued through three well spaced calls as in the standard sample survey involving personal interviews. What matters of course is the representativeness of the achieved samples. See text above and page 43.

Intensive interviews

Of the 465 respondents contacted by the ordinary interviewers, 125 were without television sets[+] and so were not eligible for interview. The remaining 340 were asked to see a second interviewer next day. Of these 15 refused; 31 were willing to have a second interview, but were not available next day; 294 agreed to an intensive interview next day. Of the 294, some 265 actually went through the intensive interview next day.

Some characteristics of those who went through the intensive interview are set out in Table 6.3. The figures in brackets are estimates for the whole of Greater London. The table footnotes give the origins of these (all-London) estimates.

Table 6.3

Characteristics of intensive interviewees

Sex	%	(%)*	Occupational level	%	(%)†
Male	49	(49)*	Professional, semi-		
Female	51	(51)	professional and		
	100	(100)	executive	5	(6)
			Highly skilled	17	(12)
Age	%	(%)*	Skilled	23	(24)
			Moderately skilled	19	(25)
20–24	7	(11)	Semi-skilled	19	(14)
25–34	18	(19)	Unskilled	12	(14)
35–44	17	(19)	Unclassifiable	5	(5)
45–54	22	(19)		100	(100)
55–64	15	(16)			
65+	21	(16)			
	100	(100)			

* Based on 1961 Census data for London (Census 1961: County Report, London, London: HMSO, 1963).

†Based on data developed by the Audience Research Department of the BBC, relating to the period 1952.

+Fieldwork was completed in the mid-sixties.There is no reason known to the author for suspecting that the level of understanding of survey questions will have changed much since that time—certainly nothing to suggest that understanding might now be better.

43

From Table 6.3 it will be seen that the respondents who went through both the ordinary and the intensive interviews were: (1) representative of those in Greater London in terms of sex distribution; (ii) somewhat over represented by persons aged 65 years and over; (iii) somewhat over-represented by the highly skilled. To the extent that understanding of questions (as put by the first interviewer) is negatively related to age and positively related to occupational level, there would be some balancing out of those two sources of possible bias. Generally speaking, however, the achieved sample is broadly representative of the adult public of London in terms of the three variables featured in Table 6.3.

METHODS OF ANALYSIS

Of the 265 intensive interviews, 19 were not used because of tape recorder failure* throughout the interview. The remaining 246 were subjected to the kind of analysis set out below.†

The four analysts, three of whom were university graduates, went through a period of training for this particular job. Throughout their analyses, their work was subject to supervision and to checking and challenging. There was a separate analysis sheet for each of the 29 test questions, and there were several stages to the analyses reported on any one of these sheets.

1 Working from the tape recording of the intensive interviewer, from the intensive interview report form, and from the first interview questionnaire, analysts entered the following details for each test question.

(a)   the respondent's first-interview answers to the test question and to the check question;

(b)   the respondent's second-interview explanation of what she

---

*Whereas there were certain entries which the intensive interviewer had to make on her report form, she had been instructed to give her full attention to the questioning of the respondent and to minimise the amount of writing down she did in the interview itself. Accordingly, the final appraisal of respondent interpretation of a question depended to a marked degree upon there being a full tape recording of the probing done in relation to that question. For 19 intensive interviews there had been a failure of tape recorder and so these 19 interviews had to be discarded. These were, of course, relatively early days in the development of portable tape-recorders and technical failures were not uncommon.

† The remaining 246 were divided fairly evenly among the four versions of the carrier questionnaire: 62 for version I, 63 for II, 57 for III and 64 for IV.

thought the question meant (see Q1 in Part II, page 194);

(c)   the respondent's second-interview explanation of exactly how she worked out her answer to the first interviewer (see Q2 in Part II, page 195);

(d)   the respondent's answers to second-interview questions designed to determine her intake/understanding, at the time of the first interview, of specific elements in the test question (e.g. what she understood by the term 'bad effects'; was she thinking of young people generally or of some particular young people when she answered the question; what ages did she have in mind in answering about young people) (see Part II, pages 198—213).

2   On the basis of this information, the analyst wrote out (see Q5 in Part II, page 217):

(a)   all special interpretations of the question, including any private meanings;

(b)   all apparent misunderstandings or errors;

(c)   all wrongful omissions of parts of the question.

3   The analysts then wrote out, on the basis of all the evidence available, exactly *what was the question which the respondent was answering in the first interview.* (See Q6 in Part II, page 217 for the instructions to analysts, and Part II, pages 2—17   for the approximately 1,600 entries made in this context.) *Each of these entries was checked and challenged against all the evidence by at least two research personnel.*

4   On the basis of the marking systems described in this report, a direct count was made of the number of instances in which each question was understood as intended, or approximately so, by those who were asked it.

5   For each question, a content analysis was made of respondent interpretations (as set out in Part II) of all the main elements in each question, and the results were presented in tabular form on pages 49—349 of this volume.

Analysts were frequently reminded (as had been the intensive interviewers) that respondents might have had *new* thoughts at the intensive interview and that it was yesterday's interpretation of the question that was wanted. On this point we should, of course, note that the intensive interviewers had the answer to the check question to use as an aid in holding the respondent to 'yesterday's' interpretation and reply, and that the analyst too could use it to help her recognise instances when a respondent was in fact talking about something other than her response 'yesterday'. It is also worth noting in this connection that intensive interviewers had reported a marked tendency in respondents to maintain earlier replies even when these were based upon serious misunderstandings.* Nonetheless, every effort was made to focus the analysts' thinking upon evidence relating to 'yesterday's' reply to the questions.

*It is well worth mentioning that intensive interviewers reported a peculiar stability to the informant's interpretation of the question in that this interpretation did not appear to undergo change in the course of the interview. Moreover, major misunderstandings continued to persist throughout the interview and to operate, when the question was re-asked at the end of the interview, to produce the same reply as was given in the first interview. It seemed that whatever lay behind a respondent's reaction and answer to the question in the first interview continued to operate and to produce the same reactions and replies in many respondents.

7 Findings: details of how each of the 29 questions was understood

On pages 49—349 are presented detailed findings for each of the 29 questions which were tested. For each of them, the presentation is in several parts: (1) the wording of the question actually asked; (2)intended definitions of the different parts of the question (used as a basis for rating respondent interpretations); (3)respondent interpretations of the question (details in Part II); (4)criteria used in marking the interpretations of respondents and the distribution of ratings allocated; (5) the detailed results of a content analysis of respondents' interpretations; (6)a summary of the results of the marking and of the content analysis. In section (5)the results of content analysis for each of various words and concepts are presented in tabular form, the table being preceded by a statement of findings (for that word or concept) and being followed by a set of *speculative* comments (labelled as such) about what may perhaps have led to the misinterpretation(s) isolated by the content analysis and presented in the tables. These two statements, namely the findings and the speculations, are offered in their own right as material likely to be of value to the reader, but they were also intended for use in the later development of hypotheses about the nature and the causes of misinterpretation of survey questions. (Such hypotheses are presented in the second part of the findings (pages 370-389).

One feature of this presentation of the findings that must be noted is the *repetition*, in each of its 29 sections, of certain vital introductory or explanatory comments. These repetitions are to be found in the first three lines under 'Definitions of the different parts of the question' (see page 49) and in points 1, 2 and 3 of 'Marking the interpretations' (page 50). The obvious query about this repetition is why it cannot be presented just once as a general introduction that relates to each of the 29 sections of the findings. However, the fact of the matter is that each of the 29 sections is likely to be read as a report in its own right and with a space of time between the reading of the 29 different sections. Accordingly, each section has been made complete and independent, each with its vital (though repetitive) introduction.

On another score altogether, the occasional reader may disagree here and there with the criteria adopted regarding what is an acceptable or correct understanding of a test question or of some of its parts. For example, in the test question 'Do you think that children suffer any ill-effects from watching programmes with violence in them, ...', the term 'you' was meant to refer to the views of the respondent alone—and not to (say) her husband's views. And the reference to 'violence' in programmes was meant to refer to violence generally—and not solely to swearing or solely to sexual violence. However, if disagreement *does* arise, that reader will find *the greater part* of the findings for each test question is in the form of tabular detail about *how* terms were understood—rather than in for form of a simple count of judgements about the understanding being right or wrong.

The distribution of overall ratings for each question (e.g. see the table on page 63) calls for two explanatory comments, as set out in Notes A and B below.

A. The overall rating given to a question was the lowest of the ratings given to any of its parts. Thus if an interpretation of the term 'impartial' in a question was rated as 'unduly different from intended', whereas the interpretation of the term 'news programmes' in that same question was rated 'somewhat different but permissible', the overall rating 'unduly different' was given to the question. This was because a total question can be no stronger than its weakest part. If one part is misunderstood, then the total question must be regarded as being misunderstood. A question is too much of a unity for us to be able to separate out any of its parts as independent of the other parts. The reader who disagrees with this point may care to re-interpret the rating 'unduly different' as 'at least part of the interpretation of the question was unduly different'. Over and above this, he has available to him the full detail of how each part of each question was interpreted.

If one element in a question was rated 'unduly general' and another element was rated 'unduly specific' (i.e. two ratings of equal value), then *both* were applied to the question. The total number of *ratings* shown in the distribution table may, therefore, be in excess of the total number of persons contributing to those ratings. But no one person will figure in that total *both* in the group of 'permissible' ratings *and* in the group of 'unduly ...' ratings.

B. The percentages given for the overall ratings of questions do not always total precisely 100 per cent, because the sub-totals making them up have been individually rounded.

7.1   QUESTION 4, QUESTIONNAIRE 1

The wording of the question

'How many days of the week do you usually watch television? I mean weekdays and Saturdays and Sundays, of course, and daytime viewing as well as evening viewing?'

Check question

'Which days do you view?'

Definitions of the different parts of the question

The following are the intended meanings of key terms in the question. *However, as indicated below, some variants of the intended interpretations were regarded as permissible and others as possibly permissible.* The reference 'how many (days)' was meant to be interpreted as 'what is the number of (days)' (i.e. inviting a numerical answer). The reference 'days of the week' was meant to refer to all seven days and not solely to the period Monday to Friday. 'Days' was meant to refer to the whole of the day and not simply to 'evenings only' or to 'daytime only'. The word 'you' was meant to be interpreted as 'you, yourself' and was not intended to include others (e.g. respondent's spouse, children, relatives, lodger(s)). The word 'usually' was meant to be interpreted as 'ordinarily', 'in the ordinary course of events', 'commonly'. Other acceptable interpretations of the term were: 'as a rule', 'generally', 'normally', 'habitually', 'as a routine', 'almost always', 'mostly', 'typically'. The reference 'watch television' was intended to mean attend to whatever is being shown on the screen or to give it at least some degree of attention.

Respondents' interpretations of the question

Respondents' interpretations of the terms in this question are set out in

49

full in the Appendix (Part II). They are based upon the replies of 59 people.

Marking the interpretations

The system used for rating or marking respondents' interpretations of questions

The following marking or rating system was used:

1 If all elements of the question were interpreted as intended, the interpretation as a whole was rated 'fully as intended' ($\checkmark$).

2 Failure to interpret any significant element of the question fully as intended was sufficient to pull the total interpretation down below the level of 'fully as intended'. The level so reached was determined by the most seriously misinterpreted (significant) element in the test question. For example, if all but one of the significant elements of the question were interpreted as intended and the interpretation of that other element was rated as 'somewhat limited but permissible' (see below), then the whole interpretation was so rated (i.e. 'somewhat limited but permissible'). The reason for this is that a question cannot be regarded as a safe one unless all its parts are interpreted as intended.

3 If a significant element of the question was obviously and substantially misinterpreted or was omitted altogether, the total interpretation was marked 'incorrect' (X).

4 In the context of this system, the following ratings were made of specific elements of respondents' interpretations.

(a) 'how many (days) ...'. Where this reference was interpreted as intended (see above), the rating 'correct' ($\checkmark$) was applied. Where something was added to a permissible interpretation without losing the latter, the rating 'extra but permissible' (ExP) was applied (e.g. 'and on which days'; 'and for how long'; 'and for what part of the day'). One respondent interpreted the reference as 'on what proportion (of the days)' and this was rated 'different but permissible' (DP). The following interpretations were rated 'unduly different' (UD): 'on which (days)'; 'on which and for what part'; 'for what part'; 'for what period'. Where the reference was omitted altogether, the rating 'incorrect' (X) was applied.

(b) 'days of the week'. Where this reference was interpreted as intended (see above), the interpretation was rated 'correct' ($\checkmark$). Where it seemed that the intended interpretation had been made, but where the evidence was not conclusive, the rating 'doubtful but permissible' (?P) was applied. Where it was interpreted as

50

'weekdays only' the interpretation was rated 'incorrect' (X). Where respondents' interpretation excluded part of the day (e.g. 'afternoons only'/'evenings only') the interpretation was also rated 'incorrect' (X).

(c) 'you'. Where this term was interpreted as intended (see above), the interpretation was rated 'correct' (√). Where it was interpreted as 'you and/or your family', or as 'you and/or some other(s)', the interpretation was rated 'unduly extended' (UE). Where the respondent answered as if to the question 'is your set on', that interpretation was rated 'unduly different' (UD).

(d) 'usually'. Where this term was interpreted as intended (see above), the rating 'correct' (√) was applied. The following interpretations were also rated 'correct' (√): 'for the average week'; 'as for about every week'; 'your weekly routine'; 'under normal circumstances'. Where the term was interpreted 'taking an average over the week', it was rated as 'different but permissible'(DP). Similarly for the interpretation 'more often than not'. The interpretation 'day in day out' was rated as 'doubtful but permissible' (?P). Where the term was omitted altogether, the rating 'incorrect' (X) was applied.

(e) 'watch television'. Where this reference was interpreted as intended (see above), the rating 'correct' (√) was applied. Where it seemed that attention had been paid to the screen but where the evidence was not conclusive, the rating 'doubtful but permissible' (?P) was applied. Where the interpretation did not necessarily involve 'giving the screen at least some degree of attention (e.g. 'had the set on'), or allowed the inclusion of periods when no attention was being given to the screen, the rating 'unduly different' (UD) was applied. In one case, a very limiting sort of addition had been made to the basic concept intended (i.e. 'watch and enjoy television') and this one was rated 'unduly different' (UD).

The ratings allocated.

Under the system described above, the following ratings were allocated to respondents' interpretations of this test question (see Table 7.1.1).

Content analysis of the interpretations

There follows an analysis of the different interpretations of elements of the test question. The emphasis in this analysis is upon the different kinds of interpretations which were found rather than upon the

51

number of them (though these numbers are given), the purpose of the content analysis being to discover the kinds of things that happen, to speculate about what caused them, and to derive hypotheses (about communication processes) for testing in the later phases of the enquiry.

Table 7.1.1

Ratings allocated to respondents' interpretations of test question (Q4, 1)

| | Number of | | % of persons |
	ratings	persons	
Correct (√)	10	10	17
Extra but permissible (ExP)	4		
Somewhat limited but permissible (LP)	0		
Somewhat too specific but permissible (SP)	0		
Somewhat too general but permissible (GP)	0	5*	8
Somewhat extended but permissible (EP)	0		
Somewhat different but permissible (DP)	3		
Doubtful but permitted (?P)	8	8	14
Unduly limited (UL)	1		
Unduly general (UG)	0		
Unduly extended (UE)	2	14	24
Unduly different (UD)	11		
Incorrect (X)	22	22	37
All persons		59	100

See Note A on page 47

Interpretations of 'how many (days)'...

The reference 'how many (days)' was meant to be interpreted as 'what is the number of 'days'' (i.e. inviting a numerical answer).

Summary of interpretations

1 'How many' was interpreted as intended by a large majority of respondents (45/59, though 7 of these added something to that interpretation (e.g. 'and for how long').

2 Amongst the other 14, there was quite a variety of interpretations. Of these, a few interpreted the term rather more specifically than was intended but in a manner which would allow the required answer to be worked out by the research analyst (e.g. 'on which days').

Others among the 14 interpreted the term more vaguely (i.e. 'how often'), some less directly (e.g. 'in what proportion') and some quite wrongly (e.g. 'are there particular afternoons when').

3 Of the 14 who misinterpreted the reference, a few added something to the misinterpretation.

Table 7.1.2

Interpretations of 'how many (days)'

How many (36)/roughly how many (2)	38	
On how many and on which (1)/on how many and for how much of (1)/on how many and for what part of (3)/what is the extent (of your viewing) and on how many (1)	6	45
For how long and for how many	1	
How often (1)/where and how often (1)		2
On what proportion and when	1	2
For what part	1	
When		3
On which (days) (2)/on which and for what periods of time (1)/ on which (days) and for what part of the day and for which programmes (1)	4	5
Are there particular afternoons when	1	
What is the pattern (of viewing)		1
Reference omitted		1
Total		59

Interpretations of 'days of the week ... I mean weekdays and Saturdays and Sundays ... and daytime viewing as well as evening viewing'

The reference 'days of the week' was meant to refer to all seven days and not solely to the period Monday to Friday. 'Days' was meant to refer to the whole of the day and not simply to 'evenings only' or to 'daytime only'.

Summary of interpretations

1 A large minority failed to interpret this reference fully as intended.

2 The main difficulty appears to have been a tendency (15 cases) to consider 'evenings only', whereas the question quite specifically said 'I mean ... daytime viewing as well as evening viewing'. In contrast to this, two respondents excluded evening viewing from consideration.

3 Three persons failed to consider all 7 days of the week in spite of being asked to do so.

4 Six persons qualified their interpretations, one by considering only days when they viewed for the whole evening and four of them only days when they viewed for a substantial period of time.

5 Two other persons, perhaps to qualify their answers, gave separate replies for separate parts of the day/year.

Table 7.1.3

Interpretations of 'days of the week'

1 *Was the phrase interpreted fully as intended?*	
Yes 33 No 22 Not clear whether yes or no	4
Total	59
2 *Did respondent consider all seven days of the week?*	
Yes, all seven	50
Five weekdays only	2
Five weekdays plus Saturday	1
Not clear how many days considered	6
Total	59
3 *Did respondent wrongly limit consideration to certain parts of the day?*	
No, respondent considered whole day	36
Respondent considered evenings only	15
Respondent considered daytime only	1
Respondent considered afternoons only	1
Not clear whether respondent considered all day or not	6
Total	59
4 *Did respondent exclude certain days, weeks or seasons from consideration?*	
No special days or weeks or seasons excluded	53
Counting only the days when you view for the whole evening	1
Counting only the days when you view for a substantial period of time (i.e. several hours)	2
Not counting days when you do only short periods of viewing (e.g. to see the news bulletins)	2
Counting only those evenings when you are at home	1
Total	59
5 *Other interpretations of note*	
Considered nights and days separately	1
Considered winter viewing and summer viewing separately	1

Speculative comment

1 One possibility is that the very effort to spell out what was meant by 'days of the week' imposed too great a load of detail on the respondent and thus fragmented intake of the question.

2 It is also possible, however, that for a question like this one, the respondent had already formulated his answer (to the originally interpreted question) before the start of the qualification or without attending to the qualification. Certainly some respondents did answer before the qualification had been finished.

Interpretations of 'you'

The word 'you' was meant to be interpreted as 'you, yourself' and not intended to include others (e.g. respondent's spouse, children, relatives, lodger(s)).

Summary of interpretations

1 In most cases, the respondent correctly interpreted the term as 'you, yourself'.

2 In at least 4 other cases, however, 'you' was interpreted collectively.

3 In 5 more instances, 'you' was interpreted in such a way that the respondent thought in terms of the *set* being turned on.

Table 7.1.4

Interpretations of 'you'

You, yourself (alone)	49
You and your wife	1
You and your family	3
You or your family	1
The set is turned on (so 'you' possibly not considered)	5

Speculative comments

1 The collective nature of television viewing may well make it difficult for the occasional respondent to work out what was *his* 'watching' and what was the 'watching of someone else in the family'.

2 However, it is also possible that some people simply think collectively when it comes to viewing behaviour—in that viewing *is done* collectively.

Interpretations of 'usually'

The word 'usually' was meant to be interpreted as 'ordinarily', 'in the ordinary course of events', 'commonly'. Other acceptable interpretations of the term were: 'as a rule', 'generally', 'normally', 'habitually', 'as a routine', 'almost always', 'mostly', 'typically'.

Summary of interpretations

1 Most respondents interpreted the term as intended or almost as intended. At the same time, the many slight variations in interpretation are worth noting.

2 Also worth noting is the fact that a few people reduced the term 'usually' to something like 'majority of occasions' or simply to 'regularly'.

3 For a few (5), the term seems to have been overlooked altogether.

Table 7.1.5

Interpretations of 'usually'

Usually (apparently as intended)	31
As a rule (1)/normally (7)/in the normal week (1)/habitually (2)/ your habit (3)/your routine (1)/your weekly routine (1)	16
What you always do (1)/day in, day out (1)	2
More often than not (2)/not just now and then (1)	3
Regularly	2
Term apparently not considered	5
Total	59

Interpretations of 'watch television'

The reference 'watch television' was intended to mean attend to whatever is being shown on the screen or to give it at least some degree of attention.

Summary of interpretations

1 The majority (44) appear to have interpreted the term 'watch television,as intended.

2 Of the remaining 15, eleven interpreted the reference simply as 'have the set on'—an interpretation which quite possibly included occasions when no attention at all was being paid to the set by the

respondent (e.g. as when he was out of the room, or reading a paper while the set was on).

3   Three respondents used a very loose interpretation indeed, the effect of which was to include occasions when they were only marginally aware of what was showing.

Speculative comment

For some people, the term 'watch' appears to be open to rather loose interpretation, at least in the television context.

Table 7.1.6

Interpretations of 'watch television' *

Did respondent interpret 'watch' as 'paying at least some attention'?

Watch, but not necessarily with full attention (3)/watch attentively (9)/
look at it with attention (1)/view with attention (1)/pay attention
to it (8)/watch in interested way (1)/actually watch (2)/actually
view (1)/actually look at screen (3)   29 ⎫
                                                                              ⎬ 44
Interpretation of 'watch' not fully established, but no reason for   ⎪
thinking other than 'watch with at least some attention' (e.g.,   ⎪
watch, look at, view)   15 ⎭

Interpreted as 'have the set on' (and so possibly included
occasions when no attention paid by respondent)   11

Watch sometimes attentively, sometimes inattentively (1)/
look at it but not necessarily pay attention (1)/glance
casually at screen without necessarily paying attention (1)   3

Not clear whether or not respondent meant 'paying attention'   1
                                                                            ——
                                                           Total   59

Other features of the interpretation (7 cases, already included above)

Sit down and attend to screen (1)/sit and watch in an interested
way (1)/sit and look at it (3)   5

(What is) the pattern of viewing carried on (by ...) (1)   1

Watch and enjoy   1

The use of raw numbers in most of the tables. Most of the many tables in this book present raw numbers rather than percentages. Thus we find in Table 7.12.8, that 24 out of 60 respondents interpreted the reference 'other than ordinary Westerns' as 'including Westerns'. To have converted the figure 24 into a percentage of 60 would have been to risk over-generalisation of the findings. With a base of only 60 cases, it is safer to present the results simply as exploratory and indicative and I consider that raw numbers are more likely to achieve this end. In rating understanding of questions *as wholes*, percentages *have* been used, but these must be seen as purely comparative in character. In any case, these overall ratings are the least important part of the findings—what matter are the tables of interpretations of words and passages and these are presented in raw number form.

Summing up the whole question

1 Of the 59 interpretations of this question, 39 per cent were allocated an overall rating of either 'as intended' or 'permissible'. This result compares with an average of 29 per cent for all the questions tested.

2 The main points of failure in this question were as follows:

(a) some respondents (15) limited their consideration of the question to evening viewing only;

(b) some interpreted 'watch television' simply as having the set on (11) or very loosely indeed;

(c) some (14) failed to answer in terms of a number or else lost the concept of number altogether; in addition there were some who excluded from consideration days when they did but little viewing (5);

(d) a few limited their consideration to less than the full 7 days of the week—in spite of a specific instruction to consider all seven;

(e) several (4) interpreted 'you' as if it included the behaviour of family members additional to the respondent;

(f) some interpreted 'usually' either too strongly (e.g. always) or too weakly (e.g. regularly) (7) and some left the concept out of consideration altogether.

3 *Speculative comments**

(a) With this question, an apparently complete sentence had been asked before a separate qualification was put forward in a second sentence. The present evidence of communication failure is consistent with some respondents formulating an answer without waiting for the qualification—though it may also be consistent with some respondents being confused by the multiplicity of concepts put to them in the total question.

(b) It may well be that the concepts 'watch' and 'you' are specially open to miscommunication in the television context, 'watch' becoming something less than 'watch with attention' and 'you' sometimes taking on a collective character.

---

*A fairly distinctive feature of this report is the presentation of what are labelled as 'Speculative comments' about each of the findings. Such comments have been presented as a basis for the later development of hypotheses about the processes or phenomena underlying the misinterpretation of questions (see pages 370 to 387). But these comments have been clearly labelled as 'Speculative comments' in order to distinguish them from 'findings'—for it would be most misleading to risk any confusion of the two.

7.2   QUESTION 9, QUESTIONNAIRE I

The wording of the question

'When you turn on your television in the evening, do you generally go on viewing till the end of the evening or do you just watch one or two programmes?' (Reply to be coded as: view till end/one or two programmes/sometimes till end, sometimes one or two.)

Definitions of different parts of the question

The following are the intended meanings of key terms in the question. *However, as indicated below, some variants of the intended interpretations were regarded as permissible and others as possibly permissible.* The word 'you' was meant to be interpreted as 'you, yourself' and was not intended to include others (e.g. respondent's spouse, children, relatives, lodger(s)). The phrase 'when (you) turn on your television' was meant to refer to the actual switching on of the television set. The reference 'in the evening' was meant to refer to the period from 6 pm onwards, on those evenings during which the respondent did at least some viewing. The word 'generally' was meant to be interpreted as: 'for the most part'; 'ordinarily'; 'in most (but not all) cases'; 'pertaining to the majority of instances'; 'usually'. The phrase 'go on viewing' was meant to be interpreted as continuing to view with at least some degree of attention. Occasional breaks of about 5 minutes were not regarded as negating continuity, but a break of half an hour or more would do so. The phrase 'till the end of the evening' was meant to convey 'till the end of all programmes for the evening', though quite a lot of variation away from this standard was regarded as permissible (see below). The word 'watch' was intended to mean to attend to what is being shown on the screen or give it at least some degree of attention. The phrase 'just ... one or two programmes' was intended to be restricted to 'one or two' only, and not to be extended to a greater number.

Respondent's interpretations of the question

These interpretations are set out in full in the Appendix (Part II). They are based on the replies of 59 people.

Marking the interpretations

The system used for rating or marking respondent's interpretations of questions

The following marking or rating system was used.

1 If all elements of the question were interpreted as intended, the interpretation as a whole was rated 'fully as intended'.

2 Failure to interpret any significant element of the question fully as intended was sufficient to pull the total interpretation down below the level of 'fully as intended'. The level so reached was determined by the most seriously misinterpreted (significant) element in the test question. For example, if all but one of the significant elements of the question were interpreted as intended and the interpretation of that other element was rated as 'somewhat limited but permissible' (see below), then the whole interpretation was so rated (i.e. 'somewhat limited but permissible'). The reason for this is that a question cannot be regarded as a safe one unless all its parts are interpreted as intended.

3 If a significant element of the question was obviously and substantially misinterpreted or was omitted altogether, the total interpretation was marked 'incorrect' (X).

4 In the context of this system, the following ratings were made of specific elements of respondents' interpretations.

(a) 'you'. Where this term was interpreted as intended (see above), the interpretation was rated 'correct' ($\sqrt{}$). Where it was interpreted as 'you and/or your family', or as 'you and some other(s)', the interpretation was rated as 'unduly extended' (UE).

(b) 'when (you) turn on your television'. Where this phrase was interpreted as intended, the rating 'correct' ($\sqrt{}$) was applied. The following interpretations of the phrase were rated 'different but permissible' (DP): 'after (you) sit down to view'; 'once (you) start viewing'. Where, as occurred in several cases, the respondent interpreted the phrase simply as 'when (you) view', the rating 'doubtful but permissible' (?P) was applied. The interpretation (once (you) switch on for a particular programme' was rated 'limited but permissible' (LP). Where the reference was omitted altogether, the rating 'incorrect' (X) was applied.

(c) 'in the evening'. Where this reference was interpreted as intended (see above), the interpretation was rated 'correct' (√). Where it was interpreted as 'from 5 pm onwards', it was rated 'extended but permissible' (EP). Where it seemed that a permissible interpretation had been made, but where the evidence was not conclusive, the rating 'doubtful but permissible' (?P) was applied. Where respondent limited his reply to some particular period (of evening), e.g. 'Monday to Friday evenings only', 'on those evenings when you know you are on early turn in the morning', that interpretation was rated 'unduly limited' (UL). Where the reference 'in the evening' was omitted altogether the rating 'incorrect' (X) was applied.

(d) 'you'. Where this term was interpreted as intended (see above), the interpretation was rated 'correct' (√). Where it was interpreted as 'you and/or your family', or as 'you and/or some other(s)', the interpretation was rated as 'unduly extended' (UE).

(e) 'generally'. Where this term was interpreted as intended (see above), the interpretation was rated 'correct' (√). Where the term was interpreted as 'habitually', 'regularly', as a matter of routine', 'on an average (evening)', the interpretation was rated 'different but permissible' (DP). Where it seemed that the term was interpreted as intended but where the evidence was not conclusive, the rating 'doubtful but permissible' was applied (?P). Where the term had been omitted altogether, the rating 'incorrect' (X) was applied.

(f) 'go on viewing'. Where this phrase was interpreted as intended (see above), the rating 'correct' (√) was applied. Also rated 'correct' were: 'go on viewing solidly'; 'watch from start to finish'; 'go on viewing more or less without stopping'. The following interpretations were rated as 'different but permissible' (DP); 'go on viewing indiscriminately'; 'sit glued to the set watching anything that comes on', 'go on viewing except for the advertisement breaks'. In several cases the interpretation seemed to be permissible but some doubt about this existed (e.g. 'watch television', 'view it', 'watch it in an unselective way'). In these cases, the rating 'doubtful but permissible' (?P) was applied. The following interpretations were rated as 'unduly different' (UD); 'stay in the room with the set'; 'leave the set on'; 'see a lot of programmes when you view': 'go on viewing except for breaks of half an hour or more'. The following interpretations were rated 'incorrect' (X): 'go on viewing on one station regardless of what is available on the other'; 'like all the programmes you see'; 'how many programmes do you watch'; 'what does your husband do about viewing'. Where the phrase was omitted altogether, the rating 'incorrect' (X) was applied.

(g) 'till the end of the evening'. Where this phrase was interpreted as intended (see above), the rating 'correct' (√) was applied. Such interpretations included: 'till the end of all programmes'; 'till close down of programmes'; 'till TV finishes'. Interpretations of the following kind were rated 'different but permissible' (DP): 'all evening'; 'for the whole of the evening'; 'till your bed time at 10 pm' (or later); 'till nearly the end of all programmes'. Where it seemed that a permissible interpretation had been made, but where the evidence was not conclusive, the rating 'doubtful but permissible' (?P) was applied. Where the phrase was omitted altogether, the rating 'incorrect' (X) was applied.

(h) 'you'. Where this term was interpreted as intended (see above), the interpretation was rated 'correct' (√). Where it was interpreted as 'you and/or your family', or as 'you and/or some other(s)', the interpretation was rated as 'unduly extended' (UE).

(i) 'watch'. Where this reference was interpreted as intended (see above), the rating 'correct' (√) was applied. Where it seemed that attention had been paid to the screen but where the evidence was not conclusive, the rating 'doubtful but permissible' (?P) was applied. Where the interpretation did not necessarily involve giving the screen at least some degree of attention (e.g. 'had the set on'), the rating 'unduly different' (UD) was applied. Where it was interpreted as 'like', that interpretation was rated 'incorrect' (X). An interpretation of the question which resulted in omission of the phrase 'or do you just watch' was similarly rated 'incorrect' (X).

(j) 'just ... one or two programmes'. Where this phrase was interpreted as intended (see above), the rating 'correct' (√) was applied. Where the interpretation was 'one or two programmes of your choosing', the rating 'somewhat specific but permissible' (SP) was applied. Where the interpretation was 'a few programmes' the rating 'somewhat general but permissible' (GP) was applied. The rating 'unduly general' (UG) was applied to the following: 'those programmes you choose or view selectively', 'only the ones you turn on for', 'do you stop viewing before that'. The rating 'incorrect' (X) was applied where the interpretation was wrong or the phrase omitted altogether.

The rating allocated

Under the system described above, the following ratings were allocated to respondents' interpretations of this test question.

Table 7.2.1

Ratings allocated to respondents' interpretations
of test question (Q9, 1)

Lowest rating allocated to any part of the interpretation	Number of Ratings	Number of Persons	% of Persons
Correct (√)	0	0	0
Extra but permissible (ExP)	0		
Somewhat limited but permissible (LP)	0		
Somewhat too specific but permissible (SP)	4		
Somewhat too general but permissible (GP)	4	12*	20
Somewhat extended but permissible (EP)	0		
Somewhat different but permissible (DP)	11		
Doubtful but permitted (?P)	3	3	5
Unduly limited (UL)	5		
Unduly general (UG)	7		
Unduly extended UE)	10	19*	32
Unduly different (UD)	6		
Incorrect (X)	25	25	42
Total		59	†

*See Note A on page 47.
†See Note B on page 48.

Content analysis of the interpretations

There follows an analysis of the different interpretations of elements of the test question. The emphasis in this analysis is upon the different kinds of interpretations which were found rather than upon the number of them (though these numbers are given), the purpose of the content analysis being to discover the kinds of things that happen, to speculate about what causes them, and to derive hypotheses (about communication processes) for testing in later phases of the enquiry.

Interpretations of 'you (turn on your television set)'

The word 'you' was meant to be interpreted as 'you, yourself', and was not intended to include others (e.g. respondent's spouse, children, relatives, lodger(s)).

Summary of interpretations

1 Some 38 of the 59 respondents interpreted this term as intended.

2 Of the rest, 15 partly by-passed the word by thinking in terms of 'when your set is turned on'—that is, the interpretation could well include the 'switching on' done by any member of the respondent's family. Several more quite clearly interpreted the term collectively (i.e. to include the family).

3 One respondent considered only the 'turning on of the set' by her husband.

4 Two persons appear simply to have overlooked the term altogether.

Table 7.2.2

Interpretations of 'you (turn on your television)'

You, yourself (as intended)	38
You and a member of your family/you and your family	2
Your set is switched on/the set is switched on	15
Your family	1
Your husband	1
Term by-passed	2
Total	59

Speculative comment

The collective (or *possibly* collective) interpretation of 'you' may spring out of the fact that the switching on of the set may be done by any member of a family and that 'you' in the viewing context may in fact have a cumulative meaning for some viewers.

Interpretations of 'when (you) turn on your television set'

The phrase 'when (you) turn on your television' was meant to refer to the actual switching on of the television set.

Summary of interpretations

1 There were 29 who interpreted this reference as intended.

2 Twenty others thought, not in terms of turning the set on, but in terms of 'starting to view'.

3 One respondent thought in terms of switching on for a *particular* programme—which was, of course, rather more pointed and specific than simply turning on the set.

4 Nine appear to have overlooked the reference altogether.

Table 7.2.3

Interpretations of 'when (you) turn on your television'

When/once (you) turn on/switch on your television set	13 ⎫
When/once your television set is turned/switched on (presumably either by you or someone else)	15 ⎬ 29
Once your family turns on the television set	1 ⎭
Once (you) start viewing/watching television	15 ⎫
When (you) view/watch television	4 ⎬ 20
After (you) sit down to view (at 5.00 pm)	1 ⎭
Once (you) switch on to watch a particular programme or set of programmes	1
Respondent did not consider the phrase	9
Total	59

Speculative comment

It may be that the first two types of interpretations would in fact yield identical answers. Nonetheless, the second of them (i.e. 'starting to view') could rule out casual noticing of the screen or half attention, or even seeing something that the respondent was not really interested in.

Interpretations of 'in the evening'

The reference 'in the evening' was meant to refer to the period from 6.00 pm onwards, on those evenings during which the respondent did at least some viewing.

Summary of interpretations

1 Practically all respondents understood 'evening' as the period from about 6.00 pm onwards.

2 There was some variety of interpretation when it came to *which* evenings were to be considered. Thus: 48 considered evenings over the whole seven day week but seven thought only of evenings in the period Monday to Friday; one limited himself to the evenings he *usually*

watched, one to evenings when he watched TV *regularly* and one to evenings when he knew he would be on 'early turn' next morning.

3 Two respondents apparently overlooked the phrase altogether.

Table 7.2.4

Interpretations of 'in the evening'

Concerning the start of the evening

Presumably from 6.00 pm onwards (no evidence to suggest other than as intended)	56
From 5.00 pm onwards	1
No evidence that the phrase had been considered at all	2
Total	59

Concerning which evenings

Any evening of the seven days of the week	48
Monday to Friday evenings only	6
On those *weekday* evenings when you watch TV regularly	1
On those evenings when you usually watch television	1
On those evenings when you know you are on early turn in the morning	1
No evidence that the phrase had been considered at all	2
Total	59

Speculative comment

There was some degree of variability in the respondents' interpretations of 'evening' with respect to *which* evenings should be considered. Presumably this arises from the fact that the question was imprecise on this account.

Interpretations of 'you (generally go on viewing)'

The word 'you' was meant to be interpreted as 'you, yourself' and was not intended to include others (e.g. respondent's spouse, children, relatives, lodger(s)).

Summary of interpretations

1 Some 47 of the 59 respondents interpreted the term 'you' as intended.

2 Of the others, 11 considered the viewing of members of the family, either as well as his/her own viewing or theirs alone.

Table 7.2.5

Interpretations of 'you (generally go on viewing)'

You, yourself, alone (apparently)		47
You and your family	3 }	
You and one or more members of your family	3 }	6
Not necessarily respondent alone (i.e. 'is the set left on')		2
Your family (and not necessarily yourself)	2 }	
Members of your family (not necessarily yourself)	1 }	3
Your husband		1
Total		59

Speculative comment

Here, as in many other instances, the term 'you' was interpreted collectively by some of the respondents. It seems possible that this springs out of the 'family' nature of the viewing of some respondents.

Interpretations of 'generally'

The word 'generally' was meant to be interpreted as 'for the most part'; 'ordinarily'; 'in most (but not all) cases'; 'pertaining to the majority of instances'; 'usually'.

Summary of interpretations

1 Of the 59 respondents, 39 interpreted this term as intended, though there was quite a lot of variability amongst their interpretations. Possibly a further 9 interpreted the term as intended, but the evidence is not conclusive.

2 Of the others, there was one who converted the term to 'regularly' and another who made it 'on an average evening'.

3 Nine seemingly overlooked the term.

Table 7.2.6

Interpretations of 'generally'

Generally (apparently as intended)	14 }	
Usually (18)/as usual (1)	19 }	39
Normally (3)/habitually (1)/as a matter of routine (2)	6 }	
Regularly		1
On an average evening		1
Not clear how the word was interpreted		9
Word seemingly not considered		9

Interpretations of 'go on viewing'

The phrase 'go on viewing' was meant to be interpreted as continue to view with at least some degree of attention. Occasional breaks of about five minutes were not regarded as negative continuity, but a break of half an hour or more *would* be so regarded.

Summary of interpretations

1 Some 46 of the 59 respondents interpreted this phrase more or less as intended, but with certain variations. Thus there were some who interpreted the term as allowing for occasional short breaks but others who interpreted it to mean viewing without break, and some of these built into the interpretation a concept of unselectivity or of indiscriminate viewing. On the other hand there were several (3) who qualified their interpretations with something like 'except for breaks' or 'provided you are not interrupted'.

2 Of the 13 unacceptable interpretations, 9 were weakened versions of the term such as 'leave the set on' (7), 'stay in the room with the set except for breaks' (1), 'see a lot of programmes when you view (1)'.

3 The others (4) were markedly incorrect (e.g. '(Do you) like all (the programmes you see)?'

Table 7.2.7

Interpretations of 'go on viewing'

Viewing interpreted more or less as intended, but sometimes with additions	
Go on viewing	26
Watch television (1)/view television (2)	3
Go on viewing solidly (1)/watch from start to finish (1)/ view everything (1)/sit glued to the set watching everything that comes on (1)	4
Go on viewing indiscriminately or unselectively (8)/watch unselectively	9
Go on viewing on one station regardless of what else is on	1
Go on viewing except for breaks (1)/go on viewing more or less without stopping (1)/go on viewing provided you are not interrupted (1)	3
	46
'Viewing' interpreted other than as intended	
Stay in the room with the set, except for breaks	1
Leave the set switched on	7
See a lot of programmes when you view	1
Like all the programmes you see	1
How many programmes do you watch	2
What does your husband do about watching	1
	13
Total	59

Speculative comment

1 The reference 'go on viewing' is to some degree imprecise: it does not indicate how the respondent should think about breaks or about interruptions to viewing. The respondent thus has to make up his own mind about such matters.

2 It was suggested by one of the intensive interviewers that many viewers don't like admitting to massive or unbroken viewing and that the conversion of 'go on viewing' into 'go on viewing indiscriminately' may allow them to opt out of the 'go on viewing' category.

Interpretations of 'till the end of the evening'

The phrase 'till the end of the evening' was meant to convey 'till the end of all programmes for the evening', though quite a lot of variation away from this standard was regarded as permissible.

Summary of interpretations

1 Whereas most of the respondents interpreted this phrase to mean 'till the end of all programmes' for the evening, there were some who appeared to have interpreted it to mean 'till the end of their evening' (i.e. till they went to bed).

2 One allowed himself a little margin with 'till nearly the end of all programmes'.

3 Several people (5) appear to have overlooked this alternative altogether (e.g. How many programmes do you usually view on a weekday evening?).

Table 7.2.8

Interpretations of 'till the end of the evening'

Till the end of all programmes (28)/till closedown (8)/to the time it finishes (1)	37
Till nearly the end of all programmes	1
All evening (5)/for the whole evening (1)	6
Till your bedtime at 11.00 pm/at about 10.00 pm/between 10.00 pm and 11.30 pm	6
Not clear how the phrase was interpreted	4
Phrase seemingly overlooked	5
Total	59

Speculative comment

Here again, the phrase is an imprecise one in that it does not specify *what* to consider as 'the end of the evening'.

Interpretations of '(or do) you (just watch)'

The word 'you' was meant to be interpreted as 'you, yourself' and was not intended to include others (e.g. respondent's spouse, children, relatives, lodger(s)).

Summary of interpretations

1 Of the 59 respondents, 41 interpreted the term just as intended.

2 There were at least 6 who brought the concept of *family* into the reference 'you', either in the sense 'you and your family' or in the more general sense 'your family'.

3 One respondent thought of her husband (only) instead of herself.

4 One person partly by-passed the reference by thinking only in terms of 'the set being on', and 10 more appear to have by-passed it in some other way, usually by overlooking the whole alternative in which it was embedded (e.g. 'How many programmes do you view on a weekday evening?')

Table 7.2.9

Interpretations of '(or do) you (just watch)

Seemingly interpreted as you, yourself alone		41
Not necessarily respondent alone (i.e. 'is the set left on')		1
You and your family	3	
You and one or more members of your family	2	5
Member of your family (not yourself—your husband)	1	
The family (not necessarily yourself)	1	2
Term not considered at all		10
Total		59

Interpretations of '(do you just) watch (one or two)'

The word 'watch' was intended to mean to attend to what is being shown on the screen or give it at least some degree of attention.

Summary of interpretations

1 In all, 42 of the respondents interpreted this term more or less as intended.

2 Two more converted it into the somewhat more precise and limiting

concept 'select' (though we should note here that others introduced this concept of 'selectivity' through other parts of the question'.

3 Three broadened the term to cover situations when the set is left on or where the respondent stays in the room with the set.

4 One converted the term into 'like'.

5 There were 11 who apparently by-passed the term altogether, mainly through overlooking the alternative in which this term was embedded.

Table 7.2.10

Interpretations of '(do you just) watch (one or two)'

Watch (apparently as intended)	32	
View (5)/viewing (3)/seeing (1)	10	42
Select (note that others introduced 'selectively' through other parts of the question—see Table 7.2.11)		2
Is the set left on (1)/(do you) leave the set on (1)/(do you) stay in the room with the set (1)		3
Like		1
Term apparently not considered (mostly through overlooking the whole alternative in which it was embedded)		11
Total		59

Interpretations of 'just (watch) one or two programmes'

The phrase 'just ... one or two programmes' was intended to be restricted to 'one or two' only and not to be extended to a greater number.

Summary of interpretations

1 Twenty-nine of the respondents properly interpreted the reference as 'one or two' and a further 9 as 'a few'.

2 There were 8, however, who tend to think only in terms of some selected set of programmes. Presumably they meant a *limited number,* but it is by no means clear that they meant only 'one or two' and in any case the tighter concept 'select' had been added.

3 Two respondents interpreted the phrase very loosely indeed, namely 'do you stop before that (i.e. before the end of the evening)'. Certainly this need not mean 'just one or two'.

4 There were 11 more respondents who disregarded the term altogether, mainly because they overlooked the whole alternative in which the reference was embedded.

5 The second part of Table 7.2.11 brings out further aspects

of the interpretations of this term. Thus 29 interpreted it numerically; 20 brought in, to some degree or other, the concept of *selected* programmes; 4 thought in terms of turning off because they had had enough.

Table 7.2.11

Interpretations of 'just (watch) one or two programmes

Some details of interpretations

One or two programmes (18)/one or two programmes of your choice (9)/one or two, turning the set off afterwards (1)/watch continuously for a short time, so that you see only one or two programmes	29
A few programmes (5)/a few programmes of your choosing (3)/(stop earlier than that, seeing) only a few programmes (1)	9
Only that selected set of programmes (and then switch off) (1)/(do you view) selectively (2)/those programmes you select (4)/those programmes you are interested in (1)	8
Stop (viewing) before that (1)/stop before that through lack of interest	2*
Phrase seemingly overlooked	11
Total	59

Other aspects of the interpretations

Phrase interpreted numerically	29
Phrase interpreted to imply a small or moderate amount of viewing	20
Phrase interpreted to imply *selecting or choosing* (e.g. one or two of your choosing ; view selectively)	11
Phrase interpreted to imply 'turn off' because he has had enough	4
Phrase seemingly overlooked	11
Total	74†

*Possibly cases of 'phrase overlooked'
†Some interpretations could be classified under more than one of the above headings.

Speculative comment

1 The temptation to deviate from a strictly numerical interpretation of 'just one or two programmes' must have been considerable, though it may well be that 'one or two' is generally interpreted to mean something 'vaguely small' or 'vaguely few'.

2 The intrusion of the notion 'selected few' and of 'turn off because had enough' could well be evidence of some established way of thinking of viewers which might then displace the possibly unrealistic alternative actually offered.

Did respondent consider both alternatives

Summary of interpretations

1 It appears that both alternatives definitely were considered by only 47 of the 59 respondents, the others considering only one (8) or neither (3).

2 When *one* of the alternatives was omitted, it tended to be the second one.

Table 7.2.12

Did respondent consider *both* alternatives?

First alternative considered	56
Second alternative considered (47) or partly considered	48
Both alternatives considered (47) or possibly considered (1)	48
Only one considered	8 } 59
Neither considered	3 }

Speculative comment

It seems reasonable to suggest that some of the respondents who left out the second alternative may have felt that they could offer an answer on the basis of the first alternative and so either answered then or stopped listening after hearing that first alternative.

Other interpretations of interest

Several people modified the question as indicated in Table 7.2.13 below.

Table 7.2.13

Other interpretations of interest

Added to the question 'watching only those programmes you are interested in	1
Added to the question 'choose the reply that is nearer to what you do'	2
Converted question to: 'when you view till the end of the evening do you see a lot of programmes or only one or two?'	1

Summary of the full question

1 Of the 59 interpretations of this question, 25 per cent were allocated an overall rating of 'as intended' or 'permissible'. This result compares with an average of 29 per cent for all the questions tested.

73

2 The main points of difficulty or of failure in this question appear to have been as follows:

(a)   The interpretation, by some respondents, of 'you' to include (or quite possibly to include) others in the family.

(b)   the tendency of some (20) to think in terms of 'starting to view' rather than in terms of 'turning the set on';

(c)   the interpretation by some of 'go on viewing' as leave the set on';

(d)   the conversion by some of 'till the end of the evening' into something equivalent to 'till the end of *your* evening' (e.g. 10.30 pm);

(e)   the interpretation of 'one or two' programmes as 'some selected set' of programmes (and not just one or two);

(f)   a failure by some respondents to consider *both* the alternatives offered;

(g)   a tendency for some respondents to overlook elements of the question, usually by overlooking the part of the question in which that element or word was embedded;

(h)   the occurrence of quite a lot of variability in the interpretation of some elements in the question (e.g. 'you'; 'generally'; 'go on viewing'; 'one or two' programmes).

3 *Speculative comments*

(a)   In this particular question, the word 'you' may have a 'family' connotation, though in some cases at least its collective interpretation may have arisen from others in the family switching on the set *on behalf of* the respondent.

(b)   The interpretation of 'when you turn on your set' as 'when you start to view' could rule out casual noticing of what is on (after turning on the set) or even something that did not happen to interest the respondent very much.

(c)   Some interpreted 'go on viewing' as 'unselective viewing' and it may possibly be that this allowed them to avoid answering 'go on viewing till the end of the evening'.

(d)   The phrase 'till the end of the evening' is probably imprecise and so is liable to facilitate loose interpretation (e.g. 'till I go to bed').

(e)   The temptation to deviate from a strictly numerical interpretation of the narrow concept 'one or two' might have been considerable and may lie behind some of the deviations that occurred.

(f)   It may be that some respondents started to answer the question on the basis of its first alternative alone and so failed to consider the second of these alternatives.

7.3   QUESTION 13b   QUESTIONNAIRE I

The wording of the question

'Do you think that the television news programmes are impartial about politics?' (To be coded as: yes/no/not sure.)

Check question

If 'yes' or 'no': 'What are your reasons for saying this?'

Definitions of different parts of the question

The intended meaning of significant elements of the question

The following are the intended meanings of key terms in the question. *However, as indicated below, some variants of the intended interpretations were regarded as permissible and others as possibly permissible.* The word 'you' was meant to be interpreted as 'you, yourself', and was not intended to include others (e.g. respondent's spouse, children, relatives, lodger(s)). The phrase 'Do (you) think (that) ... ' was intended to mean 'Is it (your) opinion (that) ...' and was not intended to mean 'What is (your) opinion *of*. The term 'television (news programme)' was intended to refer to both BBC and ITV (news programmes). The reference '(television) news programmes' was intended to mean programmes with a news content, including (but not limited to) news bulletins, other programmes with a news content such as 'Panorama', 'This Week', 'Tonight', 'Dateline', 'News Extra', 'Town and Around'. The word 'impartial was meant to be interpreted as 'unbiased', 'fair', 'treating (all parties) equally'. The term 'politics' is a broad one which was meant to refer to the affairs of Parliament and to the activities and affairs of the different political parties.

Respondents' interpretations of the question

These interpretations are set out in full in the Appendix (Part II). They are based upon the replies of 56 people.

Marking the interpretations

The system used for rating or marking respondents' interpretations of questions

The following marking or rating system was used:

1 If all elements of the question were interpreted as intended, the interpretation as a whole was rated 'fully as intended' (√).

2 Failure to interpret any significant element of the question fully as intended was sufficient to pull the total interpretation down below the level of 'fully as intended'. The level so reached was determined by the most seriously misinterpreted (significant) element of the test question. For example, if all but one of the significant elements of the question were interpreted as intended and the interpretation of that other element was rated as 'somewhat limited but permissible' (see below), then the whole interpretation was so rated (i.e. 'somewhat limited but permissible'). The reason for this is that a question cannot be regarded as a safe one unless all its parts are interpreted as intended.

3 If a significant element of the question was obviously and markedly misinterpreted or was omitted altogether, the total interpretation was marked 'incorrect' (X).

4 In the context of this system, the following ratings were made of specific elements of respondents' interpretations.

(a) 'you'. Where this term was interpreted as intended (see above), the interpretation was rated 'correct' (√). Where it seemed that a permissible interpretation had been made, but where the evidence was not conclusive, the rating 'doubtful but permissible' (?P) was applied.

(b) 'Do (you) think (that)'. Where this reference was interpreted as intended (see above), the interpretation was rated 'correct' (√). Where it seemed that a permissible interpretation had been made, the evidence was not conclusive, the rating 'doubtful but permissible' (?P) was applied. The interpretation 'what do (you) think about' was rated 'somewhat different but permissible' (DP). The following interpretations were rated

77

'unduly different' (UD): 'are (you) interested in', 'are (you) partial to', 'do (you) like to see'. Where the reference was omitted altogether the interpretation was rated 'incorrect' (X)

(c) 'television (news programmes)'. Where this term was interpreted as intended (see above), the interpretation was rated 'correct' (√). Where it seemed that a permissible interpretation had been made but the evidence was not conclusive, the rating 'doubtful but permissible' (?P) was applied. Where the interpretation was made in terms of BBC television only, or in terms of ITV programmes only, that interpretation was rated 'unduly limited' (UL). Where the term was interpreted as a comparison between BBC and ITV television, the rating 'unduly different' (UD) was applied. The interpretation 'newspapers' was rated 'incorrect' (X). Similarly where the term was omitted altogether, the rating 'incorrect' (X) was applied.

(d) 'news programmes'. Where this reference was interpreted as intended (see above), the interpretation was rated 'correct' (√). Where it was interpreted solely as news bulletins with no reference to any of the other programmes listed above, the interpretation was rated 'limited but permissible' (LP). Where the reference was interpreted as one or other of the news programmes listed above, but where news bulletins had been omitted from consideration the interpretation was rated 'limited but permissible' (LP). Where the reference was interpreted simply as 'news programmes', the rating 'doubtful but permissible' (?P), was applied. Where the reference was interpreted wholly or partly as party political broadcasts, party political interviews or other political interviews, the rating 'incorrect' (X) was applied. The rating 'incorrect' (X) was similarly applied to the interpretations 'programmes generally', 'newspapers' and where the reference was omitted altogether. Where the term was interpreted in terms of people who present broadcasts (e.g. news readers, announcers, interviewers) the rating 'unduly different' (UD) was applied.

(e) 'impartial'. Where this term was interpreted as intended (see above), the interpretation was rated 'correct' (√). The following interpretations were rated 'incorrect' (X): 'partial to'; 'interested in'; 'take sides'. An interpretation was similarly rated which was in terms of whether too much, enough, or too little (political information) was being given. Where the respondent considered whether (politics) was presented better/differently (by the BBC or ITV), this interpretation was rated 'incorrect' (X).

(f) 'politics'. Where this reference was interpreted as intended (see above), the interpretation was rated 'correct' (√). Where it seemed that a permissible interpretation had been made, but where the evidence was not conclusive, the rating 'doubtful but permissible' (?P) was applied. Where the reference was interpreted solely as 'party politics', the interpretation was rated 'limited but permissible' (LP); similarly for interpretations of 'Labour and Conservative parties (only)'. Where the reference was interpreted solely as 'the affairs of Government'; 'Parliament and MPs'; 'about Government and the way the country is run'; without consideration of party political matters; these interpretations were rated 'unduly limited' (UL).

The ratings allocated

Under the system described earlier, the following ratings were allocated to respondent interpretations of this test question.

Table 7.3.1

Ratings allocated to respondents' interpretations
of test question (QE, 1)

Lowest rating allocated to any part of the interpretation	Number of Ratings	Persons	% of Persons
Correct (√)	2	2	4
Extra but permissible (ExP)	1		
Somewhat limited but permissible (LP)	8		
Somewhat too specific but permissible (SP)	0		
Somewhat too general but permissible (GP)	0	8*	14
Somewhat extended but permissible (EP)	0		
Somewhat different but permissible (DP)	0		
Doubtful but permitted (?P)	3	3	5
Unduly limited (UL)	2		
Unduly general (UG)	0		
Unduly extended (UE)	0	7	12
Unduly different (UD)	5		
Incorrect (X)	36	36	64
Total		56	†

*See Note A on page 47.
†See Note B on page 48.

Content analysis of the interpretations

There follows an anaiysis of the different interpretations of elements of the test question. The emphasis in this analysis is upon the different kinds of interpretations which were found rather than upon the number of them (though these numbers are given), the purpose of the content analysis being to discover the kinds of things that happen, to speculate about what causes them, and to derive hypotheses (about communication processes) for testing in later phases of the enquiry.

Interpretations of 'you'

The word 'you' was meant to be interpreted as 'you, yourself' and was not intended to include others (e.g. respondent's spouse, children, relatives, lodger(s)).

Summary of interpretations

There was no clear evidence for concluding that any of these respondents misinterpreted the term 'you', though the possibility that some did so cannot be ruled out.

Table 7.3.2
Interpretations of 'you'

You (i.e. apparently as intended)	48
Unclear exactly how 'you' was interpreted but probably as intended	3
No evidence	5
Total	56

Interpretations of 'do (you) think'

The phrase 'Do (you) think (that)' was intended to mean 'Is it (your) opinion (that)' and was not intended to mean 'what is (your) opinion of'.

Summary of interpretations

1 The majority appeared to have no difficulty with this part of the question.

2 Some, however, overlooked or converted it to some degree. Thus for three it became 'are(you) interested in ...'—a conversion which fairly clearly sprang out of a mishearing of the term 'impartial' (see details below).

80

Table 7.3.3

Interpretations of 'do (you) think'

Do (you) think	39		Phrase seemingly overlooked	3
Do (you) ever think	1	40	No evidence as to nature of	
What do (you) think about	3		interpretation, if any	5
Are (you) interested in	3		Total	56
Are (you) partial to	1	5		
Do (you) like to see	1			

Speculative comment

It is quite understandable that a purely introductory phrase like 'Do (you) think' should be overlooked, and probably no harm would come of this. However in the present case, that opening phrase appears occasionally to have been converted or distorted somewhat to fit in with a misinterpretation of some other part of the question. In other words, that later misinterpretation appears to have been a dominating one as far as at least *some* other parts of the question were concerned.

Interpretations of 'television'

The term 'television (news programmes)' was intended to refer to both BBC and ITV (news programmes).

Summary of interpretations

1 Of the 56 respondents, 39 interpreted this reference as intended.

2 Of the others: some (8) interpreted it as BBC alone or ITV alone; several thought in terms of TV and/or radio; 2 thought comparatively of BBC and ITV; and one considered only newspapers.

Table 7.3.4

Interpretations of 'television (news programmes)'

Television (as intended)	39
BBC television (4)/BBC (possibly referring to radio as well) (?)	6
ITV	2
BBC television and ITV (in comparison)	2
Television and/or radio	3
Newspapers	1
No evidence	3
Total	56

81

Speculative comments

That there should be so much distortion of an apparently simple and very familiar term may seem surprising. Some of the following may possible be contributing causes.

1   The respondent was dominated by impressions about the impartiality of one or another of the two services.

2   The respondent tended to watch TV news programmes on only one station and so considered only that station in formulating an answer.

3   Some respondents thought of 'news programmes' as 'radio material' as much as (or more than) TV material and so included their radio experiences in consideration of the question. The conversion of the reference into 'newspapers' may have sprung out of the perceptual dominance (for one respondent) of the term 'news'—presumably coinciding with some weakening (or non-hearing) of the terms 'television' and 'programmes'.

Interpretations of 'news programmes'

The reference '(television) news programmes' was intended to mean programmes with a news content, including (but not limited to) news bulletins, other programmes with a news content included such as 'Panorama', 'This Week', 'Tonight', 'Dateline', 'News Extra', 'Town and Around'.

Summary of interpretations

There was considerable variation in respondents' interpretations of this reference.

1 Only 5 interpreted it in the broad way intended.

2 18 thought rather narrowly, mainly in terms of news bulletins only.

3 For 29 of the 56 respondents who were asked this question, 'news programmes' was interpreted to include political programmes of some kind.

Table 7.3.5

Interpretations of '(television) news programmes'

News programmes, apparently as intended

programmes with a news content	1	
news bulletins and other news programmes (e.g. 'Panorama', 'This Week', 'Town and Around')	3	5
television news (in general)	1	

News programmes with no mention of bulletins ... 1

News bulletins (only) (17)/news bulletins which refer to
   political events (1) ... 18

Bulletins and politics

news bulletins and political programmes	4	
news bulletins and party political broadcasts	1	5

Bulletins, politics and other news programmes

news bulletins, 'What the Papers Say', party political
   broadcasts (1)/news bulletins, 'Panorama', 'Tonight'
   and party political broadcasts (1)/news bulletins,
   'Panorama' and other political programmes (1) ... 3

Political programmes (only)

programmes about politics/political programmes	12	
political programmes and party political broadcasts	2	21
party political broadcasts (only)	3	
politics on TV	4	

Others

TV programmes (generally)	1
newspapers	1

Reference seemingly overlooked ... 1

Total	56

Speculative comments

1 It seems that for some respondents, the words 'news programmes' may have been heard only as 'the news'—with the result that the people concerned considered only news bulletins.

2 The inclusion of 'political programmes' among the programmes considered may well have sprung out of the reference, later in the question, to 'politics'—presumably through the suppression or weakening of the term 'news'.

Interpretations of 'impartial'

1 Some 25 of the 56 respondents interpreted this term more or less as intended.

2 On the other hand, 5 gave it a meaning *opposite* to that intended (i.e., unfair, biased), 9 interpreted it as implying a tendency 'to give too much time or attention to' politics (e.g. partial to; include too much about), and 2 more as inclined to give too little time to it or insufficient information about it.

3 Of the remainder, 10 appear simply to have overlooked the term and several others clearly did not know what it meant.

Table 7.3.6

Interpretations of 'impartial (about politics)'

unbiased, in sense of not favouring any one party (6)/leaning to neither left nor right (1)/giving both sides of a story (1)/not allowing personal views to colour a story (1)	9	
unbiased in presentation, reporting, interviewing	8	
unbiased both in presentation and in time allocated for party political broadcasts	5	25
unbiased in time allocated for party political broadcasts	2	
unbiased (no further definition)	1	
unfair—i.e. favouring one party rather than another	4	
biased (no further definition)	1	5
partial to (politics) in sense of concentrating unduly upon it (1)/ interested in (1)	2	
include too much (about politics)	7	9
put on enough programmes (about politics)	1	
give too little information (about political events)	1	2
presented better (by BBC or ITV)	1	
presented differently (by ITV than by BBC)	1	2
don't know the meaning of 'impartial' (see also above)		1
apparently overlooked the term		10
no evidence		2
Total		56

Speculative comment

It seemed possible that some respondents simply dropped the 'im' off the beginning of the word, so that it became something like 'partial (to)'. Others seem simply to have been unfamiliar with the term.

Interpretation of 'politics'

The term 'politics' is a broad one which was meant to refer to the affairs of Parliament and to the activities and affairs of the different political parties.

Summary of interpretations

Most respondents interpreted this word more or less as intended.

Table 7.3.7

Interpretations of '(impartial about) politics'

about party politics (generally)	17
about the Labour and Conservative parties	3
about Parliament and MPs	5
about government and the way the country is run	3
about government, Parliament and the political parties	1
about domestic and international affairs	5
politics/political matters (undefined)	22
Total	56

Other interpretations of interest

Several other interpretations are set out in the following table. In all of them, the quality of impartiality or otherwise is linked to some individual or agency (e.g. news announcer, TV authorities, those preparing the news bulletins).

Table 7.3.8

Other interpretations of interest

(do you think) TV news announcers (are impartial)	1
(do you think) newscasters and political interviewers (are impartial)	1
(do you think) newscasters (1)/announcers (1)/(are impartial)	2
(do you think) interviewers (are impartial)	2
(do you think) newsreaders and those responsible for political programmes (are impartial)	1
(do you think) those preparing news bulletins (are impartial)	1
(do you think) TV authorities (1)/management (1)/(are impartial)	2
Total	10

Summary of the full question

1 Of the 56 interpretations of this question, 23 per cent were allocated an overall rating of either 'as intended' or 'permissible'. This result com-

pares with an average of 29 per cent for all the questions tested.

2 The main sources of difficulty were as follows:

(a)   Many (18) respondents narrowed the term 'news programmes' to 'news bulletins (only)', and at least half of the 56 interpreted it either as 'political programmes (only)' (21) or as 'including political programmes' (8). In fact only five of the 56 interpreted the term just as intended.

(b)   Only about half the respondents interpreted the term 'impartial' as intended, some of the more recurrent misinterpretations being: 'unfair'; 'partial to' (in the sense of presenting too much of it).

(c)   The term 'television' was sometimes narrowed (e.g. 'BBC only' or 'ITV only') and several widened it (e.g. 'TV and/or radio').

3 There appeared to be very little difficulty over the interpretation of the terms: 'politics'; 'you'.

4 *Speculative comments*

(a)   It seems possible that some respondents heard the term 'news programmes' as 'the News' and that the injection (by many respondents) of 'political programmes' into the intended concept. may have sprung out of the reference, in the question, to 'politics'.

(b)   Quite possibly, the word 'impartial' was not understood by some respondents, and others may have heard it as 'partial'.

7.4 QUESTION 16, QUESTIONNAIRE I

The wording of the question

'Do any programmes have a *bad* effect on young people, by setting them poor moral standards?' (To be coded as: yes/no/not sure.)

Check question

If yes: 'Which ones are they?' If no: 'Why do you say that?'

Definition of the different parts of the question

The following are the intended meanings of key terms in the question. *However, as indicated below, some variants of the intended interpretations were regarded as permissible and others as possibly permissible.* The reference 'do (any programmes)' was intended to convey a question about what is in fact the case rather than what might be the case in certain special circumstances. The reference 'any programmes' was intended to mean any particular programmes, and to include both adult and children's programmes. The word 'have' (a bad effect) was meant to be interpreted as 'actually have' rather than as 'could possibly have'. The reference 'a bad effect' was intended to mean 'an effect which is undesirable in terms of established values of good and bad'. The reference 'young people' is a broad one and no single definition of it could be regarded as final. In the present context it was meant to be interpreted as 'young people in general' rather than young people in any narrow age range or special category. An acceptable definition of 'young' was one which referred to any five year span which was in the age range 8–21 years. The reference 'by setting them (poor moral standards)' was intended to mean 'by putting before them (standards) in a manner likely to cause such standards to be adopted'. However, since the question asked about bad effects actually occurring, the interpretation 'cause to adopt' must also be accepted.

The word 'poor (moral standards)' was intended to mean standards which are below those generally accepted by society. In this context, acceptable definitions included 'bad', 'wrong', 'corrupt', 'loose', 'false'. The reference 'moral standards' is a difficult one to deal with in that its dictionary definition is wider than its popular use. Strictly speaking it means 'standards of right and wrong generally', but (in its negative form) it is often used to refer to standards associated with such concepts as 'sexual immorality', 'crime', 'violence', 'drunkenness', 'swearing'.

Respondents' interpretations of the question

These interpretations are set out in full in the Appendix (Part II). They are based upon the replies of 51 people.

Marking the interpretations

The system used for rating or marking respondents' interpretations of questions

The following marking or rating system was used:

1 If all elements of the question were interpreted as intended, the interpretation as a whole was rated 'fully as intended' (√).

2 Failure to interpret any significant element of the question fully as intended was sufficient to pull the total interpretation down below the level of 'fully as intended'. The level so reached was determined by the most seriously misinterpreted (significant) element in the test question. For example, if all but one of the significant elements of the question were interpreted as intended and the interpretation of the other element was rated as 'somewhat limited but permissible' (see below), then the whole interpretation was so rated (i.e. 'somewhat limited but permissible'). The reason for this is that a question cannot be regarded as a safe one unless all its parts are interpreted as intended.

3 If a significant element of the question was obviously and substantially misinterpreted or was omitted altogether, the total interpretations was marked 'incorrect'.

4 In the context of this system, the following ratings were made of specific elements of respondents' interpretations.

(a) 'Do (any programmes)'. Where this word was interpreted as intended (see above), the interpretation was rated 'correct' (√).
The interpretation 'could (any programmes have)' was rated as 'unduly different' (UD).

(b) 'any programmes'. Where this reference was interpreted as intended (see above), the interpretation was rated 'correct' (√). Where the reference was interpreted as 'adult programmes only', this interpretation was rated as 'limited but permissible' (LP). Where it was interpreted as 'some programmes', or as 'some types of television programmes', these interpretations were rated 'somewhat general but permissible' (GP). Where the reference was interpreted as 'television generally' (i.e. no consideration of the nature of the programme content)', the interpretation was rated 'unduly general' (UG). Where it was interpreted as 'children's programmes only', the interpretation was rated 'unduly limited' (UL).

(c) 'have (a bad effect)'. Where this reference was interpreted as intended (see above), the interpretation was rated 'correct' (√). Where the reference was interpreted as 'could have (a bad effect)', or as 'are likely to have (a bad effect)', the rating 'unduly different' (UD) was applied. The interpretations 'are likely to (have a bad effect)' and 'might (affect)' were similarly rated (UD). Where the reference was not directly interpreted, but where it seemed that a permissible, if indirect, interpretation had been made, the rating 'doubtful but permissible' (?P) was applied.

(d) 'a bad effect'. Where this reference was interpreted as intended (see above), the interpretation was rated 'correct' (√). Where it seemed that a permissible interpretation had been made, but where the evidence was not conclusive, the rating 'doubtful but permissible' (?P) was applied. If the respondent was not considering a 'bad effect' at all, his interpretation was rated 'incorrect' (X).

(e) 'young people'. Where this reference was interpreted as intended (see above), that interpretation was rated 'correct' (√). Where it was interpreted as referring to young people with an age range of less than five years (though within the range of 8–21 years), the interpretation was rated 'limited but permissible' (LP); similarly for the interpretation 'your own child and his friends' and 'young people you happen to know', provided these were within the age range 8–21 years. Where the respondent interpreted 'young people' to mean children aged 7 years or less (only) or 'your own children only' or 'girls only' or 'boys only', the interpretation was rated 'unduly limited' (UL). Other interpretations rated as 'unduly limited' (UL) were: 'Teddyboy type teenagers' only; 'young people who have been properly brought up'. Where the persons considered included those aged up to 25 years as well as persons within the age range 8–21, the rating 'extended but permissible' (EP) was applied. Where the persons considered included those aged less than 8 years as well as persons within the age range 8–21 years, the rating 'extended but permissible' (EP) was similarly applied. If persons aged over 25 years (along with those within the range 8–21) were considered, the rating 'unduly extended' (UE) was applied. Where the respondent considered adults only (i.e. 21 and over only) the interpretation was rated 'incorrect' (X). Where it seemed that the respondent's interpretation of 'young people' was permissible but where some doubt nonetheless existed, the rating 'doubtful but permissible' (?P) was applied.

(f)　'by setting them (poor moral standards)'. Where this reference was interpreted as intended (see above), the interpretation was rated 'correct' (√). The interpretations: 'by causing them to copy', 'by teaching them', 'by encouraging them to adopt', 'by giving them ideas', 'by leading them', 'by affecting them', 'have an influence upon', were all regarded as acceptable (√). The interpretation 'by concentrating upon' was rated 'unduly different' (UD). The interpretations 'by showing them', 'in that they show them', were rated 'somewhat general but permissible' (GP). Where the reference was left out of consideration altogether, the rating 'incorrect' (X) was applied.

(g)　'poor (moral standards)'. Where this reference was interpreted as intended (see above), that interpretation was rated 'correct' (√). The interpretation 'undesirable' was rated 'somewhat different but permissible' (DP). Where the interpretation was in terms of a comparison between the past and the present (i.e. poorer), the interpretation was rated 'unduly different' (UD). Where the term was not considered at all, the rating 'incorrect' (X) was applied.

(h)　'moral standards'. Where this reference was interpreted as intended (see above), the interpretation was rated 'correct' (√). The following interpretations were rated 'limited but permissible' (LP): 'sex behaviour or attitudes' only referred to; 'crime/violence' only referred to; 'crime and sex' referred to without any other reference: 'crime or sex plus only one other aspect of morality' referred to. Where the interpretation was in terms only of specific moral issues other than crime or violence or sex, the interpretation was rated 'unduly limited' (UL). Where the reference was missed out altogether or the term 'standards' was not considered, the interpretation was rated 'incorrect' (X).

The ratings allocated

Under the system described above, the following ratings were allocated to respondent interpretations of this test question.

Table 7.4.1

Ratings allocated to respondents' interpretations of test question (Q16, I)

Lowest rating allocated to any part of the interpretation	Number of Ratings	Number of Persons	% of Persons
Correct (√)	1	1	1
Extra but permissible (ExP)	0		
Somewhat limited but permissible (LP)	11		
Somewhat too specific but permissible (SP)	0		
Somewhat too general but permissible (GP)	4	12*	24
Somewhat extended but permissible (EP)	1		
Somewhat different but permissible (DP)	5		
Doubtful but permitted (?P)	3	3	6
Unduly limited (UL)	11		
Unduly general (UG)	5		
Unduly extended (UE)	0	17*	33
Unduly different (UD)	9		
Incorrect (X)	18	18	35
Total		51	100

*See note A on page 47.

Content analysis of the interpretations

There follows an analysis of the different interpretations of elements of test questions. The emphasis in this analysis is upon the different kinds of interpretations which were found rather than upon the number of them (though these numbers are given), the purpose of the content analysis being to discover the kinds of things that happen, to speculate about what causes them, and to derive hypotheses (about communication processes) for testing in later phases of the enquiry.

Interpretations of 'do (any programmes)'

The reference 'do (any programmes)' was intended to convey a question about what is in fact the case rather than what might be the case in certain special circumstances.

Summary of interpretations

1 Most respondents interpreted this word as intended or nearly so.

2 On the other hand, there were 2 who gave it conditional meaning (i.e. could any programmes).

3 A few overlooked this word (along with the phrase in which it was embedded.

Table 7.4.2

Interpretations of 'do (any programmes)'

Do (any programmes) (23)/Does (any programme) (1)	24
Do (you think any programme(s))	15
Are there (any programmes)	6
Could (any programmes)	2
Term seemingly overlooked	4
Total	51

Interpretations of '(do) any programmes'

The reference 'any programmes' was intended to mean any particular programmes, and to include both adult and children's programmes.

Summary of interpretations

1 Twenty-nine of the respondents appear to have interpreted this term very generally, that is, without consideration of specific programmes and specific programme content.

2 Most of the remainder tended to think in terms of specific programme content or material. The more frequently considered of these were: material of a sexy kind and material presenting crime and violence. The other types of content considered included: hooliganism, destructiveness, bad language, swearing, drinking.

3 Two of the respondents thought in terms of TV drama.

Table 7.4.3

Interpretations of '(Do) any programmes'

Respondent considered specific programme content or material (e.g. sex, crime) (details follow)			22

Sex (5)/lovemaking (2)/ bedroom scenes (1)	8	Hooliganism	1
Sex (including sex education)	1	Teddyboyism	1
Sex presented in a very frank		Teenagers misbehaving	1
manner	1	Destructiveness	1
Aspects of sex	1	Bad language	3
Sexual looseness	1	Swearing	1
		Drinking	1
Violence	5	Wrong behaviour	1
Methods of violence	1	The seamy side of life	1
Murder	1		
Gangsterism	1	TV plays	1
Crime (robbery/stealing/thieving)	3	The drama	1
Methods of robberies	1		

Respondent did not appear to have considered specific content of programmes, but to have considered programmes rather generally	29
Total	51

Some specific interpretations of interest (from 6 of the above 51 cases)	
The coming of television	1
Programmes in comparison with other influences	1
Television alone (i.e. excluding films and newspapers)	1
Any programmes which are not fit for (children) to see	1
All programmes which deal with	1
Any of the summer programmes	1

Speculative comments

This reference appears to have been given more specific meaning by the later definition of 'bad effects' in terms of moral standards.

Interpretations of 'have (a bad effect)'

The word 'have' (a bad effect) was meant to be interpreted as 'actually have' rather than as 'could possibly have'.

Summary of interpretations

1 Eight of the 51 respondents interpreted 'have' in a conditional or a tentative sense (i.e., might, could, are likely to).

2 Fifteen apparently overlooked the concept altogether, sometimes by omission of that part of the question in which it was embedded.

Table 7.4.4

Table 7.4.4

Interpretation of 'have (a bad effect)

Have (a bad effect)	28
Might affect	
Could have	8
Are likely to have/are l[	
Term apparently overl[	15
	51

Speculative commen[

The conditional interpretation of 'have' cou[d ..] have sprung out of a respondent feeling that the effect of different sorts of TV material upon young people depends upon the young persons concerned and upon their circumstances (e.g. 'not if they have been brought up properly').

Interpretations of 'a bad effect'

The reference 'a bad effect' was intended to mean 'an effect which is undesirable in terms of established values of good and bad'.

Summary of interpretations

1 All respondents appeared to have had 'bad effects' in mind in answering the question.

2 At the same time it is well worth noting that there was much variation in the kinds of 'bad effects' which different respondents had in mind when they answered. Thus the *kinds* of bad effects considered included the following: copying poor sex standards (28 references), taking up bad behaviour, encouraging crime or violence or roughness (28 references), teaching bad language (12 references), encourage selfishness, drinking, lying (7 references).

3 At the same time, many individual respondents considered only some single aspect of bad effect.

Table 7.4.5

Interpretations of '(have) a bad effect'

The different interpretations of 'bad effect'

Affect (their) attitudes (badly (1)/be harmed in the sense of lower standards in the way of life (2)/giving standards of undesirable/ wrong/bad behaviour (8)/giving false ideas of standards of behaviour set by society (1)	12
Distorting their minds (1)/over-exciting them (1)/taking it to heart (1)	3
Encouraging them to think they can get away with poor moral behaviour	1
Copy poor sexual standards (27)/giving the idea of committing a sex crime (1)	28
Teaching about crime/delinquency (7)/teaching about robbery (5)/ teaching about gangsterism (2)	14
Teaching (them) violence	10
Teaching (them) toughness (1)/hooliganism (1)/destructiveness (1)/ teddyboyism (1)	4
Teaching (them) cruelty	2
Teaching swearing/bad language	12
Making (them) selfish (1)/encouraging bad behaviour towards others (1)	2
Encouraging drinking (2)/encouraging smoking (1)	3
Encouraging bravado (1)/encouraging lying (1)	2
Something else considered, but this was undefined	2
Reference 'bad effect' was considered, but not clear which effects were meant	4
All interpretations	99*

The number of different interpretations considered

One interpretation only considered	18
Two interpretations considered	14
Three interpretations considered	11
Four interpretations considered	4
Not clear how many interpretations were considered	4
Total	51

*As 29 respondents gave more than one interpretation, this total exceeds the number of respondents (i.e. 51).

Speculative comments

The fact that all respondents considered 'bad effect' could have sprung out of the simplicity of that concept or out of its common usage, but it also seems possible that its correct perception by all respondents was aided or made more likely by the extra reference to the same concept later on, namely *poor* (moral standards). The variability which features its more detailed interpretation does not necessarily indicate an individual narrowness in interpreting the term 'bad effect', for much depends upon what aspect of 'moral standards' they thought was affected by TV programmes.

Interpretations of 'young people'

The reference 'young people' is a broad one and no single definition of it could be regarded as final. In the present context it was meant to be interpreted as 'young people in general' rather than young people in any narrow age range or special category. An acceptable definition of 'young' was one which referred to any five-year span which was in the age range 8—21 years.

Summary of interpretations

1 There was great variability in the interpretation of this term. Thus the lower age limit to the age range considered varied all the way from 5 years to 19 years, with the upper limit running from 10 years through to 21 years. The range of ages considered was also featured by much variation.

2 Some respondents put special limits upon which young people they considered, for example: teddyboy teenagers; teenagers such as your son; your own children; children such as your own grandchildren.

3 Several of the limitations applied were extreme in character; 'those who have been brought up properly'; 'those who have been brought up properly and their viewing controlled'; 'particularly those whose moral standards are not well developed'.

Table 7.4.6
Interpretations of 'young people'

Whether interpreted in terms of age in years

Ages not indicated	11
Upper and lower limits of age span given	35
Upper age limit only given	4
Lower age limit only given	1
Total	51

Upper and lower age limits, and age spans

Lower age limits		Upper age limits		Age span considered	
5— 6 years	1	9—10 years	2	1 year	2
7— 8 years	5	11—12 years	5	2 years	5
9—10 years	9	13—14 years	5	3 years	2
11—12 years	4	15—16 years	6	4 years	5
13—14 years	6	17—18 years	6	5 years	6
15—16 years	7	19—20 years	13	6 years	4
17—18 years	3	21 years	2	7 years	3
19—20 years	1			8 years	2
				9 years	2
				10 years	2
				11 years	2
Not given	15	Not given	12	Not given	16
Total	51	Total	51	Total	51

Interpretation in non-numerical terms

Those considering specified ages

Children	7
Young children	1
Teenagers	6
Young people	11
Teddyboy type teenagers	1
Teenagers such as your son	1
Young children such as your own son	2
Children, for example your sister's child	1
Young people of the age of your son and some of his friends	1
Particularly those known to you personally	1
Those/a child who has/have been brought up properly	2
Children and teenagers who have been brought up properly and their viewing controlled	1
Young people, particularly those whose moral standards are not well developed	1
Your own children/daughters	2
Those (aged ...)	1
Not given	1
Total	40

Those not considering specified ages

Children	1
Children or teenagers	1
Young children	1
A young child	1
Youngsters	1
Young people	1
Adults	1
Children not yet in their teens	1
Children from school age upwards	1
Children such as your own grand-children	1
Children and your own children in particular	1
Total	11

Speculative comment

The term 'young people' is a broad and imprecise one in any case and this appears to have given many respondents plenty of scope to be selective with respect to the particular young people they considered.

1   This sort of freedom probably allows respondents to focus their attention upon the children they know most about.

2   The extreme limitations placed by some respondents upon this term may possibly have come out of a reaction of the kind 'it all depends'.

Interpretations of 'by setting them (poor moral standards)'

The reference 'by setting them (poor moral standards)' was intended to mean by putting before them (standards) in a manner likely to cause such standards to be adopted. However, since the question asked about bad effects actually occurring, the interpretation 'cause to adopt' must also be accepted.

Summary of interpretations

1 The majority interpreted this reference more or less as intended.

2 A few respondents, however, converted the term to something like 'by showing them', 'by concentrating upon'.

3 Twelve respondents do not appear to have considered this part of the question.

Table 7.4.7

Interpretations of 'by setting them (poor moral standards)'

By setting them (10)/it will set them (1)/because this would set them (1)/ ... are being set (1)	13
By causing them to copy (5)/cause them to copy (1)/in that they copy (1)	7
By teaching them (2)/in teaching them (1)/teach them (1)	4
By encouraging them to adopt (1)/by encouraging them to be (1)/ by encouraging them to behave (1)/by encouraging them to think (1)	4
Has caused them to have	1
By giving them (... thoughts) (1)/give them (ideas) (1)/might give them (the idea) (1)	3
By leading them (1)/lead them (1)	2
By affecting them (1)/have an influence on (1)	2
By showing them (1)/in that they show them (1)	2
By concentrating on	1
Respondent did not appear to have considered the phrase	12
Total	51

Interpretations of 'poor (moral standards)'

The word 'poor' (moral standards) was intended to mean standards which which are below those generally accepted by society. In this context, acceptable definitions included 'bad', 'wrong', 'corrupt', 'loose', 'false'.

Summary of interpretations

1 Thirty-one of the 51 respondents interpreted the term 'poor' as intended or nearly so.

2 Three appear to have converted it to 'poorer' (i.e. 'lower than pre-TV'; 'lower than when you were a child').

3 Seventeen seemingly overlooked the term.

Table 7.4.8

Interpretations of 'poor (moral standards)'

Poor	15	Undesirable	2
Bad (2)/adverse (1)	3	Declining	1 ⎫
Wrong (2)/wrong implied		Lower than pre-TV	1 ⎬ 3
(e.g. immoral) (4)	6	Lower than when you	⎪
Corrupt (2)/loose (2)	4	were a child	1 ⎭
(Giving them) a false idea	1	Respondent apparently	
		overlooked the term	17
		Total	51

Interpretations of '(poor) moral standards'

The reference 'moral standards' is a difficult one to deal with in that its dictionary definition is wider than its popular use. Strictly speaking it means 'standards of right and wrong generally', but (in its negative form) it is often used to refer to standards associated with such concepts as 'sexual immorality', 'crime', 'violence', 'drunkenness', 'swearing'.

Summary of interpretations

1 Up to 22, but quite possibly fewer, of the 51 respondents interpreted this concept in the way it was intended.

2 Sixteen more interpreted the term in a more limited way than that intended, many of these thinking solely in terms of sex behaviour.

3 Some (10) appear to have overlooked the concept altogether.

Table 7.4.9

Interpretations of 'moral standards'

Term 'moral' apparently grasped in the broad sense intended	
Moral standards (considered broadly as intended) (5)/morals (2)	7
Moral standards in relation to attitudes and general way of life	1
Moral behaviour (morals apparently considered broadly)	3
Vague references to 'moral standards' which might possibly represent intended interpretations, but by no means certain	
Standards (considered generally) (1)/standards of behaviour (3)	4
(Leading them) 'off the straight and narrow'	1
Behaviour (not known what sort)	7
Limited interpretation of the concept 'moral standards'	
Moral standards (or behaviour) interpreted solely in terms of sex	11
Moral standards (or behaviour) with respect to sex and swearing (1)/ sex and bad language (2)	3
Standards in relation to violence, drinking, smoking, bad language	1
Standards in relation to lying, cruelty and promiscuity	1
Influences their upbringing	1
Criminal behaviour	1
Reference apparently overlooked	10
Total	51

Speculative comment

Presumably the concept 'moral standards' is open to fairly specific inter
pretation, though it seems possible that where the interpretation was of
this kind, the reference to TV material may have conditioned the nature
of this specificity.

Summary for full question

1 Of the 51 interpretations of this question, 32 per cent were allocated
an overall rating of either 'as intended' or 'permissible'. This compares
with our average of 29 per cent for all the questions tested.

2 The main points of difficulty appear to have been as follows:

(a) The term 'moral standards' was frequently interpreted solely
or mainly as 'sex morality'.

(b) The reference 'any programmes' was interpreted in very
general terms (e.g. TV programmes generally) by over half the

respondents.

(c) There was considerable variation in the interpretation of the term 'young people', with respect to the bottom of the age range considered, the top of the age range considered and the total age span considered. Over and above this, some respondents appear to have put special limits upon the type of young person they considered (e.g. Teddyboy teenagers, your own child, children such as your own grandchildren, those who have been brought up properly).

(d) Some respondents overlooked entirely one or another of the elements in the question (e.g. 'poor', 'moral standards').

3 Also worth noting are:

(a) the occasional conversion of the direct concepts 'do' and 'have' into something rather conditional (e.g. could have, might affect, are likely to have);

(b) the variation in the type of programme material considered by different respondents;

(c) the occasional loosening of the concept 'setting them (poor moral standards)' into something like 'by showing them' or 'by concentrating upon';

(d) the conversion, by a few, of 'poor' into 'poorer' (e.g. lower than when you were a child).

4 All respondents considered the reference 'bad effect', though the type of bad effect considered was highly variable in going from one to another of them.

5 *Some speculative comments*

(a) Misinterpretation of one part of the question appeared to facilitate misinterpretation of another part (i.e. possibly to fit in with the other mistake).

(b) The limitation of the young people considered by any one respondent may well have sprung out of a tendency for respondents to think about the evidence closest to them—perhaps the only evidence they had.

(c) Several respondents appear to have had an 'it all depends' reaction to the question (e.g. children who have been brought up properly).

(d) The narrowness of respondent interpretation of 'moral standards' may spring in part from a general tendency to think that the term 'morals' refers mainly to 'sex morality', but it also seems possible that some of the narrowness of the interpretation was a function of the special TV context of the question—and possibly of the pre-occupation of some respondents with certain kinds of programme content.

7.5 QUESTION 19, QUESTIONNAIRE I

The wording of the question

'Remembering that advertisements pay for ITV programmes, do you think that there should be advertising on television?' (To be coded as yes/no/not sure.)

Check question

'Why do you think that?'

Definitions of different parts of the question

The following are the intended meanings of key terms in the question. *However, as indicated below, some variants of the intended interpretations were regarded as permissible and others as possibly permissible.* The reference 'remembering that' was meant to be an instruction to the respondent that the accompanying information (i.e. advertisements pay for ITV programmes) should be borne in mind while respondent answered the question. The reference 'advertisements' was meant to refer to television advertisements generally whether presented within or between programmes. The reference 'pay for' was meant to be interpreted as 'completely cover the cost of' (ITV programmes). The reference 'ITV programmes' was meant to refer to programmes presented on the ITV channel and, in the present context, to exclude the advertisements themselves. The word 'you' was meant to be interpreted as 'you, yourself' and was not intended to include others (e.g. respondent's spouse, children, relatives, lodger(s)). The reference '(do you) think there should be (advertising on television)', was intended to mean '(do you) think that (advertising should be/ought to be presented (on television)'. In this context the reference 'advertising (on television)' was meant to refer to all television advertising, whatever its type, form or placement (e.g. between or within programmes).

103

Respondents' interpretations of the question

These interpretations are set out in full in the Appendix (Part II). They are based upon the replies of 54 people.

Marking the interpretations

The system used for rating or marking respondents' interpretations of questions

The following marking or rating system was used.

1 If all elements of the question were interpreted as intended, the interpretation as a whole was rated 'fully as intended' (√).

2 Failure to interpret any significant element of the question fully as intended was sufficient to pull the total interpretation down below the level of 'fully as intended'. The level so reached was determined by the most seriously misinterpreted (significant) element in the test question. For example, if all but one of the significant elements of the question were interpreted as intended and the interpretation of that other element was rated as 'somewhat limited but permissible' (see below), then the whole interpretation was so rated (i.e. 'somewhat limited but permissible'). The reason for this is that a question cannot be regarded as a safe one unless all its parts are interpreted as intended.

3 If a significant element of the question was obviously and substantially misinterpreted or was omitted altogether, the total interpretation was marked 'incorrect' (X).

4 In the context of this system, the following ratings were made of specific elements of respondents' interpretations.

(a) 'Remembering that'. Where this reference was interpreted as intended (see above), the interpretation was rated 'correct' (√). Where it was interpreted as 'assuming that' or, 'since (i.e. because)', the interpretation was rated 'different but permissible' (DP). Where the reference was interpreted as 'if', the rating 'unduly different' (UD) was applied. Where the interpretation was omitted altogether the rating 'incorrect' (X) was applied.

(b) 'advertisements'. Where this reference was interpreted as intended (see above), the interpretation was rated 'correct' (√). The following interpretations were rated 'different but permissible' (DP): 'advertising'; 'ITV advertising'; 'advertisers'; 'manufacturers'; 'some source'. Where the reference was omitted altogether, the rating 'incorrect' (X) was applied.

(c) 'pay for'. Where this reference was interpreted as intended (see above), the interpretation was rated 'correct' (√). Where it was interpreted as 'at present pay for', this interpretation was also regarded as acceptable. Where the reference was interpreted as '(ITV) has to get (its) money (from somewhere)', or as '(money) has to come (from somewhere)', the rating 'incorrect' (X) was applied.

(d) 'ITV programmes'. Where this term was interpreted as intended (see above), the interpretation was rated 'correct' (√). Other acceptable interpretations were: 'the ITV'; 'the second channel'. Where the term was interpreted as 'the cost of the TV licence', or was omitted altogether, the rating 'incorrect' (X) was applied.

(e) 'you'. Where this term was interpreted as intended (see above), the interpretation was rated 'correct' (√). Where it seemed that a permissible interpretation had been made, but where the evidence was not conclusive, the rating 'doubtful but permissible' (?P) was applied.

(f) '(do you) think there should be (advertising on television)'. Where this phrase was interpreted as intended (see above), the interpretation was rated 'correct' (√). Where the respondents slightly altered the concept by substituting for 'should be' words such as 'must be', 'has to be', 'agree with there being', 'accept', 'approve of having', etc., that interpretation was rated as 'somewhat different but permissible' (DP). Similarly for interpretation such as: 'goods should be advertised', 'firms should be allowed to advertise'. The following interpretations were rated as 'unduly different' (UD): 'like having advertisements'; 'think there should be (a separate channel) paid for by (advertising revenue)'. Interpretations rated as 'incorrect' included the following: 'think (the advertisements) are interesting'; 'think that (the prices of products) should be included (in the advertising on TV)'.

(g) 'advertising (on television)'. Where this term was interpreted as intended (see above), the interpretation was rated 'correct' (√). Where the interpretation was limited to advertisements between programmes or to advertisements within programmes, it was rated 'limited but permissible' (LP). Where the reference was omitted altogether, the rating 'incorrect' (X) was applied.

The ratings allocated

Under the system described above, the following ratings were allocated to respondent interpretations of this test question.

Table 7.5.1
Ratings allocated to respondents' interpretations of test question (Q.19, I)

Lowest rating allocated to any part of the interpretation	Number of Ratings	Number of Persons	% of Persons
Correct (√)	10	10	19
Extra but permissible (ExP)	3		
Somewhat limited but permissible (LP)	0		
Somewhat too specific but permissible (SP)	0		
Somewhat too general but permissible (GP)	0	12*	22
Somewhat extended but permissible (EP)	0		
Somewhat different but permissible (DP)	10		
Doubtful but permitted (?P)	0	0	0
Unduly limited (UL)	0		
Unduly general (UG)	0		
Unduly extended (UL)	0	4	7
Unduly different (UD)	4		
Incorrect (X)	28	28	52
Total		54	100

*See Note A on page 47.

Content analysis of the interpretations

There follows an analysis of the different interpretations of elements of the test question. The emphasis in this analysis is upon the different kinds of interpretations which were found rather than upon the number of them (though these numbers are given), the purpose of the content analysis being to discover the kinds of things that happen, to speculate about what causes them, and to derive hypothesis about communication processes (for testing in later phases of the enquiry).

Interpretations of 'Remembering that advertisements pay for ITV programmes'

The reference 'remembering that' was meant to be an instruction to the respondent that the accompanying information (i.e. advertisements pay for ITV programmes) should be borne in mind while the respondent answered the question. The reference 'advertisements' was meant to refer to television advertisements generally, whether presented within or between programmes. The reference 'pay for' was meant to be interpreted

106

as 'completely cover the cost of' (ITV programmes). The reference 'ITV programmes' was meant to refer to programmes presented on the ITV channel and, in the present context, to exclude the advertisements themselves.

Interpretations of the whole phrase

1 Of the 54 respondents, 21 interpreted the introductory phrase as intended, 19 seemingly overlooked it and 14 interpreted it other than as intended.

2 Misinterpretations are shown in Table 7.5.2 below and include such things as: 'Remembering that the advertisements help to pay for'; 'Remembering that manufacturers pay for advertising on TV'; 'Remembering that ITV advertising might reduce the cost of the TV licence'; 'Remembering that advertisements break into programmes'.

Table 7.5.2

Interpretations of the whole phrase: 'Remembering that the advertisements pay for ITV programmes'

Whole phrase interpreted more or less as intended:

Remembering that the advertisements pay for ITV programmes (15)/ for ITV (1)	16	
Remembering that the advertisements at present pay for ITV programmes	4	21
Since the advertisements pay for ITV programmes	1	

Whole phrase seemingly overlooked 19

Phrase seemingly interpreted other than as intended:

Remembering that advertisements help to pay for ITV programmes	1	
Remembering that manufacturers pay for advertising on TV (1)/ advertisers pay for their advertisements (1)	2	
Remembering that the money for the 2nd channel has to come from somewhere (1)/since ITV has to get its money from somewhere (1)	2	
Remembering that ITV advertising might reduce the cost of the TV licence (1)/advertisements keep down the cost of the licence (1)/ advertising revenue might be used to reduce the licence fee (1)	3	14
Assuming it is not necessary to have advertisements in order to pay for ITV programmes	1	
Assuming that advertising in some form is necessary	1	
If there has to be an ITV channel	1	
Remembering that it (i.e. advertising) breaks into programmes	1	
The quantity and manner of its (i.e. advertising) presentation being what they are	1	
Bearing in mind what it may do for the national economy	1	
Total	54	

Interpretations of different parts of the opening phrase

Table 7.5.3 brings out in some detail what happened with different parts of this opening phrase. Some of the salient features are:

1 that a lot of the respondents overlooked one or another part of the opening phrase;

2 that several people converted 'remembering that' into 'assuming that' or 'if';

3 that 'pay for' became, for some, 'helps to pay for' or 'might reduce the cost (of a TV licence)';

4 'ITV programmes' was converted, by two, into 'advertising' and by three into 'a TV licence'.

Table 7.5.3

Interpretations of the various parts of the phrase: 'Remembering that the advertisements pay for ITV programmes

(a) Interpretations of 'Remembering that'		(b) Interpretations of 'advertisements'	
Remembering that (bearing in mind that	29	Advertisements	23
Since (i.e. because)	2	Advertising (4)/ITV advertising (1)	5
Assuming that	2	Advertisers	1
If	1	Manufacturers	1
The quantity and manner of advertising being what they are	1	Advertising revenue	1
		The money (for the 2nd channel)	1
Reference seemingly overlooked	19	ITV	1
Total	54	Term seemingly overlooked	21
		Total	54

(c) Interpretations of 'pay for'		(d) Interpretations of 'ITV programmes'	
Pay for	20	ITV programmes (23)/ITV (1)/the 2nd channel	25
At present pay for	4		
Helped pay for (a TV licence)	1	Advertisements on ITV (1)/advertisements (1)	2
Keep down the cost of (a TV licence)	1		
Might reduce the cost of a licence (1)/ might be used to keep down the cost of a TV licence (1)	2	(Reduce the cost of) a TV licence	3
		Reference seemingly omitted	24
(Remembering that ITV) has got to get its money from somewhere (1)/(remembering that the money) has got to come from somewhere (1)	1	Total	54
Breaks into (programmes)	1		
Reference seemingly omitted	23		
Total	54		

Speculative comment

That opening phrase is, to an important degree, just a reminder to the respondent of the present state of affairs (namely that advertisements do pay for ITV programmes) and the answering of the question itself is not really dependent upon that opening phrase being grasped or considered. Hence it may be that many of the respondents who overlooked it may have done so simply because of this. In addition, however, that opening phrase is in some ways a restricting one: it reminds the respondent that ITV programmes are paid for by advertisements and then asks if there should be advertising on television. It would be understandable if some respondents simply dropped that restrictive clause altogether.

Interpretations of '(do) you think'

The word 'you' was meant to be interpreted as 'you, yourself', and was not intended to include others (e.g. respondent's spouse, children, relatives, lodger(s)).

Summary of interpretations

1 Forty-eight of the 54 respondents interpreted this term as intended. The remaining 6 appear to have overlooked it, though at the same time there is no evidence for assuming that the respondents concerned did in fact answer for anyone but themselves.

Table 7.5.4

Interpretations of '(do) you (think)'	
You (i.e. apparently as intended)	48
No reference (but no evidence to suppose that respondent answered for anyone but him/herself personally)	6
Total	54

Interpretations of '(do you) think there should be'

The reference '(do you) think there should be (advertising on television)', was intended to mean '(do you) think that (advertising) should be/ought to be present (on television)'.

Summary of interpretations

1 About 29 of these respondents interpreted this sequence of words more or less as intended.

2 There were 20 others who were involved in varying degrees of deviation from the precise intended meaning, without being wildly wrong. These interpretations included such things as: 'do you think there has to be'; 'do you approve of having'; 'are you willing to accept'; 'do you think that firms should be allowed to'; 'are advertisers entitled to'; 'do you like having'.

3 Finally, a few respondents interpreted the reference in ways that have little or no resemblance to what was intended: 'what do you think of the timing of advertisements'; 'are (advertisements) interesting and part of an effective selling campaign'.

Table 7.5.5

Interpretations of '(do you) think there should be'

Think there should be (25)/ought to be (2)/should there be (1)/ think (goods) should be (1)	29
Think it is necessary to have (1)/think there must be (1)/must there be (1)/ think there has to be (2)	5
Agree with there being (1)/approve of having (1)/approve of the way (1)	3
Are (you) willing to accept (1)/fully accept (1)/agree with there being (1)	3
Think that firms (1)/people (1)/manufacturers (1)/should be allowed to/ are advertisers entitled to (1)	4
Like having (2)/like (2)/would (you) like (advertising) to continue (1)	5
Think (prices of products) should be included	1
(What do you) think of the amount of advertising (1)/timing of advertisements (1)	2
Are (advertisements) interesting and part of an effective selling campaign	1
Should a second channel be paid for out of advertising revenue	1
Total	54

Interpretations of 'advertising on television'

In this context, the reference 'advertising (on television)' was meant to refer to all television advertising, whatever its type, form or placement (e.g. between or within programmes).

Summary of interpretations

1 A majority (at least 47 out of 54) interpreted the reference as intended.

2 Of the others, 3 softened or qualified the reference by thinking in terms of how much advertising there should be (e.g. '(should there be) a limited amount of advertising on TV'; '(should there be) so much advertising on TV'.

3 Another respondent converted the reference into '(should there be)

110

advertising on BBC television' and one was wildly out with something like '(what do you think of) the timing of advertisements in relation to TV plays'.

Table 7.5.6

Interpretations of '(do you think there should be) advertising on television'

Advertising on TV (32)/TV advertising (2)/advertisements on TV (5)/ advertise on TV (5)/advertisements (1)	45
Advertising on ITV channel (1)/on ITV (1)	2
Also (be) advertising on BBC TV	1
So much advertising on TV	1
The amount of advertising on TV	1
A limited amount of advertising on TV	1
Advertising in order to have an ITV channel	1
An ITV channel without commercials	1
The timing of advertisements in relation to TV plays	1
Total	54

Summary for full question

1 Of the 54 interpretations of this question, 41 per cent were allotted an overall rating of either 'as intended' or 'permissible'. This compares with an average of 29 per cent for all the questions tested.

2 The main points of failure with this question were as follows:

(a)   Over half either omitted the opening phrase altogether or misinterpreted all or part of it.

(b)   The reference '(do you) think there should be' was somewhat loosely interpreted by about 20, with the deviations ranging from: 'do you think there has to be' to 'do you like having'; and several were wildly out (e.g. 'what do you think of the timing of advertisements').

(c)   The term 'advertising on television' was for the most part interpreted as intended, but some qualified it by thinking in terms of how much advertising there should be (e.g. 'should there be so much advertising on TV').

3 *Speculative comments*

Some of the misinterpretations of this question may have been forced by the rather restrictive, opening phrase. To others it may have seemed unnecessary and this may possibly lie behind it being left out by quite a lot of respondents.

7.6 QUESTION 20, QUESTIONNAIRE I

The wording of the question

'Is television advertising time used properly?' (To be coded: yes/no/not sure).

Check question

'Why do you say that?'

Definitions of different parts of the question

The following are the intended meanings of key terms in the question. *However, as indicated below, some variants of the intended interpretations were regarded as permissible and others as possibly permissible.* The reference 'television advertising' was meant to refer to all television advertising, whatever its type, form or placement (e.g. between or within programmes). The reference '(advertising) time' was meant to refer to the total amount of time spent in presenting television advertisements (whatever their type, form or placement). The reference 'used properly' was meant to refer to the use of advertising time in a manner responsibly balanced between the interests of advertisers and the comfort of viewers. This concept is a difficult one and it will be seen from below that various more limited interpretations of it were regarded as permissible.

Respondents' interpretations of the question

These interpretations are set out in full in the Appendix (Part II). They are based upon the replies of 50 people.

Marking the interpretations

The system used for rating or marking respondents' interpretations of questions

The following marking or rating system was used:

1 If all elements of the question were interpreted as intended, the interpretation as a whole was rated 'fully as intended' (√).

2 Failure to interpret any significant element of the question fully as intended was sufficient to pull the total interpretation down below the level of 'fully as intended'. The level so reached was determined by the most seriously misinterpreted (significant) element in the test question. For example, if all but one of the significant elements of the question were interpreted as intended and the interpretation of that other element was rated as 'somewhat limited but permissible' (see below), then the whole interpretation was so rated (i.e. 'somewhat limited but permissible'). The reason for this is that a question cannot be regarded as a safe one unless all its parts are interpreted as intended.

3 If a significant element of the question was obviously and substantially misinterpreted or was omitted altogether, the total interpretation was marked 'incorrect' (X).

4 In the context of this system, the following ratings were made of specific elements of respondents' interpretations.

(a) 'television advertising'. Where this reference was interpreted as intended (see above), the interpretation was rated 'correct' (√). Where the interpretation was limited to advertisements between programmes or to advertisements within programmes, it was rated 'limited but permissible' (LP). Where the reference was interpreted as 'television programmes', or where it was omitted altogether, the rating 'incorrect' (X) was applied.

(b) '(advertising) time'. Where this reference was interpreted as intended (see above), the interpretation was rated 'correct' (√). Where it was interpreted as the timing of advertisements (e.g. within the programme complex), the interpretation was rated as 'unduly different' (UD). Similarly for the interpretation 'are advertisements timed (properly)'. Where the reference was interpreted as asking if the advertising took up enough time, the rating 'incorrect' (X) was applied; similarly where the reference was omitted altogether.

(c) 'used properly?' Where this reference was interpreted as intended (see above), the interpretation was rated 'correct' (√). Where it seemed that a permissible interpretation had been made, but where the evidence was not conclusive, the rating 'doubtful but permissible' (?P) was applied. Where it was interpreted solely in terms of the interests of the advertiser, the interpretation was rated 'limited but permissible' (LP). If the interpretation was solely in terms of one aspect of the advertiser's interest, it was rated 'unduly limited' (UL). In the same way, if the interpretation was solely in terms of one aspect of the viewer's interests, it was rated 'unduly limited (UL), but 'limited but permissible' (LP) when it referred more broadly to the viewer's interests (though not at all to the advertiser's interests). Where the reference was omitted altogether or was interpreted as referring to other than advertiser's/viewer's interests, the rating 'incorrect' (X) was applied.

The ratings allocated

Under the system described above, the following ratings were allocated to respondents' interpretations of this test question.

Table 7.6.1

Ratings allocated to respondents' interpretations of of test question (Q.20, I)

Lowest rating allocated to any part of the interpretation	Number of Ratings	Number of Persons	% of Persons
Correct (✓)	3	3	6
Extra but permissible (ExP)	0		
Somewhat limited but permissible (LP)	6		
Somewhat too specific but permissible (SP)	0		
Somewhat too general but permissible (GP)	0	6*	12
Somewhat extended but permissible (EP)	0		
Somewhat different but permissible (DP)	1		
Doubtful but permitted (?P)	2	2	4
Unduly limited (UL)	6		
Unduly general (UG)	0		
Unduly extended (UE)	0	25*	28
Unduly different (UD)	23		
Incorrect (X)	14	14	28
	Total	50	100

*See Note A on page 47.

114

Content analysis of interpretations

There follows an analysis of the different interpretations of elements of the test question. The emphasis in this analysis is upon the different kinds of interpretations which were found rather than upon the number of them (though these numbers are given), the purpose of the content analysis being to discover the kinds of things that happen, to speculate about what causes them, and to derive hypotheses (about communication processes) for testing in later phases of the enquiry.

Interpretations of 'television advertising'

The reference 'television advertising' was meant to refer to all television advertising, whatever its type, form or placement (e.g. between or within programmes).

Summary of interpretations

1 Twenty-eight of the 50 respondents interpreted this reference just as intended, with up to 14 more interpreting it approximately so.

2 Four respondents put a special limit upon this reference, converting it into one or another of the following: advertisements within program mes; advertisements between programmes; different kinds of advertisements; individual advertisements.

3 Two others converted the term into 'programmes'.

Table 7.6.2

Interpretations of 'television advertising'

Television advertising (seemingly used as inteded)	28
The television advertisements (12)/advertisements (1)	13
Blocks of advertisements	1
Advertisement breaks	2
Advertisements within programmes	1
Commercials between programmes	1
Different kinds of advertisements	1
Individual advertisements	1
ITV programmes	1
TV programmes meant for adults	1
Total	50

Interpretations of 'time'

The reference '(advertising) time' was meant to refer to the total amount of time spent in presenting television advertisements (whatever their type, form or placement).

Summary of interpretations

1 Twenty-four of the respondents converted 'time' to 'timing', and 3 more modified it to 'the amount of time'.

2 Six appear to have overlooked the term 'time' altogether.

3 Only 17 of the 50 respondents appear to have grasped the term just as intended.

Table 7.6.3

Interpretations of 'time'

The time allocated for advertising (i.e. as intended)	17
The time given to individual advertisements (e.g., is it enough?)	3
The timing of advertisements (within the programme complex)	24
Respondent apparently overlooked the term	6
Total	50

Speculative comment

The conversion of 'time' into 'timing' may possibly have been a result of simple mishearing, but it is also quite possible that the conversion was assisted by a desire on the part of some respondents to refer to a feature of advertising which annoyed them, namely the timing of advertisements within the programme complex.

Interpretation of 'used properly'

The reference 'used properly' was meant to refer to the use of advertising time in a manner responsibly balanced between the interests of advertisers and the comfort of viewers. This concept is a difficult one and it will be seen from above that various more limited interpretations of it were regarded as permissible.

Summary of interpretations

1 Relatively few of these respondents (i.e.10/50) interpreted this term from the viewpoints of both viewers and advertisers. By contrast, 24 of them considered only the viewer standpoint and 14 considered only the advertiser viewpoint.

2 Another feature of the results is that individual respondents tended to consider only one narrow aspect of either the viewer standpoint or the advertiser standpoint, for example: in terms of fairness to advertisers, or in terms of making you want to try products, or in terms of ensuring that people watch them, or in terms of not interrupting at the wrong place, or in terms of taking up the right amount of time, or in terms of showing the things that consumers want to know about. Within this context of narrowness of perception and of individual variation, the most commonly used basis for judgment had to do with the timing or the placement of advertisements (23/50).

Table 7.6.4

Interpretations of 'used properly'

The many different criteria used

In terms of general efficiency: use efficiently (1)/put to good effect (1)/ come quickly to the point (not wasting time) (1)   3

In terms of advertisers advantage: put to best use from advertiser's point of view (1)/used or presented to advertiser's advantage or benefit (3)/fair to advertisers (2)   6

In terms of selling goods: sells goods (1)/makes you want to buy products (1)   2

In terms of securing attention or notice: to ensure people watch them (2)/ effective in catching public's interest (1)/efficient in reaching appropriate or large audience (5)/shown long enough for people to see them (1)   9

In terms of placement, timing and interruptions: put on at right time in relation to programmes (1)/put on at right time/right time of day (4)   5 ⎫

Not interrupting at wrong places/not interrupting   5 ⎪

Not interrupting too frequently (1)/taking the right number of breaks (1)   2 ⎬ 24

Not interfering with programmes (3)/not spoiling programmes by interrupting (8)   11 ⎪

Breaks long enough to do what you want in them   1 ⎭

In terms of the amount of time given to them: taking the right amount of time   3

In terms of viewer service, welfare, interestingness: showing the things the consumer wants to hear about (1)/in the best interests of the public (1)/put to best use from the consumer's point of view (1)/ fair to viewers (3)/interesting (1)   7

Other criteria: of the right sort (1)/'not improperly' (1)   2

Term seemingly overlooked   2

All criteria   59*

117

Table 7.6.4 (contd.)

Whether both viewer and advertiser interests were considered

Interpreted in terms of both viewer and advertiser interests	5 }	10
Possibly both, but evidence inconclusive	5 }	
Interpreted in terms of viewer interests or comfort only		23
Interpreted in terms of advertiser only	13 }	14
Possibly advertiser interests only, but evidence inconclusive	1 }	
Quite unclear what interest(s) the respondent had in mind		1
Reference seemingly overlooked		2
Total		50

*Some respondents were using more than one narrow criterion

Speculative comment

1 This result, while probably not surprising once it is known, highlights the general and imprecise nature of the term 'properly' when used in the present context. It also makes clear, however, the tendency of these respondents to be highly selective and specific in their interpretation of that word, at least in the present context. Presumably this narrowing tendency is in the direction of the respondents' preoccupations (e.g. with the interruption of his programme by advertisements).

2 These results indicated that a position could easily arise with this question where identical choices of reply could mask real differences in opinion on the matter asked about.

Summary for the full question

1 Of the 50 interpretations of this question, 22 per cent were allocated an overall rating of either 'as intended' or 'permissible'. This result compares with an average of 29 per cent for all questions tested.

2 The main sources of difficulty were as follows:

(a) Many of the respondents converted the term 'time' into 'timing'.

(b) Only 10 of the 50 respondents based their judgments (of whether or not advertising time was being used properly) upon consideration of both viewer and advertiser interests, most of the rest having made their judgments only from the viewers' standpoint or only from the advertisers' standpoint. Over and above this difficulty, there was great variability in the particular aspect of viewer or of advertiser interest considered.

118

3 Other sources of difficulty were:

(a) The conversion of 'television advertising' into either some specific type of advertisement (e.g. those that break into programmes) or into 'programmes';

(b) The occasional overlooking of some element of the question.

4 *Speculative comments*

(a) The conversion of 'time' into 'timing' may possibly have arisen out of simple mishearing, but it is also possible that this conversion was assisted by a desire of respondents to refer to something they felt strongly about (i.e. the timing of interruptions, the general placement of advertisements).

(b) It seems that this conversion may have helped a few respondents to modify other parts of the question (to fit the conversion).

(c) The term properly was apparently an imprecise term in this TV setting, in that it allowed a major degree of narrow selectivity to go on with respect to the adoption of criteria for making the necessary judgment (i.e. about TV advertising time being used properly or not). The criterion adopted by different individuals seems to have been a function of habitual but narrow ways of thinking about TV advertising.

7.7 QUESTION 21, QUESTIONNAIRE I

The wording of the question

'What do you usually do when the television advertisements come on?'

Definitions of different parts of the question

The following are the intended meanings of key terms in the question. *However, as indicated below, some variants of the intended interpretations were regarded as permissible and others as possibly permissible.* The reference 'what do (you) do' was meant to be interpreted as 'how do (you) occupy yourself during this particular period of time'. The word 'you' was meant to be interpreted as 'you, yourself' and was not intended to include others (e.g. respondent's spouse, children, relatives, lodger(s)). The word 'usually' was meant to be interpreted as 'ordinarily', 'in the ordinary course of events', 'commonly'. Other acceptable interpretations of the term were: 'as a rule', 'generally', 'normally', 'habitually', 'as a routine', 'almost always', 'mostly', 'typically'. The reference 'television advertisements' was meant to refer to television advertisements generally, whether presented within or between programmes.

Respondents' interpretations of the question

These interpretations are set out in full in the Appendix (Part II). They are based upon the replies of 53 respondents.

Marking the interpretations

The system used for rating or marking respondents' interpretations of questions

The following marking or rating system was used.

120

1 If all elements of the question were interpreted as intended, the interpretation as a whole was rated 'fully as intended' (✓).

2 Failure to interpret any significant element of the question fully as intended was sufficient to pull the total interpretation down below the level of 'fully as intended'. The level so reached was determined by the most seriously misinterpreted (significant) element in the test question. For example, if all but one of the significant elements of the question were interpreted as intended and the interpretation of that other element was rated as 'somewhat limited but permissible' (see below), then the whole interpretation was so rated (i.e. 'somewhat limited but permissible'). The reason for this is that a question cannot be regarded as a safe one unless all its parts are interpreted as intended.

3 If a significant element of the question was obviously and substantially misinterpreted or was omitted altogether, the total interpretation was marked 'incorrect' (X).

4 In the context of this system, the following ratings were made of specific elements of respondents' interpretations.

(a) 'What do (you) do'. Where this reference was interpreted as intended (see above), the interpretation was rated 'correct' (✓). Where the reference was interpreted as 'what are the different things (you) do'; what kinds/sorts of things do (you) do', the rating 'somewhat general but permissible' (GP) was applied. Where something was added to a permissible interpretation without losing the latter (e.g. 'what do (you) do to the set and what sort of thing might (you) do yourself') the rating 'extra but permissible' (ExP) was applied. Where the reference was interpreted as 'what do (you) do about the set' or 'do you go on watching', the rating 'unduly limited' (UL) was applied. The following interpretations were rated 'unduly different' (UD): what sorts of things do (you) do apart from watching'; 'what do (you) do when you stay in the room with the television set'.

(b) 'you'. Where this term was interpreted as intended (see above), the interpretation was rated 'correct' (✓). Where it was interpreted as 'you and your family', or as 'you and some other(s)', the interpretation was rated as 'unduly extended' (UE).

(c) 'usually'. Where this term was interpreted as intended, it was rated 'correct' (✓). Where it was interpreted as 'often', 'frequently', 'more often than not', 'on the majority of occasions', it was rated 'different but permissible' (DP). Where it was interpreted as 'sometimes' or was omitted altogether, it was rated as 'incorrect' (X).

(d) 'television advertisements'. Where this reference was interpreted as intended (see above), it was rated 'correct' (✓). Where the interpretation was limited to advertisements between programmes or to advertisements within programmes, it was rated 'unduly limited' (UL). Where the interpretation was omitted altogether, the rating 'incorrect' (X) was applied.

The ratings allocated

Under the system described above, the following ratings were allocated to respondent interpretations of this test question.

Table 7.7.1

Ratings allocated to respondents' interpretations of test question (Q21, I)

Lowest rating allocated to any part of the interpretation	Number of Ratings	Number of Persons	% of Persons
Correct (√)	19	19	36
Extra but permissible	3		
Somewhat limited but permissible (LP)	1		
Somewhat too specific but permissible (SP)	0		
Somewhat too general but permissible (GP)	3	8*	15
Somewhat extended but permissible (EP)	0		
Somewhat different but permissible (DP)	3		
Doubtful but permitted (?P)	0	0	0
Unduly limited (UL)	14		
Unduly general (UG)	0		
Unduly extended (UE)	2	16*	30
Unduly different (UD)	4		
Incorrect (X)	10	10	19
Total		53	100

*See Note A on page 47.

Content analysis of the interpretations

There follows an analysis of the different interpretations of elements of the test question. The emphasis in this analysis is upon the different kinds of interpretations which were found rather than upon the number of them (though these numbers are given), the purpose of the content analysis being to discover the kinds of things that happen, to speculate about what causes them, and to derive hypotheses (about communication processes) for testing in later phases of the enquiry.

Interpretations of 'What do (you) do'

The reference 'What do (you) do' was meant to be interpreted as 'how do (you) occupy yourself during this particular period of time?'

Summary of interpretations

1 Of the 53 respondents, 36 interpreted this set of words more or less as intended and there were 6 more who thought in terms of 'what sorts of things' they did.

2 Ten of the others put special limits upon their interpretations: 'what is one of the things you do?'; 'what sorts of things do you do when you are not watching?'; 'when you don't stay and watch'; 'when you stay in the room with the set'; 'what do you do to the set?'

Table 7.7.2

Interpretations of 'what do (you) do'

Reference interpreted apparently as intended	34
What are the different things (you) do (1)/what are you doing (1)	2
What sort(s) of things do (you) do (4)/kinds of things do you do (2)	6
What is one of the things (you) do	1
What sort of things do (you) do apart from watching (1)/when you are not watching (1)	2
What sort of thing do (you) do when you don't stay and watch	1
What do (you) do when you stay in the room with the set	1
What do (you) do about the set (2)/to the set (1)/in regard to the set (1)	4
What do (you) do to the set and what sort of thing might (you) do yourself	1
Do you go on watching	1
Total	**53**

Speculative comment

1 This part of the question is imprecise in that it does not make clear just what is required: all the different things, one particular thing, what sorts of things.

2 In this question, as in many others, there is some tendency for respondents to limit the reference, possibly to fit their own situations.

Interpretations of '(What do) you (do)'

The word 'you' was meant to be interpreted as 'you, yourself' and was not intended to include others (e.g. respondent's spouse, children, relatives, lodger(s)).

Summary of interpretations

1 Practically all understood this term as intended.

2 Two interpreted it as including members of their family (i.e. a collective interpretation).

Table 7.7.3

Interpretations of 'you'

You (i.e. term apparently interpreted as intended, i.e. 'you, yourself')	51
You and your family (1)/you and other members of your family (1)	2
Total	53

Interpretations of 'usually'

The word 'usually' was meant to be interpreted as 'ordinarily', 'in the ordinary course of events', 'commonly'. Other acceptable interpretations of the term were: 'as a rule', 'generally', 'normally', 'habitually', 'as a routine', 'almost always', 'mostly', 'typically'.

Summary of interpretations

1 Some 35 of the 53 interpreted the term acceptably.

2 Six seemingly overlooked it (e.g. what sort of thing might you do yourself/what sorts of things do you do when).

3 The rest (12) gave it a reduced or weakened interpretation (e.g. more often than not, more often, sometimes).

Table 7.7.4

Interpretations of 'usually'

Usually (apparently as intended, but evidence not fully conclusive)		29
Generally (1)/normally (4)/almost always (1)		6
On the majority of occasions (2)/more often than not (1)		3
Most often	1	3
Often	2	
Sometimes		6
Term apparently not considered		6
Total		53

Speculative comment

1 Some of the weakened interpretations may well have sprung out of the difficulty of naming any particular thing or things that are usually

done 'when the television advertisements come on'.

2 It is also worth suggesting that the meaning of this term may be rather vague and difficult even when it is used outside of the present context.

Interpretations of 'television advertisements'

The reference 'television advertisements' was meant to refer to television advertisements generally, whether presented within or between programmes.

Summary of interpretations

1 Whereas 39 of the respondents thought in terms of advertisements generally (i.e. as intended), there were 14 others who did not.

2 Of the latter, 10 thought in terms of advertisements that occur within programmes, and 4 in terms of advertisements that occur between programmes.

Table 7.7.5

Interpretations of 'when the television advertisements come on'

When the TV advertisements come on (38)/come on	39
When the TV advertisements come on in the middle of a programme	8
When the TV advertisements come on during a programme	1
When a programme is interrupted by TV advertisements	1
When the TV advertisements come on between programmes	4
Total	53

Speculative comment

1 This specifity in the interpretation of some respondents could of course have sprung out of a failure to hear properly.

2 It seems more likely, however, that the specificity was selective or driven 'in character'. Thus it might be that some respondents felt especially strongly about advertisements that interrupt the programme and so chose to think in terms of such advertisements. Or perhaps others only leave the room during advertisement periods between programmes or at the end of a programme and, feeling that 'out of room behaviour' was what was being asked about, chose to confine their thinking to such advertisements.

Summary for the whole question

1 Of the 53 interpretations of this question, 51 per cent were allocated an overall rating of either 'as intended' or 'permissible'. This compares with an average of 29 per cent for all the questions tested.

2 Some of the points of failure were as follows:

(a)   The interpretation by some (10) of 'what do (you) do' in a rather limited or qualified sense (e.g. what is one of the things you do, what do you do apart from watching, what do you do when you stay in the room with the set, what do you do to the set.

(b)   Twelve and probably up to 18 respondents reduced 'usually' to a weaker concept such as 'more often than not', 'often', 'sometimes'.

(c)   Quite a lot of respondents (14) interpreted the phrase 'when the television advertisements come on' in a less broad or general way than intended (e.g. advertisements that interrupt programmes (10), advertisements that come on between two programmes (4)).

3 *Speculative comment*

(a)   This question had in it relatively few concepts and this may have contributed to its *relatively* high score.

(b)   There appeared to be a tendency for some respondents to be narrowly selective in their interpretation of some terms in the question and this seems to have been facilitated by the imprecise character of one reference (namely 'what do (you) do') and by possibly strong feelings in relation to another (namely 'television advertisements').

7.8 QUESTION 5, QUESTIONNAIRE II

The wording of the question

'For how many hours do you usually watch television on a weekday? This includes evening viewing.'

Definitions of the different parts of the question

The following are the intended meanings of key terms in the question. *However, as indicated below, some variants of the intended interpretations were regarded as permissible and others as possibly permissible.* The phrase 'for how many hours' was meant to be interpreted as 'what is the number of hours' (i.e. inviting a numerical answer). The word 'you' was meant to be interpreted as 'you, yourself' and was not intended to include others (e.g. respondent's spouse, children, relatives, lodger(s)). The word 'usually' was meant to be interpreted as 'ordinarily', 'in the ordinary course of events', 'commonly'. Other acceptable interpretations of the term were: 'as a rule', 'generally', 'normally', 'habitually', 'as a routine', 'almost always', 'mostly', 'typically'. The reference 'watch television' was intended to mean attend to whatever is being shown on the screen or to give it at least some degree of attention. The reference 'on a weekday' was meant to refer solely to the period Monday to Friday. In the present case it was intended to mean 'all day' and not just some part of the day (see the qualifying clause at the end of the question). The reference 'evening viewing' was intended to refer to the period from 6 pm onwards on those evenings when the respondent did at least some viewing.

Respondents' interpretations of the question

These interpretations are set out in full in the Appendix (Part II). They are based upon the replies of 52 people.

127

Marking the interpretations

The system used for rating or marking respondents' interpretations of questions

The following marking or rating system was used.

1 If all elements of the question were interpreted as intended, the interpretation as a whole was rated 'fully as intended' (√).

2 Failure to interpret any significant element of the question fully as intended was sufficient to pull the rating for the total interpretation down below the level of 'fully as intended'. The level so reached was determined by the most seriously misinterpreted (significant) element in the test question. For example, if all but one of the significant elements of the question were interpreted as intended and the interpretation of that other element was rated 'somewhat limited but permissible' (see below), then the whole interpretation was so rated (i.e. 'somewhat limited but permissible'). The reason for this is that a question cannot be regarded as a safe one unless all its parts are interpreted as intended.

3 If a significant element of the question was obviously and substantially misinterpreted or was omitted altogether, the total interpretation was marked 'incorrect' (X).

4 In the context of this system, the following ratings were made of specific elements of respondents' interpretations.

(a) 'For how many hours'. Where this phrase was interpreted as intended (see above), the rating 'correct' (√) was applied. Where it was interpreted 'during which hours', 'over what period', the interpretation was rated as 'different but permissible' (DP). Where something was added to a permissible interpretation without losing the latter, the rating 'extra but permissible' (ExP) was applied. Where the phrase was interpreted as 'how much' (e.g. 'very little'), the interpretation was rated 'unduly different' (UD). The following interpretations were rated 'incorrect' (X): 'how many hours a week'; 'until when'; 'for which programmes'.

(b) 'you'. Where this term was interpreted as intended (see above), the interpretation was rated 'correct' (√). Where it was interpreted as 'you and/or your family' or as 'you or some other(s)', the interpretation was rated as 'unduly extended' (UE). Where the respondent answered as if to the question '... is your set on', that interpretation was rated 'unduly different' (UD).

(c) 'usually'. Where this term was interpreted as intended (see above), the rating 'correct' (√) was applied. The rating 'different but permissible' (DP) was applied to the interpretations: 'more

128

often than not', 'taking an average over the days'. The interpretation 'regularly' was rated 'doubtful but permissible' (?P). Where the term was omitted altogether, the rating 'incorrect' (X) was applied.

(d) 'watch television'. Where this reference was interpreted as intended (see above), the rating 'correct' (√) was applied. Where it seemed that attention had been paid to the screen but where the evidence was not conclusive, the rating 'doubtful but permissible' (?P) was applied. Where the interpretation did not necessarily involve 'giving the screen at least some degree of attention' (e.g. 'had the set on') or allowed the inclusion of periods when no attention was being given to the screen, the rating 'unduly different' (UD) was applied.

(e) 'on a weekday'. Where this reference was interpreted as intended (see above), the rating 'correct' (√) was applied. Where it seemed that the intended interpretation had been made, but where the evidence was not conclusive, the rating 'doubtful but permissible' (?P) was applied. An interpretation where respondent based his estimate upon 'viewing at this time of year' (only), was rated 'different but permissible' (DP). An interpretation was rated 'unduly limited' (UL) where 'weekday' was taken to refer to days in the period Monday to Friday with the exception of days when the respondent did not view at all or viewed occasionally or for only a short period, or viewed away from home. An interpretation was similarly rated (UL), where respondent restricted his consideration to those weeks when he was on night-shift. The interpretation was rated 'incorrect' (X) where respondent: gave a total for the whole period of five days (Monday to Friday); or considered all seven days of the week; omitted the reference (i.e. 'on a weekday') altogether.

(f) 'evening viewing'. Where this reference was interpreted as intended, the rating 'correct' (√) was applied. Where it was omitted, the rating 'incorrect' (X) was applied.

Table 7.8.1

Ratings allocated to respondents' interpretations
of test question (Q5, II)

Lowest rating allocated to any part of the interpretation	Number of Ratings	Number of Persons	% of Persons
Correct (√)	3	3	6
Extra but permissible (ExP)	0		
Somewhat limited but permissible (LP)	0		
Somewhat too specific but permissible (SP)	0		
Somewhat too general but permissible (GP)	0	5*	10
Somewhat extended but permissible (EP)	0		
Somewhat different but permissible (DP)	6		
Doubtful but permitted (?P)	4	4	8
Unduly limited (UL)	15		
Unduly general (UG)	0		
Unduly extended (UE)	5	22*	42
Unduly different (UD)	10		
Incorrect (X)	18	18	35
Total		52	†

*See Note A on page 47.
†See Note B on page 48.

Content analysis of the interpretations

There follows an analysis of the different interpretations of elements of the test question. The emphasis in this analysis is upon the different kinds of interpretations which were found rather than upon the number of them (though these numbers are given), the purpose of the content analysis being to discover the kinds of things that happen, to speculate about what causes them, and to derive hypotheses (about communication processes) for testing in later phases of the enquiry.

Interpretations of '(For) how many hours'

The phrase '(For) how many hours' was meant to be interpreted as 'what is the number of hours' (i.e. inviting a numerical answer).

Summary of interpretations

1 Forty-two of the 52 respondents interpreted the reference as intended.

2 There were 7 more who gave starting and finishing times, leaving it to the interviewer to work out the duration of viewing.

3 Of the other 3, one appears to have thought only in terms of terminal viewing time, one in terms of which programmes he viewed, and one interpreted the concept as asking for a non-numerical interpretation of 'how much viewing was done' (e.g. very little).

Table 7.8.2

Interpretations of '(For) how many hours'

For how many hours (26)/for about (3)/ roughly (3)/ approximately (1)/ how many hours	33	
For how long (in hours) (1)/what is the number of hours or duration in hours (7)	8	42
At what time do you start and for how long do you continue	1	
Between what times/hours (i.e. from when to when)		7
Until when (do you view)		1
For which programmes (do you view)		1
How much viewing (e.g. very little)		1
Total		52

Speculative comments

1 An interesting possibility raised by some of these interpretations is that some respondents may *not be able* to *work out* a numerical answer.

2 On the other hand it may simply be that a respondent will 'think aloud' up to the point of naming starting and finishing times and simply stops work having done that, leaving the rest to the interviewer.

Interpretations of 'you'

The word 'you' was meant to be interpreted as 'you, yourself' and was not intended to include others (e.g. respondent's spouse, children, relatives, lodger(s)).

Summary of interpretations

1 Forty-four of the 52 interpreted this term as intended.

2 Of the rest, 4 interpreted it to include family members, one interpreted it as meaning himself or his family and 3 interpreted the word as 'is your set on'.

Table 7.8.3
Interpretations of 'you'

You, yourself		44
You and your husband	2	
You and your family	1	4
You and others in the house	1	
You or your family		1
(For how many hours) is your set on		3
Total		52

Speculative comment

It seems that 'you' is prone to collective (i.e. family) interpretation when used in the television context.

Interpretations of 'usually'

The word 'usually' was meant to be interpreted as 'ordinarily', 'in the ordinary course of events', 'commonly'. Other acceptable interpretations of the term were: 'as a rule', 'generally', 'normally', 'habitually', 'as a routine', 'almost always', 'mostly', 'typically'.

Summary of interpretations

1 Thirty-one of the 52 interpreted this term as intended.

2 Four gave it a less demanding or intense meaning (i.e. 'more often than not', 'often', 'regularly').

3 Fourteen converted it into something that meant 'taking an average over a period of days' and one just looked for an average day and considered that.

4 Two apparently by-passed the term, without it being clear what they did in its absence.

Table 7.8.4

Interpretations of 'usually'

Usually (apparently as intended) (21)/usual for you (1)/usual number of hours) (1)	23
Generally (1)/normally (6)/habitually (1)	8
More often than not	1
Often	1
Regularly	2
The average (weekday) (1)/on average (9)/taking an average (over 5 days) (2)/taking an average (over 7 days) (2)/taking an average (over weeks) (1)	15
Term apparently not considered	2
Total	52

Speculative comment

1 The term 'usually' may have put some respondents into special difficulty in that there may not have been, for them, any 'usual' number of hours, and conceivably this could lead them to taking an average over several days or converting the term 'usually' into 'often' or 'more often than not'.

2 It seems possible also that the term 'usually' is either imprecise or poorly understood.

Interpretations of 'watch television'

The reference 'watch television' was intended to mean attend to whatever is being shown on the screen or to give it at least some degree of attention.

Summary of interpretations

1 This reference was interpreted as intended by up to 35 of the 52 respondents. Even amongst these, however, there were qualifications and elaborations such as 'sit down and pay attention', 'watch except for advertising', 'listen and look'.

2 There were 14 for whom this reference became 'have the set on'.

133

Table 7.8.5

Interpretations of 'watch television'

Did respondent interpret 'watch' as 'paying at least some attention'?

Watch with at least some attention (14)/watch attentively (1)/look at it with attention (3)/view with attention (1)/pay attention to it (8)/concentrate on television in an interested way (1)/take an interest in what is showing (1)	29
Interpretation of 'watch' not fully established, but no reason for thinking other than 'with at least some attention' (e.g. 'look at')	6
Interpreted as 'have the TV set on' (and so possibly included occasions when no attention was being paid by respondent)	14
Watch without necessarily paying attention	1
Not clear whether respondent was paying attention or not	2
Total	52

Other features of the interpretation (6 cases, already included above)

Sit down and pay attention	1
(Begin) looking at screen and ... continue viewing	1
Attentively watch except for advertising breaks	1
(Fit in) your viewing	1
Listen and look	1

Speculative comment

The term 'watch' appears to be a rather imprecise one, for some people at least, when used in the television context. It may well be that this instability is increased by the fact that people *happen* to be in the TV room when the set is turned on.

Interpretations of 'on a weekday? This includes evening viewing'

The reference 'on a weekday' was meant to refer solely to the period Monday to Friday. In the present case it was intended to mean 'all day' and not just some part of the day (see the qualifying clause at the end of the question).

Summary of interpretations

1 This whole set of words appears to have been interpreted as intended by only 15 of the 52 respondents.

2 While 38 correctly interpreted the term 'weekday', there were 12 who considered the whole week.

3 While 32 quite properly considered the whole weekday in working out an answer, some 17 considered evenings only.

4 Various of the respondents applied their own limitations to the period and to the occasions considered in working out an answer. Thus two excluded days when they did only a little viewing; one considered only the days when he/she viewed regularly; one considered only the period when his wife was alive; two limited their consideration to certain parts of the year (e.g. winter viewing period).

5 One respondent interpreted the question as a request for the total viewing time over five weekdays.

Table 7.8.6

Interpretations of 'on a weekday? This includes evening viewing'

1 *Was the phrase interpreted fully as intended?*

| Yes | 15 | No | 32 | Not clear | 5 | (Total | 52) |

2 *Did the respondent consider only the five weekdays?*

Yes, five weekdays only	38
No, all seven days of the week	12
Not clear whether weekdays only considered	2
Total	52

3 *Did the respondent wrongly limit consideration to certain parts of the day?*

No, respondent considered whole day	32
Respondent considered evenings only	17
Not clear whether respondent considered all day or not	3
Total	52

4 *Did respondent exclude certain days, weeks or seasons from consideration?*

No special days or weeks or seasons wrongly excluded	38
Counting only those weekdays when you view for a substantial period of time (1)/excluding days when you don't view much (1)	2
Counting only those days when you view at least something	6
Counting only those days when you are at home	2
Counting only those days when you view regularly	1
Considering when your wife was alive	1
Considering only viewing at this time of year (1)/only the winter viewing period (1)	2
Considering only when you are on night-shift	1
Total	53*

5 *Other interpretations of note*

Consider the period, Monday to Friday, as a whole	1

*One respondent had more than one exclusion of this kind

Speculative comment

1 For some, the reference 'this includes evening viewing' appears to

have become something like 'consider evening viewing only' and may indicate that an appended instruction is a risky way to try to communicate or to underline something that the question designer wants to have 'driven home'.

2 'Weekday' appears to be an unstable term, at least when presented in a sentence already somewhat crowded with concepts each of which calls for respondent effort of some kind.

3 There appears to be a tendency for some respondents to modify the question to suit their own special situations or possibly even to give the interviewer 'a more balanced view of what actually happens'.

Other interpretations of interest

One respondent added to the question as follows: And what about last night?

Summary for full question

1 Of the 52 interpretations of this question, 24 per cent were allotted an overall rating of either 'as intended' or 'permissible'. This compares with an average of 29 per cent for all the questions tested.

2 The main points of failure in the question were as follows:

(a)   the interpretation of 'usually' as 'the average over a period of days' (14 cases);

(b)   the interpretation (by some) of 'watch television' as something other than 'you, personally, giving the screen at least some attention' (e.g. as 'the set being on');

(c)   probably closely related to (b), the collective interpretation of 'you', so that the term includes or could include other members of the family as well;

(d)   the extension of 'weekdays' to 'days of the week' (i.e. 7-day week) (12 cases);

(e)   the wrongful limiting of the part of day considered to evenings;

(f)   the exclusion of certain days and seasons from consideration (e.g. days when you view but a little; counting only winter viewing).

3 Speculative comments

It may possibly be that:

(a)   the term 'watch' is specially unstable in the TV context, being interpreted by some as 'just having the set on';

(b)   the term 'you' is specially open to collective interpretation when used in the TV setting;

(c)   the term 'usually' may put a respondent into a specially difficult position (i.e. if there is not some usual hourage) and virtually forces him to calculate an average or to convert the term in some way;

(d)   the addition of an instruction at the end of a sentence which would seem complete without the addition may lead to careless perception of that addition (in the present case converting 'this includes' to something like 'this means' or 'considering only');

(e)   the term 'weekday' was too much buried in the sequence of concepts for its '5-day' character to be perceived.

7.9 QUESTION 10, QUESTIONNAIRE II

The wording of the question

'On an average evening, how often do you switch from one station to the other?'

Definition of the different parts of the question

The following are the intended meanings of key terms in the question. *However, as indicated below, some variants of the intended interpretations were regarded as permissible and others as possibly permissible.* The word 'average' in the present context is descriptive of the word 'evening' (rather than of 'number of times') and it was intended to refer to those evenings on which viewing is normal. Acceptable definitions of the word were 'usual' (evening), 'normal', 'general', 'most', 'typical', 'ordinary'. The word 'evening' was meant to refer to the period from 6 pm onwards, on those evenings during which the respondent did at least some viewing. The reference 'how often' was intended to mean 'how frequently' or 'how many times'. An acceptable form of answer was a number or a verbal indication of frequency such as: 'very seldom'; 'quite often'; 'not very often'. The word 'you' was meant to be interpreted as 'you, yourself' and was not intended to include others (e.g. respondent's spouse, children, relatives, lodger(s)). The reference 'switch from one station to the other' was intended to mean 'turn the knob (or push the button) on the television set in order to change from one station to the other', whether the change was made: at the beginning of a viewing session (because the set was not tuned in to the desired station); for exploratory purposes; for picking up a selected programme.

Respondents' interpretation of the question

These interpretations are set out in full in the Appendix (Part II). They

138

are based upon the replies of 53 people.

Marking the interpretations

The system used for rating or marking respondents' interpretations of questions

The following marking or rating system was used:

1 If all elements of the question were interpreted as intended, the interpretation as a whole was rated 'fully as intended' (√).

2 Failure to interpret any significant element of the question fully as intended was sufficient to pull the total interpretation down below the level of 'fully as intended'. The level so reached was determined by the most seriously misinterpreted (significant) element in the test question. For example, if all but one of the significant elements of the question were interpreted as intended and the interpretation of that other element was rated as 'somewhat limited but permissible' (see below) then the whole interpretation was so rated (i.e. 'somewhat limited but permissible'). The reason for this is that a question cannot be regarded as a safe one unless all its parts are interpreted as intended.

3 If a significant element of the question was obviously and substantially misinterpreted or was omitted altogether, the total interpretation was marked 'incorrect' (X).

4 In the context of this system, the following ratings were made of specific elements of respondents' interpretations.

(a) 'average'. Where this term was interpreted as intended (see above), the interpretation was rated 'correct' (√). Where the interpretation seemed to be as intended but where the evidence was not conclusive, the interpretation was rated 'doubtful but permissible (?P). Where the respondent related the term 'average' to the number of switchings instead of to 'evening', the interpretation was rated 'unduly different' (UD). Where the term was not considered at all, the rating 'incorrect' (X) was applied.

(b) 'evening'. Where this reference was interpreted as intended (see above), the rating 'correct' (√) was applied. The following interpretations were rated 'unduly limited' (UL): 'on a weekday evening'; 'on a Wednesday evening'. The following interpretations were rated 'incorrect' (X): 'on those evenings when you do any switching at all'; 'during the whole day'. Where the reference was omitted altogether, the rating 'incorrect' (X) was also applied.

(c) 'how often'. Where this reference was interpreted as intended (see above), the rating 'correct' (√) was applied. The following interpretations were rated 'incorrect' (X); 'on how many nights'; 'at what times'; 'for how long'; 'for which programmes'; 'under what circumstances'. Where the reference was not considered at all, the rating 'incorrect' (X) was applied.

(d) 'you'. Where this term was interpreted as intended (see above), the interpretation was rated 'correct' (√). Where it was interpreted as 'you and your family', or as 'you and some other(s)', the interpretation was rated as 'unduly extended' (UE). Where the term was omitted altogether, the rating 'incorrect' (X) was applied.

(e) 'switch from one station to the other'. Where this reference was interpreted as intended (see above), the rating 'correct' (√) was applied. Where something was added to a permissible interpretation without losing the latter (e.g. (do you) stay on one station or (do you) switch from one station to the other) the rating 'extra but permissible' (ExP) was applied. The following interpretations were rated 'incorrect' (X): 'switching from one station to the other and back again' counted as one switch; counting as 'one' the turning on of the set: excluding exploratory switching from the count. The interpretations: '(watch) one station before switching to the other' and '(when you) do not switch from one station to the other at all' were also rated 'incorrect' (X); similarly where the reference was omitted altogether.

Table 7.9.1

Ratings allocated to respondents' interpretations of test question (Q10, II)

Lowest rating allocated to any part of the interpretation*	Number of Ratings	Number of Persons	% of Persons
Correct (√)	12	12	23
Extra but permissible (ExP)	0		
Somewhat limited but permissible (LP)	0		
Somewhat too specific but permissible (SP)	0	0	0
Somewhat too general but permissible (GP)	0		
Somewhat extended but permissible (EP)	0		
Somewhat different but permissible (DP)	0		
Doubtful but permitted (?P)	1	1	2
Unduly limited (UL)	6		
Unduly general (UG)	0	14	26
Unduly extended (UE)	5		
Unduly different (UD)	5		
Incorrect (X)	26	26	49
Total		53	100

*See Note A on page 47.

Content analysis of the interpretations

There follows an analysis of the different interpretations of elements of the test question. The emphasis in this analysis is upon the different kinds of interpretations which were found rather than upon the number of them (though these numbers are given), the purpose of the content analysis being to discover the kinds of things that happen, to speculate about what causes them, and to derive hypotheses (about communication processes) for testing in later phases of the enquiry.

The interpretations of 'average (evening)'

The word 'average' in the present context is descriptive of the word 'evening' (rather than of 'number of times') and it was intended to refer to those evenings on which viewing is normal. Acceptable definitions of the word were 'usual' (evening), 'normal', 'general', 'most', 'typical', 'ordinary'.

Summary of interpretations

1 Twenty-two of the 53 interpreted this term as intended.

2 There were 9 who interpreted it as an average of the number of switchings on different evenings.

3 In addition, there were 9 for whom the interpretation was not clear and there were 13 who seemingly overlooked the term altogether.

Table 7.9.2

Interpretations of 'average (evenings)'

Usual (5)/usually (5)/usual for you (1)	11 ⎫	
Ordinary (1)/normal (3)/typical (4)/as a rule (1)/generally (1)/ most (1)	11 ⎬	22
Taking an average of the number of switches (i.e. on different evenings) (4)/averaging it out (4)/average (of the number of switches)		9
Not clear how the term was interpreted		9
Term not apparently considered		13
	Total	53

Speculative comment

1 This concept was a difficult one in that it required the respondent to identify an average evening (if there was one that could be called 'average') and to base his count on that particular evening. In the circumstances, it is not surprising that some respondents thought instead of the average number of switchings over some spread of evenings.

2 At the same time, it is also possible that the difficulty over this word lay simply in mishearing it, or in not knowing what it meant.

Interpretations of 'on an (average) evening'

The word 'evening' was meant to refer to the period from 6 pm onwards, on those evenings during which the respondent did at least some viewing.

Summary of interpretations

1 Over 40 persons interpreted this reference as intended.

2 Three persons wrongly limited their thinking to weekday evenings, and another to Wednesday evening.

3 There were two who counted only periods when they did at least some switching (and one of these thought only in terms of daytime viewing).

4 Several (5) apparently overlooked the term altogether.

Table 7.9.3

Interpretations of 'on an (average) evening'

On (or during or in the course of) an evening	29	
On (or in) evenings	2	33
On nights	2	
During (in the course of) evening viewing	4	
On those evenings when you watch television (3)/on a viewing evening (1)/on evenings during time spent viewing (1)	5	9
On a weekday evening (1)/on a weekday evening in recent weeks (1)/in the course of weekday evenings on which you view (1)		3
On a Wednesday evening		1
On those evenings when you do any switching	1	2
During the day, on the days when you do any switching	1	
Reference seemingly overlooked		5
Total		53

Interpretations of 'how often'

The reference 'how often' was intended to mean 'how frequently' or 'how many times'. An acceptable form of answer was a number or a verbal indication of frequency such as: 'very seldom'; 'quite often'; 'not very often'.

Summary of interpretations

1 A majority (45/53) interpreted the term more or less as indicated (e.g. how often, how many times, on how many).

2 Amongst the few misinterpretations were: at what time, about how long, for which programmes, under what circumstances.

3 Several respondents appear to have by-passed the reference altogether (4).

Table 7.9.4

Interpretations of 'how often'

How often (i.e. apparently as intended)	16	
How many times (23)/about how many times (1)/how many times altogether (3)	27	45
On how many	2	
At what times (i.e. when)		1
About how long		1
For which programmes		1
Under what circumstances		1
Reference apparently overlooked		4
	Total	53

Speculative comment

It seems possible that the several misinterpretations (and the by-passing) of the term 'how often' sprang out of the sheer difficulty of working out a meaningful number and that the several misinterpretations are, in a sense, substitute information.

Interpretations of 'you'

The word 'you' was meant to be interpreted as 'you, yourself' and was not intended to include others (e.g. respondent's spouse, children, relatives, lodger(s)).

Summary of interpretations

1 Of the 53 respondents, 41 interpreted the term as intended (i.e. you, yourself).

2 Almost all the rest interpreted it collectively, mostly in terms of the respondent's family.

Table 7.9.5

Interpretations of 'you'

You only	41	You and others	1
You and your husband	2	You or your wife	1
You and your family	7	Term not considered	1
		Total	53

Speculative comment

1 The collective interpretation of 'you' may well have sprung out of

switching behaviour being a family activity (e.g. with someone doing your switching for you or vice versa, or a joint decision to switch being made).

2 Perhaps, too, the collective nature of viewing gives a collective meaning to 'you' when used in the viewing context.

Interpretations of 'switch from one station to the other'

The reference 'switch from one station to the other' was intended to mean 'turn the knob (or push the button) on the television set in order to change from one station to the other', whether the change was made: at the beginning of a viewing session (because the set was not tuned in to the desired station); for exploratory purposes; or for picking up a selected programme.

Summary of interpretations

1 The majority of respondents (42/53) interpreted this phrase as intended.

2 Of the rest there were 6 who interpreted it to mean switching away from one particular channel (without it being clear at all that switching back to that channel would also count as a separate switching act).

3 Three persons counted 'switch to another station and then switch back again' as a single switching act.

4 One person converted the term to a major degree and another apparently by-passed it altogether.

Table 7.9.6
Interpretations of 'switch from one station to the other'

As intended	38
Counting as one, the original switching on of the set	4
Switch over to the BBC/from ITV to BBC	6
Excluding switching just to see what is on	1
Counting as one, switching from one station to the other and back again	3
How long do you watch one station before switching to the other	1
Phrase seemingly overlooked	1
Total	54*

*One respondent was counted under two of the above headings.

Some special interpretations

Some of the following interpretations represent additions to the intended interpretation and others are distortions of it.

Table 7.9.7

Some interpretations of interest

Do you stay on one station or do you switch from one station to the other (1)
Do you switch from one station to the other during the time you are viewing (1)
Do you view on the BBC channel and on the ITV channel
How long do you watch one station before switching to the other (1)
Are there nights when you do not switch from one station to the other at all (1)

Respondent added to the question, as:

... regarding your viewing on Monday and Tuesday evening as normal (1)

Summary for full question

1 Of the 53 interpretations of this question, 25 per cent were allocated
an overall rating of either 'as intended' or 'permissible'. This result compares with an average of 29 per cent for all the questions tested.

2 The main sources of failure were as follows:

(a) tendency to convert 'average evening' into 'average of the
number of switchings over different evenings' (9) or to by-pass
this term ('average') altogether (13);

(b) a tendency to interpret 'you' collectively (e.g. to include the
respondent's family as well as himself) (11);

(c) a tendency to interpret 'switch from one station to another'
in such a way that some switching acts are liable to be left uncounted (e.g. switch to the other channel and back again counted
as one switching act; excluding exploratory switching (10);

(d) the interpretation of evening in a limited sense (e.g. on a
weekday evening, on those evenings when you do any switching
at all) (6).

3 *Some speculative comments*

(a) The term 'average' could have been specially difficult for
people for whom there was no 'average evening' (as far as switching was concerned) and this may have forced them to convert this
concept into 'what is the average number of switchings over different nights.

(b) The term 'you', used in the context of switching behaviour,
seems somewhat prone to collective interpretation.

7.10 QUESTION 11b, QUESTIONNAIRE II

The wording of the question

'Amongst the programmes you watch at weekends, which ONE do you find the most interesting?'

Definitions of different parts of the question

The following are the intended meanings of key terms in the question. *However, as indicated below, some variants of the intended interpretations were regarded as permissible and others as possibly permissible.* 'Amongst (the programmes) you watch' was intended to mean 'considering the programmes to which you pay at least some degree of attention'. The word 'programmes' was intended to refer to any television programmes irrespective of channel or times of presentation. The word 'you' was meant to be interpreted as 'you, yourself' and was not intended to include others (e.g. respondent's spouse, children, relatives, lodger(s)). The reference '(at) weekends' was meant to refer to Saturdays and Sundays only, and to refer to the whole day on these days. The reference 'which one' was meant to refer to a single programme and not, for example, to a kind or type of programme or to more than one programme. The reference 'most (interesting)' was meant to be interpreted as 'of greatest (interest)'; 'specially (interesting)'. The word 'interesting' was meant to be interpreted as 'attention-holding'.

Respondents' interpretations of the question

These interpretations are set out in full in the Appendix (Part II). They are based upon the replies of 59 people.

Marking the interpretations

The system used for rating or marking respondents' interpretations of questions

The following marking or rating system was used.

1 If all elements of the question were interpreted as intended, the interpretation as a whole was rated 'fully as intended' ($\checkmark$).

2 Failure to interpret any significant element of the question fully as intended was sufficient to pull the total interpretation down below the level of 'fully as intended'. The level so reached was determined by the most seriously misinterpreted (significant) element in the test question. For example, if all but one of the significant elements of the question were interpreted as intended and the interpretation of that other element was rated as 'somewhat limited but permissible' (see below) then the whole interpretation was so rated (i.e. 'somewhat limited but permissible'). The reason for this is that a question cannot be regarded as a safe one unless all its parts are interpreted as intended.

3 If a significant element of the question was obviously and substantially misinterpreted or was omitted altogether, the total interpretation was marked 'incorrect' (X).

4 In the context of this system, the following ratings were made of specific elements of respondents' interpretations.

(a) 'Amongst (the programmes) you watch'. Where the reference was interpreted as intended (see above), the interpretation was rated 'correct' ($\checkmark$). Where it seemed that attention had been paid to the screen but the evidence was not conclusive, the rating 'doubtful but permissible' (?P) was applied. Where the reference was interpreted as 'amongst the programmes you see and whose names you can remember' the interpretation was rated 'limited but permissible' (LP). The interpretations 'amongst the programmes available' and 'amongst the programmes showing' were rated 'unduly different' (UD). The interpretation 'among the programmes you are interested in' was rated 'unduly limited' (UL). Where the word 'watch' was omitted altogether, or where the whole reference was omitted, the interpretation was rated as 'incorrect' (X).

(b) 'programmes'. Where this term was interpreted as intended (see above), the interpretation was rated 'correct' ($\checkmark$). Where it was interpreted as 'evening programmes', the interpretation was rated 'unduly limited'. Where the term was interpreted as 'types of programmes' or as 'ITV presentations' or as 'channel', the interpretation was rated 'unduly different' (UD).

(c) 'you'. Where this term was interpreted as intended (see above), the interpretation was rated 'correct' ($\checkmark$). Where it was interpreted as 'you and your family', or as 'you and some other(s), the interpretation was rated as 'unduly extended' (UE).

(d) '(at) weekends'. Where this reference was interpreted as intended (see above), the rating 'correct' ($\checkmark$) was applied. Where the reference was interpreted as 'weekend evenings', the interpretation was rated 'unduly limited' (UL). Where the reference was interpreted as 'Saturday (only)' or 'Sunday (only)', or as weekends in winter', the interpretation was similarly rated (UL). Where the reference was interpreted as the whole week, (i.e. 'Sunday to Saturday'), or as 'an unspecified period of time', or where the reference was not considered at all, the interpretation was rated 'incorrect' (X).

(e) 'which one'. Where this reference was interpreted as intended, the interpretation was rated 'correct' ($\checkmark$). Where the reference was interpreted as 'which ones'; or 'which kind'; or 'which kinds'; the rating 'unduly different'(UD) was applied. Where the reference was interpreted as 'which TV channel/station' the interpretation was rated 'incorrect' (X). Where the reference had been omitted altogether the rating 'incorrect' (X) was also applied.

(f) 'most (interesting)'. Where this reference was interpreted as intended (see above), the interpretation was rated 'correct' ($\checkmark$). Where the reference was interpreted as 'best' or as 'prefer', the interpretation was also regarded as acceptable. Where the reference was omitted altogether, the rating 'incorrect' (X) was applied.

(g) 'interesting'. Where this term was interpreted as intended (see above), the rating 'correct' ($\checkmark$) was applied. Where the term was interpreted as 'holding your attention and enjoyable' or as 'entertaining and gripping', this interpretation was rated 'somewhat extended but permissible' (EP). Where the term was interpreted as 'like' or as 'enjoyable' or as 'favourite' or as 'prefer to watch' or as 'like to watch' or as 'make a special point of viewing', the interpretation was rated 'different but permissible (DP). Where the term was omitted altogether, the rating 'incorrect' (X) was applied.

The ratings allocated

Under the system described above, the following ratings were allocated
to respondents' interpretations of this test question.

Table 7.10.1

Ratings allocated to respondents' interpretations
of test question (QE1, II)

Lowest rating allocated to any part of the interpretation	Number of Ratings	Persons	% of Persons
Correct (√)	1	1	2
Extra but permissible (ExP)	0		
Somewhat limited but permissible (LP)	0		
Somewhat too specific but permissible (SP)	0		
Somewhat too general but permissible (GP)	0	5	8
Somewhat extended but permissible (EP)	1		
Somewhat different but permissible (DP)	4		
Doubtful but permitted (?P)	0	0	0
Unduly limited (UL)	3		
Unduly general (UG)	0		
Unduly extended (UE)	1	22*	37
Unduly different (UD)	21		
Incorrect (X)	31	31	52
	Total	59	†

* See Note A on page 47.
† See Note B on page 48.

Content analysis of the interpretations

There follows an analysis of the different interpretations of elements
of the test questions. The emphasis in this analysis is upon the different kinds of interpretations which were found rather than upon the
number of them (though these numbers are given), the purpose of the
content analysis being to discover the kinds of things that happen, to
speculate about what causes them, and to derive hypotheses (about
communication processes) for testing in later phases of the enquiry.

Interpretations of 'amongst (the programmes) you watch'

'Amongst (the programmes) you watch', was intended to mean 'considering' the programmes to which you pay at least some degree of attention'. 'You' was meant to be interpreted as 'you, yourself' and was not intended to include others (e.g. respondent's spouse, children, relatives, lodger(s)).

Summary of interpretations

1 Only 8 of the 59 interpreted this phrase just as intended, though there were several more (6) who added to it by considering 'programmes you *have* watched' as well.

2 Quite a lot of the remaining 45 converted the concept 'programmes you watch' into something else, for example: 'programmes you see' (2); 'programmes you are interested in' (1); 'programmes which are showing or are available' (18).

3 Others again appear to have concerned themselves with programmes generally (12), and there were 10 more who thought simply in terms of 'which programme or channel' (do you like).

Table 7.10.2

Interpretations of 'amongst (the programmes) you watch'

Amongst/of (the programmes) you watch	8
Amongst/of (the programmes) you have watched (3)/of (the programmes) you watch and have watched (2)	6
Amongst/of (the programmes) you see (i.e. without necessarily making a a point of watching)	2
Amongst (the programmes) you see and whose names you can remember	1
Amongst (the programmes) you are interested in	1
Amongst/of (programmes) available (3)/showing (15)	18
Of the (programmes)	12
Which (programme, channel)	10
No reference (e.g. 'When there's something you don't like')	1
Total	59

Speculative comment

It would seem from the evidence that the term 'watch' is a very unstable one when considered in the television context. It appears to take on meanings all the way from 'attend to' to 'showing or available', and it seems that quite often it can be overlooked altogether.

Interpretations of 'programmes'

The word 'programmes' was intended to refer to any television programme irrespective of channel or of times of presentation.

Summary of interpretations

1 Whereas a majority (40/59) interpreted this term as intended (namely, in terms of specific programmes), there were some (14) who interpreted it solely as 'kinds' or 'types' or programmes.

2 Of the others, one limited himself to evening programmes and three thought partly in terms of specific channels.

Table 7.10.3

Interpretations of 'programmes'

Programmes (as intended)	36 ⎫
Currently (showing) programmes	1 ⎬ 40
Current and past programmes	3 ⎭
Evening programmes	1
Different types or kinds of programmes	14
(which) channel (do you like the more) (1)/and which programmes on that channel (1)/and which types of programmes on that channel	3
Something you don't like on ITA	1
Total	59

Speculative comment

It may be that some of these respondents thought more easily or naturally in terms of programme types or kinds (e.g. sports programmes, plays) than they did of specific programmes.

Interpretations of 'Weekends'

The reference '(at) weekends' was meant to refer to Saturdays and Sundays only, and to refer to the whole day on these days.

Summary of interpretations

There were 20 (out of 59) who did not interpret this term as intended. Six of these apparently overlooked the term altogether and 8 considered the whole week. The remaining 6 misinterpretations were spread between: Saturdays only; Sundays only; Sunday evenings; weekend evenings; weekends in the winter; an unspecified 'period of time'.

Table 7.10.4

Interpretations of 'weekend'

Weekends (as intended)	39
Saturdays (only) (1)/Sundays (only)(1)/Sunday evenings (1)	3
The whole week	8
Weekend evenings	1
Weekends in the winter	1
A period of time (duration not specified)	1
Reference apparently overlooked	6
Total	59

Interpretations of 'which one'

The reference 'which one' was meant to refer to a single programme and not, for example, to a kind or type of programme or to more than one programme.

Summary of interpretations

Of the 59 respondents, there were 34 who interpreted this term in the singular, as intended. On the other hand, there were 24 who interpreted the term in the plural (e.g. which ones, which kinds).

Table 7.10.5

Interpretations of 'which ones'

Which one	20	Which ones and which channel	1
Which ones	19	Which TV channel/station	2
Which one kind	12	Reference overlooked	1
Which kinds	4	Total	59

Some speculative comments

The word *one* could easily have been heard as *ones*, though we should note that the word was printed *one* in the question and the interviewers were told to stress its singular character.

Interpretations of 'Must'

The reference 'most (interesting)' was meant to be interpreted as 'of greatest (interest)', 'especially (interesting)'.

Summary of interpretations

1 Thirteen of the respondents apparently overlooked this term.

2 Up to 37 interpreted the term more or less as intended (i.e. most, favourite, best, prefer).

3 There were 9 who converted 'most' into a looser concept which did not involve identifying any single programme (e.g. really (interesting), specially, particularly).

Table 7.10.6

Interpretations of 'most (interesting)'

Most	29 } 30	Favourite	1 }
More (of 2 channels)	1	Best	3 } 6
Most consistently	1	Prefer	2 }
Really	3 }	Concept apparently	
Specially	4 } 9	overlooked	13
Particularly	2 }	Total	59

Speculative comment

Several things may possibly have contributed to the overlooking of the qualification 'most': the difficulty of identifying a single programme as most interesting; a desire to mention more than one programme or type of programme; a simple mishearing; the fact that the question had at least 6 concepts in it.

Interpretations of 'interesting'

The word 'interesting' was meant to be interpreted as 'attention-holding'.

Summary of interpretations

1 Eleven of the interpretations were more or less as intended.

2 The rest could not really be considered equivalent to 'interesting': 'enjoyable', 'entertaining', 'like', 'appeals', 'prefer', 'favourite'.

3 Three persons overlooked the term (e.g. which programme do you ... usually watch at weekends?')

Table 7.10.7

Interesting/interested in/can learn something of interest	8	Appeals to you	2
		Prefer/prefer to watch	3
Attention holding (2)/gripping (1)/	3	Make a special point of viewing	1
Enjoyable	9	Favourite	1
Entertaining (3)/regard as entertainment (1)	4	Concept seemingly overlooked	5
Like or like to watch (24)/like and enjoy (2)	26	Total	62*

*Three respondents offered multiple (though related) interpretations

Some speculative comments

1 It seems that the term 'interesting' is rather unstable and open to loose interpretation, at least in the television context where so often the criterion of success is something much more akin to 'enjoyment' than to 'interest'.

2 In addition, it seems unlikely that mention of the programme which meant most to a respondent will be suppressed by consideration of the precise meaning of 'interest'.

3 Finally, it is well to remember that the concept 'interesting' is about the sixth which the respondent was required to fit into his grasp of the questioner's intention.

Summary for the whole question

1 Of the 59 interpretations of this question, 10 per cent were allocated an overall rating of either 'as intended' or 'permissible'. This compares with an average of 29 per cent for all the questions tested.

2 The main points of failure were as follows:

(a) for many, the term 'watch' tended to be interpreted very loosely and quite frequently was lost altogether (e.g. amongst the programmes that are showing);

(b) for most, the word 'watch' was interpreted as something more like 'enjoyment' or 'entertainment';

(c) there was a tendency for some to interpret 'programmes' as 'types' or 'kinds' of programmes (e.g. plays, westerns, documentaries);

(d)   there was a failure by some to think solely and wholly in terms of weekend programmes (e.g. the whole week, parts of the weekend);

(e)   there was a tendency in some to convert the singular concept 'one' into a plural concept;

(f)   some overlooked the qualification 'most' and there was a reduction of its stringency by others (e.g. 'really' (like)).

3 *Speculative comments*

(a)   In all likelihood, terms such as 'watch', 'interesting' are especially unstable in the television context.

(b)   It is possibly asking a lot of a respondent to request him to nominate *one* programme and only *one* as 'tops' in some way— especially in a brief and possibly unexpected interview.

(c)   It must be noted that this particular question had in it at least 6 different concepts, all of which the respondent had to grasp in order to answer the question—though this is by no means rare in survey interviews.

7.11   QUESTION 14b, QUESTIONNAIRE II

The wording of the question

'Do you think that television programmes seen by children are appropriate for them?' (To be coded as: yes/no/not sure).

Check question

'Why do you say that?'

Definitions of different parts of the question

The following are the intended meanings of key terms in the question. *However, as indicated below, some variants of the intended interpretations were regarded as permissible and others as possibly permissible.* The word 'you' was meant to be interpreted as 'you, yourself' and was not intended to include others (e.g. respondent's spouse, children, relatives, lodger(s)). The phrase 'television programmes (seen by children)' was intended to mean television programmes in general and, in the present context, to include both children's programmes and those adult programmes which children might see. The reference '(programmes) seen by (children)' was meant to limit respondents' consideration to programmes which children do in fact watch. The reference 'children' is a broad one and no single definition of it could be regarded as final. In the present context, it was meant to be interpreted as 'children in general' rather than children in any narrow age range or special category. An acceptable definition was one which considered the age range 5—14 years, or some extension of that range towards 2—17 years. The word 'appropriate' was intended to mean suitable generally, rather than suitable (for) in some rather specific sense.

157

Respondents' interpretations of the question

These interpretations are set out in full in the Appendix (Part II). They are based upon the replies of 60 people.

Marking the interpretations

The system used for rating or marking respondents' interpretations of questions

The following marking or rating system was used.

1 If all elements of the question were interpreted as intended, the interpretation as a whole was rated 'fully as intended' (√).

2 Failure to interpret any significant element of the question fully as intended was sufficient to pull the total interpretation down below the level of 'fully as intended'. The level so reached was determined by the most seriously misinterpreted (significant) element in the test question. For example, if all but one of the significant elements of the question were interpreted as intended and the interpretation of that other element was rated as 'somewhat limited but permissible' (see below), then the whole interpretation was so rated (i.e. 'somewhat limited but permissible'). The reason for this is that a question cannot be regarded as a safe one unless all its parts are interpreted as intended.

3 If a significant element of the question was obviously and substantially misinterpreted or was omitted altogether, the total interpretation was marked 'incorrect' (X).

4 In the context of this system, the following ratings were made of specific elements of respondents' interpretations.

(a) 'you'. Where this term was interpreted as intended (see above), the interpretation was rated as 'correct' (√). Where it seemed that a permissible interpretation had been made, but where the evidence was not conclusive, the rating 'doubtful but permissible' (?P) was applied.

(b) 'television programmes (seen by children)'. Where this phrase was interpreted as intended (see above), the interpretation was rated 'correct' (√). Where the interpretation seemed to be the one intended but where the evidence was inconclusive, the rating 'doubtful but permissible' (?P) was applied. Where the phrase was interpreted as 'children's programmes (only)' or as 'adult programmes (only)' or as 'some specific children's programmes (such as Children's Hour programme)', the interpretation was rated 'unduly limited' (UL).

(c) '(programmes) seen by (children)'. Where this reference was interpreted as intended (see above), the interpretation was rated 'correct' ($\checkmark$). Where it seemed that a permissible interpretation had been made, but where the evidence was not conclusive, the rating 'doubtful but permissible' (?P) was applied. Where the reference was interpreted as 'showing', 'shown on', 'meant for', 'for', the rating 'unduly different' (UD) was applied. Where the reference was interpreted as 'might see', 'might be seen by', the rating 'unduly different' (UD) was similarly applied.

(d) 'children'. Where this reference was interpreted as intended (see above), that interpretation was rated 'correct' ($\checkmark$). *Other* interpretations were rated 'limited but permissible' (LP) if they covered an age span of 4 years or more and included at least 2 years in the range 8—12 years. Where it seemed that a permissible interpretation had been made, but where the evidence was not conclusive, the rating 'doubtful but permissible' (?P) was applied. An interpretation of the reference which was only partly within the range 2—17 years was rated 'unduly extended' (UE). An interpretation of the term as less than 2 years (only) or as over 17 years (only) was rated 'incorrect' (X). Where the respondent interpreted 'children' as 'very young children (only)', the interpretation was rated 'unduly limited' (UL). Other interpretations were also rated 'unduly limited' (UL), namely: 'your own children (only)'; 'your own grandchildren (only)'. Where the respondent considered 'adults only' (i.e. those aged 21 years and over only), the interpretation was rated 'incorrect'.

(e) 'appropriate'. Where this term was interpreted as intended (see above), it was rated 'correct' ($\checkmark$). In a lot of cases, the rating 'limited but permissible' (LP) was applied to the respondents' interpretation. These interpretations included: 'enjoyable and understandable'; 'educational'; 'in good taste'; 'good for their morals'; 'not frightening'. In other cases, the interpretation was rated 'extended but permissible' (EP): 'good for them'; 'enjoyed by them'. Where the reference was interpreted as 'good or bad (for)'; 'have any good or bad effects (on)', the rating 'unduly extended' (UE) was applied. Where the reference was interpreted as 'detrimental to their conduct'; 'go on too long to be good (for)'; 'is it right that (children ...) should stay up late and see ... ', these interpretations were rated 'incorrect' (X). Where the reference was omitted altogether the rating 'incorrect' (X) was similarly applied.

The ratings allocated

Under the system described above, the following ratings were allocated to respondent interpretations of this test question.

Table 7.11.1

Ratings allocated to respondents' interpretations
of test question (QE2, II)

Lowest rating allocated to any part of the interpretation	Number of Ratings	Persons	% of Persons
Correct (√)	0	0	0
Extra but permissible (ExP)	0		
Somewhat limited but permissible (LP)	4		
Somewhat too specific but permissible (SP)	0		
Somewhat too general but permissible (GP)	0	4	7
Somewhat extended but permissible (EP)	0		
Somewhat different but permissible (DP)	0		
Doubtful but permitted (?P)	0	0	0
Unduly limited (UL)	37		
Unduly general (UG)	0		
Unduly extended (UE)	3	41*	68
Unduly different (UD)	30		
Incorrect (X)	15	15	25
Total		60	100

*See Note A on page 47.

Content analysis of interpretations

There follows an analysis of the different interpretations of elements of the question. The emphasis in this analysis is upon the different kinds of interpretations which were found rather than upon the number of them (though these numbers are given), the purpose of the content analysis being to discover the kinds of things that happen, to speculate about what causes them, and to derive hypotheses (about communication processes) for testing in later phases of the enquiry.

Interpretations of 'you'

The word 'you' was meant to be interpreted as 'you, yourself' and was not intended to include others (e.g. respondent's spouse, children, relatives, lodger(s)).

Summary of interpretations

There is no evidence for concluding that any of these respondents misinterpreted the word 'you'.

Table 7.11.2

Interpretations of 'you'	
You, yourself, alone (apparently)	59
Not clear whether 'you' was considered	1
Total	60

Interpretations of '(television) programmes'

The phrase 'television programmes (seen by children)' was intended to mean television programmes in general and, in the present context, to include both children's programmes and those programmes which children might see.

Summary of interpretations

1 Nineteen (possibly 20) of these respondents interpreted the term 'programmes' in the broad way intended.

2 Of the remaining respondents, 26 thought only in terms of children's programmes and of these, 11 considered only certain groupings of sections or types of children's programmes (e.g. those in 'Children's Hour', children's programmes in the afternoon from 3 pm, puppet shows) or even (only) specific programmes (e.g. 'Andy Pandy', 'Popeye').

3 Twelve respondents considered only adult programmes and some only particular kinds of adult programmes (e.g. adult plays, plays with sex and violence in them).

Table 7.11.3

Interpretations of '(television) programmes'

Programmes considered generally		
Programmes	13	
Programmes including both children's and adult programmes	3	19
Programmes including adult programmes	3	
Programmes considered with some degree of selectivity		
Programmes including adult programmes and particularly those presenting violence		1
Children's programmes considered generally		
Children's programmes (14)/on children's television (1)		15
Children's programmes considered selectively or with limited coverage		
Children's hour programmes	4	
Morning and afternoon children's programmes and children's hour	1	
Children's programmes in the afternoon from 3 pm	1	
Children's programmes such as 'Andy Pandy', 'Popeye' (1)/'Pussy Cat, Willum and Puppet' programmes (1)/'Superman', 'Fireball X15', spy stories (1)	3	11
Children's programmes in the early evening containing horror and a lot of gunplay	1	
Some of the children's programmes	1	
Adult programmes considered generally		
Adult programmes		7
Adult programmes considered selectively or with limited coverage		
Adult programmes such as plays	1	
Adult programmes such as plays that incorporate sex and violence	2	
Adult programmes such as gangster programmes and late night documentaries containing violence	1	5
Adult programmes concerned with sex (e.g. some plays)	1	
Other: Some programmes in the evening		1
Not clear what was considered		1
Total		60

Speculative comment

1 The term 'programme' is broad and the very variability of programmes (in terms of their appropriateness for children), seems likely to have ruled out a simple reply of 'yes' or 'no'. To offer a meaningful reply of either kind, a respondent would very likely have to limit the range or type of programme on which he based that reply. His only (honest) alternative

may well have been 'no opinion' or 'not sure' or impossible to say'. One could well sympathise with any attempt (if that is what happened) to reduce to manageable form an otherwise over-general question.

2 Quite possibly the tendency of a lot of the respondents to think only in terms of children's programmes sprang out of the later reference to 'appropriateness for children'—in the same sense that the word 'children' seemed to indicate the sort of programmes that were meant.

3 Another possible factor in the situation—perhaps the most potent—is the existence of some degree of preoccupation, on the part of respondents, with child reactions to certain kinds of programmes, or the impact upon children of some classes of programme.

Interpretations of '(programmes) seen by'

The reference '(programmes) seen by (children)' was meant to limit respondents' consideration to programmes which children do in fact watch.

Summary of interpretations

1 For 24 of the 60 respondents, there was no clear evidence as to how this reference had been interpreted. However, less than half of the remaining 36 interpreted it as intended.

2 A lot of the others (i.e. 14/36) seemed to limit the reference in some way. Examples are: programmes which children might see; programmes you allow your children to see; programmes meant for children; programmes recently seen by ... .

3 There were also some respondents who widened the reference to something like 'programmes showing on TV'.

Table 7.11.4

Interpretations of '(programmes) seen by'

Seen by (14)/watched by (1)	15 ⎫	16
Recently seen by	1 ⎭	
(programmes) which (children) might see (1)/which might be seen by (1)/which (children) might look at (1)/might watch (1)		4
(programmes) you allow (your children) to see		1
(programmes meant for (2)/put on for (2)/particularly those for (1)/ programmes *recently* seen by (4)		9
(programmes) showing (3)/shown on (1)/being shown to (1)/what is shown on (1)		6
Possibly one of the above categories but evidence as to which is not clear		23
Interpretation quite unclear		1
	Total	60

Speculative comment

1 Since most respondents could not be expected to know what programmes were seen by children—perhaps even children close to them—some degree of qualification might well be expected (e.g. programmes children might see, programmes meant for children, programmes you allow your children to see). This absence of knowledge (on the part of respondents) might also lie behind the seemingly non-committal responses such as 'programmes showing on TV'.

2 Difficulties relating to the whole question seem to stem from the vagueness and non-specificity of the term 'programmes', and the interpretation of the expression 'seen by' appears to have been influenced by this.

Interpretations of '(programmes seen by) children'

The reference 'children' is a broad one and no single definition of it could be regarded as final. In the present context, it was meant to be interpreted as 'children in general' rather than children in any narrow age range or special category. An acceptable definition was one which considered the age range 5—14 years, or some extension of that range towards 2—17 years.

Summary of interpretations

1 Seven of the 60 interpreted the reference as intended, with 23 more coming within permissible limits of that interpretation.

2 Twenty-six of the 60 interpretations were unduly limited or unduly extended, one was wrong, and for 3 of them the evidence was unclear.

3 There was great variability, in going from respondent to respondent, in terms of the lower limit of the age range considered, in terms of the upper limit of the age range considered, and in terms of the span of years considered.

4 Some respondents thought in terms of specific children, for example: your own children; your grandchildren; children aged about the same as your own; children such as your own.

Table 7.11.5

Interpretations of '(programmes seen by) children'

The permissibility or otherwise of the ratings

Correct ( )	7	Unduly limited (UL)	18
Limited but permissible (LP)	22	Unduly extended (UE)	8
Extended but permissible (EP)	1	Incorrect (X)	1
Unclear, but rated 'doubtful but permitted (?P)	3	Total	60

Upper and lower age limits and age spans

Lower age limits		Upper age limits		Age spans considered	
0— 2 years	2	Under 8 years	8	1 year	3
3— 4 years	6	8 years	2	2 years	2
5— 6 years	12	9—10 years	10	3 years	4
7— 8 years	12	11—12 years	10	4 years	3
9—10 years	1	13—14 years	11	5 years	5
11—12 years	4	15—16 years	3	6 years	5
13—14 years	2	17—18 years	2	7 years	4
		19—20 years	1	8 years	4
				9 years	2
				10 years	2
				11 years	3
				13 years	1
Not given	21	Not given	13	Not given	22
Total	60	Total	60	Total	60

Non-numerical aspects of interpretations

Children	37	
Children, including young girls	1	38
Young children (3)/small children (1)/kiddies (1)		5
Very young children and older children (1)/children of different ages (1)		2
Children aged about the same as your own	2	
Children such as your own	1	4
Children, your own grandchildren in particular	1	
Your own children (6)/your own small children (1)	7	
Your grandchildren	1	8
All such references		57

Speculative comment

The term 'children' appears to be a fairly imprecise one, open to varying interpretations. Its imprecise nature may well have provided scope for the specialised interpretations which other aspects of the question tended to demand. For example, the difficulty of generalising about *all* 'children' (when one does not know about the viewing of children generally) may have encouraged respondents to base replies upon children known well to them.

Interpretations of 'appropriate'

The word 'appropriate' was intended to mean suitable generally, rather than suitable (for) in some rather specific sense.

Summary of interpretations

1 Whereas many of these respondents interpreted the term in a fairly general sense, there were others whose interpretation was quite specific.

2 Moreover, these specific interpretations tended to vary from respondent to respondent: good for them; good for their minds; understood by them; educational; interesting; enjoyable.

3 Almost all grasped at least some aspect of the intended meaning.

Table 7.11.6

Interpretations of 'appropriate'

Suitable (for them) (35)/fit (for them) (6)	41	42
The sort of thing they should view	1	
Are suited to their particular ages (1)/are right for their respective ages (1)		2
Suit them		2
Good (for them) (6)/good or bad (for them) (1)/have any good or bad effects (on them) (1)/harmless (1)	9	12
Good for (their) minds (1)/detrimental to their conduct (1)/in good taste or proper (1)	3	
Understood (by them)		2
Educational (2)/instructive (1)/teach something useful (1)		4
Interest (them (1)/are interesting (to them) (3)/equally interesting to (children of all ages) (1)		5
Enjoyed (by them) (3)/enjoyable (3)/can enjoy (them) (1)/liked (1)		8
Entertaining		2
Go on too long to be good (for them)		1
Is it right that (children ...) should stay up late and see (adult programmes)		1
Not clear what question was considered		1
Total		83*

*Some of the 60 respondents had more than one interpretation of the term.

Speculative comment

1 The word 'appropriate' is a very broad one and we may reasonably expect some degree of selectivity to occur in terms of the specific aspect of it which individual respondents consider.

166

(b)   Perhaps, too, the particular programmes (or types of programmes) considered by them conditioned their interpretations
of 'appropriate' to at least some degree.

Some other interpretations of interest (3 cases)

These are shown in Table 7.11.7.

Table 7.11.7

Interpretations of interest

Respondent added to the question 'going by those you have seen'	1
Respondent was unable to decide between two versions of the question	1
It was not possible to tell what question was being answered (except that it referred to children aged 5—15)	1

Summary for full question

1 Of the 60 interpretations of this question, 7 per cent were allocated
an overall rating of either 'as intended' or 'permissible'. This compares
with an average of 29 per cent for all the questions tested.

2 The main points of difficulty or of failure were as follows:

(a)   26 of the 60 respondents wrongly eliminated adult programmes from consideration and 12 wrongly eliminated children's
programmes.

(b)   Some respondents narrowed 'seen by' into something rather
conditional (e.g. which children might see, which you allow children to see, programmes meant for children). Others widened the
reference to something like 'programmes showing on TV'.

(c)   30 of the 60 respondents interpreted children at least
approximately as intended, though the remaining 30 were fairly
widely out. Some of the latter considered only very limited
groups of children, e.g. your own child; your grandchild; children
such as your own; children, your own grandchildren in particular.
Moreover, the age range of the children considered by individual
respondents was highly varied.

(d)   The word 'appropriate' was interpreted fairly broadly (as
intended) by many of the respondents, but there were some who
interpreted it in terms of only one of its numerous aspects. Moreover, the aspect considered varied quite a lot in going from one to
another respondent.

167

3 Speculative comments

(a) Short of answering 'don't know' or 'not sure', some respondents may have had no alternative to basing their answers upon just one class or type of programme—since two different classes of programme may have warranted different answers. At the same time, it also seems possible that the high degree of selectivity that appeared to occur amongst respondents on this issue may have been due to the apparent indications of other parts of the question (e.g. appropriateness 'for children') or to the preoccupation of some respondents with the suitability (for children) of specific types of programmes.

(b)   The tendency of some respondents to convert 'seen by' into the more conditional form 'might see' or 'meant for', may have sprung out of the fact that most respondents could not be expected to know what programmes children (generally) do in fact watch.

(c)   It may have been the imprecise nature of the term 'children' which provided scope for some respondents to base their replies upon the viewing behaviour of children (or classes of children) known to them.

(d)   The word 'appropriate' is similarly broad and imprecise and may well have provided scope for selectivity in line with the apparent indications of other parts of the question or with the preoccupations of respondents concerning the 'appropriateness' for children of particular classes of programme material.

7.12   QUESTION 15, QUESTIONNAIRE II

The wording of the question

'Do you think that children suffer any ill effects from watching programmes with violence in them, other than ordinary Westerns?' (To be
coded: yes/no/not sure.)

Check question

'Will you tell me your reasons for saying that?' If 'yes': 'Which programmes are you thinking of?'

Definitions of different parts of the question

The following are the intended meanings of key terms in the question.
*However, as indicated below, some variants of the intended interpreta-
tions were regarded as permissible and others as possibly permissible.*
The word 'you' was meant to be interpreted as 'you, yourself' and was
not intended to include others (e.g. respondent's spouse, children, relatives, lodger(s)). The reference 'children' is a broad one and no single
definition of it could be regarded as final. In the present context, it was
meant to be interpreted as 'children in general' rather than children in
any narrow age range or special category. An acceptable definition was
one which considered the age range 5—14 years, or some extension of
that range towards 2—17 years: The popular use of the term 'suffer (any
ill effects)' is often wider than its dictionary definition: in this context
it was intended to mean 'undergo'. The reference '(suffer) any ill
effects' was intended to mean '(undergo) any mental, moral or physical
harm, including harm to character'. The word 'programme' was intended
to mean 'programmes in general' and to include both adult and children's
programmes. The word 'violence' was intended to refer to the use of
physical force, particularly against other people, and acceptable interpretations will include (among others) 'fighting', 'shooting', 'murder', 'war',
'brutality'. The phrase 'other than ordinary Westerns' was intended to

169

signify that Westerns were not to be considered in the answer.

Respondents' interpretations of the question

These interpretations are set out in full in the Appendix (Part II). They are based upon the replies of 60 people.

Marking the interpretations

The system used for rating or marking respondents' interpretations of questions

The following marking or rating system was used.

1 If all elements of the question were interpreted as intended, the interpretation as a whole was rated 'fully as intended' (√).

2 Failure to interpret any significant element of the question fully as intended was sufficient to pull the total interpretation down below the level of 'fully as intended'. The level so reached was determined by the most seriously misinterpreted (significant) element in the test question. For example, if all but one of the significant elements of the question were interpreted as intended and the interpretation of that other element was rated as 'somewhat limited but permissible' (see below), then the whole interpretation was so rated (i.e. 'somewhat limited but permissible'). The reason for this is that a question cannot be regarded as a safe one unless all its parts are interpreted as intended.

3 If a significant element of the question was obviously and substantially misinterpreted or was omitted altogether, the total interpretation was marked 'incorrect' (X).

4 In the context of this system, the following ratings were made of specific elements of respondents' interpretations.

(a) 'you'. Where this term was interpreted as intended (see above), the interpretation was rated 'correct' (√). Where it seemed that a permissible interpretation had been made, but where the evidence was not conclusive, the rating 'doubtful but permissible' (?P) was applied.

(b) 'children'. Where this reference was interpreted as intended (see above), that interpretation was rated 'correct' (√). Other interpretations were rated 'limited but permissible' (LP) if they covered an age span of 4 years or more and included at least 2 years in the range 8—12 years. Where it seemed that a permissible

170

interpretation had been made, but where the evidence was not conclusive, the rating 'doubtful but permissible' (?P) was applied. An interpretation of the reference which was only partly within the range 2—17 years was rated 'unduly extended' (UE). An interpretation of the reference as less than 2 years old (only) or as more than 17 years old (only) was rated 'incorrect' (X). Where the respondent interpreted 'children' as 'very young children (only)' or as 'teenagers (only)' or as 'older children (only)' or as 'your own child (only)', that interpretation was rated 'unduly limited' (UL). Other interpretations were also rated 'unduly limited', namely 'nervous children', 'impressionable but not average children', 'children who have been brought up properly'.

(c) 'suffer (any ill effects)'. Where this term was interpreted as intended (see above), it was rated 'correct' (√). The interpretation 'have suffered' was rated 'different but permissible' (DP). In some cases the term appeared to have been by-passed. Where the interpretation of the rest of the question seemed to imply the intended interpretation of 'suffer' (but where the evidence was not conclusive) the rating 'doubtful but permissible' (?P) was applied. Where the interpretation of the rest of this question made it clear that the word 'suffer' had been omitted altogether, the interpretation was rated incorrect (X).

(d) '(suffer) any ill effects'. Where this reference was interpreted as intended (see above), it was rated 'correct' (√). Where it seemed that a permissible interpretation had been made, but where the evidence was not conclusive, the interpretation was rated 'doubtful but permissible' (?P). If the respondent was not considering 'ill effects' at all, his interpretation was rated 'incorrect' (X).

(e) 'programmes'. Where this term was interpreted as intended (see above), it was rated 'correct' (√). Where it was interpreted as 'adult programmes only', the interpretation was rated 'limited but permissible' (LP). Where the term was interpreted as 'children's programmes (only)', the rating 'unduly limited' (UL) was applied. Where Westerns were included in the interpretation, the rating 'incorrect' (X) was applied.

(f) 'violence'. Where this term was interpreted as intended (see above), it was rated 'correct' (√). Some interpretations included both the intended meaning of violence and other meanings such as 'horror', 'rudeness', 'sexiness', 'swearing': these interpretations were rated as 'unduly extended' (UE). Other interpretations left out the violence concept altogether (possibly substituting a concept such as swearing, rudeness, sexiness): these interpretations

171

were rated 'incorrect' (X).

(g) 'other than ordinary Westerns'. Where this reference was interpreted as intended (see above), it was rated 'correct' (√). The interpretations 'other than Westerns' and 'excluding Westerns' were similarly rated 'correct' (√). Where the interpretation given included Westerns, the interpretation was rated 'incorrect' (X). The interpretation 'other than children's programmes' was also rated 'incorrect'. Similarly, where the reference was not considered at all, the rating 'incorrect' was applied.

The ratings allocated

Under the system described above, the following ratings were allocated to respondents' interpretations of this test question.

Table 7.12.1

Ratings allocated to respondents' interpretations of of test question (Q.15, II)

Lowest rating allocated to any part of the interpretation	Number of Ratings	Persons	Persons
Correct (√)	0	0	0
Extra but permissible (ExP)	0		
Somewhat limited but permissible (LP)	2		
Somewhat too specific but permissible (SP)	0		
Somewhat too general but permissible (GP)	0	2	3
Somewhat extended but permissible (EP)	0		
Somewhat different but permissible (DP)	0		
Doubtful but permitted (?P)	3	3	5
Unduly limited (UL)	13		
Unduly general (UG)	0		
Unduly extended (UE)	3	16*	27
Unduly different (UD)	1		
Incorrect (X)	39	39	65
Total		60	100

*See Note A on page 47.

Content analysis of the interpretations

There follows an analysis of the different interpretations of elements of the test question. The emphasis in this analysis is upon the different

172

kinds of interpretations which were found rather than upon the number of them (though these numbers are given), the purpose of the content analysis being to discover the kinds of things that happen, to speculate about what causes them, and to derive hypotheses (about communication processes) for testing in later phases of the enquiry.

Interpretations of 'you'

The word 'you' was meant to be interpreted as 'you, yourself' and was not intended to include others (e.g. respondent's spouse, children, relatives, lodger(s)).

Summary of interpretations

There was little or no evidence to suggest that the term 'you' had been interpreted other than as intended. At the same time the check made in thi special case was not a complete one (see note to Table 7.12.).

Table 7.12.2
Interpretations of 'you'

Respondent appeared to have interpreted the word 'you' as intended (i.e. 'you, yourself, alone')	59*
Unclear exactly how the word 'you' was interpreted but probably acceptable	1
	60*

*Whereas the intensive interview yielded information about respondent interpretations of the word 'you', such interpretations were not made the subject of direct and focused probing (as was in fact done for this word in some of the other questions). Accordingly, all defective interpretations of the word in its present context have not necessarily been picked up.

Interpretations of 'children'

The reference 'children' is a broad one and no single definition of it could be regarded as final. In the present context, it was meant to be interpreted as 'children in general' rather than children in any narrow age range or special category. An acceptable definition was one which considered the age range 5—14 years, or some extension of that range towards 2—17 years.

Summary of interpretations

Details are given in Table 7.12.3.

1 This table exhibits marked variability in respondents' interpretations of the word 'children'. Thus: while 14 had the lower age limit (of children) fixed at about 5–6 years, there were two respondents who had it at 0–2 years and 10 who fixed it at 11 years or older. Indeed, one respondent had the lower limit fixed at 15–16 years. The same great variability applied to the upper age limit of those considered as 'children': 9 had it at 8 years or less, though none went beyond 20 years. There was also a great range in the span of years considered as encompassing 'children', with 12 respondents limited it to a 3-year span and 3 respondents thinking of 'children' as spanning at least 10 years.

2 Considered in non-numerical terms, the same picture emerged—namely great variability in the interpretation of this word: very young children, children, teenagers, older children, young people.

3 Some respondents interpreted the term 'children' rather narrowly and personally, for example: children such as your own or such as your grandchildren; your own two children; children and your own in particular.

4 Three respondents applied rather special qualifications or limits to their interpretations of this term: children who are brought up properly; impressionable but not average children; nervous children. These are interpretations which allowed them to say 'yes' to the question when otherwise some of them at least might quite possibly have said 'no'.

Table 7.12.3

Interpretations of 'children'

Whether or not interpreted in terms of ages

Ages not indicated	14
Upper and lower limits of age span given	40
Upper limit only given	5
Lower limit only given	1
Total	60

Upper and lower age limits and age spans

Lower age limits		Upper age limits		Age spans considered	
0– 2 years	2	Under 8 years	4	1 year	1
3– 4 years	2	8 years	5	2 years	4
5– 6 years	14	9–10 years	3	3 years	7
7– 8 years	7	11–12 years	15	4 years	9
9–10 years	6	13–14 years	8	5 years	4
11–12 years	6	15–16 years	5	6 years	3
13–14 years	3	17–18 years	4	7 years	3
15–16 years	1	19–20 years	1	8 years	4
				9 years	2
				10 years	1
				11 years	2
Not given	19	Not given	15	Not given	20
Total	60	Total	60	Total	60

Interpretations in non-numerical terms

Those considering specific ages		Those not considering specific ages	
Children	28	Children	5
Young children	1	Young children	2
Younger children	1	Younger children	1
Very young children	1	Young people other than very	
Older children	2	young children	1
Teenagers	1	Children of various ages	1
Young people	2	Your own children	2
Children such as your own		Your young children	1
children	2	Nervous children	1
Children such as your own			
grandchildren	1	Total	14
Children and your own in			
particular	1		
Your own children	1		
Your own two children	2		
Your grandchildren	1		
Children who are brought up			
properly	1		
Impressionable but not average			
children	1		
Total	46		

Speculative comment

1   That the range of interpretations of this word should be so great is probably not surprising because in popular use the term appears to have quite a wide range in meaning.

2   Quite possibly, many more respondents than we were able to identify were thinking of particular children (e.g. their own children) in answering the question and so might have had the ages of those particular children in mind.

3   The limiting of 'children' to those 'who have been brought up properly' could well allow a respondent to answer 'no' to the question whereas otherwise he might have said 'yes'. And vice versa for the interpretation 'impressionable but not average children' or 'nervous children'.

4   It also seems possible that some respondents tended to think of age ranges which in their opinion were (or were not) open to influence by programmes with violence in them.

Interpretations of 'suffer (any ill effects)'

In this particular context, the term 'suffer' was intended to mean 'undergo'.

Summary of interpretations

1 Five respondents did not consider the term directly (e.g. 'Do you think that programmes with violence in them ... are fit for children to watch?').

2 One respondent converted the term into the past tense (i.e. 'have suffered').

3 The great majority (54/60) apparently understood the term just as intended.

Table 7.12.4

Interpretations of 'suffer (any ill effects)'

'Suffer' (any ill effects) (i.e. interpreted as intended)	54
Have 'suffered' (any ill effects)	1
Concept not directly considered but sense of the concept at least partly communicated	5
Total	60

Interpretations of '(suffer) any ill effects'

The reference '(suffer) any ill effects' was intended to mean '(undergo) any mental, moral or physical harm, including harm to character'.

Summary of interpretations

1 In the first place, all 60 respondents appear to have considered the term 'ill effects' (at least indirectly), and to have grasped at least part of its essential character (i.e. 'ill effects' was intended to mean any mental, moral or physical harm, including harm to character).

2 It is noteworthy, however, that not all limited themselves to those ill effects which one might consider possible consequences of exposure to programmes with violence in them. Thus, whereas 47 of the 60 appear only to have been considering (and judging in terms of) ill effects possibly stemming from violence programmes, there were 10 who thought also of ill effects seemingly other than those likely to stem from seeing violence on television (e.g. become rough and learn to swear; become violent and rude), and there were 3 who appeared to consider only (or mainly) ill effects other than those that might stem from seeing violence in programmes (e.g. swearing, loose sex morality).

3 Even amongst respondents who stuck to 'ill effects possibly stemming from violence in programmes', there was considerable variability, respondent by respondent, in terms of what ill effect was being considered— and, presumably, forming the basis for judgment. For all 60 persons,

176

these different criteria ranged from having nightmares, becoming nervous, copying violent or rough behaviour, having criminal ideas, copying bad behaviour, learning to swear, being cruel. Moreover, amidst this variability, many respondents appeared to have had only one criterion mainly in mind.

Table 7.12.5

Interpretations of '(suffer) any ill effects'

The different interpretations of 'ill effects'

Have bad dreams (7)/nightmares (5)/disturbed nights (1)		13
Made nervous (5)/disturbed (1)/worried (1)/mental effects (4)	11	16
Become frightened (4)/are frightened when they go to bed (1)	5	
Have their emotions aroused		1
Copy or imitate violence (12)/learn violence (2)/become violent (4)/ use violence (1)	19	21
Get ideas about shooting (1)/about being warlike (1)	2	
Are made unruly	1	
Rough with each other (1)/brutal to each other (1)	2	4
Hooliganism	1	
Learn criminal ideas	4	6
Become delinquent	2	
Are led astray (1)/mislead (1)	2	
Copy bad behaviour/bad things (7)/copy undesirable behaviour (1)	8	14
Have their lives altered in a bad way	1	
Copy what they see	3	
Take it to heart		1
Learn swearing		2
Pick up bad manners		1
Suffer bad moral effects		1
Being cruel		1
Total		81*

Were the ill effects considered, related to violence?

Ill effects related solely to violence	47
Ill effects related to violence and to things other than violence	10
Ill effects related to things other than violence	3

* As some respondents gave more than one interpretation, this total exceeds the number of respondents.

Speculative comment

The most important thing about this set of findings is its indication that, possibly unknown to the interviewer, one respondent may be answering/judging in terms of a criterion at least partly different from the criterion guiding another respondent. Often enough, their respective criteria will be substantially different.

177

Interpretations of 'programmes (with violence in them)'

The word 'programmes' was intended to mean 'programmes in general' and to include both adult and children's programmes.

Summary of interpretations

1 Forty-six of the 60 interpreted this term in its intended breadth—i.e. as programmes in general, and including both adult and children's programmes.

2 Some 14, however, interpreted the term very much more specifically: 'children's programmes only'; 'adult programmes only'; 'adult medical programmes and adult programmes'.

Table 7.12.6

Interpretations of 'programmes (with violence in them)'

Any programmes (i.e. as intended)	46
Children's programmes	7
Adult programmes (5)/other than childrens' programmes (1)	6
Adult medical programmes and adult programmes	1
Total	60

Speculative comment

1 It seems possible that the interpretation 'children's programmes' (7 cases) sprang out of respondent assumption that this is what must have been meant since the question asked about the effects of programmes on children.

2 It may also be that the 6 who thought in terms of adult programmes only, considered that only this sort of programme (i.e. adult) contained much violence and hence was what was being asked about. Certainly there were respondent comments to that effect.

3 In each case (i.e. 1 and 2), I am suggesting that the question was possibly not specific enough on this point and may even have encouraged respondents to work out what sort of programme was probably meant.

4 Another possibility, of course, is that the respondent's interpretation of this term reflected or was influenced by the sort of programme that the respondent wanted to report upon.

Interpretations of 'violence'

The word 'violence' was intended to refer to the use of physical force, particularly against other people, and acceptable interpretations would include (amongst others) 'fighting', 'shooting', 'murder', 'war', 'brutality'.

Summary of interpretations

1 Forty-six of the 60 respondents interpreted 'violence' solely in terms of physical force, particularly against other people. Of the others, 7 interpreted the word in terms both of physical force and of behaviour not involving physical force. There there were 3 who interpreted the word solely or mainly in terms of something other than physical force (e.g. programmes presenting swearing, smut, rudeness).

2 Over and above such deviations from what was intended, there was evidence of a great deal of variability in the meaning given to the term 'violence'. Thus in Table 7.12.7 it will be seen that these interpretations included Westerns(!), gunfighting, knifings, robberies, crime, holdups, beating people up, sadism, wrestling, horror, swearing, smut, rudeness, sex, bad morals. Moreover, the great majority had in mind only one of the criteria shown in Part II of Table 7.12.7.

3 Specially noteworthy is the fact that so many, 24 out of 60, should have been thinking in terms of Westerns, when this interpretation was specifically ruled out by a qualifying clause in the question.

Table 7.12.7

Interpretations of 'violence'

Part I: Did the respondent interpret 'violence' as something concerned with the use of physical force, particularly against other people?

Respondent interpreted 'violence' solely in terms of physical force, particularly against others (see list (i) below)	46
Respondent interpreted 'violence' in terms both of physical force (see (i) below) and of behaviour other than physical force (see list (ii) below)	7
Respondent interpreted 'violence' only in terms of behaviour other than physical force (see list (ii) below)	3
Not clear how violence was interpreted	4
Total	60

Part II: Details of interpretations *

(i) Interpretations apparently relating to physical force particularly against other people

Westerns	24	Hold-ups (1)/gangsters (7)	8
Gunfighting (2)/shooting (4)	6	Beating people up (2)/thuggery	
Fighting	1	(1)	3
Murders (7)/killings (4)	11	Sadism	1
Bank robberies (3)/robberies (1)/		Wrestling	2
burglaries (1)	5	Horror	1
Crime	5		

179

(ii) Interpretations not obviously related to physical force

Swearing (3)/bad language (2)/		Rudeness	1
swear words (1)	6	Sex	2
Smut	1	Bad morals as in glamorous	
Rough behaviour	1	side of life	1

*Some respondents qualified under more than one sub-heading and so the totals exceed the number of respondents.

Speculative comment

1 Here, just as for the concept 'ill effects', it appears that different people may have been making judgments on the bases of at least partly different views about what sorts of programmes were being asked about in the question. Some of the differences were quite marked.

2 That so many (24/60) should have been thinking in terms of Wes rns is remarkable in the circumstances. Comments on this omission are made below.

Interpretations of 'other than ordinary westerns'

The phrase 'other than ordinary Westerns' was intended to signify that Westerns were not to be considered in the answer.

Summary of interpretations

1 Of the 60 respondents, 4 clearly included Westerns in making a judgment and there were 12 more who seemingly overlooked the phrase 'other than ordinary Westerns'.

2 On the other hand, 22 clearly excluded Westerns.

Table 7.12.8

Interpretations of 'other than ordinary Westerns'

Other than ordinary Westerns (1)/other than Westerns (12)/excluding Westerns (9)	22
Including Westerns (20)/such as Westerns (1)/particularly/especially Westerns (2)/namely Westerns (1)	24
Other than children's programmes	1
Respondent did not consider phrase as she did not understand 'other than'	1
Phrase seemingly overlooked	2
Total	60

Speculative comment

There seem to be several possible reasons for the inclusion of Westerns by many of the respondents:

(a)   that some respondents started to work out an answer before the interviewer got to this qualifying clause;

(b)   that some converted 'other than' (which can be a complex concept) into 'including' or 'I mean' or some such terms;

(c)   that some (not hearing or not dwelling on the qualifying clause) assumed that a major source of violence in programmes seen by children was the Western;

(d)   that some excluded ordinary Westerns, but included Westerns of the less ordinary kind.

These 'reasons' are, however, but speculations and they should not be regarded as otherwise.

Some further interpretations of interest

Table 7.12.9

Other interpretations of interest (3 cases)

Interpretations of 'do you think (children) suffer any ill effects from watching programmes . . .		
Do you think children should watch programmes . . .?	1	
Do you think that children's programmes ... are fit for children to watch?	1	2
Added to the question		
Thinking about all possible effects		1
Total		3

Summary of whole question

1   Of the 60 interpretations of this question, 8 per cent were allocated an overall rating of either 'as intended' or 'permissible'. This compares with an average of 29 per cent for all the questions tested.

2   The main sources of failure appear to have been as follows:

(a) a tendency of many respondents to have a very limited idea of what ages encompass 'childhood' (e.g. 3–5 years, 12–16 years, 5–7 years, 14–17 years) or to put some rather special or personal limit upon *which* children they considered (e.g. nervous children, impressionable but not average children, your own children, your grandchildren, children who have been brought up properly);

(b)   a tendency to include Westerns in their considerations in spite of being asked to exclude them (at least 24 of the 60 did this);

(c)   the inclusion of programme content additional to (7) or other than (3) violence in their interpretations of '(programmes with) violence (in them)';

(d)   the narrowing of the term 'programme' to some more specific category of programme material (14) (e.g. children's programmes, adult programmes).

3   It is also well worth noting that there was a high degree of variability in the interpretation of terms like 'children', 'ill effects', 'violence'— such that respondents who offer identical choice of answer may well have been considering rather different aspects of the matter concerned.

4   *Speculative comments*

(a)   A lot of different concepts were built into this question and this may possibly have contributed to its being so poorly grasped.

(b)   The inclusion of Westerns in spite of a specific instruction not to do so may possibly have sprung out of one or more of the following: respondents starting to answer an apparently complete question before the final (and limiting) instruction was voiced by the interviewer; respondents assuming that Westerns were meant because they felt that these were the main focus of violence seen by children on television; the words 'other than' may have been specially prone to communication failure.

(c)   Respondents who narrowed the term 'programme' to mean 'children's programmes' may have assumed that since the question was about children's programmes, children's programmes must have been meant. Others, narrowing the term to 'adult programmes', may have felt that these were the main source of violence seen by children and hence were what was meant.

(d)   Perhaps the variability in the interpretation of 'ill-effects' might have been reduced if the context-setting word 'violence' had been introduced before the term 'ill effects'.

(e)   The term 'children' seems to have been a specially unstable term, at least in this setting.

(f)   It seems possible that some of these respondents have narrowed or modified different terms in the question in order to fit the question to their own experience or to allow them, to express strong feelings on some matter which the question did not ordinarily bear directly upon. This may be what happened with the terms 'children' and 'ill effect'.

7.13 QUESTION 20, QUESTIONNAIRE II

The wording of the question

'Do you think that people who plan the advertising programmes are using the advertising time properly, or do you think that this time is being used badly?' (To be coded: Used properly/used badly/sometimes properly/sometimes badly.)

Check question

'Why do you say that?'

Definitions of different parts of the question

The following are the intended meanings of key terms in the question. *However, as indicated below, some variants of the intended interpretations were regarded as permissible and others as possibly permissible.* The phrase 'people who plan the advertising programmes' was intended to refer generally to those who are responsible for the form, the content, and the general presentation of advertising on television. The term 'advertising (time)' was meant to refer to all television advertising, whatever its type, form or placement (e.g. between or within programmes). The reference '(advertising) time' was meant to refer to the total amount of time spent in presenting television advertisements (whatever their type, form or placement). The reference 'using ... properly' was meant to refer to the use of advertising time in a manner responsibly balanced between the interest of the advertisers and the comfort of the viewers. This concept is a difficult one and it will be seen from below that various more limited interpretations of it were regarded as permissible. The reference 'used badly' was meant to imply a disregard or a failure with respect to the interests of viewers or advertisers or both.

Respondents' interpretations of the questions

These interpretations are set out in full in the Appendix (Part II). They are based upon the replies of 60 people.

Marking the interpretations

The system used for rating or marking respondents' interpretations of questions

The following marking or rating system was used.

1 If all elements of the question were interpreted as intended, the interpretation as a whole was rated 'fully as intended' (√).

2 Failure to interpret any significant element of the question fully as intended was sufficient to pull the total interpretation down below the level of 'fully as intended'. The level so reached was determined by the most seriously misinterpreted (significant) element in the test question. For example, if all but one of the significant elements of the question were interpreted as intended and the interpretation of that other element was rated 'somewhat limited but permissible' (see below), then the whole interpretation was so rated (i.e. 'somewhat limited but permissible'). The reason for this is that a question cannot be regarded as a safe one unless all its parts are interpreted as intended.

3 If a significant element of the question was obviously and substantially misinterpreted or was omitted altogether, the total interpretation was marked 'incorrect' (X).

4 In the context of this system, the following ratings were made of specific elements of respondents' interpretations.

(a) 'people who plan the advertising programmes'. Where this reference was interpreted as intended (see above), the rating 'correct' (√) was applied. Interpretations such as 'the advertisers', 'those in charge of advertising', were regarded as acceptable. Where the reference was interpreted as 'the manufacturers', the interpretation was rated 'different but permissible' (DP). Where it seemed that the intended interpretations had been made, but where the evidence was not conclusive, the rating 'doubtful but permissible' (?P) was applied.

(b) 'advertising (time)'. Where this term was interpreted as intended (see above), the interpretation was rated 'correct' (√). Where the interpretation was limited to advertisements between programmes or to advertisements within programmes, it was rated 'limited but permissible' (LP). Where this term was interpreted as 'some (i.e. certain) television advertisements', the rating 'unduly limited' (UL) was applied. Where the term was omitted altogether, the rating 'incorrect' (X) was applied.

(c)   '(advertising) time'. Where this reference was interpreted as intended (see above), the interpretation was rated 'correct' (√). Where it was interpreted as 'timing of advertisements' (e.g. within the programme complex), the interpretation was rated 'unduly different' (UD). Similarly for the interpretation 'are advertisements timed (properly)?'. Where the reference was interpreted as asking if advertising took up too much time, the rating 'incorrect' (X) was applied; similarly where the reference was omitted altogether.

(d)   'using ... properly'. Where this reference was interpreted as intended (see above), the interpretation was rated 'correct' (√). Where it seemed that a permissible interpretation had been made, but where the evidence was not conclusive, the rating 'doubtful but permissible' (?P) was applied. Where it was interpreted solely in terms of the interests of the advertiser the rating 'limited but permissible' (LP) was allotted. Where it was solely in terms of *one aspect* of the advertiser's interest, it was rated 'unduly limited' (UL). In the same way, if the interpretation was solely in terms of *one aspect* of the *viewer's* interests, it was rated 'unduly limited' (UL). Where the reference was omitted altogether or was interpreted as referring to other than advertiser/viewer interests, the rating 'incorrect' (X) was applied.

(e)   'used badly?' Where this reference was interpreted as intended (see above), the interpretation was rated 'correct' (√). Where it was interpreted solely in terms of the interests of the advertiser, the interpretation was rated 'limited but permissible' (LP). If the interpretation was solely in terms of *one aspect* of the advertiser's interests, it was rated 'unduly limited' (UL). In the same way, if the interpretation was solely in terms of *one aspect* of the *viewer's* interests, it was rated 'unduly limited' (UL). The interpretation of the reference was rated 'incorrect' (X), where the respondent answered 'used badly' on the grounds that: (the total amount of time used for advertising) was too great; advertisements should not be shown at all on television. Where the reference was omitted altogether the rating 'incorrect' (X) was applied.

The ratings allocated

Under the system described above, the following ratings were allocated to respondent interpretations of this test question.

Table 7.13.1

Ratings allocated to respondents' interpretations
of test question (Q20, II)

Lowest rating allocated to any part of the interpretation	Number of Ratings	Number of Persons	% of Persons
Correct (√)	0	0	0
Extra but permissible (ExP)	0		
Somewhat limited but permissible (LP)	11		
Somewhat too specific but permissible (SP)	0		
Somewhat too general but permissible (GP)	0	18*	30
Somewhat extended but permissible (EP)	0		
Somewhat different but permissible (DP)	15		
Doubtful but permitted (?P)	2	2	3
Unduly limited (UL)	19		
Unduly general (UG)	0	20*	33
Unduly extended (UE)	0		
Unduly different (UD)	6		
Incorrect (X)	20	20	33
	Total	60	†

*See Note A on page 47.
†See Note B on page 48.

Content analysis of respondents' interpretations

There follows an analysis of the different interpretations of elements of
the test question. The emphasis in this analysis is upon the different
kinds of interpretations which are found rather than upon the number
of them (though these numbers are given), the purpose of the content
analysis being to discover the kinds of things that happen, to speculate
about what causes them, and to derive hypotheses (about communication processes) for testing in later phases of the enquiry.

Interpretations of 'people who plan the advertising programmes'

The phrase 'people who plan the advertising programmes' was intended
to refer generally to those who are responsible for the form, the content, and the general presentation of advertising on television.

Summary of interpretations

1 Most respondents appear to have omitted consideration of this phrase altogether.

2 Of those considering it, there were 7 who thought, as intended, in terms of 'those who plan the advertising or the advertisements'.

Table 7.13.2

Interpretations of 'people who plan the advertising in programmes'

People who plan the advertising (3)/the advertisements (4)	7
Those in charge of advertising	1
The advertisers	2
The manufacturers	1
Respondent did not appear to consider the phrase	49
Total	60

Speculative comment

In all probability, this phrase could have been discarded without much damage to the meaning of the question. Because of this, a failure to consider it was not brought into the overall rating for grasp of the question (see above).

Interpretations of 'advertising (time)'

The term 'advertising (time)' was meant to refer to all television advertising, whatever its type, form or placement (e.g. between or within programmes).

Summary of interpretations

1 Practically all of the 60 respondents grasped this term as intended.

2 There were several, however, who gave it a rather more specific meaning than was intended: advertisement breaks, the individual advertisements, certain advertisements.

Table 7.13.3

Interpretations of 'advertising (time)'

advertising (interpretation apparently as intended)	56
advertisement breaks	1
advertisements (i.e. considered generally)	1
the individual television advertisements (i.e. ads considered separately)	1
some (i.e. certain) television advertisements	1
Total	60

187

Interpretations of '(advertising) time'

The reference '(advertising) time' was meant to refer to the total amount of time spent in presenting television advertisements (whatever their type, form or placement).

Summary of interpretations

1 Whereas the majority understood this term as intended, there were some (12) who interpreted it as (the) timing (of advertisements).

2 A few respondents overlooked the concept of 'time' altogether.

Table 7.13.4

Interpretations of '(advertising) time'	
The time allocated to advertising (as intended)	44
The timing of advertisements (within the programme complex)	12
Respondent apparently overlooked the term	4
Total	60

Speculative comment

The interpretation of 'time' as 'timing' seemingly served to limit the criteria in terms of which the respondent made a choice of answer. The reasons for this narrowing of the term are by no means clear, but one possibility is that it has been helped along by the annoyance of some viewers by what they regard as the spoiling of programmes by the interruption of these with advertisements at the wrong places (i.e. a timing issue).

Interpretations of 'using ... properly'

The reference 'using ... properly' was meant to refer to the use of advertising time in a manner responsibly balanced between the interest of the advertisers and the comfort of the viewers. This concept is a difficult one and it will be seen that various more limited interpretations of it were regarded as permissible.

Summary of interpretations

1 The outstanding feature of Table 7.13.5 is the sheer variety of the criteria in terms of which respondents judged whether or not advertising time was being used properly.

2 As perhaps one might expect from the previous table, the most

frequently adopted criterion concerned the placement and timing of advertisements in the programme complex and the broad issue of programme interruption (33 of the 84 uses of criteria).

3 The other criteria used vary widely and were in terms of one or another of the following: selling goods; impact; providing useful information or a service to viewers; general quality of advertisements; the repetitions and the number of them; viewer enjoyment and/or viewer rights.

4 Most people thought in terms of only one narrow criterion and there were relatively few who thought in terms of more than two criteria.

5 No more than 14 respondents thought in terms of both viewer and advertiser interests, most of the others limiting their consideration of the question to either viewer interests alone or advertiser interests alone.

6 A few people appear to have overlooked the reference altogether.

Table 7.13.5

Interpretations of 'using ... properly'

The many different criteria used by respondents

In terms of selling goods: selling goods, persuading to buy (6)/ advertisers getting value for money (1) — 7

In terms of impact: producing greatest impact on viewer (1)/successful in catching people's interests (2)/in sense that advertisements are appealing (1)/realism (1) — 5

In terms of providing useful information or service to viewers: providing useful information about products, about available goods (6)/gives viewers a service (1)/advertisements are instructive (1) — 8

In terms of general quality of advertisements: putting on good advertisements (1)/skilfully presented (1)/good content (1)/well designed and compiled (1) — 4

In terms of repetitiveness and total number of them: non-repetitiveness of advertisements (4)/total amount of time devoted to advertising, the amount of advertising (6)/the total number of advertisements (1) — 11

In terms of placement, timing, interruptions: well placed (1)/put on at right time of night (1)/well timed (4)/well timed so as not to spoil programmes by interrupting programmes too often (4)/not interrupting programmes at the wrong time (e.g. at points of interest) (8)/not confusing through intruding into a play (1) — 33

In terms of viewer enjoyment/viewer rights: from standpoint of viewer enjoyment of programmes (2)/liked by you (2)/not a waste of time (2)/not sacrificing interests of viewers to those of advertisers (1)/not forcing people to watch (because advertisement is in middle of programme) (2) — 9

Not clear how term was interpreted — 2
Term was not considered at all — 5

Total — 84*

*Some respondents considered in terms of more than one of the above elements

189

Whether both viewer and advertiser interests considered

Interpreted reference in terms of both viewer and advertiser interests	4 ⎫
Possibly both but evidence inconclusive	5 ⎬ 12
Both considered, but mainly viewer interests	3 ⎭
Interpreted in terms of viewer interests/comfort only	30 ⎫
Possibly considered viewer interests/comfort only, but evidence inconclusive	1 ⎬ 31
Interpreted in terms of advertiser interests only	8 ⎫
Possibly considered advertisers interests only, but evidence inconclusive	2 ⎬ 10
Not clear whether considered viewer interests only or advertisers interests only or both	2
Reference apparently not considered at all	5
Total	60

Speculative comment

It would seem that certain dominant aspects of viewer reactions to TV advertising have also dominated the choice of criteria in deciding whether or not advertising time is used properly. It may be that this tendency was strengthened by the use of the word 'time' (which for some became 'timing').

Interpretations of 'used badly'

The reference 'used badly' was meant to imply a disregard or a failure with respect to the interests of viewers or advertisers or both.

Summary of interpretations

1 Understandably, there is much similarity between these results and those presented in Table 7.13.5.

2 Here too, the outstanding feature of the findings is the variety of the criteria in terms of which respondents judged whether or not advertising time was being 'used badly'.

3 Here too, the most frequently adopted criterion concerned the placement of advertisements in relation to programmes (34 of the 76 interpretations).

4 The other criteria used were in terms of defect: in selling power; in impact; in informativeness; in quality of advertisements; in regard to repetitiveness; in regard to the number of them; in regard to viewer enjoyment/rights.

5 Just as with the previous concept, most respondents thought only in

190

terms of one of these criteria (60 thought of 76 between them).

6 No more than 11 thought in terms of both viewer and advertiser interests.

7 A few of the 60 respondents appear to have overlooked the concept 'used badly'.

Table 7.13.6

Interpretations of 'used badly'

(i) Various criteria considered by respondents

Not selling
Failing to sell goods/products	5	
Advertisers not getting value for money	1	6

Impact defects
Lack realism	1

Not sufficiently informative
Not providing useful information about products	2	
Uninformative advertisements	1	4
Too many (packed into small time) for them to impart meaning individually	1	

Poor quality of advertisements
Rubbishy	1	
Not presented skilfully	1	3
Designed and compiled badly	1	

Repetitiveness
Repeating the same advertisements too often/too often in the one evening	4

Number, amount of time given to them
Too many advertisements	3	
As many as possible packed into allotted time	1	7
Too much time spent on it in evening/too much of it	2	
Exceeding the permitted time	1	

Placement of advertisements and interruptions
Badly placed/badly placed in relation to programmes	2	
Badly timed/presented at wrong time in the evening	4	
By interrupting programmes	12	
Interferes with programmes through interrupting them/spoils programmes through interrupting them/spoils viewing through interrupting	4	34
Badly timed with respect to when they interrupt programmes/interrupt programmes at ill-advised moments/interrupt when you are interested in the programme	6	
Too many interruptions	5	
Confusing the viewer by intruding into the programme itself	1	

Viewer enjoyment/viewer rights
Spoils viewer enjoyment of programmes	2	
Not liked by viewer	1	
Wasting TV time	2	8
Sacrificing interests of viewers to the interest of the advertiser	1	
Forcing viewers to watch by putting them in middle of programme	2	

Not clear how the phrase was interpreted	3
Phrase apparently not considered at all	6
Total	76*

*Some of the 60 respondents offered more than one criterion.

Table 7.13.6 continued:

(ii) Whether both viewer and advertiser interest considered

Interpreted in terms of both viewer and advertiser interests (4)/ possibly both, but evidence inconclusive (3)	7
Interpreted in terms of viewer interests/comfort only (29)/ possibly considered only viewer interests/comfort, but evidence not conclusive (8)	37
Interpreted in terms of advertiser interests only (4)/possibly considered only advertiser interests, but evidence not conclusive	6
Not clear whether considered viewer interests only or advertiser interests only or both	4
Reference apparently not considered at all	6
Total	60

Summary for the whole question

1 Of the 60 interpretations of this question, 33 per cent allocated an overall rating of either 'as intended' or 'permissible'. This compares with an average of 29 per cent for all of the questions tested.

2 The main points of difficulty or failure were as follows:

(a)   the interpretation (by 14) of (advertising) time as the 'timing' (of advertisements);

(b)   the failure of most respondents to reach a judgment on the basis of consideration of both viewer and advertiser interests, coupled with a tendency to consider only some single criterion (of 'done properly' or 'done badly').

3 It is also worth noting that most respondents overlooked the opening phrase (though this was not regarded as sufficient to count against a permissible grasp of the question); that a few respondents overlooked one or both of the concepts 'used properly' and 'used badly'; that the criteria used by respondents to judge whether advertising time was being used properly or badly varied widely from one respondent to another, so that two seemingly similar answers might well refer to quite different aspects of television advertising.

4 *Speculative comments*

It seems quite possible that the matters about which this question asks for respondent judgement are emotionally loaded in the sense that the interruption of programmes by advertisements is a rather sore point with respondents. If this is so, it could well explain the conversion of 'time' to 'timing' and the dominance of the criterion 'placement of advertisements in programmes'/'interruption' among the judgement criteria of respondents.

7.14 QUESTION 21, QUESTIONNAIRE II

The wording of the question

'When the advertisements come on between two programmes, what do you usually do when you stay in the room with the television?'

Definitions of the different parts of the question

The following are the intended meanings of key terms in the question. *However, as indicated below, some variants of the intended interpretations were regarded as permissible and others as possibly permissible.* The phrase 'advertisements ... between 2 programmes' was meant to refer only to television advertisements that come between one programme and the next, and not to those which occur within programmes. The word 'you' was meant to be interpreted as 'you, yourself', and was not intended to include others (e.g. respondent's spouse, children, relatives, lodger(s)). The word 'usually' was meant to be interpreted as 'ordinarily', 'in the ordinary course of events', 'commonly'. Other acceptable interpretations of the term were: 'as a rule', 'generally', 'normally', 'habitually', 'as a routine', 'almost always', 'mostly', 'typically'. The reference '... what do (you ...) do ...' was meant to be interpreted as 'how do (you) occupy yourself during this particular period of time'. The phrase 'when you stay in the room with the television' was meant to be interpreted as 'considering only those occasions when you stay in the same room as the television set, and excluding from consideration any occasions when you leave the room'.

Respondents interpretations of the question

These interpretations are set out in full in the Appendix (Part II). They are based upon the replies of 56 people.

Marking the interpretations

The system used for rating or marking respondents' interpretations of questions

The following marking or rating system was used.

1 If all elements of the question were interpreted as intended, the interpretation as a whole was rated 'fully as intended' (√).

2 Failure to interpret any significant element of the question fully as intended was sufficient to pull the total interpretation down below the level of 'fully as intended'. The level so reached was determined by the most seriously misinterpreted (significant) element in the test question. For example, if all but one of the significant elements of the question were interpreted as intended and the interpretation of that other element was rated as 'somewhat limited but permissible' (see below), then the whole interpretation was so rated (i.e. 'somewhat limited but permissible'). The reason for this is that a question cannot be regarded as a safe one unless all its parts are interpreted as intended.

3 If a significant element of the question was obviously and substantially misinterpreted or was omitted altogether, the total interpretation was marked 'incorrect' (X).

4 In the context of this system, the following ratings were made of specific elements of respondents' interpretations.

(a) 'advertisements ... between 2 programmes'. Where this phrase was interpreted as intended (see above), the rating 'correct' (√) was applied. Where it seemed that the interpretation was as intended, but where the evidence was not conclusive, the rating 'doubtful but permissible' (?P) was applied. Where it was interpreted as 'television advertisements generally' (i.e. irrespective of whether between or within programmes) it was rated 'unduly general' (UG). Where the phrase was interpreted as 'advertisements which break into programmes', or where it was omitted altogether, the rating 'incorrect' (X) was applied.

(b) 'you'. Where this term was interpreted as intended (see above), the interpretation was rated 'correct' (√). Where it was interpreted as 'you and your family', or as 'you and some other(s)', the interpretation was rated as 'unduly extended' (UE).

(c) 'usually'. Where this term was interpreted as intended (see above), the rating 'correct' (√) was applied. The rating 'different but permissible' (DP) was applied to the interpretations: 'often', 'more often than not'. Where the term was interpreted as 'sometimes' or omitted altogether, the rating 'incorrect' (X) was applied.

(d) 'what do (you ...) do'. Where this reference was interpreted as intended (see above) the interpretation was rated 'correct' (√). Where the reference was interpreted as 'what sort/kind of thing do (you) do', the rating 'somewhat general but permissible' (GP) was applied. Where the reference was interpreted as 'what do (you) do to the TV set' or as 'do (you) watch them' or as 'do (you) carry on viewing or switch over to BBC' the rating 'unduly limited' (UL) was applied. The interpretation 'what do (you) think (of the advertisements)' was rated 'incorrect' (X).

(e) 'when you stay in the room with the television'. Where the respondent interpreted this phrase as intended (see above), the interpretation was rated 'correct' (√). An interpretation was rated 'incorrect' (X) where the respondent answered in terms of things done outside the room in which the set was located, and similarly rated (X) where the reference was omitted altogether.

The ratings allocated

Under the system described above, the following ratings were allocated to respondents' interpretations of this test question.

Table 7.14.1

Ratings allocated to respondents' interpretations
of test question (Q21, II)

Lowest rating allocated to any part of the interpretation	Number of Ratings	Number of Persons	% of Persons
Correct (√)	2	2	4
Extra but permissible (ExP)	0		
Somewhat limited but permissible (LP)	0		
Somewhat too specific but permissible (SP)	0		
Somewhat too general but permissible (GP)	0	0	0
Somewhat extended but permissible (EP)	0		
Somewhat different but permissible (DP)	0		
Doubtful but permitted (?P)	0	0	0
Unduly limited (UL)	1		
Unduly general (UG)	13		
Unduly extended (UE)	0	13*	23
Unduly different (UD)	0		
Incorrect (X)	41	41	73
Total		53	100

*See Note A on page 47.

Content analysis of the interpretations

There follows an analysis of the different interpretations of elements of the test question. The emphasis in this analysis is upon the different kinds of interpretations which were found rather than upon the number of them (though these numbers are given), the purpose of the content analysis being to discover the kinds of things that happen, to speculate about what causes them, and to derive hypotheses (about communication processes) for testing in later phases of the enquiry.

Interpretations of ... 'advertisements between two programmes ...'

The phrase 'advertisements ... between 2 programmes' was meant to refer only to television advertisements that come between one programme and the next, and not to those which occur within programmes.

Summary of interpretations

Only 10 of the 56 respondents clearly limited their consideration of advertisements to those between two programmes. Of the others, most (30) simply ignored the restriction to 'between programmes' advertisements and considered advertisements generally. But there were some (11) who limited themselves to advertisements within programmes—a major distortion of the question.

Table 7.14.2

Interpretations of 'advertisements between two programmes'

Respondent considered only advertisements between two programmes	10
Respondent considered only advertisements within programmes (e.g. in middle of programmes (10)/of good programmes (1))	11
Respondent considered both advertisements between two programmes and advertisements within programmes (i.e. advertisements generally)	30
Not clear whether or not respondent considered only advertisements between programmes	4
Did not consider advertisements at all	1
Total	56

Speculative comment

1 Whereas there may be something about the sound of the word 'between' that works against it being heard, it seems much more likely that something more positive and directional has gone on.

2 Bearing in mind the hostility of many viewers towards advertisements

cannot resist including in their replies reference to these interruption advertisements—perhaps even to the extent of considering them alone. Certainly other explanations may be possible, but distorted perception in the setting of strong feeling is in fact a well established phenomenon.

Interpretations of '(what do) you (do)'

The word 'you' was meant to be interpreted as 'you, yourself', and was not intended to include others (e.g. respondent's spouse, children, relatives, lodger(s)).

Summary of interpretations

Whereas practically all interpreted this term as intended, a few extended it to include others/other members of the family as well.

Table 7.14.3
Interpretations of '(what do) you (do)'

Apparently as 'you, yourself, alone' (i.e. as intended)	52
Term interpreted as 'you and member of your family'	3
You and others	1
Total	56

Interpretations of 'usually'

The word 'usually' was meant to be interpreted as 'ordinarily', 'in the ordinary course of events', 'commonly'. Other acceptable interpretations of the term were: 'as a rule', 'generally', 'normally', 'habitually', 'as a routine', 'almost always', 'mostly', 'typically'.

Summary of interpretations

1 Some 33 of the 56 interpreted the term either as intended or in a way closely similar to intended.

2 Of the others, a few reduced it to something like 'often' or 'more often than not' and two regarded it simply as 'sometimes'.

3 A large number of respondents (18), appear to have overlooked the term altogether, tending instead to refer to some form of behaviour which, by its very nature, can occur but infrequently (e.g. make a cup of tea).

Table 7.14.4

Interpretations of 'usually'

Usually (apparently as intended but evidence not fully conclusive)	27
As a rule (1)/generally (1)/normally (2)/mostly (1)/typically (1)	6
More often than not (1)/often (2)	3
Sometimes	2
Terms 'usually' apparently not considered at all	18
Total	56

Speculative comment

The overlooking of the term 'usually' may well have been helped along by the sheer difficulty of finding some one thing that the respondent usually did in the situation described. There are many different things that people do when 'the advertisements come on', but it is doubtful that many do some one thing usually. Thus the question probably put many a respondent in a difficult position—whereby either he said something about the various things he seemingly did when 'between advertisements' came on or he said, quite correctly, that there was no particular thing that he usually did at such times.

Interpretations of 'what do (you) do'

The reference 'what do (you) do' was meant to be interpreted as 'how do (you) occupy yourself during this particular period of time'.

Summary of interpretations

1 While a majority interpreted this set of words as intended, there were some (10) who converted the question into the 'easier to answer question': 'What kind or sort of thing do you do?'.

2 A few answered, also rather generally, in terms of what they do to the set.

200

Table 7.14.5

Interpretations of 'what do (you) do'

Reference interpreted apparently as intended		34
What sort(s) of thing do (you) do (8)/kind of thing do (you) do (2)		10
What is one of the things (you) do		2
What sort of thing might (you) do		1
What do (you) do to the TV set	3	
Do (you) leave the set on or do you switch it off	1	4
Do (you) watch them	3	
Do (you) carry on viewing or switch over to BBC	1	4
What do (you) think (of the advertisements)		1
Total		56

Speculative comment

This part of the question could be extremely difficult to deal with, for it refers to 'usual behaviour' when in fact there may be no specific behaviour which is usual, but only some broad type of behaviour which tends to recur (e.g. 'find something else to do'), or some class of behaviour which the respondent sometimes does.

Interpretations of 'when you stay in the room with the television'

The phrase 'when you stay in the room with the television' was meant to be interpreted as 'considering only those occasions when you stay in the same room as the television set, and excluding from consideration any occasions when you leave the room'.

Summary of interpretations

Less than half gave evidence of having heard or correctly grasped this phrase, with the result that frequently replies were not limited solely to behaviour in the TV room. Indeed, a few converted this limited condition to its opposite, namely 'when you do not stay in the room with the set'.

Table 7.14.6

Interpretations of 'when you stay in the room with the television'

Phrase apparently interpreted as intended	24
When you do not stay in the room with the television set (2)/ when you leave the viewing room (1)	3
Phrase seemingly overlooked	29
Total	56

Speculative comment

1   These results would be consistent with the question seeming to be complete before the final qualifying clause was added by the interviewer (i.e. 'When the advertisements come on between programmes, what do you usually do?')

2   But the results might also be consistent with respondents wanting to answer broadly about their behaviour when the advertisements come on—so that they ignored the restricting clause.

Other interpretations of interest

One respondent added (to the question) a request for an explanation of why he did whatever it was he did (in fact, why he left the set on).

Summary for the full question

1 Of the 56 interpretations of this question, 4 per cent were allocated an overall rating of either 'as intended' or 'permissible'. This compares with an average of 29 per cent for all the questions tested.

2 Serious miscommunication occurred on quite a number of points. Thus:

(a)   only 10 clearly limited their consideration to advertisements between two programmes;

(b)   over 20 either omitted consideration of the term 'usually' or gave it a meaning rather like 'sometimes or often'; 10 limited their thinking to some 'sort' or 'kind' of thing;

(c)   over half seemingly failed to limit their replies to occasions when they stayed in the room with the set.

3 Speculative comments

Part of the trouble with this question appears to have been that for many respondents there really was no particular thing that they usually did when 'between programme advertisements' came on, but only a lot of different things that they 'sometimes' or 'often' did, and which they felt they wanted to mention. In addition to this, however, the question attempted to put a rather tight and specific restriction upon the thinking required of the respondent, namely:

(a)   advertisements between programmes only;

(b)   behaviour when they stayed in the room with the set.

202

Perhaps the generality and the strength of peoples' reactions in relation to advertising was too much for these restrictions. Perhaps the second of them suffered because a seemingly complete question had been formulated before the final restriction was made.

7.15   QUESTION 21b, QUESTIONNAIRE II

The wording of the question

'What is your general impression of television advertising?'

Definition of the different parts of the question

The following are the intended meanings of key terms in the question. *However, as indicated below, some variants of the intended interpretations were regarded as permissible and others as possibly permissible.* The word 'your' was meant to be interpreted as 'of you, yourself' and not as 'of you and others'. The reference 'general (impression)' was meant to refer to respondent's opinion of television advertising, taking into consideration all its different aspects. This overall opinion is to be contrasted with an opinion about some single aspect of television advertising. This concept is a difficult one and it will be seen below that various more limited interpretations of it were regarded as permissible. The reference 'television advertising' was meant to refer to all television advertising, whatever its type, form or placement (e.g. between or within programmes).

Respondents' interpretations of the question

These interpretations are set out in full in the Appendix (Part II). They are based upon the replies of 47 people.

Content analysis of interpretations

The system used for rating or marking respondents' interpretations of the question

The following marking or rating system was used.

204

1 If all elements of the question were interpreted as intended, the interpretation as a whole was rated 'fully as intended' ($\checkmark$).

2 Failure to interpret any significant element of the question fully as intended was sufficient to pull the total interpretation down below the level of 'fully as intended'. The level so reached was determined by the most seriously misinterpreted (significant) element in the test question. For example, if all but one of the significant elements of the question were interpreted as intended and the interpretation of that other element was rated as 'somewhat limited but permissible' (see below), then the whole interpretation was so rated (i.e. 'somewhat limited but permissible') The reason for this is that a question cannot be regarded as a safe one unless all its parts are interpreted as intended.

3 If a significant element of the question was obviously and substantially misinterpreted or was omitted altogether, the total interpretation was marked 'incorrect' (X).

4 In the context of this system, the following ratings were made of specific elements of respondents' interpretations.

(a) 'your'. Where this term was interpreted as 'of you, yourself', the interpretation was rated as 'correct' ($\checkmark$). Where it was interpreted as 'of you and other(s), the interpretation was rated as 'unduly extended' (UE).

(b) 'general impression'. Where this reference was interpreted as intended (see above), the rating 'correct' ($\checkmark$) was applied. The rating 'limited but permissible' (LP) was applied to the following kinds of interpretation: (i) interpretations in terms of the general value (of advertising) to the viewer but not to the advertiser (e.g. 'what do you think of the value of advertising to the viewer', 'how do you rate advertisements from the point of view of their usefulness to the housewife'); (ii) interpretations in terms of their general value to the advertiser (e.g. 'what do you think of advertising in terms of the efficiency of selling', 'from the point of view of selling, how well or badly are the television advertisements presented'); (iii) interpretations in terms of some broad aspect of television advertising (e.g. its 'entertainment value', 'its necessity', 'its quality of presentation') as distinct from some narrow aspect such as repetitiveness, timing'. The rating 'unduly limited' (UL) was applied to interpretations in terms of some narrow aspects of television advertising such as 'the amount of time spent on it', 'the number of advertisements presented', 'the timing of advertisements (i.e. in relation to interruption of programmes'), 'repetitiveness of some advertisements', 'accuracy of claims made', 'kinds of product advertised'. The same rating (i.e. (UL)) was also applied to interpretations such as 'what are some examples of stupid advertisements'.

Where the interpretation was clearly wrong or where it was omitted altogether, the rating 'incorrect' was applied (X).

(c) 'television advertising'. Where this reference was interpreted as intended (see above), it was rated 'correct' (√). Where it was interpreted as 'the advertisements', this interpretation was rated as 'limited but permissible' (LP). Where the interpretation was limited to advertisements between programmes or where it was limited to advertisements within programmes the interpretation was rated 'limited but permissible' (LP). The rating 'unduly limited' (UL) was applied where the interpretation was in terms of certain categories of advertisement. Where the reference was omitted altogether, the rating 'incorrect' (X) was applied. See also the marking instructions under 'general impression'.

The ratings allocated

Under the system described above, the following ratings were allocated to respondent interpretations of this test question.

Table 7.15.1

Ratings allocated to respondents' interpretations
of test question (QE3, II)

Lowest rating allocated to any part of the interpretation	Number of Ratings	Persons	% of Persons
Correct (√)	0	0	0
Extra but permissible (ExP)	2		
Somewhat limited but permissible (LP)	26		
Somewhat too specific but permissible (SP)	0	26*	55
Somewhat too general but permissible (GP)	0		
Somewhat extended but permissible (EP)	0		
Somewhat different but permissible (DP)	2		
Doubtful but permitted (?P)	1	1	2
Unduly limited (UL)	14		
Unduly general (UG)	0	18	38
Unduly extended (UE)	0		
Unduly different (UD)	4		
Incorrect (X)	2	2	4
Total		47	†

*See Note A on page 47.
†See Note B on page 48.

Content analysis of the interpretations

There follows an analysis of the different interpretations of elements of the test question. The emphasis in this analysis is upon the different *kinds* of interpretations which were found rather than upon the number of them (though these numbers are given), the purpose of the content analysis being to discover the kinds of things that happen, to speculate about what causes them, and to derive hypotheses (about communication processes) for testing in later phases of the enquiry.

Interpretations of 'your'

The word 'your' was meant to be interpreted as 'of you, yourself' and not as 'of you and other(s))'.

Summary of interpretations

There is no reason for concluding that this term was interpreted other than as intended.

Table 7.15.2

Interpretations of 'your'

Of you	38
Term appears to have been interpreted as 'of you', but evidence not conclusive	9
Total	47

Interpretations of 'general impression'

The reference 'general impression' was meant to refer to respondents' opinion of television advertising, taking into consideration all its different aspects. The overall opinion is to be contrasted with an opinion about some single aspect of television advertising. This concept is a difficult one and it will be seen below that various more limited interpretations of it were regarded as permissible.

Summary of interpretations

1 There was a lot of variability, between individuals, in terms of the particular aspect(s) of TV advertising which they considered in saying what was their 'general impression': the efficiency of TV advertising in selling goods (3); the power of advertisements to give you a good impression of a product (2); how well or badly they are presented (2); their

silliness or sense (2); the repetitiveness of them (2); their entertainment value for the viewer (2); their usefulness to the housewife (1); the desirability of having advertising on television (3); the soap powder advertisements (1).

2 Not only was there overall variability in what different respondents considered, but there was marked narrowness in terms of the different aspects of 'television advertising' that any one respondent considered. Thus 37 of the 47 respondents appear to have offered a 'general impression' on the basis of only one aspect of television advertising. Moreover that one aspect was itself usually quite often a narrow one.

Table 7.15.3

Interpretations of 'general (impression of)'

(a) *The many different aspects considered*

From the point of view of selling goods

Of the efficiency of TV ads in selling goods (3)/from point of view of selling goods (1)/in terms of efficiency in selling to you (3)/ in terms of getting people to try new products (1)	8	
Of their efficiency in getting people to take notice of them	1	
Of their power to give you a good impression of the product	2	14
Of how basic is the impact	1	
Of their function from the business man's point of view (1)/from the seller's point of view (1)	2	

In terms of basic features (of TV advertising) and of (its) presentation

Of the way they are designed	1	
Of how well or badly they are presented (2)/of how well or badly presented, from viewer standpoint (2)/of quality of presentation (2)/of things wrong with the way they are presented (1)	7	
Of their silliness or sense	2	16
Of the (large) number of them (2)/of the amount of time given to them (1)	3	
Of the repetitiveness of them	2	
Of their timing (i.e. in relation to interruption of programmes)	1	

In terms of viewer benefits, viewer standpoint

In terms of one of the things from viewer's standpoint/from viewer's standpoint	2	
In terms of its entertainment value (2)/in terms of liking or disliking it generally (1)/ in terms of the interestingness of its content (1)/ in terms of things of interest to the viewer (1)	5	
In terms of the worthwhileness of what they present	1	16
In terms of their usefulness to the housewife (1)/of their value to the viewer (1)/of telling the public about goods available (2)	4	
In terms of the quality or value of the goods advertised	1	
In terms of the accuracy of claims made	1	
In terms of its social and aesthetic impact (1) of its possible harmfulness in view of the kinds of goods advertised (1)	2	

In terms of the principle of having TV advertising at all

Of the desirability of having it	3	
Of the desirability of having it if it is selling goods (1)/causing people to buy new goods (1)	2	9
In terms of your liking or disliking having it on TV	1	
In terms of the necessity of having advertising on TV	3	

In terms of other concepts or other aspects of TV advertising

Of the soap powder commercials	1	
What is one of the things wrong with the TV ads you dislike	1	
Of how they could be improved	1	
One of (your impressions)	1	6
Of some (TV ads)	1	
And what are examples of stupid ones (i.e. ads)	1	

Did not appear to consider the term or some substitute for it	1
Total	62*

(b) Breadth of interpretation of term 'general'

Interpreted term in a single (limited) context:

(solely) from the point of view of selling goods	8	
(solely) in terms of basic features of the advertisements	10	
(solely) in terms of viewer standpoint, benefits	11	37†
(solely) in terms of principle of advertising on TV at all	5	
(solely) in terms of some other rather specific consideration	3	

Interpreted term with reference to two or more of the above contexts

(Two) only	8
Three	1

Did not appear to consider the term at all	1
Total	47

---

*Some of the 47 respondents interpreted the term in more than one of the above categories (giving 62 references in all). See (b).

†Some respondents contributed more than once to a *single* category.

Speculative comment

It seems that the word 'general' did not serve to spread or widen or generalise the judging processes of these respondents. One possibility is that this word ('general') does not have for people the broad meaning intended. Another possibility is that respondents tend ordinarily to be preoccupied with fairly narrow aspects of TV advertising—perhaps even to the extent of habitually judging television advertising solely in terms of these particular aspects of it.

Interpretations of 'television advertising'

The reference 'television advertising' was meant to refer to all television advertising, whatever its type, form or placement (e.g. between or within programmes).

Summary of interpretations

1 About half the respondents interpreted this reference as intended (26).

2 There were 20 more who narrowed the concept somewhat to mean 'television advertisements'.

3 Three respondents went much further in this narrowing tendency and considered only some/some kinds of advertisements (i.e. 'stupid ones', 'soap powder commercials', 'some' television advertisements).

Table 7.15.4

Interpretations of 'television advertising'

Television advertising (apparently as intended)		26
Television advertisements		20
'Stupid ones' (i.e. advertisements)	1*	
'Some' television advertisements	1*	3
Soap powder commercials	1*	
Reference apparently overlooked		1
Total		50

*The 3 cases marked with asterisks also contributed to the first and second category in this table.

Speculative comment

What is particularly interesting—over and above the narrowing tendency referred to in my summary—is the absence of evidence that respondents tended to think solely of interruption advertisements as distinct from 'between programmes' advertisements, or vice versa. One possibility is that the generality of the word 'advertising' acted as a stopper to the operation of any narrowing tendency in this additional direction. Another possibility is that the term 'general', got transferred from 'impression' to 'advertising'—a possibility which might fit in with the results set out in Table 7.15.3.

Summary for full question

1 Of the 47 interpretations of this question, 57 per cent were allocated an overall rating of either 'as intended' or 'permissible'. This compares with an average of 29 per cent for all the questions tested.

2 The various points of difficulty in this question included the following.

(a)   There was considerable variability, in going from one respondent to another, in terms of the particular aspect of television advertising which formed the basis of the impression reported to the interviewer. For most respondents, the basis of the reply given appears to have been some single aspect of TV advertising and very often a very narrow aspect of it at that.

(b)   There was a tendency for the reference 'television advertising' to be narrowed, mainly to 'television advertisements'.

3 On the other hand, there was no evidence to suggest that the word 'your' had been misinterpreted or that the reference 'TV advertising' had been converted into 'advertising between programmes' or 'advertising within programmes'.

4 *Speculative comment*

(a)   It seems possible that the term 'general' may for some respondents have become attached to the word 'advertising' (i.e. advertising in general, advertisements in general) rather than being taken to qualify 'impression' (as intended).

(b)   Whether this be so or not, it seems possible that some of these respondents were habituated to base their reactions to television advertising upon some single, rather narrow, aspect of television advertising.

7.16 QUESTION 5, QUESTIONNAIRE III

The wording of the question

'For how many hours do you usually watch television on a weekday?
This means Monday to Friday but not Saturday or Sunday, and includes
daytime viewing as well as evening viewing?'

Definitions of different parts of the question

The following are the intended meanings of key terms in the question.
*However, as indicated below, some variants of the intended interpreta-
tions were regarded as permissible and others as possibly permissible.*
The phrase 'for how many hours' was meant to be interpreted as 'what
is the number of hours' (i.e. inviting a numerical answer). The word
'you' was meant to be interpreted as 'you, yourself' and was not intended to include others (e.g. respondent's spouse, children, relatives,
lodger(s)). The word 'usually' was meant to be interpreted as 'ordinarily', 'in the ordinary course of events', 'commonly'. Other acceptable
interpretations of the term were: 'as a rule', 'generally', 'normally',
'habitually', 'as a routine', 'almost always', 'mostly', 'typically'. The
reference 'watch television' was intended to mean attend to whatever is
being shown on the screen or to give it at least some degree of attention.
The reference 'on a weekday' was meant to refer solely to the period
Monday to Friday. In the present case it was intended to mean all day
and not just some part of the day (see the qualifying clause at the end
of the question). The phrase '... includes daytime viewing as well as the
evening viewing' was intended to be interpreted as an instruction to take
into account both the viewing done during the day (i.e. up to 6.00 pm)
and the viewing done in the evening (i.e. after 6.00 pm).

Respondents' interpretations of the question

These interpretations are set out in full in the Appendix (Part II). They

are based upon the replies of 54 people.

Marking the interpretations

The system used for rating or marking respondents' interpretations of questions

The following marking or rating system was used.

1 If all elements of the question were interpreted as intended, the interpretation as a whole was rated 'fully as intended' ($\checkmark$).

2 Failure to interpret any significant element of the question fully as intended was sufficient to pull the total interpretation down below the level of 'fully as intended'. The level so reached was determined by the most seriously misinterpreted (significant) element in the test question. For example, if all but one of the significant elements of the question were interpreted as intended and the interpretation of that other element was rated as 'somewhat limited but permissible' (see below), then the whole interpretation was so rated (i.e. 'somewhat limited but permissible'). The reason for this is that a question cannot be regarded as a safe one unless all its parts are interpreted as intended.

3 If a significant element of the question was obviously and substantially misinterpreted or was omitted altogether, the total interpretation was marked 'incorrect' (X).

4 In the context of this system, the following ratings were made of specific elements of respondents' interpretations.

(a) 'for how many hours'. Where this phrase was interpreted as intended (see above), the rating 'correct' ($\checkmark$) was applied. Where it was interpreted as 'between which hours', or 'over what period', the rating 'different but permissible' (DP) was applied. Where something was added to a permissible interpretation without losing the latter, the rating 'extra but permissible' (ExP) was applied (e.g. 'and for which hours', 'and on which days', 'and between what times'). The interpretations 'how often' and 'how much' (e.g. 'occasionally', 'very little') were rated 'unduly different' (UD), as was the interpretation 'for which part of the day'. The following interpretations were rated 'incorrect' (X): 'for how many hours over a full week', 'for which programmes'.

(b) 'you'. Where this term was interpreted as intended (see above), the interpretation was rated 'correct' ($\checkmark$). Where it was interpreted as 'you and your family', or as 'you and some other(s))', the interpretation was rated as 'unduly extended' (UE). Where the respondent answered as if to the question 'is your set on', that interpretation was rated 'unduly different' (UD).

(c) 'usually'. Where this term was interpreted as intended (see above), the rating 'correct' (√) was applied. Similarly for the interpretation 'mainly'. Where the term was interpreted as: 'more often than not'; 'taking an average over the days' ; the rating 'different but permissible' (DP) was applied. The interpretation 'regularly' was rated 'doubtful but permissible' (?P). Where the term was omitted altogether, the rating 'incorrect' (X) was applied.

(d) 'watch television'. Where this reference was interpreted as intended (see above), the rating 'correct' (√) was applied. Where it *seemed* that attention had been paid to the screen but where the evidence was not conclusive, the rating 'doubtful but permissible' (?P) was applied. Where the interpretation did not necessarily involve 'giving the screen at least some degree of attention (e.g. 'had the set on') or allowed the inclusion of periods when attention was not being given to the screen, the rating 'unduly different' (UD) was applied.

(e) 'on a weekday'. Where this reference was interpreted as intended (see above) the rating 'correct' (√) was applied. Where it seemed that the intended interpretation had been made, but where the evidence was not conclusive, the rating 'doubtful but permissible' (?P) was applied. An interpretation in which respondent based his estimate upon 'summer viewing' (only), was rated 'different but permissible' (DP). Where respondent considered each day separately, the interpretation was also rated 'different but permissible' (DP). An interpretation was rated 'unduly limited' (UL) where 'weekday' was taken to refer to days in the period Monday to Friday with the exception of days when respondent viewed for only a short period, or viewed away from home. The interpretation was similarly rated (UL) where the respondent only counted those weeks when he was able to view in the evenings. The interpretation was rated 'incorrect' (X) where respondent: gave a total for the whole period of five days (Monday to Friday); considered all seven days of the week; considered all days of the week except Saturday; omitted the reference (i.e. 'on a weekday') altogether.

(f) 'includes daytime viewing as well as evening viewing'. Where this reference was interpreted as intended (see above), this rating 'correct' (√) was applied. Where this instruction had been bypassed altogether (i.e. not even implied by the interpretation of other parts of the question), the rating 'incorrect' (X) was applied. Where there was some doubt as to whether or not the respondent had acted upon this instruction, the rating 'doubtful but permissible' was applied (?P).

The ratings allocated

Under the system described above, the following ratings were allocated to respondent interpretations of this test question.

Table 7.16.1
Ratings allocated to respondents' interpretations
of test question (Q5, III)

Lowest rating allocated to any part of the interpretation	Number of Ratings	Number of Persons	% of Persons
Correct (✓)	2	2	4
Extra but permissible (ExP)	2		
Somewhat limited but permissible (LP)	0		
Somewhat too specific but permissible (SP)	0	8*	15
Somewhat too general but permissible (GP)	0		
Somewhat extended but permissible (EP)	0		
Somewhat different but permissible (DP)	6		
Doubtful but permitted (?P)	5	5	9
Unduly limited (UL)	2		
Unduly general (UG)	0	9*	17
Unduly extended (UE)	0		
Unduly different (UD)	8		
Incorrect (X)	30	30	56
Total		54	†

*See Note A on page 47.
†See Note B on page 48.

Content analysis of the interpretations

There follows an analysis of the different interpretations of elements of the test question. The emphasis in this analysis is upon the different kinds of interpretations which were found rather than upon the number of them (though these numbers are given), the purpose of the content analysis being to discover the kinds of things which happen, speculate about what causes them, and to derive hypotheses (about communication processes) for testing in later phases of the enquiry.

215

Interpretations of 'for how many hours'

The phrase 'for how many hours' was meant to be interpreted as 'what is the number of hours' (i.e. inviting a numerical answer).

Summary of interpretations

1   Of the 54 respondents, 37 interpreted this reference numerically, as intended, though 4 of them gave additional information (e.g. *'and* for *which* hours'; *'and which* weekdays').

2   Another 9 interpreted it as 'between which hours' (giving replies which could, of course be converted into a total hourage) and 2 more answered as to 'for what different lengths of time'.

3   Of the remainder, 4 converted the reference into something like 'for which parts of the day' (e.g. evenings only), one into 'how often' and one into 'for which programmes'.

Table 7.16.2

Interpretations of 'for how many hours'

For how many hours (21)/for about how many hours (1)/for roughly how many hours (3)/for approximately how many hours (2)	27	
For how long in hours (3)/for what total of hours (3)	6	
For how many hours and until what time (1)/for how many hours and for which hours (1)/for roughly how many hours and for what times (1)/on which weekdays and for how many hours (1)	4	37
When (i.e. between which hours)	9	11
For what different lengths of time	2	
For which part(s) of the day (e.g. evenings only)		4
How often		1
For which programmes		1
Total		54

Interpretations of 'you'

The word 'you' was meant to be interpreted as 'you, yourself' and was not intended to include others (e.g. respondent's spouse, children, relatives, lodger(s)).

Summary of interpretations

Ten of the 54 interpreted this term as if they had been asked 'is your set on?' (i.e. so that the viewing of others in the family group might well be included in such answers as were given).

Table 7.16.3

Interpretations of 'you'

You, yourself, alone	44
Is your set on (so possibly you and others)	10
Total	54

Speculative comments

In this television context, the term 'you' seems to be specially open to collective interpretation.

Interpretations of 'usually'

The word 'usually' was meant to be interpreted as 'ordinarily', 'in the ordinary course of events', 'commonly'. Other acceptable interpretations of the term were: 'as a rule', 'generally', 'normally', 'habitually', 'as a routine', 'almost always', 'mostly', 'typically'.

Summary of interpretations

1 Up to 21 of the 54 interpreted this term more or less as intended.

2 Dubious interpretations included: 'more often than not' (which could quite possibly mean only a slight majority of times); 'on average'.

3 Some (9) respondents appear to have overlooked the term altogether.

Table 7.16.4

Interpretations of 'usually'

Usually (apparently as intended, but evidence not fully conclusive) (3)/ usual for you (1)	4	
Generally (3)/normally (4)/habitually (2)/your practice (1)	10	16
Mostly (1)/mainly (1)	2	
More often than not		8
Regularly		5
On average (13)/on a rough average (2)/taking a broad average (1)		16
Term apparently not considered		9
Total		54

Speculative comment

1 If a respondent did not have any usual behaviour with respect to 'hours spent viewing TV on weekdays', he may well have felt it necessary to convert or overlook that term. This would be consistent with some of

the details set out in Table 7.16.4.

2 If this particular speculation is correct, then the word 'usually' would seem to have been an undesirable one to have used in this particular context at least.

Interpretations of 'watch television'

The reference 'watch television' was intended to mean attend to whatever is being shown on the screen or to give it at least some degree of attention.

Summary of interpretations

Thirty-six (possibly 38) interpreted this term as intended, but 16 converted it into something like 'have the set on'—which, of course, does not necessarily mean that the respondent was giving the set 'at least some degree of attention'.

Table 7.16.5

Interpretations of 'watch television'

(a) Did the respondent interpret 'watch' as paying at least some attention?	
Watch with at least some attention	36
Interpretation of 'watch' not fully established but no reason for thinking other than 'with at least some attention'	1
Interpreted as 'the television set is turned on' and so possibly included times when no attention was paid by respondent	16
Not clear whether or not the respondent considered paying attention or not	1
Total	54

(b) Other features of the interpretation (2 cases, already indicated above)	
Settle down to really watch	1
Sit down in front of the television set	1

Speculative comment

Two possible reasons for the misinterpretations that occurred may be:

(a) that the term 'watch' was interpreted collectively (i.e. in terms of the whole family);

(b) that, in the television context, the term 'watch' became a vague term—a situation quite possibly furthered by the fact that respondents may happen to be in the viewing room when the set is on (i.e. without being there with the purpose of viewing) or that they may perhaps look at the set just now and then.

Interpretations of 'on a weekday?' This means Monday to Friday but not Saturday or Sunday and includes daytime viewing as well as evening viewing

The reference 'on a weekday' was meant to refer solely to the period Monday to Friday. In the present case it was intended to mean 'all day' and not just some part of the day (see the qualifying clause at the end of the question).

Summary of interpretations

1 At least 11 of the respondents ignored the instruction that only Monday to Friday be considered.

2 Twelve respondents wrongly limited their consideration of the question to evenings only.

3 Five of the 54 excluded certain days or periods from their consideration of the question, for example: 'excluding days on which you view only a little', 'counting summer time only'.

4 It is also noteworthy that 6 respondents considered the period Monday to Friday as a whole—that is, as if the question asked for the total amount of viewing over that 5 day period.

Table 7.16.6

Interpretations of 'on a weekday'
This means Monday to Friday but not Saturday and Sunday
and includes daytime viewing as well as evening viewing

1 *Was the phrase (plus statement) interpreted as intended?*

| Yes | 20 | No | 30 | Not clear | 4 | (Total = 54) |

2 *Did the respondent consider weekdays only?*

Yes, weekdays only	42
Five weekdays plus Sunday	1
All seven days of the week	10
Not clear which days were considered	1
Total	54

3 *Did the respondent wrongly limit consideration to certain parts of the day?*

No, respondent considered whole day	39
Respondent considered evenings only	12
Not clear whether respondent considered all day	3
Total	54

4 *Did the respondent exclude certain days, weeks or seasons from consideration*

No special days or weeks or seasons excluded	49
Excluding days on which you view only a little	1
Counting only those weekdays on which you view most	1
Counting only those weeks when you are able to watch in the evenings	1
Counting only when you are at home	1
Counting summer time only	1
Total	54

5 *Other interpretations of note (8 cases)*

Considered the total period (Monday to Friday) as a whole	6
Considered each of the days/evenings separately	2
Total	8

Speculative comment

1 The qualifying clause, despite its specificity and its emphatic nature, appears to have no affect on a number of these respondents and it remains a possibility that: it confused them; they had started to work out an answer before the qualification was made.

2 The collective interpretation of 'weekday' may have sprung out of the phrase 'this means Monday to Friday' (i.e. respondent may have worked out a total for the whole viewing period).

Interpretations of 'includes daytime viewing as well as evening viewing

This phrase was intended as an instruction to take into account both viewing done during the day (i.e. up to 6.00 pm) and the viewing done during the evening (i.e. after 6.00 pm).

Summary of interpretations

These were presented in the context of Table 7.16.6, section 3.

Summary for the full question

1 Of the 54 interpretations of this question, 28 per cent were allocated an overall rating of either 'as intended' or 'permissible'. This result compares with an overall average of 29 per cent for all the questions tested.

2 The main points of failure in this question were as follows:

(a)   In spite of a direct instruction to exclude Saturday and Sunday from consideration, at least eleven failed to do so;

similarly, twelve considered evenings only in spite of an instruction to the contrary. Some wrongly excluded certain days or periods from consideration and several accumulated their viewing hours over the whole of the period considered.

(b) The reference 'watch television' was quite frequently (16 persons) converted into something like 'have the set on'.

(c) The term 'you' was sometimes broadened so as to include the viewing behaviour of persons other than the respondent alone.

(d) The majority failed to interpret the term 'usually' as intended, the main distortions being: 'on average', 'more often than not', 'regularly'. Some appeared to by-pass it altogether.

(e) The numerical reference 'for how many hours' sometimes lost its tight numerical character (e.g. becoming something like 'between which hours'), and occasionally was lost altogether.

3 *Speculative comments*

(a) All or part of the lengthy qualifying sentence (i.e. 'This means ...') appears to have been overlooked by some respondents and this may have been the result of:

 (i) these respondents starting to think out an answer before the qualifying phrase was voiced;

 (ii) the qualifying phrase being specially difficult to grasp.

(b) The weakening of the term 'watch television' (e.g. have the set on) may have sprung out of the collective character of a family's exposure to television (e.g. respondent may happen to see something watched or turned on by others in the family).

(c) The word 'you' may also have a specially collective connotation when used in the context of television viewing.

(d) The frequent misinterpretation of 'usually' could have arisen out of there being no usual (number of hours) for quite a lot of these respondents, but rather some range of more recurrent hourages. On the other hand, some respondents may simply have been evading the effort of giving a proper answer to a thought demanding question.

7.17   QUESTION 10, QUESTIONNAIRE III

The actual wording of the question

'How many times do you usually switch from one station to the other, when viewing on a weekday evening?'

Definition of the different parts of the question

The following are the intended meanings of key terms in the question. *However, as indicated below, some variants of the intended interpretations were regarded as permissible and others as possibly permissible.* The reference 'how many times' was meant to be interpreted as 'what is the number of times' (i.e. inviting a numerical answer). The word 'you' was meant to be interpreted as 'you, yourself' and was not intended to include others (e.g. respondent's spouse, children, relatives, lodger(s)). The word 'usually' was meant to be interpreted as 'ordinarily', 'in the ordinary course of events', 'commonly'. Other acceptable interpretations of the term were: 'as a rule', 'generally', 'normally', 'habitually', 'as a routine', 'almost always', 'mostly', 'typically'. The reference 'switch from one station to the other' was intended to mean 'turn the knob (or push the button) on the television set in order to change from one station to the other', whether the change was made: at the beginning of a viewing session (because the set was not tuned in to desired station); for exploratory purposes; for picking up a selected programme. The reference 'on a weekday' was meant to refer solely to the period Monday to Friday. The word 'evening' was meant to refer to the period from 6.00 pm onwards, on those evenings during which the respondent did at least some viewing.

Respondents' interpretations of the question

These interpretations are set out in full in the Appendix (Part II). They are based upon the replies of 52 people.

222

Marking the interpretations

The system used for rating or marking respondents' interpretations of the question

The following marking or rating system was used.

1 If all elements of the question were interpreted as intended, the interpretation as a whole was rated 'fully as intended' (√).

2 Failure to interpret any significant element of the question fully as intended was sufficient to pull the total interpretation down below the level of 'fully as intended'. The level so reached was determined by the most seriously misinterpreted (significant) element in the test question. For example, if all but one of the significant elements of the question were interpreted as intended and the interpretation of that other element was rated as 'somewhat limited but permissible' (see below), then the whole interpretation was so rated (i.e. 'somewhat limited but permissible'). The reason for this is that a question cannot be regarded as a safe one unless all its parts are interpreted as intended.

3 If a significant element of the question was obviously and substantially misinterpreted or was omitted altogether, the total interpretation was marked 'incorrect' (X).

4 In the context of this system, the following ratings were made of specific elements of respondents' interpretations.

(a) 'how many times'. Where this reference was interpreted as intended (see above), the rating 'correct' (√) was applied. The interpretation 'roughly how many times' was also regarded as acceptable. The following interpretations involved a non-numerical interpretation, and were rated 'different but permissible' (DP): 'how often'; 'how frequently'. The following interpretations were rated 'unduly different' (UD): 'do you often'; 'do you ever'; 'do you (usually)'; 'are there many times'. The rating 'incorrect' (X) was applied to the interpretations: 'at what time is the set switched on'; 'on what occasions do you ... '; 'under what circumstances do you ...', 'do you view ... or do you switch ...'; 'to which station is your set mostly tuned'.

(b) 'you'. Where this term was interpreted as intended (see above), the interpretation was rated 'correct' (√). Where it was interpreted as 'you and your family', or as 'you and some other(s))', the interpretation was rated as 'unduly extended' (UE). Where the respondent answered as if to the question ' how many times is your set switched', the interpretation was rated 'unduly different' (UD). Where, as in one case, respondent did not know whether the question meant 'yourself alone', or 'you and your family', the rating 'doubtful but permissible' (DP) was applied.

(c) 'usually'. Where this term was interpreted as intended (see above), the rating 'correct' (√) was applied. The rating 'different but permissible' (DP) was applied to the interpretations: 'on average', 'taking an average', 'a rough average'. The interpretation 'over a period of viewing' was rated 'incorrect' (X).

(d) 'switch from one station to the other'. Where this reference was interpreted as intended (see above) the rating 'correct' (√) was applied. The rating 'different but permissible' (DP) was applied to the interpretations: 'decide to switch etc'; 'switch to the other station'; 'switch over to the other channel'. Where the respondent interpreted the phrase as 'which channel do you watch/view', the rating 'incorrect' (X) was applied. The following interpretations were also rated 'incorrect' (X): 'switch from one station to the other and back again'; 'switch from one station to the other, excluding all exploratory switching'; 'switching from one station to the other for exploratory purposes only (i.e. excluding switching for selected programmes)'. Where the reference was omitted altogether, the rating 'incorrect' (X) was similarly applied.

(e) 'on a weekday'. Where this reference was interpreted as intended (see above), the rating 'correct' (√) was applied. Where the interpretation included Saturday and/or Sunday in the period considered, or where the reference was omitted altogether, the rating 'incorrect' (X) was applied.

(f) 'evening'. Where this reference was interpreted as intended (see above), the rating 'correct' (√) was applied. Where it seemed that the intended interpretation had been made, but where the evidence was not conclusive, the rating 'doubtful but permissible' (?P) was applied. Where the interpretation was limited to 'those evenings when you view alone' (i.e. by yourself), the rating 'unduly limited' (UL) was applied. Where the reference was interpreted as 'an evening when the set is on', the interpretation was rated 'unduly different (UD). Where the reference was interpreted as 'all times of the day', or was omitted altogether, the rating 'incorrect' (X) was applied.

The ratings allocated

Under the system described above, the following ratings were allocated to respondent interpretations of this test question.

224

Table 7.17.1

Ratings allocated to respondents' interpretations
of test question (Q10, III)

Lowest rating allocated to any part of the interpretation	Number of Ratings	Persons	% of Persons
Correct (√)	1	1	2
Extra but permissible (ExP)	0		
Somewhat limited but permissible (LP)	0		
Somewhat too specific but permissible (SP)	0		
Somewhat too general but permissible (GP)	0	4	8
Somewhat extended but permissible (EP)	0		
Somewhat different but permissible (DP)	4		
Doubtful but permitted (?P)	1	1	2
Unduly limited (UL)	1		
Unduly general (UG)	0		
Unduly extended (UE)	5	6	12
Unduly different (UD)	0		
Incorrect (X)	40	40	77
	Total	52	†

†See Note B on page 48.

Content analysis of interpretations

There follows an analysis of the different interpretations of elements of the test question. The emphasis in this analysis is upon the different kinds of interpretations which were found rather than upon the number of them (though these numbers are given), the purpose of the content analysis being to discover the *kinds* of things that happen, to allow speculation about what causes them, and to derive hypotheses about communication processes (for testing in later phases of the enquiry).

Interpretations of 'How many times'

The reference 'how many times' was meant to be interpreted as 'what is the number of times' (i.e. inviting a numerical answer).

Summary of interpretations

1   Of the 52 respondents, 21 interpreted the reference in the numerical

sense intended.

2   Of the others, a large number (17) interpreted it as 'how often' or 'how frequently', going from this to a non-numerical reply (e.g. 'not very often').

3   Then there were some (6) who misinterpreted to a major degree with such things as 'on what occasion', 'at what time', 'under what conditions'.

4   Finally, 8 persons appear to have overlooked the concept altogether.

Table 7.17.2

Interpretations of 'how many times'

How many times (i.e. as intended) (19)/roughly how many times (2)	21
How often (16)/how frequently (1)	17
On what occasions (2)/under what circumstances (1)	3
Are there many times (when)	1
What is the largest number of times	1
At what time	1
Phrase not considered	8
Total	52

Speculative comment

It appears that saying how many times he/she 'switched from one station to another when viewing on a weekday evening' is a difficult question to answer with anything like numerical exactness, and it may be that some respondents looked for (and found) an easier (and non-numerical) way of dealing with the question (e.g. on what occasions?)

Interpretations of 'you'

The word 'you' was meant to be interpreted as 'you, yourself', and was not intended to include others (e.g. respondent's spouse, children, relatives, lodger(s)).

Summary of interpretations

1   Only 34 of the 52 interpreted this term as intended (i.e. you, yourself).

2   Of the rest, 14 appeared to interpret the term as involving family members (i.e. a collective interpretation) and there were 3 who thought only in terms of the set being switched on—by someone.

226

Table 7.17.3
Interpretations of 'you'

You, yourself, alone (i.e. as intended)	34
You and your wife (3)/You and your husband (1)	4
You and your family (8)/You or your family (1)/Your family (1)	10
The set is switched (so 'you' possibly not considered)	3
Respondent did not know if 'you' meant himself alone or the whole family	1
Total	52

Speculative comment

1   It could well be difficult for a respondent to recall how much of the switching he himself did and how much of it was done by other members of his family. His difficulty might be increased if others in the family had switched on his behalf. In such conditions, a collective or family interpretation of 'you' might seem to the respondent to be the more obvious interpretation.

2   It is also possible that, for anything as collective as set switching, a respondent might assume that we meant 'you' to be interpreted collectively.

Interpretations of 'usually'

The word 'usually' was meant to be interpreted as 'ordinarily', 'in the ordinary course of events', 'commonly'. Other acceptable interpretations of the term were: 'as a rule', 'generally', 'normally', 'habitually', 'as a routine', 'almost always', 'mostly', 'typically'.

Summary of interpretations

1 About half of the respondents appear to have overlooked this concept altogether.

2 Of the rest, 12 interpreted the term more or less as intended, 11 interpreted it as something like 'taking an average' and 2 considered what happened on 'an average evening'.

Table 7.17.4
Interpretations of 'usually'

Usually (i.e. apparently as intended)	10
Mostly	2
On an average (evening)	2
Taking an average/taking a rough average/on average	11
Term seemingly overlooked altogether	27
Total	52

Speculative comment

1   If there was not some usual behaviour when viewing on a
weekday evening—and this seems possible for some respondents—
then a respondent might either say just that or overlook the concept 'usual' in order to give the interviewer some idea of his or
her switching behaviour. The high degree of 'overlooking' that
occurred may well have some such explanation.

2   The attempt to calculate an average could have sprang out
of the very same difficulty—namely that there was no usual number of switching.

Interpretations of 'switch from one station to the other'

The reference 'switch from one station to the other' was intended to
mean 'turn the knob or push the button on the television set in order
to change from one station to the other', whether the change is made at
the beginning of the viewing session (because the set was not tuned into
the desired station), for exploratory purposes, or for picking up a selected programme.

Summary of interpretations

1 Of the 52 interpretations, 35 were seemingly as intended. There were
four more which might have been as intended but which, on the other
hand, possibly put a limit upon the particular switchings which were to
be counted (e.g. only those which were made because of lack of satisfaction with what was being viewed).

2 Ten of the remaining 13 interpreted it other than as intended. They
included: purely exploratory switching (i.e. excluding changes made to
view specific programmes); switching other than purely exploratory
switching; switching exclusive of any initial switching away from the
station to which the set was tuned when first turned on; switching from
BBC to ITV; switching from one station to the other and back again.

3 There were three cases when the concept was missed altogether (e.g.
which station do you watch?)

Table 7.17.5

Interpretations of 'switch from one station to the other'

Switch from one station to the other (29)/to another (2)	31	
Switch over to see the other station/channel (3)/decide to switch from one station to the other (1)	4	35
Switch over to the other channel because of dissatisfaction with a programme	1	
Switch over to see if there is anything better on the other channel (1)/ to see if the programme on the other station is better (1)/to find a programme to watch (1)	3	4
Switch from one station to the other with the express purpose of exploration (i.e. excluding changes made to pick up specific programmes) (1)	1	
Switch from one station to the other, excluding any initial switching over (because set on wrong station)	2	10
Switch from one station to the other, excluding any initial switch over and excluding exploratory switching	1	
Switch from BBC to ITV (1)/from ITV to BBC (2)/over to BBC (1)	4	
Switch from one station to the other and back again	2	
Which station or channel do you watch/tune to	3	
Total	52	

Speculative comment

Up to 13 of the 52 respondents interpreted the phrase in such a way that some of their switching was likely to go uncounted. Misinterpretations of concepts do not have to be only in a direction leading to loss of instances, but in this case the initial concept was a maximum one and misinterpretation could operate only in the limiting direction.

Interpretations of 'on a weekday (evening)'

The reference 'on a weekday' was meant to refer solely to the period Monday to Friday.

Summary of interpretations

1 Only 28 of the 52 respondents definitely interpreted this reference as intended.

2 Of the rest, 14 included Saturday and Sunday in their considerations and two more excluded only either Saturday or Sunday.

3 In several cases (3) it was not clear how 'weekday' was interpreted and there were five people who appeared to leave it out of consideration altogether.

Table 7.17.6

Interpretations of 'on a weekday (evening)'

From Monday till Friday (only) or presumably so	28
From Monday till Saturday	1
From Sunday till Saturday (i.e. 7 days)	14
Apparently all seven days except Saturdays	1
Not clear which days were considered	3
Reference not considered at all	5
Total	52

Speculative comment

This short question is really crowded with concepts—at least seven of them—and it seems possible that the perception of 'weekday' was thereby interfered with in the case of some respondents.

Interpretations of '(on a weekday) evening'

The word 'evening' was meant to refer to the period from 6.00 pm onwards, on those evenings during which the respondent did at least some viewing.

Summary of interpretations

1 One respondent considered only those weekday evenings when he viewed alone, and five appeared to overlook the term altogether.

2 The majority (45) interpreted the term as intended.

Table 7.17.7

Interpretations of '(on a weekday) evening'

Evening interpreted as intended	45
Those evenings when you view alone	1
Not clear which part of the day considered	1
Term not considered at all	5
Total	52

Other interpretations of interest

One respondent interpreted the question as: What station do you watch mostly and for what ITV programmes do you switch over?

230

Summary for the full question

1 Of the 52 interpretations of this question, 12 per cent were allocated an overall rating of 'as intended' or 'permissible'. This compares with an average of 29 per cent for all the questions tested.

2 The main points of failure in interpreting this question were:

(a) a marked tendency to overlook the term 'usually' (27 of the 52 did this) or to interpret it as an average over the different evenings when respondent views (11);

(b) a tendency to interpret 'how many times' as allowing a non-numerical response;

(c) a tendency to interpret 'weekday' as including weekends (14 cases);

(d) a tendency to interpret 'you' in a collective sense (e.g. you and your family) (14);

(e) a tendency to interpret 'switch from one station to another' in a way which left out at least some 'switching behaviour'.

3 In addition there were several specific interpretations which, though not individually numerous, are worth noting:

(a) several respondents by-passed 'you' by thinking in terms of 'how often the set is switched';

(b) two respondents regarded as one switching the act of switching from one station to the other and back again; others either disregarded purely exploratory switching or counted only exploratory switching, and three simply overlooked the reference (i.e. 'switched from one station to the other').

4 *Speculative comments*

(a) To the extent that a respondent had no usual 'number of switchings', that respondent could be in a very difficult position in trying to answer this question and it may be that a difficulty of this sort lay behind the frequent overlooking or distortion of the terms 'usually' and 'how many times'.

(b) The collective nature of switching behaviour in some homes may have been responsible for the relatively large number (compared with other questions) who interpreted 'you' in a family sense.

231

7.18   QUESTION 12, QUESTIONNAIRE III

The wording of the question

'What are the things you dislike about programmes on television?'

Definitions of the different parts of the question

The following are the intended meanings of key terms in the question. *However, as indicated below, some variants of the intended interpretations were regarded as permissible and others as possibly permissible.* The reference 'what are the things (about programmes)' was to features of programmes rather than *which* programmes. The word 'you' was meant to be interpreted as 'you, yourself' and was not intended to include others (e.g. respondent's spouse, children, relatives, lodger(s)). The term 'dislike' was intended to mean 'find disagreeable', 'unsatisfactory', 'unattractive', or 'do not enjoy'. The term '(about) programmes' was meant to refer to television programmes generally and not to just some single programme or type of programme. It was not meant to refer to advertisements.

Respondents' interpretations of the question

These interpretations are set out in full in the Appendix (Part II). They are based upon the replies of 51 people.

Marking the interpretations

The system used for rating or marking respondents' interpretations of questions.

The following marking or rating system was used.

1 If all elements of the question were interpreted as intended, the interpretation as a whole was rated 'fully as intended' ($\sqrt{}$).

232

2 Failure to interpret any significant element of the question fully as intended was sufficient to pull the total interpretation down below the level of 'fully as intended'. The level so reached was determined by the most seriously misinterpreted (significant) element in the test question. For example, if all but one of the significant elements of the question were interpreted as intended and the interpretation of that other element was rated 'somewhat limited but permissible' (see below), then the whole interpretation was so rated (i.e. 'somewhat limited but permissible'). The reason for this is that a question cannot be regarded as a safe one unless all its parts are interpreted as intended.

3 If a significant element of the question was obviously and substantially misinterpreted or was omitted altogether, the total interpretation was marked 'incorrect' (X).

4 In the context of this system, the following ratings were made of specific elements of respondents' interpretations.

(a) 'what are the things (about programmes)'. Where this reference was interpreted as intended (see above), it was rated 'correct' (√). Where it was interpreted as 'what is one of the things', it was rated 'limited but permissible' (LP). Where it was interpreted as 'what (types of programmes)', or 'which (particular programme)', the rating 'unduly different' (UD) was applied. Where something was added to a permissible interpretation without losing the latter, (e.g. 'what are the things and (types of programmes)', the rating 'extra but permissible' (ExP) was applied. The interpretation was rated 'incorrect' (X) where it took one of the following forms: 'what do you do'; 'are you satisfied'. Where the reference was omitted altogether, the rating 'incorrect' was also applied (X).

(b) 'you'. Where this term was interpreted as intended (see above), the interpretation was rated 'correct' (√). Where it was interpreted as 'you and your family', or as 'you and some other(s)' the interpretation was rated as 'unduly extended' (UE).

(c) 'dislike'. Where this word was interpreted as intended (see above), the interpretation was rated 'correct' (√). Where it was interpreted as 'dislike most', 'annoys you most', or 'partly dislike', it was rated as 'different but permissible' (DP). Where the respondent added 'and like' to the interpretation, the rating 'extra but permissible' (ExP) was applied. Where the term was interpreted solely as 'like' or solely as 'satisfied with' or solely some other form of approval, the rating 'incorrect' (X) was applied.

(d) '(about) programmes'. Where this term was interpreted as intended (see above), the interpretation was rated 'correct' (√). When it was interpreted as 'types of programmes', the rating 'different but permissible' (DP) was applied. The rating DP also applied to the following interpretations: 'types of programme and programme content'; 'type of programme and particular programmes'. Where the reference was interpreted solely as a single type of programme (e.g. 'plays' only considered), the rating 'unduly limited' (UL) was applied. Similarly where the respondent considered only some single programme (e.g. 'Sunday Night at the London Palladium'). Where the term was interpreted as 'the BBC only' or as 'ITV only', the rating 'unduly limited' (UL) was also applied. In some cases, the respondent appeared to have omitted the reference altogether (e.g. 'things on television') and in this case, the rating 'incorrect' (X) was applied. When the term was interpreted as 'advertising only', that interpretation was also rated 'incorrect' (X).

The ratings allocated

Under the system described above, the following ratings were allocated to respondents' interpretations of this test question.

Table 7.18.1

Ratings allocated to respondents' interpretations
of test question (Q10, III)

Lowest rating allocated to any part of the interpretation	Number of Ratings	Number of Persons	% of Persons
Correct (√)	1	1	2
Extra but permissible (ExP)	2		
Somewhat limited but permissible (LP)	4		
Somewhat too specific but permissible (SP)	0		
Somewhat too general but permissible (GP)	0	9	18
Somewhat extended but permissible (EP)	0		
Somewhat different but permissible (DP)	3		
Doubtful but permitted (?P)	0	0	0
Unduly limited (UD)	5		
Unduly general (UG)	0		
Unduly extended (UE)	1	26*	51
Unduly different (UD)	22		
Incorrect (X)	15	15	29
	Total	51	100

*See Note A on page 47.

234

Content analysis of the interpretations

There follows an analysis of the different interpretations of elements of test questions. The emphasis in this analysis is upon the different kinds of interpretations which were found rather than upon the number of them (though these numbers are given), the purpose of the content analysis being to discover the kinds of things that happen, to speculate about what causes them, and to derive hypotheses (about communication processes) for testing in later phases of the enquiry.

Interpretations of 'what are the things (about programming)'

The reference 'what are the things (about programmes)' was intended to mean 'what aspects' or 'what facets' of programmes, rather than which programmes.

Summary of interpretations

1 Nineteen of the 51 respondents interpreted this reference as intended; there were five more who limited the interpretation to something like 'what is one of the things' or 'what is the thing'.

2 Sixteen respondents converted the reference to 'what kinds of programmes' and 3 more converted it to 'what particular programmes.'

3 A number of the remaining 8 interpreted the concept as intended but added something to it (e.g. 'and what types of programmes'/'what programmes'/'what channels'.

4 Two respondents by-passed the concept altogether.

Table 7.18.2

Interpretations of 'what are the things (about programmes)'

What are the things (11)/what are all the things (1)/what sorts of things (1)/what (i.e. what things) (6)	19
What is one of the things (4)/what is the thing (1)	5
What types (of programmes) (14)/what kind of programme (1)/what kind of programme content (1)	16
What (programme) (2)/what particular programme (1)	3
What are the things and what types of programmes	1
What types (of programmes) and what particular (programmes)	1
What are the things, including particular (programmes)	1
What type of (programme) and what else	1
Which channel and what are the things	1
What do you do and what is an example of the kind of (programme you dislike)	1
What do you do	1
Are you generally satisfied	1
Total	51

Speculative comment

It is probably more difficult for respondents to generalise about features of television they dislike than it is to name specific programmes (or types of programmes) they dislike. Perhaps too, the vagueness of the term 'things' is likely to have facilitated any respondent tendency to take this easier line.

Interpretations of 'you'

The word 'you' was meant to be interpreted as 'you, yourself' and was not intended to include others (e.g. respondent's spouse, children, relatives, lodger(s)).

Summary of interpretations

1 Practically all respondents interpreted this term as intended.

2 One (possibly 2) converted it to include another person as well.

Table 7.18.3

Interpretations of 'you'	
You (i.e. apparently as intended)	49
You and your wife	1
You (apparently including others, but unclear whom)	1
Total	51

Interpretations of 'dislike'

The word 'dislike' was intended to mean to find 'disagreeable', 'unsatisfactory', 'unattractive', or 'do not enjoy'.

Summary of interpretations

1 Forty-three of the 51 respondents interpreted this term as intended.

2 The remaining 8 modified it in various ways; 'dislike most'; 'things that should not be on television'; 'partly dislike'; '(what do you) dislike and (what) like'; 'like'; 'satisfied with'.

Table 7.18.4

Interpretations of 'dislike'

Dislike (as intended	43	Partly dislike	1
Dislike most (1)/annoys you		Dislike and like	2
most (1)	2	Like	1
Things should not be on television	1	(Are you) satisfied with	1
		Total	51

Interpretations of '(about) programmes on television'

The term '(about) programmes on television' was meant to refer to television programmes generally and not to just some single programme or type of programme. It was not meant to refer to advertisements.

Summary of interpretations

1 Only 17 considered this term in the way intended.

2 Some broadened it to include anything on television (i.e. possibly including advertisements).

3 Others (24) narrowed it to mean particular types of programmes or programme content, programmes on one of the two channels.

4 One respondent even limited consideration to 'advertising'.

Table 7.18.5

Interpretations of '(about) programmes'

Television as a whole (3)/things about TV (1)	4
Things on television	4
Programmes (considered broadly as intended)	17
Types or kinds of programme(s)	16
Type of programme content	2 } 19
Types of programme and particular programmes	1
Things you watch on television	1
ITV programmes (1)/BBC TV programmes (1)/things on your channel (1)	3
Plays	2
Advertising	1
Total	51

Speculative comment

Where respondents thought only of what they disliked about certain kinds of programmes, it seems possible that they were in the grip of a preoccupation with their dislike of that kind of programme and so did not get round to a wider consideration of the matter.

Concerning the basic form of the question

Five persons appeared to alter the basic form of the question as shown in Table 7.18.6.

Table 7.18.6

The form of the question

Question form basically unaltered		46
Alterations and additions		
Are you generally satisfied (with the programmes on TV)	1	
What do you do (when programmes you dislike appear)	1	
What do you do about programmes you dislike on TV (and		5
what is an example of programmes you dislike)	1	
(What do you dislike) and give your reasons	2	
Total		51

Summary of full question

1 Of the 51 interpretations of this question, 20 per cent were allocated an overall rating of either 'as intended' or 'permissible'. This compares with an average of 29 per cent for all the questions tested.

2 The main forms of misinterpretation were as follows:

(a)   the conversion (by 16) of 'what are the things' into 'what kind(s) of programme(s)';

(b)   the narrowing of the reference 'programmes' (19) into 'type' or 'kind of programme', and its broadening into 'television generally' (8).

3 Noteworthy also were:

(a)   the alteration of the basic nature of the question by five respondents;

(b)   the distortion of the word 'dislike' (by 8 persons) into things such as: 'dislike most'; 'partly dislike'; 'like'; 'satisfied with';

(c)   the conversion of 'programmes' into the programmes on only one of the channels.

4 *Speculative comments*

Some respondents may have found it easier to talk about specific programmes they disliked or to limit themselves to considering things they

238

disliked about certain kinds of programmes—easier, that is, than considering matters generally. Another possibility is that some respondents were preoccupied with certain kinds of programmes or with particular programmes and automatically answered the question in terms of these.

7.19   QUESTION 14b, QUESTIONNAIRE III

The wording of the question

'What proportion of your evening viewing time do you spend watching
news programmes?'

Definitions of different parts of the question

The following are the intended meanings of key terms in the question.
*However, as indicated below, some variants of the intended interpreta-
tions were regarded as permissible and others as possibly permissible.*
In the reference 'what proportion of your (evening viewing) time', the
word 'proportion' was intended to mean 'fraction' (e.g. half, quarter,
tenth). In the present context, this fraction would reflect the size relationship of the amount of time spent by the viewer watching (evening)
news programmes and the total time he spent watching (evening) television programmes of any kind. Acceptable interpretations were: 'part',
'fraction', 'percentage'. The reference 'evening viewing (time) was meant
to refer to the period from 6.00 pm onwards, on those evenings during
which the respondent did at least some viewing. The word 'you' was
meant to be interpreted as 'you, yourself' and was not intended to include others (e.g. respondent's spouse, children, relatives, lodger(s)).
The reference 'news programmes' was intended to mean programmes
with a news content, including (but not limited to) news bulletins. Thus
news programmes other than news bulletins would include: 'Panorama',
'This Week', 'Tonight', 'Dateline', 'Town and Around'.

Respondents interpretations of the question

All interpretations are set out in full in the Appendix (Part II). They are
based upon the replies of 53 people.

Marking the interpretations

The system used for rating or marking respondents' interpretations of the question

The following marking or rating system was used.

1 If all elements of the question were interpreted as intended, the interpretation as a whole was rated 'fully as intended' (√).

2 Failure to interpret any significant element of the question fully as intended was sufficient to pull the total interpretation down below the level of 'fully as intended'. The level so reached was determined by the most seriously misinterpreted (significant) element in the test question. For example, if all but one of the significant elements of the question were interpreted as intended and the interpretation of that other element was rated as 'somewhat limited but permissible' (see below), then the whole interpretation was so rated (i.e. 'somewhat limited but permissible'). The reason for this is that a question cannot be regarded as a safe one unless all its parts are interpreted as intended.

3 If a significant element of the question was obviously and substantially misinterpreted or was omitted altogether, the total interpretation was marked 'incorrect' (X).

4 In the context of this system, the following ratings were made of specific elements of respondents' interpretations.

(a) 'what proportion of your (evening viewing) time'. Where this reference was interpreted as intended (see above), it was rated 'correct' (√). Where it was interpreted as 'how much time' (i.e. inviting replies such as: 'as much as we can'; 'quite a lot'; 'about a quarter of an hour'), the interpretation was rated as 'unduly different' (UD). Where 'what proportion of your (evening viewing) time' was interpreted as 'what proportion of the news programmes', the rating 'incorrect' (X) was applied. Similarly where 'proportion' was omitted altogether (e.g. 'how often do you watch news programmes', 'which news programmes do you watch/like').

(b) 'evening viewing (time)'. Where this reference was interpreted as intended (see above), the rating 'correct' (√) was applied. Where the reference was interpreted as 'weekday evening viewing (time) only', the interpretation was rated 'unduly limited' (UL). The following interpretations were rated 'incorrect' (X): 'including daytime viewing'; 'leisure time'; 'on the occasions when you are viewing' ('evening' not considered). Where the reference was omitted altogether, the rating 'incorrect' (X) was also applied.

(c) 'you'. Where this term was interpreted as intended (see above), the interpretation was rated 'correct' (√). Where it was interpreted as 'you and your family', or as 'you and some other(s)', the interpretation was rated as 'unduly extended' (UE).

(d) 'news programmes'. Where this reference was interpreted as intended (see above), the interpretation was rated 'correct' (√). Where it was interpreted solely as news bulletins with no reference to any of the other programmes listed above, the interpretation was rated 'limited but permissible' (LP). Where the reference was interpreted as one or other of the news programmes listed above, but where news bulletins had been omitted from consideration, the interpretation was rated 'limited but permissible' (LP). Where it was interpreted as 'the main nine o'clock news bulletin', the interpretation was rated as 'unduly limited' (UL). If 'sports programmes' was added to a permissible interpretation, the rating 'extra but permissible' (ExP) was applied. Where the reference was interpreted as 'sports programmes only', the rating 'incorrect' (X) was applied.

The ratings allocated

Under the system described above, ratings (shown in Table 7.19.1) were allocated to respondent interpretations of this test question.

242

Table 7.19.1

Ratings allocated to respondents' interpretations of test question (Q.E1, III)

Lowest rating allocated to any part of the interpretation	Number of Ratings	Number of Persons	% of Persons
Correct (√)	0	0	0
Extra but permissible (ExP)	0		
Somewhat limited but permissible (LP)	0		
Somewhat too specific but permissible (SP)	0		
Somewhat too general but permissible (GP)	0	0	0
Somewhat extended but permissible (EP)	0		
Somewhat different but permissible (DP)	0		
Doubtful but permitted (?P)	1	1	2
Unduly limited (UL)	0		
Unduly general (UG)	0		
Unduly extended (UE)	0	5	9
Unduly different (UD)	5		
Incorrect (X)	47	47	89
	Total	53	100

Content analysis of interpretations

There follows an analysis of the different interpretations of elements of the test question. The emphasis in this analysis is upon the different kinds of interpretations which were found rather than upon the number of them (though these numbers are given), the purpose of the content analysis being to discover the kinds of things that happen, to speculate about what causes them, and to derive hypotheses (about communication processes) for testing in later phases of the enquiry.

Interpretations of 'What proportion (of your ... time)'

In the reference 'what proportion of your (evening viewing) time', the word 'proportion' was intended to mean 'fraction' (e.g. half, quarter, tenth). In the present context, this fraction would reflect the size relationship of the amount of time spent by the viewer watching (evening) news programmes and the total time he spent watching (evening) television programmes of any kind. Acceptable interpretations were: 'part', 'fraction', 'percentage'.

Summary of results

1 Only 14 of the 53 respondents interpreted this reference more or less as intended, and two more appear to have interpreted it in a vaguely proportionate sense (i.e. (Do you spend) much/all (of your time)?).

2 Of the remaining 37 respondents, 11 interpreted the term in a broadly quantitative (but not proportionate) sense with things like: (for) how long; how many hours; how often.

3 Seventeen respondents answered in terms of 'which' (news programmes), 5 in terms of 'when' (i.e. at what times), and one respondent in terms of 'on which channel'.

4 Then there were 2 who converted the reference into 'do you like (to watch)' and 2 more who changed it into simply 'do you (watch)?'.

Table 7.19.2

Interpretations of 'what proportion (of your time)'

What proportion (i.e. as intended) (2)/and which (1)	3	
What fraction (1)/part (2)/percentage (1)	4	14
How much of	7	
(Do you spend) much/all (of your time)	2	
(For) how long (do you watch)	3	
How many (news programmes) (2)/how often (do you watch) (2)/ how many times (2)/how consistently (1)/do you like to watch and how often (1)	8	
When (i.e. at what times)	5	
Which (news programmes) (15)/which and how much of (2)	17	
On which channel	1	
Do you like to watch	2	
Do you watch	2	
Total	54*	

*One interpretation was in tw   parts which fell into 2 different categories.

Speculative comment

1 At least 2 of the   reasons for this major   failure seemed to be: that many respor   dents did not understand the word 'proportion'; that working out the   proportion' is difficult or de manding and that respondents found some e.   substitute for it.

2 There may also have en a tendency for people to be over-informative (e.g. by listing the dit erent news programmes they see instead of offering a proportion), but th may be no more than part of a tendency

to evade the difficult task of working out some overall proportion.

Interpretations of 'evening viewing (time)'

The reference 'evening viewing (time)' was meant to refer to viewing in the period from 6.00 pm onwards, on those evenings during which the respondent did at least some viewing.

Summary of interpretations

1 Some 42 of the 53 respondents interpreted this reference as intended.

2 Of the remaining 11 interpretations, 8 received narrowing and/or broadening treatment of some kind. Thus for 3 of them, the period of the week considered was narrowed to weekday only; others (5) considered the whole of the day rather than just evenings; one thought in terms of evening news programmes.

Table 7.19.3

Interpretations of 'evening viewing (time)'

Evening viewing (41)/viewing on an average evening (1)	42
Weekday evening viewing	2
Daily viewing (both day and evening)	1
Weekday viewing (both day and evening)	1
Your leisure time, both day and evening	1
Evening news programmes	1
When you are actually viewing (1)/during the time you are tuned in (1)	2
Reference gly overlooked	3
Total	53

Interpretations of 'you'

The word 'you' was meant to be interpreted as 'you, yourself' and was not intended to include others (e.g. respondent's spouse, children, relatives, lodger(s)).

Summary of interpretations

Whereas 51 of 53 interpreted this term as intended, there were 2 who broadened it to mean 'you and your family'.

Table 7.19.4

Interpretations of 'you'	
Term apparently interpreted as 'you, alone'	51
You and your family	2
Total	53

Interpretations of 'news programmes'

The reference 'news programmes' was intended to mean programmes with a news content, including (but not limited to) news bulletins.

Summary of interpretations

1 Eleven (possibly 12) interpreted this reference as intended.

2 Another respondent broadened it to include party political talks.

3 Thirty-seven considered only 'news bulletins' (and 2 of these only the main news bulletins).

4 Of the remaining 3, one thought in terms of TV programmes generally, one in terms of sports programmes only and one in terms of 'television, especially news and sport'.

Table 7.19.5

Interpretations of 'news programmes'	
News bulletins (only) (35)/the main news bulletins (2)	37
News bulletins plus one or more of the following: current affairs programmes; 'Tonight'; 'Panorama'; 'This Week'; 'Town and Around'; 'Dateline'; 'Gallery'; 'What the Papers Say'	11
News programmes (no further definition)	1
News programmes and party political talks	1
Television, especially news and sport	1
Sports programmes	1
Television programmes	1
Total	53

Speculative comment

It seems that many of the respondents may have heard this reference as 'the News'.

Summary for the full question

1 Of the 53 interpretations of this question, 2 per cent were allocated an overall rating of either 'as intended' or 'permissible'. This compares with an average of 29 per cent for all the questions tested.

2 The main sources of difficulty were as follows:

(a) only 14 of the 53 interpreted the term 'proportion' as intended and there were 27 where interpretations did not have even a quantitative element to them;

(b) no more than 12 interpreted 'news programmes' as intended, with 37 of the 53 considering only 'news bulletins';

(c) eight respondents either widened or narrowed some aspect of the reference 'evening viewing' (e.g. considered all day instead of just evening, considered evening viewing on weekdays only).

3 *Speculative comments*

(a) While it may be that many respondents did not properly understand the word 'proportion', the major failure of respondents to give this word its intended meaning may be the result of the sheer demandingness of working out the overall proportion called for. This explanation seems to tie in with the findings in Table 7.19.2.

(b) The considerable tendency to interpret 'news programmes' as 'news bulletins' may well have arisen out of 'news programmes' being heard as 'the News'.

7.20   QUESTION 16, QUESTIONNAIRE III

The wording of the question

'Do you think any programmes have bad effects on young people's morals?' (To be coded as: yes/no/not sure.)

Check question

If 'yes': 'Which ones?' If 'no': 'Why do you say that?'

Definition of the different parts of the question

The following are the intended meanings of key terms in the question. *However, as indicated below, some variants of the intended interpretations were regarded as permissible and others as possibly permissible.* The word 'you' was meant to be interpreted as 'you, yourself', and was not intended to include others (e.g. respondent's spouse, children, relatives, lodger(s)). The reference 'any programme' was intended to mean any particular programmes, and to include both adult and children's programmes. The word 'have (bad effects)' was meant to be interpreted as 'actually have', rather than 'could possibly have'. The reference 'bad effects' was intended to mean 'effects which are undesirable in terms of established values of good and bad'. The reference 'young people' is a broad one and no single definition of it could be regarded as final. In the present context it was meant to be interpreted as 'young people in general' rather than young people in any narrow age range or special category. An acceptable definition of 'young' was one which referred to any five year span which was in the range of 8–21 years. The term 'morals' is a difficult term to deal with in that its dictionary definition is wider than its popular use. Strictly speaking, it means 'standards of right and wrong generally' but (in its negative form) it is often used to refer to such concepts as sexual immorality, crime, violence, drunkenness, swearing.

248

Respondents' interpretations of the question

These interpretations are set out in full in the Appendix (Part II). They are based upon the replies of 50 people.

Marking the interpretations

The system used for rating or marking respondents' interpretations of the question

The following marking or rating system was used.

1 If all elements of the question were interpreted as intended, the interpretation as a whole was rated 'fully as intended' (√).

2 Failure to interpret any significant element of the question fully as intended was sufficient to pull the total interpretation down below the level of 'fully as intended'. The level so reached was determined by the most seriously misinterpreted (significant) element in the test question. For example, if all but one of the significant elements of the question were interpreted as intended and the interpretation of that other element was rated 'somewhat limited but permissible' (see below), then the whole interpretation was so rated (i.e. 'somewhat limited but permissible'). The reason for this is that a question cannot be regarded as a safe one unless all its parts are interpreted as intended.

3 If a significant element of the question was obviously and substantially misinterpreted or was omitted altogether, the total interpretation was marked 'incorrect' (X).

4 In the context of this system, the following ratings were made of specific elements of respondents' interpretations.

(a) 'you'. Where this term was interpreted as intended (see above), the interpretation was rated 'correct' (√). Where it seemed that a permissible interpretation had been made, but where the evidence was not conclusive, the rating 'doubtful but permissible' (?P) was applied.

(b) 'any programmes'. Where this reference was interpreted as intended (see above), the interpretation was rated 'correct' (√). Where the reference was interpreted as 'adult programmes only', this interpretation was rated as 'limited but permissible' (LP). Where it was interpreted as 'some types of programmes', the interpretation was rated 'somewhat general but permissible' (GP). Where the reference was interpreted as 'television programmes generally(i.e. no consideration of nature of programme content)' the interpretation was rated 'unduly general' (UG). Where it was interpreted as 'children's programmes only', the interpretation was rated 'unduly limited' (UL).

(c) 'have (bad effects)'. Where this reference was interpreted as intended (see above), the interpretation was rated 'correct' (√). The interpretations 'cause (bad effects)', 'are responsible for (bad effects)', 'are (detrimental) to', were also regarded as acceptable. In some cases the respondent did not interpret the reference directly, but nevertheless an interpretation in the sense of 'actually have' was implicit. Such interpretations were rated 'doubtful but permissible' (?P). The interpretations: 'might (have)'; 'could (have)'; 'are likely to (have)'; 'might (cause)'; 'would be (adversely affected, i.e. if)' were rated 'unduly different' (UD). Where the reference was omitted altogether, the rating 'incorrect (X) was applied.

(d) 'bad effects'. Where this reference was interpreted as intended (see above), the interpretation was rated 'correct' (√). Where it seemed that a permissible interpretation had been made but where the evidence was not conclusive, the rating 'doubtful but permissible' (?P) was applied. If the respondent was not considering 'bad effects' at all, his interpretation was rated 'incorrect' (X).

(e) 'young people'. Where this reference was interpreted as intended (see above), that interpretation was rated 'correct' (√). Where it was interpreted as referring to young people with an age span of less than five years (though within the range 8–21 years), the interpretation was rated 'limited but permissible' (LP); similarly for the interpretation 'your own child and his associates', provided these were aged within the range 8–21 years. Where the respondent interpreted 'young people' to mean children aged 7 years or less (only), or 'your own child only', or 'girls only' or 'boys only', that interpretation was rated 'unduly limited' (UL). Other interpretations rated as UL were: 'young people whose viewing is properly controlled'; 'young people who have been properly brought up'. Where the persons considered included those aged up to 25 years as well as persons within the age range 8–21, the rating 'extended but permissible' (EP) was applied. Where the persons considered included those aged less than 8 years as well as persons within the age range 8–21 years, the rating 'extended but permissible' (EP) was similarly applied. If persons over 25 years (along with those within the range 8–21) were considered, the rating 'unduly extended' (UE) was applied.

Where the respondent considered adults only (i.e. 21 and over only), the interpretation was rated 'incorrect' (X). Where it seemed that the respondent's interpretation of 'young people' was permissible but where some doubt nonetheless existed, the rating 'doubtful but permissible' (?P) was applied.

(f) 'morals'. Where this term was interpreted as intended (see above), the interpretation was rated 'correct' (√). The following interpretations were rated 'limited but permissible' (LP): 'sex attitudes or behaviour only referred to'; 'crime/violence only referred to'; 'crime and sex referred to without any other reference'; 'crime or sex plus only one other aspect of morality referred to'. When the interpretation was in terms only of specific moral issues other than crime, violence, sex, the interpretation was rated 'unduly limited' (UL). Where the term was missed out altogether, the rating 'incorrect' (X) was applied.

The ratings allocated

Under the system described above, the following ratings were allocated to respondent interpretations of this test question.

Table 7.20.1

Ratings allocated to respondents' interpretations
of test question (Q.16, III)

Lowest rating allocated to any part of the interpretation	Number of Ratings	Number of Persons	% of Persons
Correct (√)	4	4	8
Extra but permissible (ExP)	1		
Somewhat limited but permissible (LP)	11		
Somewhat too specific but permissible (SP)	0	12*	24
Somewhat too general but permissible (GP)	2		
Somewhat extended but permissible (EP)	3		
Somewhat different but permissible (DP)	1		
Doubtful but permitted (?P)	9	9	18
Unduly limited (UL)	14		
Unduly general (UG)	3	22*	44
Unduly extended (UE)	0		
Unduly different (UD)	9		
Incorrect (X)	3	3	6
		50	100

*See Note A on page 47.

251

Content analysis of interpretations

There follows an analysis of the different interpretations of elements of the test question. The emphasis in this analysis is upon the different kinds of interpretations which were found rather than upon the number of them (though these numbers are given), the purpose of the content analysis being to discover the *kinds* of things that happen, to speculate about what causes them, and to derive hypotheses (about communication processes) for testing in later phases of the enquiry.

Interpretations of 'you'

The word 'you' was meant to be interpreted as 'you, yourself' and was not intended to include others (e.g. respondent's spouse, children, relatives, lodger(s)).

Summary of interpretations

All respondents apparently interpreted this term as intended.

Table 7.20.2

Interpretations of 'you'

Apparently as intended (i.e. you, yourself, only)	50

Speculative comment

In view of what happened to this term in other questions (i.e. its collective interpretation), it may well be worth noting that in this question the respondent was asked, not about viewing behaviour, but about his/her opinion on a particular issue.

Interpretations of 'any programmes'

The reference 'any programmes' was intended to mean any particular programmes, and to include both adult and children's programmes.

Summary of interpretations

1 Twenty-six of the 50 respondents did not appear to have considered specific programmes or specific contents of programmes, but to have considered programmes rather generally.

2 On the other hand, there were 24 who tended to think in terms of one or more sorts of programme content: sex immorality or violence

or crime or bad language or misbehaviour or ... Since the interpretations of the 24 were spread over 34 such specifications, it appears that many of these respondents thought only of one sort of programme. It is interesting to note that 12 of these 24 respondents thought in terms of sex.

3 Among the 50 respondents, there were 6 who put other kinds of limitations on the reference: adult plays only, plays, detective programmes.

Table 7.20.3.

Interpretations of 'any programmes'

Respondent did not appear to have considered specific content of programmes, but to have considered programmes rather generally			26
Respondent considered specific programme content or material (e.g. sex, crime). (Details follow)			24 *
Sex (10)/Sex immorality (2)	12	Crime	1
Programmes about prostitution	1	Murder	1
'Near the knuckle' material	1	Theft	1
'Kitchen sink' material	1	Stealing and shoplifting	1
Violence	5	Bad language	2
Brutality	1	Swearing	3
		Misbehaviour (unspecified)	4
		Total	50

Some special interpretations of interest (from 6 of the above cases)	
Adult programmes only	1
Television plays (3)/particularly TV plays (1)	4
Detective programmes	1

*Some respondents considered more than one element of content.

Speculative comment

It seems fairly clear that various of these 50 respondents answered the questions from an over-general standpoint—though it is doubtful that an interviewer would know that this was going on. Though the question quite possibly invites this situation, it seems well worth asking how many questions involve the same sort of difficulty—or what a question designer should do to keep respondents strictly to whatever question they are required to answer.

Interpretations of 'have (bad effects)'

The word 'have (bad effects)' was meant to be interpreted as 'actually have', rather than 'could possibly have'.

Summary of interpretations

Whereas 39 of the 50 interpreted this word as intended, there were 9 who interpreted it more loosely; might have, could have, are likely to have, would be (adversely affected).

Table 7.20.4

Interpretations of 'have (bad effects)'

Have (bad effects) (35)/cause (1)/are responsible for (2)/ are (detrimental)(1)	39
Might have (2)/might cause (1)	3 ⎫
Could have	4 ⎬ 9
Are likely to have (1)/would be (adversely affected) (i.e. if) (1)	2 ⎭
Respondent seemingly overlooked the reference	2
Total	50

Speculative comment

It appears that some of the 9 deviating respondents were interpreting the term so as to allow for certain qualifications they were making (e.g. 'It depends on the girl'; 'It depends on the parents' outlook'; 'not the average person of average intelligence').

Interpretations of '(have) bad effects'

The reference 'bad effects' was intended to mean 'effects which are undesirable in terms of established values of good and bad'.

Summary of interpretations

1 There was considerable variability (in going from one respondent to another) in the way 'bad effects' was interpreted. These interpretations included: decline in sex morality (34 of the 86 interpretations); 'teach dishonesty and crime' (8 references); 'teach violence or make it acceptable' (14 references); 'teach swearing or bad language' (9).

2 Whereas 18 clearly had more than one sort of 'bad effect' in mind in giving an answer to the question, there were 22 or more who appear to have had only one sort of 'bad effect' in mind in working out an answer.

Table 7.20.5

Table 7.20.5

Interpretations of '(have) bad effects'

The different interpretations of 'bad effects'

Adversely affect (their) outlook (2)/adversely affect (their) conduct (3)/teach bad behaviour (3)	8
Cause a decline in sexual morality (13)/set sexually immoral example (1)	14
Teach sexual misbehaviour (15)/teach (them) to be 'Bohemian in (their) ... ' (1)/ teach sexual looseness (2)/promiscuity (1)	19
	1
	2
...heft (2)/shoplifting (1)	6
...ce (8)/encourage a violent attitude (2)/ ... 'as an every day thing' (1)/teach	14
...urage hooliganism (1)	2
	1
Teach swearing (5)/teach bad language (4)	9
Cause drunken parties	1
Cause rudeness	1
Cause disrespect for parents	1
Frighten	1
Something else considered (in addition to one or more above) but not specified	4
Bad effects considered, but not clear which	3
Bad effects apparently not considered	1
Total	86*

The number of different interpretations per respondent

One interpretation only considered	22
Two interpretations considered	9
Three interpretations considered	8
Four interpretations considered	1
Not clear how many interpretations were considered	10
Total	50

*As up to 28 respondents gave more than one interpretation, this total exceeds the number of respondents.

Speculative comment

Here too, then, the question appears to have allowed respondents considerable freedom with respect to what bad effect(s) they considered in formulating a reply to the question.

255

Interpretations of 'young people'

The reference 'young people' is a broad one and no single definition of it could be regarded as final. In the present context it was meant to be interpreted as 'young people in general' rather than young people in any narrow age range or special category. An acceptable definition of 'young' was one which referred to any five year span which was in the age range 8—21 years.

Summary of interpretations

1 Up to 39 of the 50 respondents interpreted this term as intended. Amongst these, however, there was quite a lot of variability as indicated in Table 7.20.6.

2 Ten respondents were highly specific in their interpretations of this term, for example: your own child; males only; young people who have been properly brought up.

3 One respondent overlooked the reference altogether.

Table 7.20.6a

Interpretations of 'young people'

Covering a 5 year span within the range 8—21 years	13	⎞
Within the range 8—21 years	10	⎟
Young people (1)/teenagers only (2)	3	⎬ 39
Up to 25 years but also within the range 8—21 years	4	⎟
Within some part of the range 8—21 years but extending below it	9	⎠
Less than 8 years (only)	1	
Your own child/children (only)	4	
Females only	1	
Males only	2	
Young people who have been properly brought up	1	
Young people whose viewing is properly controlled	1	
Term overlooked (i.e. 'Do you have any complaints about any of the programmes that are presented on television	1	
Total	50	

Speculative comments

1 It seems that this term has rather different meanings for different people.

2 At the same time, there does seem to be scope for its special context to influence the interpretation of this term. This seems to have happened with interpretations such as 'males only' or 'young people who have

256

been brought up properly', but this tendency may well have gone further and affected the ages of the young people considered.

3 Especially noteworthy is the limitation of the term 'young people' to 'your own child or children' (or the like). This is a limitation that is understandable in that people are likely to draw upon what they actually know about in order to answer a question, but one may wonder how many of the other interpretations are similarly conditioned.

Table 7.20.6b

Interpretations of 'young people'

Whether interpreted in terms of age in years

Ages not indicated	9
Upper and lower limits of age span given	40
Upper age limit only given	1
Lower age limit only given	0
Total	50

Upper and lower age limits, and age spans

Lower age limits		Upper age limits		Age span considered	
4 years	3	7 years	1	1 year	1
5– 6 years	4	11–12 years	3	2 years	2
7– 8 years	5	13–14 years	6	3 years	2
9–10 years	5	15–16 years	10	4 years	3
11–12 years	4	17–18 years	10	5 years	6
13–14 years	8	19–20 years	7	6 years	8
15–16 years	11	21–22 years	1	7 years	3
Not given	10	23–24 years	1	8 years	4
		25–26 years	1	9 years	2
		31 years	10	10 years	3
				11 years	3
				12 years	1
				15 years	1
				20 years	1
				Not given	10
Total	50	Total	50	Total	50

Table 7.20.6b (continued)

Non numerical interpretations
(whether ages given or not)

Children	3	
'Present day' children	1	
School children	1	8
Young children	3	

Your own children/your own young children/your own young sons	3
Teenage children (your own for example)	1
Teenagers	5
Teenagers from the average family	1
Especially teenagers	1
Teenage girls	1
Young people	17
Young people, especially girls	1
Young males	2
Young people (going mainly by what happens to your own daughters)	1
Boys and girls (going by your own experience with your own children)	1
Those who are properly controlled over what they see	1
Those who have been properly brought up	1
Young children who have been properly guided by parents	1
Those (aged)	3
Children in your home	1
Your	1
	50

Interpretations of 'morals'

The term 'morals' is a difficult term to deal with in that its dictionary definition is wider than its popular use. Strictly speaking it means 'standards of right and wrong generally' but (in its negative form) it is often used to refer to such concepts as sexual immorality, crime, violence, drunkenness, swearing.

Summary of interpretations

1 Eleven of the 50 respondents quite properly interpreted this term in the broad sense intended and there were five more who may have done so, though the evidence for claiming this is not very firm.

2 Of the remaining 34, some 31 appear to have interpreted the term

'moral' in a relatively limited way. Thus 16 only considered sexual morality, whilst others considered only sex and swearing or only sex and violence or only violence and crime, and so on.

3 Three respondents appear to have overlooked the concept altogether.

Table 7.20.7

Interpretations of 'morals'

The term 'morals' quite possibly interpreted in the broad sense intended

Moral standards (5)/moral behaviour (2)/morals (4)	11

*Vague references which might mean that respondent interpreted 'morals'
    as intended, but by no means certain*

Morals in relation to copying wrongful behaviour	1	
Morals, particularly sex morality	1	
Relating to the bad things they see done on TV	1	5
Morals or behaviour (evidence of meaning not available)	1	
Standards of conduct or of outlook	1	

Limited interpretations of 'morals'

Sexual morality (only)	16	Swearing (1)/bad language (2)	3
Sex and swearing (only)	2	Violence (only)	1
Sex and violence (only)	4	Violence and crime (only)	2
Sex or violence or theft	1	Criminal ideas and behaviour	
Sex and respect for parents	1	in relation to society	1
Concept apparently omitted altogether			3
		Total	50

Speculative comments

1 Specially noteworthy is the interpretation of morals in terms of sexual morality only (16 of the 50 did this).

2 Ordinarily a researcher might not be aware that his different respondents were basing their answers on rather different interpretations of 'morals'.

Summary for the full question

1 Of the 50 interpretations of this question, 50 per cent were allocated an overall rating of 'as intended' or 'permissible'. This compares with an average of 29 per cent for all the questions tested.

2 The main sources of misinterpretation were as follows:

(a)   there was a tendency for some respondents to think in terms of a limited number of rather specific kinds of programme content, rather than to think of specific programmes;

(b) some respondents (9) converted the term 'have' (in the context 'do ... any programmes have bad effects') into a conditional form such as 'might have', 'could have';

(c) There were 10 who interpreted the concept 'young people' in a very specific way, for example: males only; young people who have been brought up properly; your own child.

3 A noteworthy feature of the findings was the high degree of variability in the way certain terms were interpreted: 'any programmes'; 'bad effects'; 'young people'; 'morals'. Some of these interpretations were broad and some were narrow (e.g. 'morals' interpreted as 'standards of right and wrong generally' versus 'sexual morality'). In addition, specific interpretations were frequently different in character (e.g. 'bad effects' was interpreted as 'frighten' versus 'teach criminal ideas').

4 In terms of success:

(a) all respondents appear to have interpreted 'you' as intended;

(b) all but one respondent considered the concept 'bad effects';

(c) only three respondents failed to consider at least some aspect of 'morals'.

5 *Speculative comments*

(a) The term 'you' was not presented in a family context and this may have facilitated its successful interpretation in this case, this contrasts with what happened in family contexts.

(b) The very variability of respondent interpretation of major terms in this question should be noted because it suggests that similar replies may not always represent similar views on the particular matter asked about.

7.21   QUESTION 20, QUESTIONNAIRE III

The wording of the question

'On the ITV, a certain amount of time is spent showing cartoon advertisements. Do you think that this sort of advertising is done properly?' (To be coded: yes/no/not sure.)

Check question

'Why do you say that?'

Definitions of the different parts of the question

The following are the intended meanings of key terms in the question. *However, as indicated below, some variants of the intended interpretations were regarded as permissible and others as possibly permissible.* The reference '(on the) ITV' was intended to refer only to the commercial television channel. The reference 'cartoon advertisements' was meant to refer solely to those advertisements featuring animated drawings. There was no intention to differentiate between cartoon advertisements presented between programmes and those presented within programmes. The word 'you' was meant to be interpreted as 'you, yourself' and was not intended to include others (e.g. respondent's spouse, children, relatives, lodger(s)). The reference 'done properly' was meant to refer to the use of this form of advertising in a manner which was responsibly balanced between the interests of the advertiser and those of the viewer. This concept is clearly a difficult one and it will be seen below that various more limited interpretations of it were regarded as permissible.

Respondents' interpretations of the question

These interpretations are set out in full in the Appendix (Part II). They

are based upon the replies of 51 people.

Marking the interpretations

The system used for rating or marking respondents' interpretations of questions

The following marking or rating system was used.

1 If all elements of the question were interpreted as intended, the interpretation as a whole was rated 'fully as intended' (√).

2 Failure to interpret any significant element of the question fully as intended was sufficient to pull the total interpretation down below the level of 'fully as intended'. The level so reached was determined by the most seriously misinterpreted (significant) element in the test question. For example, if all but one of the significant elements of the question were interpreted as intended and the interpretation of that other element was rated as 'somewhat limited but permissible' (see below), then the whole interpretation was so rated (i.e. 'somewhat limited but permissible'). The reason for this is that a question cannot be regarded as a safe one unless all its parts are interpreted as intended.

3 If a significant element of the question was obviously and substantially misinterpreted or was omitted altogether, the total interpretation was marked 'incorrect' (X).

4 In the context of this system, the following ratings were made of specific elements of respondents' interpretations.

(a) '(On the) ITV'. Where this reference was interpreted as intended (see above), the interpretation was rated 'correct' (√). Where it was interpreted as 'television generally', it was rated 'unduly extended' (UE). Where the reference was omitted altogether, the rating 'incorrect' (X) was applied.

(b) 'cartoon advertisements'. Where this reference was interpreted as intended (see above), the interpretation was rated 'correct' (√). Where it was interpreted as 'including humorous advertisements along with cartoon advertisements', the interpretation was rated 'unduly extended' (UE). Where a reference was interpreted as 'advertisements done in a deliberately silly way' (i.e. non-cartoon advertisements), the interpretation was rated 'unduly different' (UD). Where it was interpreted as 'advertisements in general', the interpretation was rated as 'incorrect' (X). The interpretation 'cartoon programmes' was rated 'incorrect' (X) as was the interpretation 'cartoons (generally) in newspapers, magazines and on television. Where the interpretation was omitted altogether, the rating

262

'incorrect' (X) was applied.

(c) 'you'. Where this term was interpreted as intended (see above), the interpretation was rated 'correct' (√). Where it seemed that a permissible interpretation had been made, but where the evidence was not conclusive, the rating 'doubtful but permissible' (?P) was applied.

(d) 'done properly'. Where this reference was interpreted as intended (see above), the interpretation was rated 'correct' (√). Where the interpretation was solely from the viewer's standpoint or solely from the advertiser's standpoint, the interpretation was rated 'limited but permissible' (LP). In some cases, respondent interpreted the phrase solely in terms of one aspect of advertisers' interests (e.g. draws attention to the product) or solely in terms of one aspect of the viewers' interests (e.g. amusing). In spite of this narrowness, these interpretations were rated 'limited but permissible' (LP), the reason being mainly that the concept itself (i.e. cartoon advertisements) is a narrow one and that many viewers traditionally judge the merits of cartoon advertisements from rather specific standpoints. In some cases the respondent judged in terms of the basic power of cartoon advertisements to present information accurately or to sell products, in terms of their positioning in relation to programmes, or in terms of preference for this form of advertising to other forms. These interpretations were rated 'doubtful but permissible' (?P). In a few cases where the respondent considered only the rightness or wrongness of having this sort of advertising at all, the rating 'incorrect' (X) was applied (e.g. 'are they really necessary or just a waste of time'; 'are they a proper way of using the talents of those who do them'). Where the reference was omitted altogether, the rating 'incorrect' (X) was applied.

The ratings allocated

Under the system described above, the following ratings were allocated to respondents' interpretations of this test question.

Table 7.21.1
Ratings allocated to respondents' interpretations
of test question (Q.20, III)

Lowest rating allocated to any part of the interpretation	Number of Ratings	Number of Persons	% of Persons
Correct (✓)	2	2	4
Extra but permissible (ExP)	0		
Somewhat limited but permissible (LP)	18		
Somewhat too specific but permissible (SP)	0		
Somewhat too general but permissible (GP)	0	18*	35
Somewhat extended but permissible (EP)	0		
Somewhat different but permissible (DP)	2		
Doubtful but permitted (?P)	7	7	14
Unduly limited (UL)	1		
Unduly general (UG)	0		
Unduly extended (UE)	4	6	12
Unduly different (UD)	1		
Incorrect (X)	18	18	35
Total	51	51	100

*See Note A on page 47.

Content analysis of the interpretations

There follows an analysis of the different interpretations of elements of
the test question. The emphasis in this analysis is upon the different
kinds of interpretations which were found rather than upon the number
of them (though these numbers are given), the purpose of the content
analysis being to discover the kinds of things that happen, to speculate
about what caused them, and to derive hypotheses (about communication processes) for testing in the later phases of the enquiry.

Interpretations of '(on the) ITV'

The reference '(on the) ITV' was intended to refer only to the commercial television channel.

Summary of interpretations

Three (and possibly five) of the 51 respondents broadened this reference
beyond ITV.

Table 7.21.2

Interpretations of '(on the) ITV'

On ITV (as intended)	46
On television generally	3
Term apparently omitted (i.e. no evidence that respondent understood the question to be about television in particular)	2
Total	51

Interpretations of 'cartoon advertisements'

The reference 'cartoon advertisements' was meant to refer solely to those advertisements featuring animated drawings. There was no intention to differentiate between those cartoon advertisements presented between programmes and those presented within programmes.

Summary of interpretations

1 Thirty-one of the respondents understood the term more or less as intended.

2 Thirteen broadened the term to 'advertisements generally'.

3 Three went further and converted 'advertisements' into 'programmes'. Noteworthy also were the following misinterpretations: 'cartoon advertisements' was shortened to 'cartoons' (1), became 'humorous advertisements' (1), became 'silly advertisements' (1).

Table 7.21.3

Interpretations of 'cartoon advertisements'

Cartoon advertisements (as intended)	29 }	30
Television advertisements of the Kennomeat kind	1 }	
Cartoon advertisements as in Shop Window		1
Humorous advertisements including but not limited to cartoon advertisements	1 }	2
Advertisements done in a deliberately silly way	1 }	
Advertisements in general	11 }	13
The different advertisements/some things advertised	2 }	
Cartoon programmes (on TV)	3 }	4
Cartoons (respondent did not know whether reference was to television programmes or to newspapers or to magazines)	1 }	
No information about the nature of the interpretation		1
Total		51

Speculative comment

1 The widening of the term to 'advertisements in general' would be consistent either with the non-perception of the word 'cartoon' or with its 'half deliberate' neglect (e.g. because respondent was not sure of its meaning, because of a desire to talk about a class of advertisements broader than cartoons or more irritating than cartoons).

2 For several others, it may well have been that the term 'cartoon' was sufficiently odd in combination with 'advertisements' for only its more expected or usual object to be perceived (i.e. 'programme') or for the dropping of the ill-fitting word (i.e. 'advertisements') altogether.

3 At least two respondents appeared not to know the meaning of the word 'cartoon'.

Interpretations of 'you'

The word 'you' was meant to be interpreted as 'you' yourself' and was not intended to include others (e.g. respondent's spouse, children, relatives, lodger(s)).

Summary of interpretations

There was no evidence that any of the respondents misinterpreted this term.

Table 7.21.4

Interpretations of 'you'

You, apparently as intended	50
No evidence as to interpretation	1
Total	51

Interpretations of 'done properly'

The reference 'done properly' was meant to refer to the use of this form of advertising in a manner which was responsibly balanced between the interests of the advertiser and those of the viewer. This concept is clearly a difficult one and it will be seen above that various more limited interpretations of it were regarded as permissible.

Summary of interpretations

1 Table 7.21.5 makes it clear that there was a lot of variation, in going from one person to another in terms of the criteria being used to decide

whether or not cartoon advertisements were being done 'properly'. Thus judgments were made on the basis of things like: power to communicate, accuracy of claims, viewer enjoyment, efficiency in selling, whether or not respondent approved of there being advertising, whether or not advertisements were in good taste.

2 In spite of this overall variability, however, many individuals appeared to judge on the basis of some single, and usually narrow, criterion. Even more to the point, no more than 14 considered the matter from the point of view of both viewers and advertisers, and the figure is possibly nearer to 4. By contrast, at least 21 judged from the standpoint of viewers alone.

3 Against the 21 (at least) who judged from viewers' standpoint only, there were 7 (at least) who judged from advertisers viewpoint only.

Table 7.21.5
Interpretations of 'done properly'

(i)   *The many different interpretations*

Well done   3

Relating to standard of presentation: well presented or well put out (2)/
   technically sound (1)/well drawn (1)/of good standard (1)/in good
   taste and suitable for most viewers (1)   6

Relating to power to communicate: lucid (1)/informative (1)/gives
   detailed description of product (1)/have properly planned order of
   presentation (1)/stick to the point (1)   5

Accurate   2

For adult intelligence: sensible (1)/fit for adult intelligence (2)/clever (3)   6

Viewer enjoyment or interest: interesting (3)/pleasing or enjoyed or liked
   (7)/amusing (6)/entertaining (2)/entertaining for small children (1)/
   different (1)/such that you don't mind seeing them (1)   21

Relating to efficiency in selling: efficient (1)/ effective in selling products
   (3)/effective in selling to people other than yourself (2)/presented in a
   manner likely to sell products (2)/ convincing (1)/attention getting (3)/
   memorable (1)/a good way of advertising (1)   14

Compared with other forms: more attention getting or more convincing
   than other forms of advertising (2)/preferable to other forms of
   advertising (2)   4

Approved of otherwise: do you approve of them (3)/do you like them or
   like the use of them (5)/are they necessary and not just a waste of time
   (1)/a proper use of the talents of those who do it?(1)   10

What is your opinion of them   3

Their timing in relation to programmes: should they be timed so as not to
   interrupt programmes (2)/are they timed in best way for viewer enjoyment (1)/don't take up too much viewing time (1)   4

Other interpretations   3
                                                                          Total   81*

(ii)   *Some global aspects of interpretations*

The phrase was omitted altogether	2
The phrase was apparently given some consideration	49
Total	51
Viewer standpoint only considered	21
Advertiser standpoint only considered	7
Both standpoints considered	4
Unclear whether only one or both considered	10
Neither standpoint considered	1
Unclear whether either standpoint considered	6
Apparently omitted altogether	2
Total	51

*Some respondents had more than one interpretation.

268

Some speculative comments

1 The term 'properly' is very broad and unspecific and it appears to have given these respondents considerable freedom in interpreting it.

2 That this freedom should have taken such a narrow form for the individual, quite possibly reflects a normally narrow or rigid way of thinking about or judging whatever form of advertising they had in mind.

3 Whatever the reason for the narrowness of the criterion used by the individual, it is apparent that identical choice of answers may very well mask differences of opinion.

Summary for full question

1 Of the 51 interpretations of this question, 53 per cent were allocated an overall rating of either 'as intended' or 'permissible'. This compares with an average of 29 per cent for all the questions tested.

2 The main sources of difficulty in this question was as follows:

(a) Quite a lot of the respondents broadened the term 'cartoon advertisements' to mean 'advertisements generally' (13), and a few even converted it into 'programmes' (3).

(b) Relatively few considered both viewer and advertiser standpoints in deciding whether or not cartoon advertisements were done 'properly', many judging from a viewer's standpoint alone. Even the latter seemed to be talking in terms of some rather narrow aspect of the viewer's standpoint.

(c) A few converted the term ITV into 'TV generally'.

3 *Speculative comments*

(a) The misinterpretation of the term 'cartoon advertisements' could possibly spring out of non-perception of the word 'cartoon', or out of the over-riding of it by the later use of the word 'advertising' (on its own). On the other hand, it is possible that some viewers wanted to talk in terms of advertisements generally (they may have had strong feelings on the matter) rather than about anything as narrow as cartoon advertisements.

(b) The narrowness and variability of the criterion used by respondents in deciding whether or not cartoon advertisements were done properly suggests the existence of a normally narrow way of regarding or judging in this particular setting. On the other hand, the vagueness of the term 'properly' probably gave respondents plenty of scope for being as specific as they cared to be.

7.22 QUESTION 21, QUESTIONNAIRE III

The wording of the question

'Do you go on watching the screen when the television advertisements come on or do you do something else at that time?' (To be coded as: go on watching/do something else/sometimes one, sometimes other/not sure.)

Check questions

If 'do something else': 'What do you do?' If 'go on watching': 'Why do you do this?'

Definitions of different parts of the question

The following are the intended meanings of key terms in the question. *However, as indicated below, some variants of the intended interpretations were regarded as permissible and others as possibly permissible.* The word 'you' was meant to be interpreted as 'you, yourself' and was not intended to include others (e.g. respondent's spouse, children, relatives, lodger(s)). The reference 'watching television' was intended to mean attending to what is being shown on the screen or giving it at least some degree of attention. The reference 'television advertisements' was meant to refer to television advertisements generally, whether presented within or between programmes. The phrase 'or do you do something else at that time' was meant to refer to the respondent's own behaviour (i.e. mental and physical activities) during the time that the advertisements were being shown on the screen. Relevant behaviour would include behaviour either in the same room as the set or elsewhere, wherever the respondent might be.

Respondents' interpretation of the question

These interpretations are set out in full in the Appendix (Part II). They

271

are based upon the replies of 54 people.

Marking the interpretations

The system used for rating or marking respondents' interpretations of questions

The following marking or rating system was used:

1 If all elements of the question were interpreted as intended, the interpretation as a whole was rated 'fully as intended' (√).

2 Failure to interpret any significant element of the question fully as intended was sufficient to pull the total interpretation down below the level of 'fully as intended'. The level so reached was determined by the most seriously misinterpreted (significant) element of the test question. For example, if all but one of the significant elements of the question were interpreted as intended and the interpretation of that other element was rated as 'somewhat limited but permissible' (see below), then the whole interpretation was so rated (i.e. 'somewhat limited but permissible'). The reason for this is that a question cannot be regarded as a safe one unless all its parts are interpreted as intended.

3 If a significant element of the question was obviously and substantially misinterpreted or was omitted altogether, the total interpretation was marked 'incorrect' (X).

4 In the context of this system, the following ratings were made of specific elements of respondents' interpretations.

(a) 'you'. Where this term was interpreted as intended (see above), the interpretation was rated 'correct' (√). Where it was interpreted as 'you and your family', or as 'you and some other(s)', the interpretation was rated as 'unduly extended' (UE).

(b) 'watching television'. Where this reference was interpreted as intended (see above), the rating 'correct' (√) was applied. Where it seemed that attention had been paid to the screen but where the evidence was not conclusive, the rating 'doubtful but permissible' (?P) was applied. Where the interpretation did not necessarily involve giving the screen at least some degree of attention (e.g. 'have the set on') or allowed the inclusion of periods when no attention was being given to the screen, the rating 'unduly different' (UD) was applied.

(c) 'television advertisements'. Where this reference was interpreted as intended (see above), it was rated 'correct' (√). Where the interpretation was limited to advertisements between programmes or to advertisements within programmes, it was rated as 'unduly limited' (UL). Where the interpretation was omitted altogether, the rating 'incorrect' (X) was applied.

(d) 'or do you do something else at that time'. Where this phrase was interpreted as intended (see above), the interpretation was rated 'correct' (√). The interpretations 'or do you switch off and do something else then', 'or do you get up and do something else then' were rated 'limited but permissible' (LP). Where the phrase was interpreted as 'or do you switch off', or as 'or do you get up and leave the room', the interpretations were rated 'unduly limited' (UL). Where the phrase was omitted altogether, the rating 'incorrect' (X) was applied.

The ratings allocated

Under the system described above, the following ratings were allocated to respondents' interpretations of this test question.

Table 7.22.1

Ratings allocated to respondents' interpretations
of test question (Q.21, III)

Lowest rating allocated to any part of the interpretation	Number of Ratings	Number of Persons	% of Persons
Correct (√)	13	13	24
Extra but permissible (ExP)	0		
Somewhat limited but permissible (LP)	0		
Somewhat too specific but permissible (SP)	0		
Somewhat too general but permissible (GP)	0	0	0
Somewhat extended but permissible (EP)	0		
Somewhat different but permissible (DP)	0		
Doubtful but permitted (?P)	16	16	30
Unduly limited (UL)	17		
Unduly general (UG)	0	23*	43
Unduly extended (UE)	4		
Unduly different (UD)	7		
Incorrect (X)	2	2	4
Total		54	†

*See Note A on page 47.
†See Note B on page 48.

273

Content analysis of the interpretations

There follows an analysis of the different interpretations of elements of the test question. The emphasis in this analysis is upon the different kinds of interpretations which were found rather than upon the number of them (though these numbers are given), the purpose of the content analysis being to discover the *kinds* of things that happen, to speculate about what causes them, and to derive hypotheses (about communications processes) for testing in later phases of the enquiry.

Interpretations of 'you'

The word 'you' was meant to be interpreted as 'you, yourself' and was not intended to include others (e.g. respondent's spouse, children, relatives, lodger(s)).

Summary of interpretations

Most respondents interpreted this term as intended, but there were a few (4) who interpreted it to include one or more members of the family as well.

Table 7.22.2

Interpretations of 'you'

Apparently interpreted as 'you, alone' (i.e. as intended)	50
You and your wife (2)/you and your husband (1)/you and your family (1)	4
Total	54

Speculative comment

The inclusion of others in the interpretation of 'you' could possibly spring out of viewing being a family or collective activity for the respondents concerned.

Interpretations of '(go on) watching (the screen)'

The reference 'watching (the screen)' was intended to mean attending to what is being shown on the screen or giving it at least some degree of attention.

Summary of interpretations

1 Most respondents (47/54) appeared to grasp this term as intended.

274

At the same time there was quite a lot of variability in the meaning that people gave to the word: watching attentively (22); giving the screen at least some degree of attention; looking but perhaps only casually; noticing the screen in an automatic (but not interested) way. We should note too that of these 47 people who appeared to grasp the term more or less as intended, there were 15 about whom the evidence was inconclusive.

2 The other seven of the 54 respondents misinterpreted the term (e.g. keep the set on, stay in the room with the set).

Table 7.22.3

Interpretations of '(go on) watching (the screen)'

Interpretations actually or possibly as intended

Watching attentively (or to that effect) (9)/attending to, giving attention to, deliberately looking (10)/watching with interest (3)	22
Keep eyes on screen/fixed on screen	2
Giving the screen at least some attention	2
Look at or watch screen, though not necessarily with full attention (3)/ though not necessarily with much attention (1)	4
Looking but perhaps only casually	1
Noticing the screen in an automatic (but not interested) way	1
Reference apparently interpreted as intended, but evidence not conclusive	15

47

Interpretations not as intended

Keep or have the set on (without necessarily looking at it)	5
Keep the set tuned to ... even if volume turned down	1
Stay in the room with the set on (without necessarily paying attention)	1
Did not grasp term (i.e. could be either 'keep set on' or 'attend to screen')	1
Total	54

7*

*Some respondents made more than one interpretation

Speculative comment

The present use of the term 'watching' is probably more definitive than were various uses of the term 'watch' in this inquiry (in that it was used in the context 'go on watching the screen') and this may account partly for the greater degree of success in communicating it on this occasion. Nonetheless, error and variability in this interpretation do occur.

Interpretations of 'television advertisements'

The reference 'television advertisements' was meant to refer to television advertisements generally, whether presented within or between programmes.

Summary of interpretations

1 Most respondents interpreted this reference as intended but there were 10 who limited it either to mean advertisements occurring between programmes (5) or advertisements that break into programmes (5).

2 Nobody appeared to overlook the reference altogether.

Table 7.22.4

Interpretations of 'television advertisements'

Television advertisements generally (i.e. as intended)	44
Those television advertisements that break into the middle of a programme	5
Those television advertisements that occur between programmes	5
Total	54

Interpretations of 'or do you do something else at that time'

The phrase 'or do you do something else at that time' was meant to refer to the respondent's own behaviour (i.e. mental and physical activities) during the time that the advertisements were being shown on the screen. Relevant behaviour would include behaviour either in the same room as the set or elsewhere, wherever the respondent might be.

Summary of interpretations

1 A majority understood this part of the question as intended, but there were 17 who either overlooked it (2) or misinterpreted it.

2 The misinterpretations were varied, as indicated in Table 7.22.5

Table 7.22.5

Interpretations of 'or do you do something else at that time'

Or do you do something else then		37
Or do you switch off and do something else then	3	
Or do you get up and do something else then	3	6
Or do you get up and leave the room then/go out then		3
Or do you switch off		6
Phrase apparently overlooked		2
Total		54

Speculative comment

The 15 misinterpretations could well make a difference to the respondent's eventual answer. Thus *'switching off* and doing something else'

276

is a much more definite action than simply 'doing something else', and a person who just 'did something else' might feel disqualified from choice of the second alternative (offered in the question) if he or she had interpreted the reference as *switching* off as well as doing something else.

Summary for full question

1 Of the 54 interpretations, 54 per cent were allocated an overall rating of either 'as intended' or 'permissible'. This compares with an average of 29 per cent for all the questions tested.

2 The different points of failure by some respondents included the following:

(a) interpreting 'you' to include family members (4);

(b) interpreting 'watching' as 'keeping the set on' (5);

(c) limiting consideration of 'television advertisements' to only those occurring between programmes or to only those occurring within programmes (10);

(d) limiting or converting the question 'do you do something else then' (e.g. do you get up and do something else then; do you go out then; do you switch off then) (15).

3 *Speculative comment*

Fewer misinterpreted 'watching' (in this question) than did so in other questions, and this may perhaps have sprung out of the present setting being the more definitive.

The actual wording of the question

'How many days of the week do you usually watch television?' Let them answer, then say 'I'm including Saturday and Sunday of course—does that make any difference?'

Definitions of the different parts of the question

The following are the intended meanings of key terms in the question. *However, as indicated below, some variants of the intended interpretations were regarded as permissible and others as possibly permissible.* The reference 'how many (days)' was meant to be interpreted as 'what is the number of days' (i.e. inviting a numerical answer). The reference 'days of the week' was meant to refer to all seven days and not solely to the period Monday to Friday. 'Days' was meant to refer to the whole of the day and not simply to 'evenings only' or to 'daytime only'. The word 'you' was meant to be interpreted as 'you, yourself' and was not intended to include others (e.g. respondent's spouse, children, relatives, lodger(s)). The word 'usually' was meant to be interpreted as 'ordinarily', 'in the ordinary course of events', 'commonly'. Other acceptable interpretations of the term were: 'as a rule', 'generally', 'normally', 'habitually', 'as a routine', 'almost always', 'mostly', 'typically'. The reference 'watch television' was intended to mean attend to whatever is being shown on the screen or to give it at least some degree of attention.

Respondents' interpretations of the question

These interpretations are set out in full in the Appendix (Part II). They are based upon the replies of 60 people.

Marking the interpretations

The system used for rating or marking respondents' interpretations of questions

The following marking or rating system was used.

1 If all elements of the question were interpreted as intended, the interpretation as a whole was rated 'fully as intended' (√).

2 Failure to interpret any significant element of the question fully as intended was sufficient to pull the total interpretation down below the level of 'fully as intended'. The level so reached was determined by the most seriously misinterpreted (significant) element in the test question. For example, if all but one of the significant elements of the question were interpreted as intended and the interpretation of that other element was rated as 'somewhat limited but permissible' (see below), then the whole interpretation was so rated (i.e. 'somewhat limited but permissible'). The reason for this is that a question cannot be regarded as a safe one unless all its parts are interpreted as intended.

3 If a significant element of the question was obviously and substantially misinterpreted or was omitted altogether, the total interpretation was marked 'incorrect' (X).

4 In the context of this system, the following ratings were made of specific elements of respondents' interpretations.

(a) 'how many (days)'. Where this reference was interpreted as intended (see above), the rating 'correct' (√) was applied. Where something was added to a permissible interpretation without losing the latter, the rating 'extra but permissible' (ExP) was applied (e.g. 'and on which'; 'and during what part of the day'). One respondent interpreted the reference as 'on what proportion of days' and this was rated 'different but permissible' (DP). Similarly for the interpretation 'with what frequency'. The following were rated 'unduly different' (UD): 'what has been the extent of your viewing'; 'how much (of the time the TV is avaialble)'. Where the term was omitted altogether, the rating 'incorrect' (X) was applied.

(b) 'days of the week'. Where this reference was interpreted as intended (see above), the interpretation was rated 'correct' (√). Where the respondent considered weekdays and weekend separately, giving a different answer for each, the rating 'different but permissible' (DP) was applied. Where the reference was interpreted in terms of 'summer only', the rating 'different but permissible' (DP) was also applied. The rating 'unduly limited' (UL) was applied to the following interpretations: 'excluding days when you do not view much'; 'counting only days when you regularly view at least something'. The same rating (UL) was applied where respondent limited his consideration to winter only/last winter, or where the reference was interpreted as 'evenings' only. Where the reference was interpreted as 'weekdays' only (i.e. Monday to Friday); or as a six-day period, the rating 'incorrect' (X) was applied. The rating 'incorrect' (X) was similarly applied where the term was omitted altogether.

(c) 'you'. Where this term was interpreted as intended (see above), the interpretation was rated 'correct' (√). Where it was interpreted as 'you and your family', or as 'you and some other(s)', the interpretation was rated as 'unduly extended' (UE). Where the respondent answered as if to the question 'is your set on', that interpretation was rated 'unduly different' (UD).

(d) 'usually', Where this term was interpreted as intended (see above), it was rated 'correct' (√). Similarly for the interpretations: 'in most weeks', 'for the average week', 'as for almost every week'. Where the interpretation was interpreted as 'taking an average over some weeks', it was rated as 'different but permissible' (DP). Where it was interpreted as 'taking a weekly average for the summer', the interpretation was rated 'unduly specific' (US). When the respondent considered which particular days he usually watched TV and totalled these, that interpretation was rated as 'incorrect' (X). Where the term was omitted altogether, the rating 'incorrect' (X) was applied.

(e) 'watch television'. Where this reference was interpreted as intended (see above), the rating 'correct' (√) was applied. Where it seemed that attention had been paid to the screen but where the evidence was not conclusive, the rating 'doubtful but permissible' (?P) was applied. Where the interpretation did not necessarily involve giving the screen at least some degree of attention (e.g. 'had the set on'), the rating 'unduly different' (UD) was applied.

The ratings allocated

Under the system described above, the following ratings were allocated to respondents' interpretations of this test question.

Table 7.23.1

Ratings allocated to respondents' interpretations of test question (Q.4, IV)

Lowest rating allocated to any part of the interpretation	Number of Ratings	Number of Persons	% of Persons
Correct (√)	13	13	22
Extra but permissible (ExP)	3		
Somewhat limited but permissible (LP)	0		
Somewhat too specific but permissible (SP)	0	6*	10
Somewhat too general but permissible (GP)	0		
Somewhat extended but permissible (EP)	0		
Somewhat different but permissible (DP)	4		
Doubtful but permitted (?P)	5	5	8
Unduly limited (UL)	19		
Unduly general (UG)	0	28*	47
Unduly extended (UE)	7		
Unduly different (UD)	7		
Incorrect (X)	8	8	13
Total		60	100

*See Note A on page 47.

Content analysis of the interpretations

There follows an analysis of the different interpretations of elements of the test question. The emphasis in this analysis is upon the different *kinds* of interpretations which are found rather than upon the number of them (though these numbers are given), the purpose of a content analysis being to discover the *kinds* of things that happen, to speculate about what causes them, and to derive hypotheses (about communication processes) for testing in later phases of the enquiry.

Interpretations of 'how many (days)'

The reference 'how many (days)' was meant to be interpreted as 'what is the number of (days)' (i.e. inviting a numerical answer).

Summary of interpretations

1 Almost all the respondents (56/60) interpreted the phrase as intended. Of the whole 60, a few added extra (i.e. not asked for) details to

their replies.

2 The four deviant interpretations allowed for replies other than some number of days.

Table 7.23.2

Interpretations of 'how many (days)'

How many (51)/roughly how many (3)	54
On how many (days) and on which (1)/during what parts (of the day) and on how many (1)	2
	56
On what proportion (of days)	1
Over how much of the time that television is available	1
What has been the extent (of viewing)	1
With what frequency and when	1
Total	60

Speculative comment

It seems possible on the evidence available, that some of the four deviant cases adapted the interpretation to fit their rather irregular viewing behaviour.

Interpretations of 'days of the week ... including Saturdays and Sundays'

The reference 'days of the week' was meant to refer to all seven days and not solely to the period Monday to Friday. 'Days' was meant to refer to the whole day and not simply to 'evenings only' or to 'daytime only'.

Summary of interpretations

Thirty-four of the 60 respondents interpreted this reference fully as intended. The remaining 26 went wrong in one or more of the following ways.

(a)   They did not consider all seven days of the week (5 cases);

(b)   They considered evenings only, excluding viewing in earlier part of the day (18 cases);

(c)   They excluded some weeks or seasons or some special days from their considerations (14 cases).

282

Table 7.23.3

Interpretations of 'days of the week ... including Saturdays and Sundays'

1 *Was the phrase interpreted fully as intended?*			
Yes 34	No 26		(Total = 60)

2 *Did respondent consider all seven days of the week?*

Yes, all seven	55
Five weekdays only	3
Five weekdays plus Saturday	1
Considered' any one evening'	1
Total	60

3 *Did respondent wrongly limit consideration to certain parts of the day?*

No, respondent considered whole day	42
Respondent considered evenings only	18
Total	60

4 *Did respondent exclude certain days, weeks or seasons from consideration?*

No special days or weeks or seasons excluded	48
Counting only days when you regularly view at least something	1
Excluding days when you don't view much (i.e. less than half an hour, only a few minutes, only for the news)	4
Counting only weeks when you are at home every night	5
Counting winter only/last winter only	3
Counting summer only	1
Respondent interpreted phrase as 'any one evening'	1
Total	63*

5 *Other interpretations of note (3 cases)*

Considered the 5 weekdays and 2 days of the weekend separetely	1
Considered each of the 7 days/evenings separately	2

*Several respondents applied more than one exclusion of this kind.

Speculative comment

1 One possible reason for the exclusion (by some) of Saturday and Sunday is that the several respondents concerned heard 'including' as 'excluding'. Then again, some respondents may have already begun working out a reply before the interviewer started to read out this qualification.

2 There were 18 people who did not consider periods of the day other than evenings. It seems unlikely that this was due, for so many, to a mishearing of the question.

3 The fact that 14 people excluded from consideration certain weeks, seasons and particular days is also noteworthy: 4 respondents, it will

be remembered, did not consider days when they did less than some minimum of viewing; 5 persons kept out of consideration weeks when they were not at home each night; 4 limited themselves to certain seasons. Between them, and on the basis of the evidence available, these omissions suggest one or more of the following processes: a tendency to overlook 'hard to sum up' details and to stick to a simpler pattern of behaviour if possible; a tendency in some to try to 'do justice' to themselves and/or to the question (e.g. by overlooking periods when they did little or no viewing); a tendency in some to avoid looking like TV addicts (i.e. as might seem to be so if they counted days on which they did but little viewing).

Interpretations of 'you'

The word 'you' was meant to be interpreted as 'you, yourself' and was not intended to include others (e.g. respondent's spouse, children, relatives, lodger(s)).

Summary of interpretations

Fourteen of the 60 interpreted this term in such a way that viewing by other members of the family was or could have been included in the count.

Table 7.23.4

Interpretations of 'you'

You, yourself (alone)		46
You and your wife (4)/you and your husband (2)	6	
You and one or more of your family	1	8
You and your friend	1	
The set is turned on (so 'you' possibly not considered)		5
At least someone in your family (not necessarily 'you')		1
Total		60

Speculative comment

As a good deal of viewing takes place as joint viewing by the family, it may well be easier to think in terms of 'when the set is turned on', or it may come naturally to think of 'you' as 'any of you'.

Interpretations of 'usually'

The word 'usually' was meant to be interpreted as 'ordinarily', 'in the ordinary course of events', 'commonly'. Other acceptable interpretations of the term were: 'as a rule', 'generally', 'normally', 'habitually', 'as a routine', 'almost always', 'mostly', 'typically'.

Summary of interpretations.

Forty-eight of the respondents interpreted the term 'usually' either as intended or approximately as intended (e.g. normal, typical, almost every, most). Most of the rest of the interpretations were in terms of taking an average for a week, though some of these put a special limitation on the weeks from which that average might be calculated (e.g. in the summertime, in the last six months, in the weeks when you don't go out).

Table 7.23.5
Interpretations of 'usually'

Usually (i.e. apparently as intended) (41)/usual (for you) (2)/ (in the) usual (week) (1)	44
(In a) normal (week) (1)/(In a) typical (week) (1)/most (weeks) (1)/ almost every (week) (1)	4
For the average (week)	1
Taking a (weekly) average (2)/rough (weekly) average (2) 4	
Taking a (weekly) average for summertime (1)/(weekly) average over the last six months (1)/(weekly) average for the weeks you don't go out (1) 3	7
At least sometimes	1
Term apparently not considered	3
Total	60

Interpretations of 'watch television'

This reference 'watch television' was intended to mean attend to whatever is being shown on the screen or to give it at least some degree of attention.

Summary of interpretations

Whereas over 50 of the respondents appear to have interpreted the term as intended, there were 5 who thought only in terms of whether or not the set was turned on.

Table 7.23.6

Interpretations of 'watch television'

Did respondent interpret 'watch' as 'paying at least some attention'

Watch with at least some attention (42)/look at the screen with at least some attention (1)/might watch with at least some attention (1)/free to watch with at least some attention (1)	45	
Interpretation of 'watch' not fully established, but no reason for thinking other than 'with at least some attention'	9	54
TV set turned on (and so respondent possibly included times when no attention was being paid)		5
Not clear whether or not respondent considered paying attention		1
Total		60

Some other interpretations of 'watch television' (3 cases)

Watch at least something on television	1
Watch at least for the news	1
(The extent of) the viewing which (you) have done	1

Some speculative comments

Interpretation solely in terms of the set being on (5 cases) may have sprung out of those respondents being the only ones who watched the set concerned. But it is also possible that some of these five thought about the family and themselves collectively.

Some other interpretations of interest

Four respondents added to the question as shown in Table 7.23.7.

Table 7.23.7

Other interpretations of interest

Additions to the question (4 cases)

'And how does your summer time viewing compare with this?'	2
'And with what exceptions'	1
'If you wish to do so'	1
Total	4

Summary for the full question

1 Of the 60 interpretations of this question, 40 per cent were allocated an overall rating of either 'as intended' or 'permissible'. This compares with an average of 29 per cent for all of the questions tested.

2 Some of the points of failure were as follows.

286

(a) Some respondents (14) excluded from consideration some weeks, or some seasons, or certain days (e.g. days when you don't view much, counting only days when you regularly view, counting only weeks when you are home every night, counting winter only).

(b) Quite a lot of respondents (18) wrongly limited their consideration to evening viewing only.

(c) Some did not consider all seven days of the week in spite of a specific instruction to do so (5).

(d) Some respondents (8) interpreted 'you' as including one or more persons in addition to themselves (mainly family members) and others (5) partly bypassed the term by thinking only of whether or not the set was on.

(e) In dealing with the word 'usually', 7 thought in terms of an average calculated over some weeks.

(f) For a few people (5), 'watch television' became 'the set turned on'.

3 On the other hand, there was a high degree of success in communicating the term 'how many'.

4 *Speculative comments*

(a) The exclusion (by 14 respondents) of certain days or weeks or seasons may possibly have sprung out of: a tendency to eliminate factors or situations that would make it hard to work out a reply; a tendency to avoid looking like an addict (i.e. ruling out days when but little viewing was done); a tendency by respondents to try to give the interviewer a not atypical picture of their viewing.

(b) Since viewing often just occurs in one's presence, it may be difficult for that person to determine how much was his own viewing and how much was that of someone else in the family. Such a difficulty might lie behind the collective interpretation of 'you' (by some respondents) and the vague interpretation of 'watch' by others.

(c) The request for 'usual' behaviour may have posed special difficulties for respondents with no usual pattern of viewing during the week—and so may have forced some into trying to calculate an average. On the other hand the people who interpreted 'usually' as average may quite sincerely have thought of these two terms as equivalent.

7.24   QUESTION 8, QUESTIONNAIRE IV

The wording of the question

'Do you use weekly printed programmes regularly when deciding what to view?' (To be coded: yes/no/not sure.)

Check question

If 'yes': 'Which ones do you use?' If 'no': 'How do you decide, then?'

Definitions of the different parts of the question

The following are the intended meanings of key terms in the question. *However, as indicated below, some variants of the intended interpretations were regarded as permissible and others as possibly permissible.* The word 'you' was meant to be interpreted as 'you, yourself' and was not intended to include others (e.g. respondent's spouse, children, relatives, lodger(s)). In the present context the word 'use' was meant to be interpreted as 'make reference to (weekly printed material)', or 'look up (programmes in weekly printed material)'. The reference 'weekly printed programmes' was intended to mean publications containing printed information about available programmes for a full week (e.g. *Radio Times* and *TV Times*). The reference was not intended to mean newspaper lists presenting programmes available for a single day or for less than a full week. The word 'regularly' means 'recurring uniformly' and acceptable definitions included 'each day', 'each week', 'every time the TV set is turned on'. The phrase 'when deciding what to view' was meant to be interpreted as 'when selecting programmes for viewing, or making up one's mind to view particular programme material'. This phrase could be related to selections made several times daily, or made each week in order to plan ahead for the whole week.

288

Respondents' interpretations of the question

These interpretations are set out in full in the Appendix (Part II). They are based upon the replies of 56 people.

Marking the interpretations

The system used for rating or marking respondents' interpretations of questions

The following marking or rating system was used.

1 If all elements of the question were interpreted as intended, the interpretation as a whole was rated 'fully as intended' (✓).

2 Failure to interpret any significant element of the question fully as intended was sufficient to pull the total interpretation down below the level of 'fully as intended'. The level so reached was determined by the most seriously misinterpreted (significant) element in the test question. For example, if all but one of the significant elements of the question were interpreted as intended and the interpretation of that other element was rated as 'somewhat limited but permissible' (see below), then the whole interpretation was so rated (i.e. 'somewhat limited but permissible'). The reason for this is that a question cannot be regarded as a safe one unless all its parts are interpreted as intended.

3 If a significant element of the question was obviously and substantially misinterpreted or was omitted altogether, the total interpretation was marked 'incorrect' (X).

4 In the context of this system, the following ratings were made of specific elements of respondents' interpretations.

(a) 'you'. Where this term was interpreted as intended (see above), the interpretation was rated 'correct' (✓). Where it was interpreted as 'you and your family', or as 'you and some other(s)', the interpretation was rated as 'unduly extended' (UE).

(b) 'use'. Where this term was interpreted as intended (see above), it was rated 'correct' (✓). When it was interpreted as 'look at', the interpretation was rated 'different but permissible' (DP). Where it was interpreted as 'buy', 'take', 'get', it was rated as 'unduly different' (UD). Where it was interpreted as 'buy and use', 'take and use', or 'get and use', or 'take and look at', the interpretation was rated as 'unduly extended (UE).

(c) 'weekly printed programmes'. Where this reference was interpreted as intended (see above), the interpretation was rated 'correct' (√). Where the reference was interpreted as 'daily printed programme lists (i.e. showing programmes available for just one day)', the interpretation was rated 'incorrect' (X). Similarly, where it was interpreted as 'information about a particular programme in the weekly papers', the interpretation was also rated 'incorrect' (X). Where the reference was interpreted as the *Radio Times* only, or as the *TV Times* only, the interpretation was rated 'limited but permissible' (LP).

(d) 'regularly'. Where this term was interpreted as intended, it was rated 'correct' (√). Where it was interpreted as 'usually' or 'ordinarily' the interpretation was rated 'different but permissible' (DP). Where it was interpreted as 'in the course of every week', the interpretation was similarly rated (DP). Where the term was not considered at all, the rating 'incorrect' (X) was applied. Where it seemed that a permissible interpretation had been made, but where the evidence was not conclusive, the rating 'doubtful but permissible' (?P) was applied.

(e) 'when deciding what to view'. Where this phrase was interpreted as intended, the interpretation was rated 'correct' (√). Where it was interpreted as 'to find out what programmes are showing on the following week' or as 'to decide if there is anything you particularly want to view', the interpretation was rated 'somewhat different from intended but permissible' (DP). Where the phrase was interpreted as 'to plan your activities during the following week according to the programmes that are on television', the interpretation was rated 'unduly different' (UD). Where the phrase was omitted altogether, the rating 'incorrect' (X) was applied.

The ratings allocated

Under the system described above, the following ratings were allocated to respondent interpretations of this test question.

Table 7.24.1

Ratings allocated to respondents' interpretations of test question (Q8, IV)

Lowest rating allocated to any part of the interpretation	Number of Ratings	Number of Persons	% of Persons
Correct (√)	4	4	7
Extra but permissible (ExP)	0		
Somewhat limited but permissible (LP)	0		
Somewhat too specific but permissible (SP)	0	1	2
Somewhat too general but permissible (GP)	0		
Somewhat extended but permissible (EP)	0		
Somewhat different but permissible (DP)	1		
Doubtful but permitted (?P)	1	1	2
Unduly limited (UL)	0		
Unduly general (UG)	0	11	20
Unduly extended (UE)	5		
Unduly different (UD)	6		
Incorrect (X)	39	39	70
Total		56	†

†See Note B on page 48.

Content analysis of the interpretations

There follows an analysis of the different interpretations of elements of the test question. The emphasis in this analysis is upon the different kinds of interpretations which were found rather than upon the number of them (though these numbers are given), the purpose of the content analysis being to discover the *kinds* of things that happen, to speculate about what causes them, and to derive hypotheses (about communication processes) for testing in later phases of the enquiry.

Interpretations of 'you'

The word 'you' was meant to be interpreted as 'you, yourself' and was not intended to include others (e.g. respondent's spouse, children, relatives, lodger(s)).

Summary of interpretations

Practically all respondents appear to have answered for themselves alone.

However, 3 of the 56 included other family member(s) in replying.

Table 7.24.2
Interpretations of 'you'

You, alone (i.e. term apparently interpreted as intended)	53
You or your family	1 ⎫
You or your wife	1 ⎬ 3
You and your husband	1 ⎭
Total	56

Speculative comment

The inclusion of one or more family members may possibly stem out of viewing decisions quite often being a family matter.

Interpretations of the term 'use'

In the present context, the word 'use' was meant to be interpreted as 'make reference to (weekly printed material)', or 'look up (programmes in weekly printed material)'.

Summary of interpretations

Sixteen of the 56 extended the term to include buying or taking, while another 10 converted it to 'buy' or 'take' or 'get'.

Table 7.24.3
Interpretations of 'use'

Use or make use of (29)/look at (1)	30
Buy and use (4)/take and use (4)/get and use (1)/take and look through (1)	10
Buy (11)/take (4)/get (1)	16
Total	56

Speculative comment

The extension of the term 'use' to include 'buying' or 'taking' could sell lead to an under-estimate of use, while the conversion of the concept 'use' to 'buy or take or get' could well lead to the elimination of viewers who are not the ones responsible for securing it.

Interpretations of 'weekly printed programmes'

The reference 'weekly printed programmes' was intended to mean publications containing printed information about available programmes for

292

a full week (e.g. *Radio Times* and *TV Times*). The reference was not intended to mean newspaper lists presenting programmes available for a single day or for less than a full week.

Summary of interpretations

'Weekly printed programmes' were thought of in three main ways:

(a)   the *Radio Times* and *TV Times* type of weekly programme paper (35 of the 56 respondents);

(b)   printed programmes of any kind, whether daily or weekly issued (15); programme lists in newspapers only (daily or Sunday (5).

(c)   programme lists in newspapers only (daily or Sunday)(5).

Quite a lot of the respondents appeared to have overlooked the restraining word 'weekly'.

Table 7.24.4

Interpretations of 'weekly printed programmes'

Programme information in weekly papers	1	*TV Times*	1	
		Weekly printed programmes such as *TV Times*	1	} 2
Radio Times and *TV Times*	11			
Radio Times or *TV Times*	13	Printed programmes of any kind	5	
Official or published programmes (i.e. *Radio* and *TV Times*	2 } 28	Any printed programmes (e.g. in daily newspapers, *Radio Times* or *TV Times*	10	} 15
Printed programmes such as *Radio Times* and *TV Times*	1			
Any weekly TV booklet	1			
Radio Times	2	Printed programmes in newspapers	1	
Weekly printed programmes such as *Radio Times*	3 } 5	Printed programmes in daily newspapers	2 } 5	
		Printed programmes in daily or Sunday newspapers	2	

Speculative comment

1 The concept 'weekly printed programmes' is a complex one and perhaps it is not surprising that the restricting word 'weekday' should have been lost to some of the respondents.

2 It seems possible that many respondents thought automatically of only those printed materials to which they ordinarily or usually went when seeking aids to programme selection—and that this swamped out the actual details of that part of the question.

Interpretations of 'regularly'

The word 'regularly' means 'recurring uniformly' and acceptable definitions included 'each day', 'each week', 'every time the TV set is turned on'.

Summary of interpretations

About a third of the respondents appear to have omitted this concept altogether. Most of the others (29/36) interpreted the term to mean 'recurring uniformly', though there were variations in terms of the frequency of this 'uniform recurrence'. Thus 10 thought in terms of each week, 9 in terms of each day, 2 in terms of 'whenever deciding what to view', and 2 more as weekly for buying and daily for using. Finally, there were 7 who interpreted the word 'regularly' in a somewhat loose fashion, namely 'usually' or 'ordinarily'.

Table 7.24.5

Interpretations of 'regularly'

Regularly (4)/(make) regular (use of) (2)	6
Weekly (2)/each week (4)/every week (2)/once a week (1)/in the course of every week	10
Daily (3)/each day (5)/every evening (1)	9
(Buy) every week and (use) each day 1 ⎱ (Buy) each week and (use) whenever (you use your set) 1 ⎰	2
Usually (6)/ordinarily (1)	7
Whenever (deciding what to view)	2
No reference to the concept	20

Speculative comment

1 Whether a respondent had interpreted the term 'regularly' as 'weekly' or as 'daily' appeared to depend to some extent upon his interpretation of the word 'use'. Thus those who converted the term into 'taking' or 'buying' tended to think of 'regularly' in terms of 'weekly', whereas those who interpreted 'use' as 'look at', were more likely to interpret 'regularly' as 'daily'.

2 Since the specific interpretation of 'regularly' seems to depend upon the respondent properly grasping other elements of the question, it seems better to avoid using it at all, substituting for it the precise concept actually intended.

Interpretations of 'when deciding what to view'

The phrase 'when deciding what to view' was meant to be interpreted as 'when selecting programmes for viewing, or making up one's mind to view particular programme material'. This phrase could be related to selections made several times daily, or made each week in order to plan ahead for the whole week.

Summary of interpretations

Seven of the 56 respondents appear to have overlooked this part of the question. Of the rest, most grasped it more or less as intended, though even so, there was some degree of variation: when deciding; in deciding; to help you decide; to plan (a week's viewing); to see what will be on.

Table 7.24.6

Interpretations of 'when deciding what to view'

When deciding what to view (21)/whenever deciding (2)	23
In deciding what to view (2)/for deciding (6)/in order to decide (4)/ so that you can decide (1)/for reaching decisions about (1)/to help you decide (2)/to help you select (1)/for selecting (1)/in choosing (1)/ for programme selection when you use the TV set (1)	20
To plan a week's viewing (2)/to plan your viewing for the following week (1)	3
To see what programmes will be on during the following week (1)/to find out what is being shown (1)	2
To decide if there is anything you particularly want to view	1
No reference to the term	7

Speculative comment

The evidence points to personal variability in the interpretation process, much of the variability seemingly stemming out of a tendency for the respondent to reshape this part of the question to fit his own (usual) selecting behaviour.

Summary for the full question

1 Of the 56 interpretations of this question, 11 per cent were allocated an overall rating of 'as intended' or 'permissible'. This compares with an average of 29 per cent for all the questions tested.

2 The main points of difficulty in this question were as follows:

(a)   Sixteen of the 56 extended the term 'use' to include buying or taking (i.e. as well as 'using') while 10 more converted it to 'buying' or 'taking' or 'getting'.

(b)   For most respondents, the weekly printed paper reference was interpreted in one of three different ways: the *Radio Times* and *TV Times* type of weekly paper (35 cases); printed programmes of any kind, whether daily or weekly used (15); programme lists in newspapers only (daily or Sunday) (5). Many of the respondents appear to have overlooked the restricting word 'weekly'.

(c)   About a third appeared to overlook the concept 'regularly', but most of the rest (29/36) interpreted it to mean 'recurring uniformly'—though there were variations in the frequency of this 'uniform recurrence'.

3 Other noteworthy points were as follows:

(a)   Several people (3) interpreted 'you' collectively (i.e. to include member(s) of respondent's family).

(b)   Though it occurred within permissible limits, there was a high degree of variability in respondent interpretation of references such as: 'weekly printed programmes'; 'regularly'; 'when deciding what to view'.

4 *Speculative comments*

(a)   It seems possible that in thinking about particular programmes, many respondents went automatically to the source they ordinarily used and that this process overrode the source indicated by the question.

(b)   Respondents who thought in terms of weekly printed programmes tended also to think of 'regularly' as 'weekly recurrent', whilst those thinking of daily papers tended to think of 'regularly' as 'daily recurrent'.

7.25 QUESTION 14, QUESTIONNAIRE IV

The wording of the question

'Thinking about television over the last few years, do you think that programmes are better nowadays or do you think that they are worse than they were?' (To be coded: better now/worse now/some better some worse/the same/no opinion or not sure.)

Check question

'Why do you think so?'

Definition of the different parts of the question

The following are the intended meanings of key terms in the question. *However, as indicated below, some variants of the intended interpretations were regarded as permissible and others as possibly permissible.* The phrase 'thinking about television' was meant to be interpreted as 'considering television output generally', and was not meant to be limited to some single narrow aspect of television. The phrase 'over the last (few) years' was meant to cover the whole of the period referred to, and not just to isolated occasions within it. The term ... 'few' was meant to refer to an immediately preceding period of at least three years but not more than six years duration. The word 'you' was meant to be interpreted as 'you, yourself' and was not intended to include others (e.g. respondent's spouse, children, relatives, lodger(s)). The word 'programmes' was intended to refer to television programmes in general, both ITV and BBC. The reference 'better' ... or 'worse' was intended to elicit consideration of whether programmes had improved or deteriorated (i.e. both) over the last few years. Interpretation of the phrase 'than they were' is probably closely related to the interpretation of the opening phrase 'thinking about television over the last few years', in that this phrase was intended to set the scene for the requested comparison of television programmes now and as they were.

Respondents' interpretations of the question

These interpretations are set out in full in the Appendix (Part II). They are based upon the replies of 59 people.

Marking the interpretations

The system used for rating or marking respondents' interpretations of questions

The following marking or rating system was used.

1 If all elements of the question were interpreted as intended, the interpretation as a whole was rated 'fully as intended' (√).

2 Failure to interpret any significant element of the question fully as intended was sufficient to pull the total interpretation down below the level of 'fully as intended'. The level so reached was determined by the most seriously misinterpreted (significant) element in the test question. For example, if all but one of the significant elements of the question were interpreted as intended and the interpretation of that other element was rated as 'somewhat limited but permissible' (see below), then the whole interpretation was so rated (i.e. 'somewhat limited but permissible'). The reason for this is that a question cannot be regarded as a safe one unless all its parts are interpreted as intended.

3 If a significant element of the question was obviously and substantially misinterpreted or was omitted altogether, the total interpretation was marked 'incorrect' (X).

4 In the context of this system, the following ratings were made of specific elements of respondents' interpretations.

(a) 'thinking about television'. Where this reference was interpreted as intended (see above), the interpretation was rated 'correct' (√). Where some broad, general interpretation had been made (e.g. 'general quality of programmes'), this interpretation was regarded as acceptable. Interpretations which considered a single narrow aspect of television output (e.g. 'maturity of programmes', 'realism in programmes', 'the ability of actors') were rated 'unduly limited' (UL). Where an interpretation took into account at least two such limited aspects of television, the rating 'limited but permissible' (LP) was applied. Where consideration was based on the availability of certain specified programmes (e.g. 'travel and documentary programmes'), the interpretations were rated 'unduly limited' (UL). The interpretation 'unavailability of favourite programmes when being rested in summer' was rated 'incorrect' (X). Where it seemed that the inten-

298

ded interpretation had been made, but where the evidence was not conclusive, the rating 'doubtful but permissible' (?P) was applied.

(b) 'over the last (few) years'. Where this reference was interpreted as intended (see above), the interpretation was rated 'correct' (√). Where the reference was interpreted as 'up to ... years ago', it was not possible to say how much of the total period the respondent was considering, though if the maximum span possible was in the permissible range (as indicated above) the rating 'doubtful but permissible' (?P) was applied. Where an interpretation indicated a particular point in the past and compared this with the present (clearly without any 'span' concept), the rating 'different but permissible' (DP) was applied. The interpretations 'in the past' and 'used to be' were rated 'unduly general' (UG). Where the interpretation was omitted altogether, the rating 'incorrect' (X) was applied.

(c) 'few'. Where this term was interpreted as intended (see above), the interpretation was rated 'correct' (√). Where the time period considered was between one and two years the rating 'limited but permissible' (LP) was applied. Where the period considered was less than a year, the rating 'unduly limited' (UL) was applied. Where the period considered was from seven to ten years, the rating 'extended but permissible' (EP) was applied. Where the reference was interpreted as more than ten years, the rating 'unduly extended' (UE) was applied. The interpretation 'last winter' was rated 'unduly different' (UD), and 'in the past', 'used to be', were rated 'unduly general (UG). Where the interpretation was omitted altogether, the rating 'incorrect' (X) was applied.

(d) 'you'. Where this term was interpreted as intended (see above), the interpretation was rated 'correct' (√). Where it seemed that a permissible interpretation had been made, but where the evidence was not conclusive, the rating 'doubtful but permissible' (?P) was applied.

(e) 'programmes'. Where this term was interpreted as intended (see above), the interpretation was rated 'correct' (√). Where the term was interpreted more broadly as 'television service/output', such interpretations were rated 'somewhat general but permissible' (GP). Where the interpretation was made in terms of programmes on BBC television only, or in terms of programmes on ITV only, that interpretation was rated 'unduly limited' (UL). Where the term was interpreted as referring mainly (but not solely) to programmes on either of the BBC or the ITV channels, this interpretation was rated 'limited but permissible' (LP). Where the term was interpreted as 'one particular type of programme' only (e.g. 'plays') or as 'specific programmes' (e.g. 'Sunday Night at the London Palladium'), the interpretation was rated 'unduly limited' (UL). Where the term was interpreted as more than one type of programme (e.g. plays, medical and scientific programmes), it was rated 'limited but permissible' (LP).

(f)   'better ... or worse'. Where this reference was interpreted as intended (see above), both alternatives being considered, the interpretation was rated 'correct' (√). Where the interpretation took only 'better' into consideration, it was rated 'unduly limited' (UL). Where the interpretation was not in terms of 'better or worse' but in terms of something else (e.g. seasonal variation or change), it was rated 'unduly different' (UD).

The ratings allocated

Under the system described above, the following ratings were allocated to respondent interpretations of this test question.

Table 7.25.1
Ratings allocated to respondents' interpretations of test question (Q14, IV)

Lowest rating allocated to any part of the interpretation	Number of Ratings	Persons	% of Persons
Correct (√)	0	0	0
Extra but permissible (ExP)	0		
Somewhat limited but permissible (LP)	5		
Somewhat too specific but permissible (SP)	0		
Somewhat too general but permissible (GP)	0	6*	10
Somewhat extended but permissible (EP)	1		
Somewhat different but permissible (DP)	4		
Doubtful but permitted (?P)	20	20	34
Unduly limited (UL)	23		
Unduly general (UG)	2		
Unduly extended (UE)	11	32*	54
Unduly different (UD)	3		
Incorrect (X)	1	1	2
Total	59		100

*See Note A on page 47.

Content analysis of the interpretations

There follows an analysis of the different interpretations of elements
300

of the test question. The emphasis in this analysis is upon the different kinds of interpretations which were found rather than upon the number of them (though these numbers are given), the purpose of the content analysis being to discover the kinds of things that happen, to speculate about what causes them, and to derive hypotheses (about communication processes) for testing in later phases of the enquiry.

Interpretations of 'thinking about television'

This phrase was meant to be interpreted as 'considering television generally', and was not meant to be limited to some single narrow aspect of television.

Summary of interpretations

1 In reaching their judgements about television programmes, different respondents had markedly different criteria in mind. Thus some judged in terms of variety or choice of programmes offering, some in terms of the professionalism of production, some in terms of 'quality', some in terms of the maturity/intelligence of the programmes available. Other criteria used included: goodness of content or story; interestingness; liveliness; ability of actors and artists; the form and treatment of the programme; use of new talents and new ideas. Some respondents were judging in terms of more than one such criteria (the 59 offered 86 criteria between them) but many of them had only one criterion in mind. Accordingly, the outstanding feature of this aspect of the findings is that a respondent might be thinking in terms of any one of many different criteria in reaching a judgment (about programmes being better or worse) and that this could occur without the basic selectivity of the process being in any way evident from the answers.

2 For nine of the respondents, it was not clear just what criteria if any were being used.

Table 7.25.2

Criteria used in 'thinking about television'

The standard of television output	2	Realism	2
General quality of programmes	11	Suspense	1
Professionalism of production/		Ability of actors/artists	5
techniques	8	Form of programme/treatment	5
Variety of programmes offered/		Simplicity of statement	1
choice of programmes	11	Maturity/intelligence	5
Number of repeats	1	Number of travel and documen-	
Interestingness of programmes	11	tary programmes	1
Entertainment value/humour	3	The unavailability of favourites	
Enjoyment	3	when being rested in the	
Content of programmes/story	10	summer	1
Liveliness/use of new talent and		Personal experience	1
new ideas	5	Not clear what criteria were used	9
			96*

*Some respondents used more than one criterion and so the totals in categories exceed the number of respondents.

Speculative comment

This appears to be another example of a narrowing or selection tendency and in this instance it is a marked one. The evidence may well constitute a case for studying the mechanisms whereby people select aspects of an issue in terms of which to make judgments or ratings.

Interpretations of the phrase 'over the last (few years)'

This phrase was meant to cover the whole of the period referred to and not just isolated occasions within it.

Summary of interpretations

1 A few people interpreted this reference to mean the whole of some past period, but the majority interpreted it more loosely. Thus over 40 of the 59 interpreted it as 'within' a period going back as far as ...', without necessarily considering all of that period and leaving open to doubt just what part of it they were considering.

2 A few qualified this interpretation in terms of how long they had had a set. One chose as a starting time the beginning of ITV programming (in order to base the comparison on both ITV and BBC). One odd interpretation was in terms of 'last winter' (when that person's favourite programme was available).

Table 7.25.3

Interpretations of 'over the last (few) years'

Over the last (few) years	4 ⎰	
Over about the last (few) years	2 ⎱	6
Over the last (few) years you have had a set		1
*In the past (i.e. up to (a few) years ago)	33 ⎫	
*In the past (i.e. up to (a few) years ago) when you first got a set/ became a viewer)	7 ⎬	41
*In the past (i.e. in the period up to the start of ITV)	1 ⎭	
*In the past (i.e. (a few) years ago)	4 ⎰	
*When you first got a set (i.e. (a few years ago))	2 ⎱	6
*Before ITV started		1
*In about (1947)		1
*Last winter (when your favourite programme was available)		1
*In the past (not further defined)	1 ⎰	
*Used to be (not further defined)	1 ⎱	2
Total		59

*The respondent may have overlooked the phrase 'over the last (few) years' and picked up this meaning from a later element of the question, but this is not certain.

The reference itself (i.e. 'over the last') appears to be rather vague in its implications and to have given respondents scope for varied interpretations. Presumably it should be used only when differences of the kind found here do not matter to the sense of the question.

Interpretations of the word 'few'

The term 'few' was meant to refer to an immediately preceding period of at least three years but not of more than six years duration.

Summary of interpretations

As shown in Table 7.25.4 below, there was a strikingly wide interpretation of the term 'few': 7 out of 59 interpreted it as 2 years or less, 19 as 7 years or more and 11 as 10 years or more.

Table 7.25.4

Interpretations of 'few'

1 (year)	2	7 (years)	3	More than 8 (years)	1	
2 (years	5	8 (years)	3	Couple (of years)	1	
2–3 (years)	2	9 (years)	1	Several (years)	1	4
3 (years)	6	10 (years)	3	A few (years)	2	
4 (years)	2	11 (years)	3	Last winter	1	
5 (years)	5 {25}	12 (years)	2 {12}	In the past	1	
5–6 (years)	1	13 (years)	1	Term omitted	2	
6 (years)	9	14 (years)	1	Total	59	
		16 (years)	1			

Speculative comment

In possible explanation of this finding, it is worth noting that the term 'few' is itself both vague (it has no numerical equivalent in the dictionary) and relative (e g. to an old person, 10 years may seem but a 'few' years). The important thing for the research worker is to realise that the term can have such breadth of numerical meaning.

Interpretations of the word 'you'

The word 'you' was meant to be interpreted as 'you, yourself' and was not intended to include others as well (e.g. respondent's spouse, children, relatives, lodger(s)).

Summary of interpretations

There was no evidence that this term had been misinterpreted, though a full probe into the meaning given it by respondents was not made in this case.

Table 7.25.5

Interpretations of 'you'

Respondent appeared to have interpreted the word 'you' as intended (i.e. 'you, yourself, only')	59*

*Whereas the intensive interview yielded information about respondent interpretations of the word 'you', such interpretations were not made the subject of direct and focused probing (as was done for this word in some other of the test questions). Accordingly, all defective interpretations of the word in its present context have not necessarily been picked up.

Interpretations of the word 'programmes'

This term was intended to refer to television programmes in general, both ITV and BBC.

Summary of the evidence

A majority appears to have answered in terms of television programmes in general. Nonetheless a sizeable minority interpreted the term much more narrowly, for example: 'BBC programmes only'; 'ITV programmes only'; 'specific types of programmes'; 'a particular programme'.

Table 7.25.6

Interpretations of the word 'programmes'

BBC programmes	5	
Mainly BBC programmes	2	
Types of BBC programmes that you watch	1	9
Particular types of BBC programmes (e.g. scientific, medical, plays)	1	
ITV programmes	3	
ITV programmes with which you are familiar	1	7
Particular types of ITV programmes (e.g. plays, variety, fiction)	2	
Specific ITV programmes (e.g. 'Sunday Night at the Palladium)	1	
Programmes in general without reference to BBC or ITV	35	
Programmes that you watch	1	43
Types of programmes (e.g. plays, variety, shows)	4	
Television/television output/television service	3	
Total		59

Speculative comment

In some cases, this narrowing phenomenon appears to have arisen from the respondent 'going back' to a time before he could get ITV. In that event, he may have decided to compare 'like with like' (i.e. limited himself to BBC programmes only). It also seems worth speculation that some respondents converted 'programme' to the programmes that they were familiar with (e.g. 'ITV only'; 'types of programmes you watch'), types of programmes they were specially interested in, types of programmes about which they had strong feelings (e.g. plays).

Interpretations of the reference 'better ... or worse'

This reference was intended to get respondent to consider both possibilities—i.e. of betterment and of worsening.

Summary of interpretations

Most of the respondents (52/59) appear to have considered both alternatives. Of the others, five appear to have considered only 'better' and two appear to have omitted both alternatives (e.g. 'Have programmes changed or remained much the same?'; 'Have there been any seasonal variations in their satisfactoriness?').

Table 7.25.7

Consideration of the alternatives, 'better ... or worse'

Both alternatives considered (i.e. 'better' or 'worse')	52
Only 'better' considered	5
Neither considered (e.g., has there been change or seasonal variations)	2
Total	59

Speculative comment

The long alternatives presented in the question were intended to provide a small scale and partial test of the hypothesis that respondents would lose one or another of two long alternatives (see 'Methods', pages 14, 29). It appears that for 52 of the 59 respondents, this did not happen to any noticeable degree. On the other hand, 5 respondents did appear to consider only one alternative ('better', in this case). However, because of the multiplicity of the factors possibly operating in this situation, these findings should be regarded as suggestive rather than as anything like final and they might be made the bases of several hypotheses to be tested under controlled conditions.

Interpretations of 'than they were'

Interpretation of this phrase is probably closely related to the interpretation of the opening phrase 'thinking about television over the last few years', in that this phrase was intended to set the scene for the requested comparison of television programmes now and as they were.

Summary of interpretations

Perhaps influenced by the opening phrase, some respondents (7 out of the 59) compared 'now' with 'the collective past'. By contrast, there were 11 who compared 'now' with some period of time in the past. Between these two interpretations were 41 where 'now' was compared with an indefinite period in the past ('up to so many years ago'). Conceivably respondent's answer could vary according to which of these three interpretations he adopted.

Table 7.25.8

Interpretations of 'than they were'

Than they were over the last (i.e. over a span of ...)	7
Than they were up to (but not necessarily considering all the years between)	41
Than they were in a period of time ... years ago	5
Than they were in 1947	1
Than they were in the past	1
Than they were last winter	1
Than they were before ITV started	2
Than they used to be	1
	11
Total	59

Speculative comment

It seems that the difficulty which shows up through the evidence stems in part at least from the 'scene setting' opening phrase, though the reference 'do you think that they are worse than they were' is itself ambiguous: it could refer to the collective past or to some point in time within the past.

Summary for the full question

1 Of the 59 interpretations of this question, 44 per cent were allocated an overall rating of either 'as intended' or 'permissible'. This compared with an average of 29 per cent for all the questions tested.

2 The main points of difficulty in this question were as follows:

(a)   There was a great deal of variability in terms of the criteria used by respondents in deciding whether TV had improved or not. Moreover, most respondents tended to be judging in terms of one (or another) fairly narrow criterion rather than thinking broadly about television.

(b)   Over 40 of the 59 may have interpreted 'over the last (few years) as within a period going back as far as ...', without necessarily considering all that period and leaving open to doubt just what part they were considering.

(c)   There was a startlingly wide interpretation of the term 'few', with 19 regarding it as 7 years or more and 11 as 10 years or more.

(d)   Sixteen interpreted the term 'programmes' rather narrowly (e.g. BBC only, particular types of programmes, particular programmes).

(e)   'Than they were' was variously interpreted to mean: than they were in the collective past (i.e. counting all of the last few years); than they were in some period X years ago; than they were up to X years ago.

3 *Speculative comments*

(a)   When asked to judge, respondents tended to do so in terms of some fairly limited criterion, presumably of their own choosing.

(b)   The reference 'over the last few years' is a very vague one and appears to have invited variable interpretations.

(c)   It seems that the narrowing of the term 'programme' to something like 'BBC only' sometimes arose from people going back to a time before ITV and hence dealing only with BBC in order to make a meaningful comparison; others seemed to use the term to refer to what they were most familiar with (e.g. ITV only, certain types of programmes only) or to what they were most interested in.

(d)   The term 'than they were' is probably ambiguous in that it does not indicate whether respondent should consider all or part of some specific past period, and this ambiguity is not helped by the opening phrase.

7.26   QUESTION 18, QUESTIONNAIRE IV

The actual wording of the question

'Do you think any programmes have a bad effect on young people, by teaching them slang?' (To be coded: yes/no/not sure).

Check question

If 'yes': 'Which ones are they?' If 'no': 'Why do you say that?'

Definitions of the different parts of the question

The following are the intended meanings of key terms in the question. *However, as indicated below, some variants of the intended interpretations were regarded as permissible and others as possibly permissible.* The word 'you' was meant to be interpreted as 'you, yourself' and was not intended to include others (e.g. respondent's spouse, children, relatives, lodger(s)). The reference 'any programmes' was intended to mean any particular programmes, and to include both adult and children's programmes. The word 'have' (a bad effect) was meant to be interpreted as 'actually have' rather than as 'could possibly have'. The reference 'a bad effect' was intended to mean 'an effect which is undesirable in terms of established values of good and bad'. The reference 'young people' is a broad one and no single definition of it could be regarded as final. In the present context it was meant to be interpreted as 'young people in general' rather than young people in any narrow age range or special category. An acceptable definition of 'young' was one which referred to any five year span which was in the age range 8—21 years. The reference 'by teaching' was, in this context, intended to mean by leading (young people) to copy what is presented on television, either through setting an example or presenting the idea or showing how or telling them the words. The term 'slang' was intended to mean: 'inelegant and unauthorised popular language'; 'words and phrases in common colloquial use but generally considered to be outside of standard English in some

308

or all of their senses'.

Respondents' interpretations of the question

These interpretations are set out in full in the Appendix (Part II). They are based upon the replies of 59 people.

Marking the interpretations

The system used for rating or marking respondents' interpretations of questions

The following marking or rating system was used.

1 If all elements of the question were interpreted as intended, the interpretation as a whole was rated 'fully as intended' (√).

2 Failure to interpret any significant element of the question fully as intended was sufficient to pull the total interpretation down below the level of 'fully as intended'. The level so reached was determined by the most seriously misinterpreted (significant) element in the test question. For example, if all but one of the significant elements of the question were interpreted as intended and the interpretation of that other element was rated as 'somewhat limited but permissible' (see below), then the whole interpretation was so rated (i.e. 'somewhat limited but permissible'). The reason for this is that a question cannot be regarded as a safe one unless all its parts are interpreted as intended.

3 If a significant element of the question was obviously and substantially misinterpreted or was omitted altogether, the total interpretation was marked 'incorrect' (X).

4 In the context of this system, the following ratings were made of specific elements of respondents' interpretations.

(a) 'you'. Where this term was interpreted as intended (see above), the interpretation was rated 'correct' (√). Where it seemed that a permissible interpretation had been made, but where the evidence was not conclusive, the rating 'doubtful but permissible' (?P) was applied.

(b) 'any programmes'. Where this reference was interpreted as intended (see above), the interpretation was rated 'correct' (√). Where the reference was interpreted as 'adult programmes only', this interpretation was rated as 'limited but permissible' (LP). Where it was interpreted as 'some programmes' or as 'some types of programmes', these interpretations were rated 'somewhat general but permissible' (GP). Where the reference was interpreted as 'television programmes generally (i.e. no consideration of nature of programme content)', the interpretation was rated 'unduly general' (UG). Where it was interpreted as 'children's programmes only', the interpretation was rated 'unduly limited' (UL).

(c) 'have (a bad effect)'. Where this reference was interpreted as intended (see above), the interpretation was rated 'correct' (√). Where the reference was interpreted as 'could have' or 'would … (this) be (a bad effect)', the interpretation was rated 'unduly different' (UD).

(d) 'a bad effect'. Where this reference was interpreted as intended (see above), the interpretation was rated 'correct' (√). Where the respondent did not directly interpret 'a bad effect', but nevertheless an interpretation in the sense of 'bad effect' was implicit, the rating 'doubtful but permissible' (?P) was applied. If the respondent was not considering a 'bad effect' at all, his interpretation was rated 'incorrect' (X).

(e) 'young people'. Where this reference was interpreted as intended (see above), that interpretation was rated 'correct' (√). Where it was interpreted as referring to young people within an age span of less than 5 years (though within the age range 8–21 years), the interpretation was rated 'limited but permissible' (LP). Similarly for the interpretation 'your own child and his associates', 'young people you happen to know' and 'London children', provided these were within the age range 8–21 years. Where the respondent interpreted 'young people' to mean children of 7 or less, or 'your own child only', or 'girls only' or 'boys only', that interpretation was rated 'unduly limited' (UL). Other interpretations rated 'unduly limited' (UL) were: 'young people who have learned to speak properly'; 'working-class children from places like Bermondsey'. Where the persons considered included those aged up to 25 years as well as persons within the age range 8–21 years, the rating 'extended but permissible' (EP) was applied. Where the persons considered included those aged less than 8 years as well as persons within the age range 8–21, the rating 'extended but permissible' (EP) was similarly applied. If persons over 25 years (along with those within the range 8–21) were considered, the rating 'unduly extended' (UE) was applied. Where the respondent considered adults only (i.e. 21 and over only), the interpretation was rated 'incorrect' (X). Where it seemed that the respondent's interpretation of 'young people' was permissible but where some doubt nonetheless existed the rating 'doubtful but permissible (?P) was applied.

(f) 'by teaching'. Where this reference was interpreted as intended (see above), the interpretation was rated 'correct' (√).
The following interpretations were also regarded as acceptable: 'by causing to copy'; 'by causing to adopt'; 'by encouraging to use'. The following interpretations were rated 'different but permissible' (DP): 'are likely to teach'; 'are likely to cause ... to use'; 'are likely (to cause) to copy'; 'are likely (to cause) to pick up'; 'on the grounds that this may teach'; 'if (they) learned'. Where the reference was interpreted as '(for them) to be exposed to'; or as '(do they) hear it', the interpretation was rated 'incorrect' (X). Where it seemed that a permissible interpretation had been made, but where the reference was not directly interpreted, the rating 'doubtful but permissible' (?P) was applied. Where the reference was omitted altogether, the rating 'incorrect' (X) was applied.

(g) 'slang'. Where this term was interpreted as intended (see above), the rating 'correct' (√) was applied. Acceptable interpretations included: not standard English; inelegant though not necessarily offensive expressions and words; colloquial expressions; local idioms; cockney slang. The interpretations rated 'different but permissible' (DP) included: ungrammatical speech; American isms; cockney accents; dialects; bad pronunciation; special advertising jargon. Several interpretations were rated 'unduly different' (UD): undesirable language (i.e. words that are not very nice), 'distorted spelling'. The following interpretations were rated 'incorrect' (X): 'bad words'; 'bad talk'; 'near the mark sayings'; 'crude words'; 'swear words'. Where it seemed that the interpretation was as intended, but where the evidence was not conclusive, the rating 'doubtful but permissible' (?P) was used. Where the term was interpreted in a way which was unrelated to language (e.g. 'bad manners', 'crime', 'a down to earth view of life') the rating 'incorrect' (X) was applied. The rating 'incorrect' (X) was also applied where the term was omitted altogether.

The ratings allocated.

Under the system described above, the following ratings were allocated to respondent interpretations of this test question.

Table 7.26.1

Ratings allocated to respondents' interpretations of test question (Q18, IV)

Lowest rating allocated to any part of the interpretation	Number of Ratings	Persons	% of Persons
Correct (✓)	0	0	0
Extra but permissible (ExP)	2		
Somewhat limited but permissible (LP)	1		
Somewhat too specific but permissible (SP)	0		
Somewhat too general but permissible (GP)	0	5*	8
Somewhat extended but permissible (EP)	2		
Somewhat different but permissible (DP)	3		
Doubtful but permitted (?P)	7	7	12
Unduly limited (UL)	3		
Unduly general (UG)	11	14*	24
Unduly extended (UE)	0		
Unduly different (UD)	6		
Incorrect (X)	33	33	56
Total		59	100

*See Note A on page 47.

Content analysis of the interpretations

There follows an analysis of the different interpretations of elements of the test question. The emphasis in this analysis is upon the different kinds of interpretation which were found rather than upon the number of them (though these numbers are given), the purpose of the content analysis being to discover the kinds of things that happen, to speculate about what causes them, and to derive hypotheses (about communication processes) for testing in later phases of the enquiry.

Interpretations of 'you'

The word 'you' was meant to be interpreted as 'you, yourself' and was not intended to include others (e.g. respondent's spouse, children, relatives, lodger(s)).

Summary of interpretations

There was no evidence for considering that any of the 59 respondents had misinterpreted this term. At the same time it should be noted that the full probing technique was not applied in this instance.

Table 7.26.2
Interpretations of 'you'

Respondent appeared to have interpreted the word 'you' as intended (i.e. 'you, yourself alone')	58*
Unclear exactly how the word 'you' was interpreted but probably the interpretation was as intended	1
Total	59

*'You' not fully probed for misinterpretations

Interpretations of 'any programmes'

The reference 'any programmes' was intended to mean any particular programmes, and to include both adult and children's programmes.

Summary of interpretations

1 Of the 59 respondents, 35 interpreted this reference in terms of specific programme content. Some of these appeared to have had in mind only 'slang content', but there were others who thought also or solely in terms of content other than slang (e.g. swearing, vulgarity, crime, violence).

2 On the other hand there were 24 who did not appear to have any particular programme content in mind but who considered programme matter generally.

3 In addition, there was one respondent who considered adult programmes only, three who thought in purely comparative terms (i.e. is it TV alone or specially, rather than some other sources, and two thought in terms of TV advertisements (e.g. presenting distorted language).

Table 7.26.3

Interpretations of 'any programmes'

Respondent considered specific programme content or material (e.g. slang, bad words). Details follow.			35
Slang	21	Swearing	4
Americanisms	2	'Near the mark' expressions	
Cockney dialects or Australian		or sayings	2
dialects	3	Double meanings	1
Colloquialisms	1		
		Crime	3
Ungrammatical English	2	Violence	3
Bad grammar	1		
Bad English	1	Sex education	1
Distorted language of advertisements	1		
		Over-glamourous material	1
Undesirable language	1		
Bad words/bad language/bad talk	6	Bad manners	1

Respondent did not appear to have considered specific content of programmes, but to have considered programmes rather generally	24
Total	59

Some specific interpretations of interest (from 6 of the above 59 cases)

'programmes' interpreted as 'adult programmes only'	1
television as distinct from other sources	3
television advertisements presenting distorted language/bad eating behaviour	2

Speculative comment

1 It is fairly clear that for many the later reference to 'teaching them slang' has conditioned the programme content considered.

2 At the same time, it seems that a misunderstanding of the term 'slang' (and later evidence makes it clear that this occurs for some respondents) may have set them thinking of programme content rather different from slang.

3 The conversion of 'any programmes' into 'TV versus any other source(s)' may perhaps have sprung out of a certain defensiveness about television, or perhaps, out of an acceptance of slang usage as inevitable.

Interpretations of 'have (a bad effect)'

The word 'have (a bad effect)' was meant to be interpreted as 'actually have' rather than as 'could possibly have'.

Summary of interpretations

1 19 or more of the 59 respondents interpreted this term as intended.

2 However, there were 5 who interpreted it conditionally (i.e. 'could have'; 'would have').

Table 7.26.4

Interpretations of 'have (a bad effect)'

have/had (a bad effect)	19
could have	3
would ... (this) be (a bad effect?)	2
'have' (a bad effect) was apparently not directly interpreted	35
Total	59

Interpretations of 'a bad effect'

The reference 'a bad effect' was intended to mean 'an effect which is undesirable in terms of established values of good and bad'.

Summary of interpretations

The principal interpretation of 'bad effect' was to have the viewer 'learn or copy slang'. Seemingly similar to this interpretation are various others of this kind: colloquialisms, bad grammar, bad effect on the way people speak, and so on. However, for a few, the term 'bad effect' extended also to matters far from any possible effect of hearing slang—to crime, violence, sexual behaviour.

Table 7.26.5

Interpretations of '(have a) bad effect'

Copy or learn slang	30
American slang/Americanisms	4
Cockney slang/Cockney dialect	3
Dialect/colloquialisms	3
Copy ungrammatical English/copy bad English/copy bad grammar	6
Bad effect on language/disturbing effect on language and spelling	2
Bad effect on way people speak/poor speech	2
Adopt slovenly language	1
Undesirable language	2
Bad accent	1
Copy bad words/bad language/crude words/swearing	17
'Near-to-mark' expressions	2
Bad manners (since the commercials)	1
Copy aspects of crime seen on TV/commit offences	3
Copy violence seen on TV	3
Copy sex behaviour seen on TV/commit sex offences	2
Give false impression of life/'down-to-earth' view of life	2
Learn to stop out late	1
	85*

*This figure is less than the totals for the detail because one respondent could offer more than one 'effect'.

Speculative comment.

To some, the term 'bad effect' may have seemed superfluous—in that the question was really about whether some programmes taught slang to young people. In that situation, it seems possible that some respondents treated 'bad effect' as an independent concept (e.g. relating to committing offences, etc.). If so, it raises the possibility of there being confused responses.

Interpretations of 'young people'

The reference 'young people' is a broad one and no single definition of it could be regarded as final. In the present context it was meant to be interpreted as 'young people in general' rather than young people in any narrow age range or special category. An acceptable definition of 'young' was one which referred to any five year span which was in the age range 8—21 years.

The nature of the interpretations

1 The term 'young people' was interpreted as intended by 16 of the 59 respondents.

2 A further 34 gave responses which were regarded as permissible. Of these 34 interpretations: 10 were in the range 8—21 years but were of limited span (less than 5 years); 18 were within that range but included children aged less than 8 years; 2 were in the range 8—21 years but included persons up to 25 years.

3 Five respondents interpreted 'young people' in a very limited fashion: your own child only, boys only, working-class children from places like Bermondsey, children from good homes, younger children and your own in particular.

4 Several quite possibly grasped the term more or less as intended, but the evidence available was not conclusive ('young people' (2), children (1)).

5 One person broadened the concept of 'young people' to 'people'.

Table 7.26.6 also gives some of the above details (all of them drawn from further analysis of the interpretations in Part II of the report) within another analytical structure.

6 Of the respondents who apparently thought in terms of ages, 9 included children of 5 years or less, while 9 others did not consider any below the age of 13; on the other hand, there were 4 for whom the upper age considered did not go beyond ten years.

7 There was great variety in the actual span of years considered by respondents. Thus while 2 thought in terms of three years or less and 10 in terms of 4—5 years, there were 6 for whom the average span of 'young people' was over 11 years.

Table 7.26.6

Interpretations of 'young people'

In relation to the intended meanings

Covering a span of 5 or more years in the age range 8–21 years (i.e. as intended)	15 ⎫ 16
Teenagers	1 ⎭
Covering a span of less than 5 years in the age range 8–21 years	10 ⎫
Children you know (within age range of 8–21 years)	1 ⎬ 12
Teenagers with whom you are familiar (within age range 15–21 years)	1 ⎭
In the range 8–21 years but also including those aged under 8	18 ⎫
Children and teenagers	1 ⎬ 20
8–15 year old Londoners	1 ⎭
In the range 8–21 years but also including those up to 25 years	2
Younger children and your own child in particular	1 ⎫
Your own child (only)	1 ⎪
Boys (only)	1 ⎬ 5
Working-class children from places like Bermondsey	1 ⎪
Children from good homes	1 ⎭
Young people (2)/children (1)	3
People	1
Total	59

Upper and lower age limits and age spans (where considered)

Lower age limits		Upper age limits only		Age spans	
5 years or less	9	8 years or less	1	3 years or less	2
6– 8 years	12	9–10 years	3	4– 5 years	10
9–10 years	8	11–12 years	4	6– 7 years	16
11–12 years	8	13–14 years	5	8–10 years	12
13–14 years	4	15–16 years	20	11–15 years	5
15–16 years	4	17–18 years	10	16+ years	1
17–18 years	1	19–20 years	5	Not known	13
Not known	13	21+	2		
		Not known	9		
Total	59	Total	59	Total	59

Speculative comment

1 There was great variety in the interpretation of this term, with some respondents thinking of quite different age groups from others. It is thus a very imprecise term and one, perhaps, that ought not to be used in a context such as this one.

2 Understandably, some respondents limited their thinking to young persons they knew rather than referring to young people generally (though two went much further and considered only their own children).

318

This may have had a lot to do with the variability of interpretation found to be operating.

3 The upshot of all this is that several people giving identical replies may in fact have had differing opinions on the matter at issue.

Interpretations of 'by teaching'

The reference 'by teaching' was, in this context, intended to mean by leading (young people) to copy what is presented on television, either through setting an example or presenting the idea or showing how or telling them the words.

Summary of interpretations

1 There were only minor variations in interpretations of this term, a great majority of respondents understanding it as intended.

2 A few interpreted the term more broadly than intended (i.e. 'are likely to teach').

3 Several apparently overlooked it altogether, mainly through a major alteration of the whole or part of the question.

Table 7.26.7

Interpretations of 'by teaching' (59 cases)

Part I All interpretations		
By teaching (6)/teach (3)/teaches (2)/teach to use (2)	14	
Responsible for teaching (5)/principally responsible (1)	6	23
*Will teach (1)/likely to teach (2)	3	
Will learn	1	
Responsible for (their) learning	1	3
*If (it is) learned	1	
Imitate (1)/copy (2)/copied (1)/lead to copy (1)/causing to copy (4)	9	10
*Likely to copy (1)	1	
Pick up (6)/cause to pick up (and use) (1)	7	8
*Likely to pick up	1	
Cause to use (3)/responsible for the use of (2)/cause to adopt (1)/ lead to take up (1)/by encouraging to use (1)	8	9
*Likely to cause to use	1	
(For them) to be exposed to	1	2
(Do they) hear it	1	
Term not directly considered		6
Total		61†

*See Part II
†The total of 61 is in excess of the number of respondents because 2 respondents offered two interpretations.

Part II   Seven (7) interpretations of 'by teaching' which are less definite than 'actually do teach'. These are included in I above but presented separately here.

(programmes) are likely to teach ... (slang)	2
(programmes) are likely to cause ... to use (slang)	1
(young people) are likely to copy	1
(young people) are likely to pick up (slang etc)	1 } 7
on the grounds that this will teach ... (slang)	1
If (young people) learned (slang)	1

Interpretations of 'slang'

The term 'slang' was intended to mean: 'inelegant and unauthorised popular language'; 'words and phrases in common colloquial use but generally considered to be outside of standard English in some or all of their senses'.

Summary of interpretations

1 Most (51/59) respondents interpreted this term as something to do with language, though 3 considered a non-language matter as well and 5 considered only non-language matters.

2 There was, however, a great deal of variability in the 'language type' definitions of slang which were considered. These ranged from fairly traditional interpretations to something meaning 'bad grammar or poor English' to extreme interpretations implying vulgarity of some kind (e.g. crude words, bad language, swearing, bad talk).

3 Interpretation of a 'non-language' kind were very wide of the intended meaning and took such forms as 'crime', 'violence', 'bad sex behaviour', 'a wrong view of life', 'bad manners', 'stopping out late'.

Table 7.26.8

Interpretations of 'slang'

Part I Did respondent interpret 'slang' as something to do with language?	
Respondent interpreted 'slang' solely in terms of language (see (i) below)	51
Respondent interpreted 'slang' in terms both of language (see (i) below and of behaviour other than language (see (ii) below)	3
Respondent interpreted 'slang' only in terms of behaviour other than language (see (ii) below)	5
Total	59

(i) *Interpretations relating to language* (81 in all)

Slang expressions or slang (seemingly as intended)	22	23
Inelegant, though not necessarily offensive expressions	1	
Cockney slang (1)/Cockney or rhyming slang (2)/Cockney or other accents or dialects (3)	6	12
American slang (2)/Americanisms (4)	6	
Colloquial expressions (3)/local idioms (1)	4	

(total: 39)

Speech which is not standard English (1)/ungrammatical English (1)/bad grammar (4)/poor or bad English (4)	10
Bad pronunciation (1)/bad accents (1)	2
Slovenly language (3)/any form of poor speech (1)/cutting words short (1)	5
Special jargon as used in advertisements	1
Distorted language (1)/distorted spelling (1)	2

(total: 20)

Bad words (1)/crude words (1)/bad language (9)/language you would not want your children to hear (1)/words that are not nice (1)	13
Swearing (3)/swear words (3)	6
Bad talk (1)/'near the mark' expressions with double meanings (1)/ 'near the mark' sayings (1)	3

(total: 22)

(ii) *Interpretations not relating to language* (11 in all)

Crime (2)/violence (3)	5
Bad sex behaviour	2
A down to earth view of life	1
A wrong idea of life	1
Stopping out late	1
Bad manners	1

(total: 11)

(iii) Concept seemingly overlooked	1
Total	93

Speculative comment

1 Here again the very variety of meanings given to this term made dangerous to assume comparability between seemingly identical answers.

2 It may possible be that some people are answering as to the question 'do you think any programmes have a bad effect on young people?' (i.e. with the term 'slang' somewhat overshadowed by the 'bad effects' part of the question).

Summary for the full question

1 Of the 59 interpretations of this question, 20 per cent were allocated an overall rating of either 'as intended' or 'permissible'. This compares

with an average of 29 per cent for all the questions tested.

2 The main points of difficulty or failure were as follows:

(a)   There was major variability in the interpretation of 'young people', with respect to the ages defining this class of person. In addition, some respondents were markedly specific and even conditional with respect to the children they considered.

(b)   There was also marked variability in the interpretation given to the term 'slang'. While many of these interpretations were more or less as intended, some were in terms of bad grammar or poor pronunciation, some were in terms of some form of vulgarity (swearing, bad talk) and some were as wide of the mark as crime, violence, bad sex behaviour, bad manners.

3 Other points of difficulty were:

(a)   some, in interpreting 'any programmes' thought in terms of programme content not obviously related to slang (i.e. programmes showing crime or violence);

(b)   some respondents considered 'bad effects' only obliquely or perhaps not at all;

(c)   several respondents (5) gave to 'have' a conditional interpretation (e.g. could have).

Speculative comments

1   This question may raise special difficulties because it poses what is in principle a double question: 'do ... any programmes ... teach slang?' and 'if they do teach slang, is this a bad effect?' This situation may possibly have caused some respondents to concentrate upon 'bad effects' (overlooking 'slang') and others to concentrate upon 'slang' effects, with only indirect attention to 'bad effects'.

2   It may well be the desire of respondents to think of *individuals* in answering the question helped to give to the interpretations of this term the narrowness and variability which tended to characterise them.

7.27 QUESTION 20, QUESTIONNAIRE IV

The actual wording of the question

'Is television advertising time being used efficiently?' (To be coded: yes/no/not sure.)

Check question

'What are your reasons for saying that?'

Definitions of the different parts of the question

The following are the intended meanings of key terms in the question. *However, as indicated below, some variants of the intended interpretations were regarded as permissible and others as possibly permissible.* The reference 'television advertising' was meant to refer to all television advertising, whatever its type, form or placement (e.g. between or within programmes). The reference '(advertising) time' was meant to refer to the total amount of time spent in presenting television advertisements (whatever their type, form or placement). The reference 'used efficiently' was meant to refer to the use of advertising time (a) in a manner most likely to sell the advertised goods; (b) without waste from the point of view of selling the products advertised; (c) without unnecessary side effects, of an unfortunate kind, on the viewers'enjoyment of programmes. This concept is a difficult one and it will be seen from below, that various limited interpretations of it were regarded as permissible.

Respondents' interpretations of the question

These interpretations are set out in full in the Appendix (Part II). They are based upon the replies of 56 people.

Marking the interpretations

The following marking or rating system was used.

1 If all elements of the question were interpreted as intended, the interpretation as a whole was rated 'fully as intended' (√).

2 Failure to interpret any significant element of the question fully as intended was sufficient to pull the total interpretation down below the level of 'fully as intended'. The level so reached was determined by the most seriously misinterpreted (significant) element in the test question. For example, if all but one of the significant elements of the question were interpreted as intended and the interpretation of that other element was rated as 'somewhat limited but permissible' (see below), then the whole interpretation was so rated (i.e. 'somewhat limited but permissible'). The reason for this is that a question cannot be regarded as a safe one unless all its parts are interpreted as intended.

3 If a significant element of the question was obviously and substantially misinterpreted or was omitted altogether, the total interpretation was marked 'incorrect'.

4 In the context of this system, the following ratings were made of specific elements of respondents' interpretations.

(a) 'television advertising'. Where this reference was interpreted as intended (see above), the interpretation was rated 'correct' (√). Where the interpretation was limited to 'advertisements between programmes', or to advertisements within programmes, it was rated 'limited but permissible' (LP). Where the reference was interpreted as television programmes, or where it was omitted altogether, the rating 'incorrect' (X) was applied.

(b) '(advertising) time'. Where this reference was interpreted as intended (see above), the interpretation was rated 'correct' (√). Where the intended interpretation appeared to have been implied, but where the evidence was not conclusive, the rating 'doubtful but permissible' (?P) was applied. Where it was interpreted as the timing of advertisements (e.g. within the programme complex), the interpretation was rated 'unduly different' (UD). Similarly for the interpretation 'are advertisements timed (properly)'. Where the reference was interpreted as asking if the advertising took up the right amount of time, the rating 'incorrect' (X) was applied; similarly where the reference was omitted altogether.

(c) 'used efficiently'. Where this reference was interpreted as intended (see above), the interpretation was rated 'correct' (√). Where the interpretation was broadly in terms of selling efficiency, it was also rated 'correct' (√). Where the interpretation was in terms only of one aspect of selling efficiency, it was rated

324

'limited but permissible' (LP) (e.g. 'not wasting time', 'to ensure people watch them', 'advertising well presented', 'keeping advertisements short and thereby allowing many advertisements to be shown', 'properly timed with respect to programmes', 'easy to understand', 'advertising only things which are available in the shops'). Where the interpretation referred only to the viewer's enjoyment of programmes, without any inference of possible upset to 'selling efficiency', it was rated 'unduly limited' (UL). Where the reference was omitted altogether, the rating 'incorrect' (X) was applied.

The ratings allocated

Under the system described above, the following ratings were allocated to respondents' interpretation of this test question.

Table 7.27.1
Ratings allocated to respondents' interpretations of test question (Q20, IV)

Lowest rating allocated to any part of the interpretation	Number of Ratings	Persons	% of Persor
Correct (√)	3	3	5
Extra but permissible (ExP)	1		
Somewhat limited but permissible (LP)	6		
Somewhat too specific but permissible (SP)	0	6*	11
Somewhat too general but permissible (GP)	0		
Somewhat extended but permissible (EP)	0		
Somewhat different but permissible (DP)	1		
Doubtful but permitted (?P)	22	22	39
Unduly limited (UL)	11		
Unduly general (UG)	0	17*	30
Unduly extended (UE)	0		
Unduly different (UD)	11		
Incorrect (X)	8	8	14
	Total	56	†

*See Note A on page 47.
†See Note B on page 48.

325

Content analysis of the interpretations

There follows an analysis of the different interpretations of elements of the test question. The emphasis in the analysis is upon the different kinds of interpretations which were found rather than upon the number of them (though these numbers are given), the purpose of the content analysis being to discover the kinds of things that happen, to speculate about what causes them, and to derive hypotheses (about communication processes) for testing in later phases of the enquiry.

Interpretations of 'television advertising'

The reference 'television advertising' was meant to refer to all television advertising, whatever its type, form or placement (e.g. between or within programmes).

Summary of interpretations

1 Forty-seven of the 56 interpreted the term more or less as intended.

2 Of the remaining nine, 2 put a special limit upon the concept (i.e. advertisements presented during an evening; advertisements which state the price of products).

3 Four more of them converted this concept into something like 'the practice of interrupting programmes with advertisements'.

4 Then there were 3 who got it quite wrong by thinking in terms of programmes rather than just advertising (e.g. 'Are the different programmes put on at the right time for viewers?')

Table 7.27.2
Interpretations of 'television advertising'

Television advertising (22)/advertising on television (6)/advertising (2)	30	47
Television advertisements (15)/advertisements (2)	17	
Television advertisements presented during an evening	1	2
Television advertisements which state the price of products	1	
The present arrangement of interrupting programmes by advertisements (3)/advertising breaks (1)		4
The programmes (of the channel which spends time on advertising)	1	
The different programmes	1	3
The television broadcasting	1	
Total		56

326

Speculative comment

The interpretation (by 4) in terms of the interruption of programmes by advertisements appears to have been brought about, partly at least, by their hearing 'time' as 'timing'.

Interpretations of '(advertising) time'

The reference '(advertising) time' was meant to refer to the total amount of time spent in presenting television advertisements (whatever their type, form or placement).

Summary of interpretations

1 Fourteen of the 56 respondents interpreted this term as intended.

2 There were 16, however, who appear to have interpreted it as 'timing' (e.g. in relation to the point at which advertisements interrupt a programme).

3 In addition, about half (27) appear not to have considered the term, at least not directly (e.g. 'Do you think television advertising is used properly?')

Table 7.27.3
Interpretations of 'time'

The time allocated for advertising (11)/available for (3)	14
The timing of advertisements (within the programme complex) (e.g. placement of breaks, are they being timed properly)	16
Respondent apparently overlooked the term	27
Total	57*

*One person was responsible for two interpretations

Speculative comment

1 The fact that 27 did not directly consider the word 'time' (or overlooked it altogether) may not matter to the sense of the question. What did matter however, was the conversion of 'time' or 'timing', for this narrowed the originally broad criterion in terms of which the respondent was supposed to make his judgement.

2 It may well be that the question would be better without the word 'time', for it would seem to be wide open, in its present form, to some sort of mis-hearing or to being not heard at all. Moreover, enough viewers appeared to feel strongly about the timing of advertisements to make this conversion or distortion an easy one.

327

Interpretations of 'used efficiently'

The reference 'used efficiently' was meant to refer to the use of advertising time:

(a)   in a manner most likely to sell the advertised goods;

(b)   without waste from the point of view of selling the products advertised;

(c)   without unnecessary side effects, of an unfortunate kind, on the viewers'enjoyment of programmes.

This concept is a difficult one and it will be seen from above, that various limited interpretations of it were regarded as permissible.

Summary of interpretations

1 Whereas a few respondents appeared to overlook the reference altogether (2), the rest noted it and most grasped at least some aspect of its intended meaning.

2 Nonetheless, respondents were using the term in a fairly individual way. Thus some thought in terms of whether or not programmes were being spoiled by too many interruptions; some in terms of whether or not the advertisements were likely to catch viewer attention; some in terms of the likely power of the advertisements to sell goods; some in terms of how much help they gave to viewers with shopping information, and so on.

3 Along with this variety, however, it appears that most respondents considered the matter (of efficiency of television advertising) from only one of these rather specific points of view. Thus the 56 respondents offered between them only 73 items of this kind. Indeed this narrowness or specificity was such that of the 56, only 11 appeared to have had both viewer and advertiser interests in mind (in considering efficiency), 15 had advertiser interests only in mind and 28 had in mind viewer interests only.

Table 7.27.4

Interpretations of 'used efficiently'

The many different interpretations	
Properly used: time well used (2)/used properly (1)	3
Relating to standard of presentation: well presented (8)/ satisfactory or pleasant presentation of advertisements (4)	12
Relating to interruptions: not interrupting programmes by advertisements (3)/keeping advertisements within proper limits (1)/not spoiling programmes by interruptions (5)/not spoiling programmes by interruptions at the wrong times (1)	10
Relating to timing or placement of the advertisements (and possibly to interruptions): satisfactory placement of advertisements (1)/ properly timed with respect to programmes (1)/put on at convenient times for viewers (6)/convenient because it gives viewers a break from viewing (1)	9
Relating to length or duration of advertisements: keeping ads. short so that many can be shown in the time available (1)/satisfactory length of advertisements (2)/not too much of it (2)	5
Relating to viewer attention: to ensure people watch them (2)/efficient in holding viewers' attention (1)	3
Relating to selling goods: Sells products advertised (6)/causes people to buy (6)/used well from advertiser's or manufacturer's point of view (2)/ gains your attention (1)	15
Relating to viewer comfort, service, pleasure: From the stand point of viewer comfort (3)/helpful to viewers in providing shopping information (6)/advertising things available in shops (1)/interesting (1)/don't waste viewers' time (1)	12
Relating to honesty, etc: honest (1)/justifiable (1)	2
Relating to good sense: sensible (1)/balanced (1)	2
Total	73

Some global aspects of interpretations		
Seemingly considered advertisers' interests only	13	15
Possibly considered only advertiser interests	2	
Seemingly considered viewer interests only	25	28
Possibly considered only viewer interests	3	
Seemingly considered both advertisers' and viewer interests	4	11
Possibly considered both advertisers' and viewer interests	7	
Neither viewer nor advertiser interests considered		2
Total		56

Speculative comment

1 These results indicate a certain basic narrowness and specificity to the

criteria by which viewers judge advertising efficiency. Presumably people habitually think about this matter in certain terms and these terms dictate which criterion will be brought into play in a question of this sort.

2 The results also raise a possibility that identical (coded) replies may mask rather different opinions.

3 The evidence constitutes a strong case for splitting a general question of this kind into the specific elements about which information is required.

Other points of interest

One respondent added to his interpretation of the question: 'and does the manner of their presentation spoil programmes for you?'

Summary for the full question

1 Of the 56 interpretations of this question, 55 per cent were allocated an overall rating of 'as intended' or 'permissible'. This compares with an average of 29 per cent for all the questions tested.

2 The main points of communication failure were as follows:

(a) Sixteen of the 57 respondents interpreted 'time' as something equivalent to 'timing' (e.g. placement or timing of advertisement breaks within the programme complex).

(b) 'used efficiently' was interpreted by 28 in terms of viewer interest only, and by 15 respondents in terms of advertiser interests only. Moreover, even within these categories, respondents tended to be thinking in terms of some fairly narrow aspect of efficiency (e.g. in terms of providing shopping information for viewers or in terms of their attention-getting power, or in terms of the individual length of advertisements, or spoiling programmes by interruptions, or ...).

(c) Several converted 'television advertising' into 'television programmes' and there were 2 who restricted their consideration of advertisements to those shown in the evening or to those that give the price of a product.

3 *Speculative comment*

(a) The interpretation of 'time' as 'timing' may have been prompted by a combination of mis-hearing and the fact that some viewers have rather strong feelings about the 'timing' of advertisements, namely their placement within programmes.

(b)   The individual narrowness and the person-to-person variability of interpretations of 'used efficiently' seems to point at the existence of fairly narrow mental sets in different viewers and to call for rather specifically worded questions or sequences of specific questions (that is, if ideas about the efficiency of advertising are to be properly studied).

7.28   QUESTION 21, QUESTIONNAIRE IV

The actual wording of the question

'When the advertisements come on between two television programmes on a weekday evening, do you usually watch them?' (To be coded as: yes/no/sometimes/not sure.)

Check question

If 'no': 'What do you usually do then?'

Definitions of the different parts of the question

The following are the intended meanings of key terms in the question. *However, as indicated below, some variants of the intended interpretations were regarded as permissible and others as possibly permissible.* The phrase 'advertisements ... between programmes' was meant to refer only to the television advertisements that come between one programme and the next, and not to those which occur within programmes. The reference 'on a weekday' was meant to refer to the period Monday to Friday. The word 'evening' was meant to refer to the period from 6.00 pm onwards, on those evenings during which the respondent did at least some viewing. The word 'you' was meant to be interpreted as 'you, yourself' and was not intended to include others (e.g. respondent's spouse, children, relatives, lodger(s)). The word 'usually' was meant to be interpreted as 'ordinarily', 'in the ordinary course of events', 'commonly'. Other acceptable interpretations of the term were: 'as a rule', 'generally', 'normally', 'habitually', 'as a routine', 'almost always', 'mostly', 'typically'. To 'watch (the advertisements)' was intended to mean attend to the advertisements shown on the screen or give at least some degree of attention.

Respondents' interpretations of the question

These interpretations are set out in full in the Appendix (Part II). They are based upon the replies of 59 people.

Marking the interpretations

The system used for rating or marking respondents' interpretations of questions

The following marking or rating system was used.

1 If all elements of the question were interpreted as intended, the interpretation as a whole was rated 'fully as intended' (√).

2 Failure to interpret any significant element of the question fully as intended was sufficient to pull the total interpretation down below the level of 'fully as intended'. The level so reached was determined by the most seriously misinterpreted (significant) element in the test question. For example if all but one of the significant elements of the question were interpreted as intended and the interpretation of that other element was rated 'somewhat limited but permissible' (see below), then the whole interpretation was so rated (i.e. 'somewhat limited but permissible'). The reason for this is that a question cannot be regarded as a safe one unless all its parts are interpreted as intended.

3 If a significant element of the question was obviously and substantially misinterpreted or was omitted altogether, the total interpretation was marked 'incorrect' (X).

4 In the context of this system, the following ratings were made of specific elements of respondents' interpretations.

(a) 'advertisements ... between two programmes'. Where this phrase was interpreted as intended (see above), it was rated 'correct' (√). Where it was interpreted as 'television advertisements generally' (i.e. irrespective of whether between or within programmes), it was rated 'unduly general' (UG). Where the phrase was interpreted as 'advertisements which break into programmes', the interpretation was rated 'incorrect' (X). Where the phrase was interpreted as 'the programme on each of the two channels', 'the commercial channel rather than the BBC', or where the interpretation was omitted altogether, the rating 'incorrect' (X) was applied.

(b) 'on a weekday'. Where this reference was interpreted as intended (see above), the rating 'correct' (√) was applied. Where it seemed that the intended interpretation had been made, but where the evidence was not conclusive, the rating 'doubtful but permissible' (?P) was applied. Where the interpretation included Saturday and/or Sunday in the period considered, or where the reference was omitted altogether, the rating 'incorrect' (X) was applied.

(c)   'evening'. Where this reference was interpreted as intended (see above), the rating 'correct' (√) was applied. Where it seemed that the intended interpretation had been made, but where the evidence was not conclusive, the rating 'doubtful but permissible' (?P) was applied. Where the reference was interpreted as 'all times of the day', the interpretation was rated 'incorrect' (X). Where the reference was omitted altogether the rating 'incorrect' (X) was also applied.

(d)   'you'. Where this term was interpreted as intended (see above), the interpretation was rated 'correct' (√). Where it was interpreted as 'you and your family', or as 'you and some other(s)', the interpretation was rated as 'unduly extended' (UE).

(e)   'usually'. Where this word was interpreted as intended (see above), the rating 'correct' (√) was applied. Where this term was omitted altogether, the rating 'incorrect' (X) was applied.

(f)   'watch (the advertisements)'. Where this reference was interpreted as intended (see above), the rating 'correct' (√) was applied. Where it seemed that attention had been paid to the advertisements but where the evidence was not conclusive, the rating 'doubtful but permissible' (?P) was applied. Where the interpretation did not necessarily involve giving the advertisements at least some degree of attention (e.g. 'keep the set on') or allowed the inclusion of periods when no attention was being given to the advertisements screened, the rating 'unduly different' (UD) was applied.

The ratings allocated

Under the system described above, the following ratings were allocated to respondents' interpretations of this test question.

Table 7.28.1

Ratings allocated to respondents' interpretations
of test question (Q21, IV)

Lowest rating allocated to any part of the interpretation	Number of Ratings	Number of Persons	% of Persons
Correct (✓)	0	0	0
Extra but permissible (ExP)	0		
Somewhat limited but permissible (LP)	0		
Somewhat too specific but permissible (SP)	0	0	0
Somewhat too general but permissible (GP)	0		
Somewhat extended but permissible (EP)	0		
Somewhat different but permissible (DP)	0		
Doubtful but permitted (?P)	0	0	0
Unduly limited (UL)	0		
Unduly general (UG)	5	5	8
Unduly extended *UE)	0		
Unduly different (UD)	0		
Incorrect (X)	54	54	92
Total		59	100

*See Note A on page 47.

Content analysis of interpretations

There follows an analysis of the different interpretations of elements of the test question. The emphasis in this analysis is upon the different kinds of interpretations which were found rather than upon the number of them (though these numbers are given), the purpose of the content analysis being to discover the kinds of things that happen, to speculate about what causes them, and to derive hypotheses (about communication processes) for testing in later phases of the enquiry.

Interpretations of 'advertisements (come on) between two television programmes'

The phrase 'advertisements ... between two television programmes' was meant to refer only to television advertisements that come on between one programme and the next, and not to those which occur within programmes.

Summary of interpretations

1 Only 3 of the 59 respondents interpreted this reference

as intended.

2 Of the rest, 14 considered only advertisements that occur within programmes and 40 considered advertisements in general (i.e. irrespective of whether they break into programmes or occur between programmes).

3 Two respondents apparently overlooked the reference altogether.

Table 7.28.2

Interpretations of 'advertisements (come on) between two programmes

Respondent considered only advertisements between two programmes	3
Respondent considered only advertisements within programmes	14
Respondent considered both advertisements between two programmes and advertisements within programmes	40
Did not consider advertisements at all	2
Total	59

Speculative comment

1 It seems possible that the extension of the intended reference to 'television advertisements generally' arose out of people expecting to be asked about that more general matter.

2 The conversion of the 'between programmes' reference to 'within programmes' seems to call for a different sort of explanation and one such explanation may be that quite a lot of viewers appear to think automatically and strongly of interruption advertisements when the issue of television advertising is raised at all.

Interpretations of '(on) a weekday (evening)'

The reference 'on a weekday' was meant to refer solely to the period Monday to Friday.

Summary of interpretations

1 Only 8 clearly interpreted this term as intended, though there may have been up to 4 more also in this category.

2 By contrast, there were 37 who appear to have extended the term to include Saturdays and Sundays.

3 Nine respondents appear to have by-passed the term altogether.

336

Table 7.28.3

Interpretations of '(on) a weekday (evening)'

From Monday till Friday (only) (= 5 days)	8
From Monday till Saturday (= 6 days)	1
From Sunday till Saturday (= 7 days)	36 ⎱ 37
Any day of the week	1 ⎰
Not clear which days were considered	4
Reference apparently not considered at all	9
Total	59

Speculative comment

1   This major failure in communication may have had its source partly in plain mis-hearing (in the context of a question already rather overloaded with concepts).

2   In addition however, it is worth asking if the probable irrelevance of a distinction between weekday and any day may not have encouraged the viewers to overlook that distinction.

3   Viewing the matter another way, it may have been that the crowded nature of the question forced some respondents into some degree of economy in terms of which distinctions be kept in mind.

4   One interesting possibility is that the juxtaposing of the words ... day and evening (i.e. weekday evening) may have produced a form of perceptual conflict—in which 'evening' became dominant and 'day' was blotted out.

Interpretations of '(weekday) evening'

The word 'evening' was meant to refer to the period from 6.00 pm onwards, on those evenings during which the respondent did at least some viewing.

Summary of interpretations

At least 48 of the 59 respondents interpreted this term as intended, and only one respondent extended it to cover the whole day.

Table 7.28.4

Interpretations of '(on a weekday) evening'

Evening interpreted as intended	46
Those/those few evenings when you watch television	2
All times of the day	1
Not clear which part of the evening considered	10
Total	59

Interpretations of 'you'

The word 'you' was meant to be interpreted as 'you, yourself' and was not intended to include others (e.g. respondent's spouse, children, relatives, lodger(s)).

Summary of interpretations

Six of the 59 respondents interpreted this term collectively (i.e. as you and other(s)). In five of these instances, the extension was to member(s) of the respondent's family.

Table 7.28.5

Interpretations of 'you'

You, yourself, alone		53
You and your wife (2)/you and your husband (2)	4	
You and your family	1	6
You and your friends	1	
Total		59

Speculative comment

This form of misinterpretation probably stems out of the corporate (family) nature of much viewing, with the result that the respondent answered for the viewing group rather than for himself alone.

Interpretations of 'usually'

The word 'usually' was meant to be interpreted as 'ordinarily', 'in the ordinary course of events', 'commonly'. Other acceptable interpretations of the term were: 'as a rule', 'generally', 'normally', 'habitually', 'as a routine', 'almost always', 'mostly', 'typically'.

Summary of interpretations

1 Thirteen of the 59 respondents apparently overlooked this term altogether.

2 On the other hand, 45 got it more or less as intended.

Table 7.28.6

Interpretations of 'usually'

Usually (apparently as intended, but evidence not fully conclusive)	42
Generally (1)/normally (1)/your habit (1)	3
The thing you do most often	1
Term apparently not considered	13
Total	59

Interpretations of 'watch (the advertisements)'

To 'watch' (the advertisements)' was intended to mean to attend to the advertisement shown on the screen or to give them at least some degree of attention.

Summary of interpretations

1 At least 29, but quite possibly as many as 54 (of the 59 respondents) interpreted this term as giving at least some degree of attention to what was showing on television. Most of these people seemed to have in mind 'quite a lot of attention'.

2 One of the remaining 5 interpreted 'watch' as 'have the set on' and the other 4 appear to have had very loose notions of 'watching' (e.g. giving the set only half attention).

Table 7.28.7

Interpretations of 'watch (the advertisements)'

Did respondent interpret 'watch' as 'paying at least some attention'?

Give (them) any attention (1)/pay full attention (1)/careful attention (1)/ serious attention (1)/make a point of attending (1)/pay attention to (them) (14)/watch with attention (3)/look at (them) (5)/look at (them) with interest (2)	29
Interpretation of 'watch' not fully established, but no reason for thinking other than 'watch with at least some attention' (i.e. watch (1), look at them (19), see (1), carry on watching (2)/go on looking at them (2))	25
Interpreted as 'have the TV set on' (and so possibly included occasions when no attention paid by respondent)	1
Look at (them) but not necessarily take much interest in them (1)/look at them without paying much attention (1)/without taking much notice (1)/giving them only half attention (1)	4
Total	59

Other features of interpretation (5 cases, already included above)

Stay and look at (them)	1
Sit and look (at them) (2)/continue to sit, looking at them (1)	3
Keep on watching (them) just as if they were the programme	1

Summary for the full question

1 Of the 59 interpretations of this question, 0 per cent were allocated an overall rating of either 'as intended' or 'permitted'. This compares with an average of 29 per cent for all the questions tested.

2 The main points of failure were as follows:

(a)   the majority of respondents failed to limit their thinking to 'advertisements that come on between two programmes', thinking instead of 'advertisements generally' (40) or of advertisements that occur within programmes;

(b)   a majority extended the term 'weekday' to include consideration of Saturdays and Sundays.

3 Other (but less recurrent) points of failure were:

(a)   the omission of one or another of the terms of the question;

(b)   the collective interpretation of 'you' (6 cases);

(c)   the occasional weakening of the term 'watch' to something less than giving the set attention and the occasional qualification of the term by something like 'sit and watch'.

4 Speculative comment

(a) It seems possible that the high degree of misinterpretation of 'advertisements that (come on) between two programmes' may have been produced partly by the unexpected narrowness of the 'between programmes' reference and partly by a tendency on the part of some viewers to think automatically and strongly in terms of interruption advertisements.

(b) It may also be that crowding of this question with different concepts forced respondents into some degree of economy in terms of the distinctions that they kept in mind—with the result that a possibly unnecessary one like 'weekday' was overlooked. On the other hand, this particular omission might possibly have sprung from some degree of perceptual conflict arising out of the juxtaposing of ... day and evening (i.e. weekday evenings).

7.29   QUESTION 3 (PD), QUESTIONNAIRE IV

The wording of the question

'How many people are there in your household? Do not include yourself'.

Check question

'Who are these people?'

Definitions of the different parts of the question

The following are the intended meanings of key terms in the question. *However, as indicated below, some variants of the intended interpretations were regarded as permissible and others as possibly permissible.* The reference 'how many (people)' was meant to be interpreted as 'what is the number of people' (i.e. inviting a numerical answer). There was meant to be no limit to the ages of those considered for inclusion (i.e. babies, children, elderly people were meant to be included along with all others). The term 'people' in the context of household, was meant to refer to all persons, with no limit to the ages of those considered for inclusion (i.e. babies, children, elderly people were meant to be included along with all others). The reference 'in your household' was intended to mean '(those) who live together, with you, in one unit' (i.e. those who eat together, use the same cooking utensils, are involved in a single housekeeping account and sleep in the same establishment). 'Do not include yourself' was an instruction to the respondent to exclude himself/herself in working out an answer.

Respondents' interpretations of the question

These interpretations are set out in full in the Appendix (Part II). They are based upon the replies of 57 people.

Marking the interpretations

The system used for rating or marking respondents' interpretations of questions

The following marking or rating system was used.

1 If all elements of the question were interpreted as intended, the interpretation as a whole was rated 'fully as intended' (✓).

2 Failure to interpret any significant element of the question fully as intended was sufficient to pull the total interpretation down below the level of 'fully as intended'. The level so reached was determined by the most seriously misinterpreted (significant) element in the test question. For example, if all but one of the significant elements of the question were interpreted as intended and the interpretation of that other element was rated as 'somewhat limited but permissible' (see below), then the whole interpretation was so rated (i.e. 'somewhat limited but permissible'). The reason for this is that a question cannot be regarded as a safe one unless all its parts are interpreted as intended.

3 If a significant element of the question was obviously and substantially misinterpreted or was omitted altogether, the total interpretation was marked 'incorrect' (X).

4 In the context of this system, the following ratings were made of specific elements of respondents' interpretations.

(a) 'How many people'. Where this reference was interpreted as intended (see above), the interpretation was rated 'correct' (✓). Where it was interpreted as 'who are (the people)', the interpretation was rated 'different but permissible' (DP) provided that a number could be derived from the list given. Similarly for the interpretation 'what is the size of (your family)'.

(b) 'people'. Where this term was interpreted as intended (see above), the interpretation was rated 'correct' (✓). Where respondent limited his consideration to those who watched television on his set, the rating 'unduly limited' (UL) was applied.

(c) 'in your household?'. Where this reference was interpreted as intended (see above), the interpretation was rated 'correct' (✓). Where it seemed that a permissible interpretation had been made but where the evidence was not conclusive, the rating 'doubtful but permissible' (?P) was applied. When persons not in respondent's household were included, the rating 'unduly extended' (UE) was applied (e.g. those who come into your house to watch TV; relatives living under the same roof as respondent but in a separated unit or household; a lodger who lives separately from

343

the respondent's household). Where a genuine household member was excluded, the rating 'unduly limited' (UL) was applied.

(d) 'do not include yourself'. Where this instruction had been interpreted as intended (see above), the interpretation was rated 'correct' (√). Where the respondent had included himself/herself, the interpretation was rated 'incorrect' (X).

The ratings allocated

Under the system described above, the following ratings were allocated to respondents' interpretations of this test question.

Table 7.29.1

Ratings allocated to respondents' interpretations
of test question (Q.3(PD), IV)

Lowest rating allocated to any part of the interpretation	Number of Ratings	Persons	% of Person
Correct (√)	15	15	26
Extra but permissible (ExP)	0		
Somewhat limited but permissible (LP)	0		
Somewhat too specific but permissible (SP)	0	1	2
Somewhat too general but permissible (GP)	0		
Somewhat extended but permissible (EP)	0		
Somewhat different but permissible (DP)	1		
Doubtful but permitted (?P)	17	17	30
Unduly limited (UL)	8		
Unduly general (UG)	0	10*	18
Unduly extended (UE)	2		
Unduly different (UD)	0		
Incorrect (X)	14	14	25
Total	57		†

*See Note A on page 47.
†See Note B on page 48.

Content analysis of the interpretations

There follows an analysis of the different interpretations of elements of the test question. The emphasis in this analysis is upon the different kinds of interpretations which were found rather than upon the number of them (though these numbers are given), the purpose of the content analysis being to discover the kinds of things that happen, to speculate about what causes them, and to derive hypotheses (about communication processes) for testing in later phases of the enquiry.

Interpretations of 'how many (people)'

The reference 'how many (people)' was meant to be interpreted as 'what is the number of people' (i.e. inviting a numerical answer). There was meant to be no limit to the ages of those considered for inclusion (i.e. babies, children, elderly people were meant to be included along with all others). The term 'people', in the context of household, was meant to refer to all persons, with no limit to the ages of those considered for inclusion (i.e. babies, children, elderly people were meant to be included along with all others).

Summary of interpretations

1 All but two of the 57 respondents interpreted 'how many' in a numerical sense.

2 Some respondents appear to have put a limit upon the sort of people they they considered. Thus there were 7 who considered only viewing people (e.g. people who watch television, people old enough to watch television, people who sit down here to view, your family and relations who watch your TV set regularly), and there were 8 more who limited the sort of people considered to members of the respondent's family (e.g. your family, your family group, your immediate family). Amongst the 40 who did not put an explicit limit upon the term, there were some who included people from other households, but this comes under the heading of misinterpretation of the term 'household' and is dealt with in Table 7.29.3.

Table 7.29.2

Interpretations of 'how many people'

'How many'	
How many' interpreted numerically (as intended)	55
What is the size of	1
Who are (the people)	1
Total	57

People

People (seemingly as intended—i.e. no explicit limit put upon the people considered)	40
People who watch television (4)/people old enough to watch television (1)/ people who sit down here to watch television (1)	6
Of your family and relations who watch your television set regularly	1
Of your family (5)/family members (2)/family group (1)/of your immediate family (1)/of your family including 'in-laws' (1)	10
Total	57

Speculative comment

1 The limitation of the 'people' considered to those who watch television appears to have come out of the fact that respondents had, up to this point, been thinking almost solely about viewers and viewing. It thus appears to be a 'carry over' effect.

2 The limitation of 'the people' to 'family members' may not, in most cases, make much or any difference to the answers given, but it is in principle a limitation—and one which, quite possibly, springs out of the respondent's misunderstanding of the term 'household'.

Interpretations of '(people) in your household'

The reference 'in your household' was intended to mean '(those) who live together, with you, in one unit' (i.e. those who eat together, use the same cooking utensils, are involved in a single housekeeping account and sleep in the same establishment).

Summary of interpretations

1 This term appeared to be interpreted as intended by 21 of the 57 respondents and quite possibly as intended by a further 19 (making 40 in all).

2 On the other hand, there were between 4 and 14 who did not appear to limit their thinking to 'a domestic unit'. The most obvious cases of misinterpretation of this kind included the following: 'your family living in this house, including those who live in a separate section of it'; 'people living in this house, including those who live in flats other than your own'

Table 7.29.3

Interpretations of '(people)* in your household'

1 *People living together as a unit, presumably domestic*	21
All those who live together as a unit in the house (1)/people living in the house as a unit (2)	3
Your family, taken as a unit (12)/your family, living in this house/flat (5)/your family group living in this house (1)	18
2 *Not clear (but still possible) that a domestic unit was implied*	19
People living with you in your home/house	2
People living in your home/house	7
People living in this house/maisonette	4
People living in this house including lodgers	1
Your family living in this house	3
Your family and relatives living in this house with you	2
3 *Doubtful that a domestic unit was considered at all*	10
People in your home/flat/house	6
People in your flat, including lodger	1
People present in your flat all or most of the time	1
People present in your house most of the time	1
Your family including your future daughter-in-law	1
4 *Interpretation apparently not limited to domestic unit*	4
Your family living in this house, irrespective of whether or not part of your family unit	1
People living in this house, including those who live in a separate section of it	1
People in this house, including those who live in flats other than your own	1
'Household' not considered at all	1
5 *No evidence of whether or not term was considered*	3
Total	57

*See Table 7.29.2

Speculative comment

1   It appears that some respondents thought of 'household' as 'house' whilst others thought of it as 'family' (see Table 7.29.2).

2   This term appears to represent a difficult concept and one which calls for special attention by the question designer.

Interpretations of 'do not include yourself'

'Do not include yourself' was an instruction to the respondent to exclude himself/herself in working out an answer.

Summary of interpretations

Whereas 43 of the 57 quite rightly did not include themselves in the count, there were 13 who did so—in spite of specific instruction to the contrary.

Table 7.29.4

Interpretations of 'do not include yourself'

Excluding yourself/not counting yourself/apart from yourself	43
Including or counting yourself (10)/counting yourself as well (3)	13
Phrase did not appear to be considered at all	1
Total	57

Speculative comment

1 One possible reason for 13 of the respondents including themselves in the count is that they thought automatically of themselves as part of their own household and so did not perceive the final instruction to exclude themselves from the count.

2 Others, perhaps, had started to work out an answer, or to give it, before the interviewer had got to or through her qualification.

3 Perhaps some respondents just did not hear the vital word 'not'.

Summing up for the full question

1 Of the 57 interpretations of this question, 58 per cent were allocated an overall rating of 'as intended' or 'permissible'. This compares with an average of 29 per cent for all the questions tested.

2 The main sources of difficulty were as follows:

(a) The term 'people' was given a somewhat restricted meaning by some respondents. Thus 7 thought in terms of 'those people who watch television' and 10 in terms of people in the respondent's *family*.

(b) 'Household' became for some something other than 'a domestic unit' and possibly something more like 'house'.

(c) The instruction 'do not include yourself' did not stop 13 from doing so.

3 On the other hand, the reference 'how many' was numerically interpreted (as intended) by all but 2 respondents. This should be contrasted with what happened to the same reference in the context of other of

the questions studied in this enquiry.

4 *Speculative comments*

(a)   The very successful interpretation of 'how many' may have been a result of the directness of the question and of its apparent easiness (e.g. there seemed to be no case for an evasive or qualified response).

(b)   It seems quite possible that the interpretation of 'people' was, in some instances, influenced by an incorrect interpretation of the term 'household'.

(c)   For some, 'household' appears to have become 'house' and for others to have become 'family'.

(d)   The overlooking of the final qualifying phrase (i.e. do not include yourself) may have sprung out of respondents starting to answer before the qualification was made, or out of a fixed way of thinking (i.e. always including oneself in the count) or out of simple mishearing of the word 'not'.

8   Findings: at a more general level

Proportion of respondents who understood the test question as intended

The outstanding feature of the findings from this enquiry is the high degree of misinterpretation of questions which occurred. Table 8.1 gives details, for each of the 29 questions, of the percentage of respondents whose interpretation of a question came within permissible limits of the intended interpretation.

Table 8.1

The degree to which the 29 questions were
interpreted as intended

Percentage of respondents interpreting a question within permissible limits of what was intended	Number of questions interpreted with this degree of success
0— 5%	3
6—10%	3
11—15%	2
16—20%	2
21—25%	5
26—30%	1
31—35%	2
36—40%	2
41—45%	2
46—50%	1
51—55%	4
56—60%	2
Total	29 questions

For all the questions tested, the proportion falling within permissible limits was, on average, only 29 per cent. Moreover, going behind this average, we find that for 8 of the test questions, the percentage within permissible limits was less than 16 per cent and for one of them not a single respondent out of the 59 persons tested on it came within those limits. Moreover, the highest score for any of the questions tested was only 58 per cent.

In appraising this particular finding, we must be extremely careful to note that many of the questions tested were designed to present the respondent with difficulties of a kind found in current questioning procedure. The point in so doing was to examine the extent and the nature of communication failure with respect to such difficulties, rather than to develop anything like a representative picture of respondent understanding of survey questions. At the same time, certain other things must be noted:

1 The special features built into 24 of the test questions (on the grounds that they would probably involve the respondent in some degree of difficulty) were of a kind which occurred quite frequently in the wide range of questions and questionnaires analysed as a preliminary to this enquiry.

2 Leaving aside the issue of whether or not these special features were indeed sources of major miscommunication, the detailed analyses reported in this document* indicated that a great deal of communication failure arose from misinterpretation of words and phrases which are very commonly used in current question design.

3 The five test questions which were not meant to present any special sort of difficulty but which were taken more or less at random from the carrier questionnaires, were interpreted only somewhat more accurately than were the 24 others.

4 The system used for marking question elements (i.e. as permissible or not) was by no means tough and allowed a considerable amount of latitude in interpretation.

Accordingly, the least that can be said of the details in Table 8.1 is that they constitute a case for considering the possibility that survey respondents frequently misinterpret some aspects of the questions they are asked. The body of information presented on pages 49–349 gives a high degree of support to this contention.

The relationship between respondent characteristics and tendency to understand the test questions as intended

Since each respondent was put through tests on up to seven questions,

---

*See the Summary on pages 350–389 and the Content analysis of interpretations on pages 49–349.

it was possible to calculate, for each respondent, the proportion of these questions for which the interpretation used was either 'as intended' or 'permissible'. For the purposes of further analysis, this proportion was expressed as a percentage score. A comparison was then made of the distribution of 'percentage scores' in different sections of the population   Details of the results are set out in Table 8.2.

In general, the differences between population sectors are small to negligible. They indicate slightly better understanding of the test questions by those who ceased further education aged 16 or over; by those who have had some degree of further education since leaving school; by those from the more skilled occupational backgrounds; by those aged 20—39 years. The striking thing about the findings is the similarity of the findings for the different population sectors.

Respondent interpretation of a number of commonly used words

The detailed analyses presented on pages 49—349 in this book provide evidence about the extent and the nature of respondent distortion of quite a lot of different terms. Details of the analysis of each of thirteen of these terms have been brought together in this section mainly on the grounds that they are of a sufficiently recurrent kind to be of interest, in their own right, to the question designer. Their selection for presentation here was also conditioned by the fact that for some of them the study of respondent interpretation had been made in the setting of each of a number of different questions, so that there was scope for speculation about the way in which the interpretation of these terms varied with context.

Table 8.2

Performance according to respondent characteristics

Percentage correct or permissible (%) (In the range)*	All persons	By age		By size of household		By sex	
	n	20–39 n	40+ n	1–3 n	4+ n	Men n	Women n
0– 10	34	9	25	24	10	15	19
11– 20	57	15	42	41	16	31	26
21– 30	58	23	35	45	13	28	30
31– 40	22	6	16	18	4	10	12
41– 50	48	17	31	33	15	26	22
51– 60	16	7	9	13	3	5	11
61– 70	2	1	1	1	1	2	0
71– 80	3	1	2	2	1	3	0
81– 90	3	1	2	1	2	0	3
91–100	3	1	2	2	1	1	2
Weighted average score	29.0%	31.3%	27.9%	28.7%	29.8%	28.5%	29.5%

*In fact, individual scores are clustered at the following percentage points: 0, 13, 14, 25, 29, 38, 43, 50, 57, 63, 71, 75, 86, 100%. Averages are based on these percentage points. See paragraph 1 on page 352.

Table 8.2 (continued)

Percentage correct or permissible (%) (In the range)*	All persons	By occupational state		By occupational level		
	n	Full-time employment n	Others n	Skilled and above n	Moderately skilled and below n	Others n
0— 10	34	20	14	13	17	4
11— 20	57	33	24	23	29	5
21— 30	58	41	17	24	34	0
31— 40	22	9	13	8	12	2
41— 50	48	31	17	28	19	1
51— 60	16	8	8	9	7	0
61— 70	2	2	0	1	1	0
71— 80	3	2	1	2	1	0
81— 90	3	1	2	2	1	0
91—100	3	1	2	1	2	0
Weighted average score	29.0%	28.4%	29.9%	31.6%	28.0%	

*In fact, individual scores are clustered at the following percentage points: 0, 13, 14, 25, 29, 38, 43, 50, 57, 63, 71, 78, 86, 100%. Averages are based on these percentage points. See paragraph 1 on page 352.

354

Table 8.2 (continued)

Percentage correct or permissible (%) (In the range)*	All persons n	By age of ceasing full-time school		By further-education or training	
		15 years of less n	16+ years n	Yes n	No n
0— 10	34	26	8	6	28
11— 20	57	43	14	18	39
21— 30	58	38	20	21	37
31— 40	22	16	6	3	19
41— 50	48	26	22	17	31
51— 60	16	7	9	6	10
61— 70	2	2	0	1	1
71— 80	3	1	2	0	3
81— 90	3	1	2	1	2
91—100	3	2	1	2	1
Weighted average score	29.0%	26.3%	34.2%	31.7%	27.8%

*In fact, individual scores are clustered at the following percentage points: 0, 13, 14, 25, 29, 38, 43, 50, 57, 63, 71, 75, 86, 100%. Averages are based on these percentage points. See paragraph 1 on page 352.

For each of the thirteen terms featured in this section, the presentation is in two parts: (i) a short statement of the facts emerging from the analysis; (ii) speculative comments about the possible causes of such misinterpretations as occurred.

The term 'you'

In this enquiry, the term 'you' was interpreted as intended (i.e. as 'you', yourself, only') by the great majority of respondents. Nonetheless there were various deviations from the intended meaning, as indicated in the cumulative table below (based upon 22 tests of the word).

Table 8.3

Interpretations of 'you'

Interpretations	Number of instances
You, yourself, alone (i.e. as intended	1,071 (87%)
Evidence not conclusive, but probably as intended	11
You and your wife	13
You and your husband	11
You and your family	31
You and one or more of your family	12
You and others	4
You and your friend	6
You or your wife	2
You or your family	4
At least someone in your family (not necessarily you)	2
Your family (not necessarily you)	5
Your husband	3
Term omitted or possibly overlooked	43
No evidence as to how interpreted	7
Total	1,225

Thus there were some who broadened this term so that it included not only the respondent but one or more others as well, mostly members of the respondent's own family (6 per cent of all interpretations of the term). A few took the widening process even further, thinking of one or more family members, no matter which ones (e.g. possibly excluding themselves). There were also cases where the term 'you' was by-passed or possibly overlooked, sometimes through the whole phrase in which 'you' was embedded being overlooked, but in other instances through a question about 'how often you watch television' being converted into one about 'how often your television set is watched' or about 'how often it is turned on'.

The extent of the deviation from the intended meaning of this term varied with the question in which it appeared. This seems to indicate that some contexts facilitated more than did others, the misinterpretation of the term 'you'. For instance, there was considerable distortion of this term in the setting of the question 'How many times do you switch from one station to the other when ...?' (only 34/52 got it right) and no distortion of it at all (by the same people) when it was used in the setting of the question 'Do you think any programmes have bad effects on young people's morals?' There was also variation, from one question to another, in the nature of the deviation from the intended meaning of the term.

Speculative comments

The widening of the term 'you' tends to occur in the setting of questions about viewing behaviour (rather than in the setting of questions about personal opinions) and this may well be a reflection of the corporate nature of viewing (i.e. 'you' means the whole viewing group). On the other hand the distortion of this term may be no more than a result of some respondents avoiding the difficult task of sorting out their own behaviour from that of others in the viewing group (e.g. 'How many days of the week do you usually watch television?'/'How many times do you usually switch from one station to the other, when ...?'/'When you turn on your television set in the evening, do you generally go on viewing till the end of the evening ...?').

Whereas the widening of the term 'you' found in various of the tests made could be simply a feature of its use in questions about television behaviour, the survey research practitioner cannot rule out the possibility that it occurs in other group settings as well.

The term 'usually'

Eight separate tests were made of the interpretation of this term, each based upon over fifty persons (445 interpretations in all). Only 60 per cent of these interpretations were as intended or approximately so. Table 8.4 presents details.

The word 'usually' was meant to be interpreted as 'ordinarily', 'in the ordinary course of events', 'commonly'. Other acceptable interpretations

357

of the term were 'as a rule', 'generally', 'normally', 'habitually', 'as a routine', 'almost always', 'mostly', 'typically', and various others closely similar to these.

Table 8.3
Interpretations of 'usually'

Interpretations	Number of instances
Usually	210
What you always do	2
Almost always/almost every week	2
Generally	7
Normally/in the normal week	19
Habitually/your habit	9
Your routine/as a rule/your practice	5
Typically	2
Mostly/most/most often	7
Mainly	1
On an average evening	4
On the majority of occasions	2
More often than not	13
Often	5
Not just now and then	1
At least sometimes	1
Sometimes	8
Regularly	9
Taking an average/on average	45
Taking an average for summertime	1
Taking an average over the last six months	1
Taking a weekly average for weeks when you don't go out	1
Term omitted or overlooked	85
Others	5
Total	445

The bracket on the right groups the interpretations from 'Generally' through 'Mainly' with the figure 268.

Many of the respondents had altogether overlooked or disregarded the term 'usually', with the result that their answers were not constrained by it at all. Another section of respondents variously weakened the term into one or another of the following forms: 'more often than not', 'not just now and then', 'at least sometimes', 'sometimes'. Another group of respondents thought in terms of taking an average over some period (as distinct from saying what 'usually' happens). A few converted the term into 'regularly' (which could of course include infrequent behaviour, for example 'once every month'). There was in addition quite a lot of variation, *from one question to another*, in the degree to which the term 'usually' was interpreted as intended. It was at its worst in the question 'How many times do you usually switch from one station to the other, when viewing on a weekday evening?' (12 out of 52 got it as intended) and at its best (for very similar respondents) in the question: 'How many days of the week do you usually watch television?' (49/59).

Speculative comments

The term 'usually' is a rather strong one in that it specified behaviour or occurrences which occur rather more often than on a mere majority of occasions. Where there *is* some usual form of behaviour, the respondent should be able to answer the question without special difficulty. But where there is not any usual form of behaviour, he is placed in a rather difficult position. Strictly speaking he should opt out of answering altogether, saying that there is nothing that he *usually* does. However, the helpful respondent or the one who wants to say something, may feel forced either to ignore the term 'usually' or to weaken it to some degree (e.g. 'often' or even 'sometimes'). By so doing he can report his behaviour. This particular suggestion as to the partial cause of the trouble would fit in well with the evidence of how the extent and the nature of the distortion varies as we go from one form of question to another.

The conversion of 'usually' into the concept 'taking an average' could well be a process of a similar kind: the respondent provides information describing his own position in spite of there being no usual form of behaviour in his particular case.

On the other hand some of the distorted interpretations of the word 'usually' may spring out of a genuine misunderstanding of what the word means. Perhaps some respondents ordinarily think of it as meaning 'often', 'on average', 'regularlay'.

Mishearing of the term and perhaps not hearing it at all, ought also to be considered as possibly contributory factors.

Whatever the full set of reasons are for what has happened, the evidence of this enquiry provides clear warning that this particular term should be used with great care. It is probably fairly safe in areas of human activity where people adopt usual lines of behaviour, though even in those cases we cannot rule out the possibility that respondents may have a genuine misunderstanding of the meaning of the term or that they

359

will simply mishear it.

(Some uses of) the word 'have'

The word 'have' was tested in the context of several questions. On each occasion it was meant to be interpreted as 'actually have' rather than as 'could possibly have'.

Table 8.5

Interpretations of 'have'

Interpretations	Number of instances
Have (i.e. as intended)	86
Might have/might cause/might affect	5
Could have	10
Would be	2
Are likely to have/are likely to be/would be adversely affected if	5
Term considered only indirectly or overlooked	52
Total	160

Some 86 of the 160 interpretations tested were clearly as intended. On the other hand, 22 of them had been given either a weakened or a conditional character. For instance, the question 'Do any programmes have a bad effect on young people by setting them poor moral standards?' became, for several different respondents: 'Do you think any of the television programmes could have a bad effect on ...?'/'Are any programmes likely to have bad effects on ...?'/'Provided they are brought up properly and their viewing is controlled, will children be harmed by ...?'/'could any programmes have a bad influence ...?' A very similar question 'Do you think any programmes have bad effects on young people's morals?' became, for several, one or another of: 'With proper parental control over what they see, do you think that those aged 4 to 14 years would be adversely affected by ...?'/'Do you think that any programmes might cause ...?' etc.

Speculative comments

Some respondents may have felt themselves in a difficult position when asked to say whether or not television has in fact had the specified effect—in that they did not really know what the effect was and so felt constrained to answer a weaker question such as 'Do you think any programmes could have/might have ...?' Others were clearly in difficulty in that they felt that the answer depended upon the type of young person and the type of situation involved (e.g. 'It depends on the girl'/'It depends on the parents' outlook'.) This reaction appears to have lead them to convert the question into a conditional form of the sort given above (e.g. 'Provided they are brought up properly, will children ...?').

The reference 'on a weekday'

This reference was tested in four contexts. The aggregated results (217 interpretations from four contexts) are set out in Table 8.6.

The outstanding indication of this table is that in a large number of instances (73/217) 'weekday' was interpreted as referring to any of the seven days of the week. In other words, many respondents did not exclude Saturdays and Sundays from their consideration of the question.

Table 8.6

Interpretations of 'on a weekday'

Interpretations	Number of instances
From Monday till Friday (only) (= 5 days)	116
From Monday till Saturday (6 days)	2
From Monday till Friday plus Sunday)	2
From Sunday till Saturday (7 days)	72
Any day of the week	1
Not clear which days were considered	10
Reference apparently not considered at all	14
Total	217

There is, however, one other important feature of these results to which attention should be drawn, namely the way the test results for the term in one of its four contexts differed from those for the term in its other three contexts. In particular, for that fourth context of the term, 37 of the 59 respondents tested had interpreted the term as if it were any day of the week, compared with 10/54, 12/52, and 14/52 for the other three uses of it. Some possible reasons for this finding are suggested below.

Speculative comments

The fourth setting of the word (i.e. 'weekday') was as follows:

> When the advertisements come on between two television
> programmes on a weekday evening, do you usually watch
> them. (To be coded as: yes/no/sometimes/not sure.)

In looking for an explanation of what happened to the interpretation of 'weekday' when used in this setting, several things may be worth noting.

1 This particular question was rather crowded with concepts (all of them necessary for the proper interpretation of the question) and it may be that the effort of trying to grasp them all distracted the respondent from one or more of them, 'weekday' included.

2 Another point worth considering is that this question offered respondents a simple choice of answers (yes/no/sometimes/not sure), whereas the other questions required respondents to give an open response—e.g. 'For how many hours do you usually watch television on a weekday? This includes evening viewing'. In the circumstances, the possibility seems to exist that the latter type of question calls for the operation of the respondent's thought processes upon the specific elements of the question (i.e. 'How many hours on a weekday?')—more so, that is, than a question offering a fairly standard choice of answers'. Though this point is made purely at the speculative level, it is one which may well be worth further consideration and study.

Whatever the reasons for the conversion of 'weekday' into 'any day of the week', the occurrence of such a conversion—even at the lowest level of frequency at which it occurred in the four usages which were tested, could be of considerable import for general practice in question design.

The term 'weekends'

One test of this word was made, in the setting of the question:

> Amongst the programmes you watch at weekends, which one
> do you find the most interesting.

Whereas 39 of the 59 persons tested interpreted the term 'weekends' as intended, there were at least 11 who were in error. Of these, 3 considered only Saturdays or only Sundays, and 8 considered 'the whole week'. Another respondent limited his thinking to 'weekends in the winter'.

Speculative comments

The extent of this conversion is more or less in line with what happened, in the setting of similar question forms, to the term 'weekday'. This particular set of conversions may have sprung out of no more than mishearing or carelessness. But another possibility is that the request for the nomination of some one programme as the most interesting one known to the respondent may have led the respondent to break out of the narrow confines of weekend programmes—as,.for instance, when the respondent's favourite programme occurred on a weekday. Such a process would probably rank as interference of one part of the question with another part. Interference of any such kind is, of course, to be differentiated from intended interaction between the different elements of a question.

The term 'children'

This term was meant to be interpreted as 'children in general' rather than children in any narrow age range or special category. The term was tested in two separate questions, leading to 120 interpretations, details of which are given on pages 164—165 and 173—175.

The outstanding feature of these results is the marked variability, from one respondent to another, in the ages of the persons about whom an answer was formulated: 4—10; 9—11; 11—14; 6—14; 3—5; up to 5; 7—17; up to 10; from babyhood to 13; 'young children'; 'very young children; 'older children'; 'teenagers',etc. Considering all 120 interpretations together:

(a)   there were 16 which excluded those aged 10 years or less;

(b)   there were 32 which did not include those aged over ten years;

(c)   there were 8 which extended the ages considered beyond 16 years;

(d)   there were 33 which were limited to an age span of 4 years or less.

Another feature of the results was the apparent selectivity with respect to the categories of 'children' considered by some respondents: 'children such as your own children'; 'children, and your own in particular'; 'your own children'; 'your grandchildren'; 'children who have been brought up properly'; 'nervous children'; 'impressionable but not average children'. Some 20 of the 120 interpretations were of this kind.

The import of all this is, of course, that respondents who gave more or less similar answers may well have been referring to very different sorts of 'children'.

Speculative comments

Some of these variations in interpretation of the term 'children' may perhaps represent real differences between people in terms of what they consider are 'children'. However, it seems more likely that the wide variation in interpretations sprang out of a tendency for respondents to answer in terms of children they actually knew, or of sorts of children they thought they knew about, or in terms of the particular children with whom they were pre-occupied (e.g. as parents or grandparents). Perhaps some felt that this was the only safe way to answer. However, the immediate effect of any such tendency (i.e. to answer only within the limits of one's own confidence) would be to render the term 'children' very unstable as a communication medium.

The term 'young people'

In the context of the questions in which it was used, this term was meant to be interpreted as 'young people in general' rather than young people in any narrow age range or special category. The term was tested in the context of three separate questions, yielding 160 interpretations in all (from that number of respondents).

Just as with the interpretation of 'children', there was great variability, from one respondent to another, in the category of persons considered by respondents in reaching a reply: those aged 12—16 years; 5—8; 5—15; 16—25; those aged up to 16; 7—10; 7—15; 15—20; children under 21; 14—19; infancy to 18; 10—12; 16—17.

Bringing these interpretations together in collective form the emergent points include the following.

1 In the first place, there was a lot of variation in the lower limit of the age ranges considered: at least 10 of the 160 respondents included people aged 5 or less; approximately 25 had the lower age limit set in the range of 6—8 years; approximately 27 did not consider any aged less than 15 years.

2 Turning to the upper age limit of those considered as 'young people', we find that: 19 respondents did not consider those aged over 12 years; 36 had the upper limit at 15—16 years; 25 took the upper limit as being between 19 and 20 years and there were 7 who had it higher (21—25 years).

3 The ranges of ages considered were also highly varied: 16 respondents limited the 'young people' range to 3 years or less; 27 had thought in terms of a range of 8 to 10 years, several had it wider than 15 years.

In addition, there appeared to be some rather specialised selectivity entering into the interpretation processes of approximately 35 respondents. The main forms of this selectivity follow: children you know or are familiar with; particularly those known to you personally; children such as your own; your own children; boys only; girls only; children from good homes; working class children from places like Bermondsey; those who have been properly brought up; those whose viewing has been controlled; particularly those whose moral standards are not well developed.

Speculative comments

Several of the interpretations referred to in the previous paragraph appear to be selective in the extreme (e.g. children from good homes, those whose viewing has been controlled), and this could well have made a major difference to the answer given. These interpretations appear to be reactions to a situation in which the respondent feels that the impact of television on young people depends very much upon the personal background and character of the young people concerned.

Other of the variations listed above (e.g. children you know or are familiar with, children such as your own, your own children) could well have sprung from an understandable tendency of some respondents to want to limit their opinions to young people whose behaviour they are fairly familiar with. The wide variation in the ages of the young people considered may have sprung from a similar process, namely from people tending to formulate an answer in terms of young people they know personally or in terms of sorts of young people they feel they know about.

Whatever the reasons for the great variability which showed up through this analysis, it is clear that 'young people' is an imprecise term, just as is the term 'children' and it seems that its use can allow a great deal of variation in the kinds of people about whom an answer is formulated—without the interviewer necessarily being aware that this variability exists.

One further point is worth making. The actual form of the variability brought out in the analyses of respondent interpretation of the term 'young people', suggests some degree of influence by other parts of the question. For instance, in the question 'Do any programmes have a bad effect upon young people, by setting them poor moral standards?', it does appear that the reference to 'poor moral standards' has conditioned some of the interpretations of 'young people' (e.g. those who have been brought up properly/those whose moral standards are not well developed).

The reference 'morals' and 'moral standards'

The term 'morals' was tested in the context of Question 16, III (50 respondents) and 'moral standards' in the context of Question 16, I (51 respondents). In each case, the term was intended to refer to standards of right and wrong generally and not to some single aspect of morality (e.g. not violence only, not sexual morality only, not crime only, not swearing only, not drunkenness only).

Less than half of the respondents interpreted this term in the broad way intended, most of the rest interpreting it in a relatively limited way. Of the latter, 27 interpreted it in terms of sexual morality (only). On the other hand, there were some for whom that particular aspect of it did not enter at all into the interpretation (e.g. crime and violence only, violence only, bad language only).

Speculative comments

It seemed, from some of the details presented in Part II, that the use of this term in a question about television may have helped to slant some interpretations more one way than another (e.g. violence only, sex only), but over and above this, it seems that the term is open to variable interpretation, with quite a lot of people (but certainly not all) thinking of it as referring solely to sexual morality.

The term 'generally'

This term was tested only once, and in the context of the question:

> When you turn on your television in the evening, do you
> generally go on viewing till the end of the evening or do
> you just watch one or two programmes? (To be coded:
> view till end/one or two programmes/sometimes till end,
> sometimes one or two.)

In this particular test, there was evidence of only two of the 59 people tested definitely misinterpreting the term. They thought of it as 'regularly' and as 'on an average evening' respectively. It is worth noting that acceptable interpretations were nonetheless subject to some degree of variability: generally; usually; as usual; normally; habitually; as a matter of routine.

There were 9 (out of 59 people tested) who appeared to by-pass the word, almost all of them seemingly because the term 'generally' could not be applied to their own behaviour.

Speculative comments

This, of course, was one test in one context and we should not too readily give the word 'generally' a 'clean bill of health'. Thus it may well be that many people *do* generally do one or another of the alternatives outlined in this particular question. In other words, this question and its offer of answers may introduce but little pressure to distort or modify this term in some way. At the same time, the word 'generally' came through its single test much better than did the term 'usually' or various of the other terms presented in this section.

The term 'regularly'

This term was tested only once, in the context of the question:

> Do you use weekly printed programmes regularly when deciding what to view?' (To be coded as: yes/no/not sure.)

About a third of the 56 respondents tested appear to have left this term out of consideration altogether, turning the question into one about whether or not they used printed programmes for deciding what to view—thereby making it possible to answer 'yes' for even occasional uses of printed programmes.

Some (7) interpreted the term as 'usually' or as 'ordinarily' and there were 2 more who thought only of 'whenever deciding what to view'.

Of those who interpreted this term as intended, there was quite a lot of variation in the detail of interpretation: regularly; regularly each week; once a week; each day; each evening. All these carried the (intended) notion of 'recurring uniformly', and the variability seems to have sprung out of the particular form of behaviour which happened to fit individual cases (e.g. the person who reads a printed programme guide daily thought in terms of 'daily regularity' while the 'once a week' user thought in terms of 'weekly regularity'). Clearly, however, 'daily regularity' is a much more stringent sort of regularity than is 'weekly regularity.

Speculative comments

Quite possibly, the provision of a simple 'yes/no/not sure' choice of answer facilitated a respondent's escape from the strictures of this word. On top of this, the temptation to answer 'yes' for behaviour which was not quite regular could well have been strong for some respondents. And at what point, we may ask, does 'regularity' become 'non-regularity'?

The term 'few'

This term was tested in the context of only one question, namely:

> Thinking about television over the last few years, do you think that programmes are better nowadays or do you think they are worse than they were? (To be coded as: better now/some better, some worse/the same/no opinion or not sure.)

In this context, the term was meant to refer to a period of at least three years but not of more than six years duration.

There was in fact much variation in the interpretation of the term 'few': 7 out of the 59 people tested interpreted it as two years or less, 19 as seven years or more and 11 as ten years or more.

Speculative comments

In possible explanation of this finding, it is worth noting that the term 'few' is itself both vague (it has no numerical equivalent in the dictionary) and relative (e.g. to an old person, ten years may seem but a 'few' years). The important thing for the research worker is to realise that the term can have such breadth of numerical meaning.

In the present context, it seems quite possible that the stretching of the term to cover a period of over ten years may have been helped along by some respondents feeling their way back to a time when (in their opinion) programmes were different from 'now'.

The term 'impartial'

This term was tested only once (56 respondents) and in the context of the question:

> Do you think that the television news programmes are impartial about politics? (To be coded as: yes/no/not sure)

In this context, the word 'impartial' was meant to be interpreted as 'unbiased', 'fair', 'treating (all parties) alike'.

Of the 56 respondents tested, 25 interpreted this term more or less as intended. On the other hand, 5 gave it a meaning opposite to that intended (i.e. unfair, biased), 9 interpreted it as implying a tendency 'to give too much time or attention to' politics (e.g. partial to; include too much about) and 2 more as inclined 'to give too little time to' it or 'insufficient information about' it. Of the remainder, 10 appear simply to have overlooked the term (e.g. 'What do you think of BBC television news bulletins which refer to political events?') and several others clearly did not know *what* it meant.

Speculative comments

It is not impossible that some respondents simply heard the word as 'partial'. Others apparently were not familiar with the word. The overlooking of the term (10 respondents) usually went with considerable modification of the total question and the possibility exists that this represents a re-making of the question from some of its elements, because of a failure to understand its central term. In other words, the respondent misses the meaning of the question (because he fails to perceive some important part of it), but then does what he can by reassembling some of its bits and pieces and answering that assemblage as a question.

The term 'proportion'

The term 'proportion' was tested in the context of the following question through 53 people.

> What proportion of your evening viewing time do you spend watching news programmes?

In this context, 'proportion' was meant to mean 'fraction' (e.g. half, quarter, tenth) and it would reflect the size of the relationship of the amount of time spent by the viewer watching (any) news programmes and the total time he spent viewing (any) television programmes of any kind. Acceptable interpretations included: part; fraction; percentage.

Only 14 of the 53 respondents interpreted this reference more or less as intended, and two more appear to have interpreted it in a vaguely proportionate sense (i.e. 'Do you spend much/all of your time ... ?'). Of the remaining 37 respondents, 11 interpreted the term in a broadly quantitative (but not proportionate) sense, with things like: (for) how long ...; how many hours; how often.

The others (26 of the 53) appeared to have overlooked the reference. Thus 17 of them answered in terms of 'which (news programmes)', 5 in terms of 'when' (i.e. at what times), and one in terms of 'on which channel'. Several even thought in terms of something of the sort 'Do you like to watch ...?' or 'Do you watch ...?'

Speculative comments.

At least two of the possible reasons for this major failure seemed to be: that many respondents did not understand the word 'proportion'; that working out the 'proportion' is difficult or demanding and that respondents found some easier substitute for it.

There may also have been a tendency for people to be over-informative (i.e. by answering in terms of 'which' different news programmes they see instead of offering a proportion), but this may be no more than part of a tendency to evade the difficult task of working out some overall proportion.

Fifteen sets of hypotheses about the nature and the causes of respondent misunderstanding of the questions

In the course of the analyses presented on pages 49 to 349 in this volume, many different speculative comments (clearly labelled in the text as 'speculations') were put forward. They were put forward not only in relation to rather specific findings, but also as a source of material from which hypotheses about the nature and causes of misinterpretation might later be formulated. For the latter purpose an analysis was made of all the speculative material, using the technique of content analysis.

This led to the formulation of the 15 hypotheses set out in the following pages. The 15 are presented in order, according to the volume of the supporting evidence and, understandably, much more is written about the first two or three of them than is written about those appearing later in the list of 15.

In studying these hypotheses, it must be remembered at all times that they are no more than hypotheses, and that a lot of them tend to rest upon material which is not entirely unambiguous. If they are to progress beyond being hypotheses, the next step must be to subject them to rigorous tests, and this it was proposed to do as a follow-up to this enquiry.

To the psychologist working in communication research, some of these hypotheses will come as no surprise and he may even feel that in some contexts at least, some of them have been sufficiently well verified. However, be that as it may, the necessary verification has not yet been attempted with respect to survey questions asked in the context of the survey interview. Moreover, what we need to know is not simply whether an hypothesised process occurs to at least some degree, but the actual extent of its operation in the survey situation and the particular way in which the hypothesised process works in that situation.

Overlap of evidence. The evidence presented as a basis for any one hypothesis consists largely of examples drawn from the analyses on pages 49–349 of this volume. It will be noted by the careful reader that some one finding may figure somewhere amidst the speculative bases of *more than one* hypothesis. This is simply a reflection of the fact that more than one cause or perhaps 'alternative causes' might on occasions be speculated as lying behind some single finding. At the same

370

time, any single hypothesis tends to be based upon quite a wide range of separate findings and speculations.

Overlap of hypotheses. t is very likely that readers will begin to feel, as they go through one hypothesis after another, that some of them overlap each other or are repetitive to at least some degree. For instance, Hypothesis 1, which deals with the distortion of questions which respondents find specially difficult to cope with, refers, amongst other things, to the narrowing of some of the question elements—which is what Hypothesis 2 is about (i.e. the narrowing of elements of a question). However, the emphasis in Hypothesis 1 is upon distortion *when the question poses difficulties,* and that distortion might take the form of narrowing or of widening, or of 'clause dropping' etc. In other words, Hypothesis 2 is very much more specific than Hypothesis 1, and it deals with a specific *form* of distortion, whereas Hypothesis 1 deals with a broad *cause* of distortion.

Take another case. Hypothesis 7, which deals with people answering what they regard as the 'spirit' or the 'sense' of a question, may involve people in narrowing or broadening or qualifying. Or a mistaken idea about the 'spirit' or 'sense' of the question may have been produced by its context. But answering the 'spirit' of the question is, nonetheless, a process in its own right and it will not necessarily lead to narrowing or to broadening or to qualification; nor will it necessarily spring out of misinterpretation of context.

Accordingly, I believe the reader will find that though the 15 hypotheses do or could have areas of overlap, they are basically different hypotheses.

> *Hypothesis 1: When a respondent finds it difficult to answer a question, he is likely to modify it in such a way as to be able to answer it more easily*

The most recurrent cause of misinterpretation appears to have been asking a respondent a question which put that respondent in difficulty of some kind. Thus:

1 The question may call for very careful thought or even for a certain amount of mental arithmetic (e.g. the calculation of the proportion of one's time which is spent viewing certain kinds of programmes).

2 The question may put the respondent in an impossible position (e.g. as when he is asked about his usual behaviour when in fact he has no usual form of behaviour with respect to the subject of the question).

3 The respondent may be asked for an opinion about a matter

with respect to which he has only partial information (e.g. a question about the effects of television on children generally, when all he thinks he knows about are the effects of television on his own children).

4 The question may be so broad in its area of reference that the answer, according to the respondent, could be 'yes' for one aspect of it and 'no' for another (e.g. the appropriateness, for children, of programmes seen by children, would depend very much upon which programmes one considers).

5 The question may seem to ask for an answer to two conflicting questions (e.g. when respondent is asked if television has a bad effect by teaching slang—where respondent agrees that television teaches slang but does not think that this is a bad effect).

The respondent who is put into difficulty in one or another of these ways, could of course register 'no opinion'. But very often, it seems, respondents are sufficiently well motivated to try to give an answer, and in this situation they may resolve their difficulties in one or another of the ways listed below.

1 When a respondent finds the question difficult or burdensome or even impossible to answer:

(a)　he may distort it to make it easier/possible to answer;

(b)　he may soften or weaken the question elements which produce his difficulty;

(c)　he may omit the difficult element(s) altogether;

(d)　he may qualify some part of the question in order to make it easier to give an answer;

(e)　he may convert the question to cover his giving the interviewer some or all of the detail necessary for formulating a reply (leaving the interviewer to finish the job).

The following appear to be examples of one or another of these processes.

(i)　A respondent is asked to work out what proportion of his evening viewing time he spends watching news programmes. Assuming that he knows the meaning of 'proportion', this question could well involve the respondent in close thinking and in calculation. In this situation he may convert the question into something like 'for *roughly* what proportion of your evening viewing time ...?' or 'for how long in all do you watch news programmes?' or 'at what times do you watch news programmes?'

(ii)　The respondent who is asked what he 'usually' does when the TV advertisements come on may be in difficulty because he has no usual form of behaviour in this situation and so may convert this term into something like 'often', or 'sometimes', or 'all the different things'.

(iii) When a respondent is asked for the name of the one programme he finds most interesting amongst those he watches at weekends: he may widen 'one' into 'ones'; he may ease 'most interesting' into 'specially interesting' or even into 'like'; he may rid himself of the restriction 'weekend' and so think in terms of any day of the week.

(iv) A person asked 'how many times he switches from one station to the other ...' may change that question to a request for 'about how many times' or into a request for 'the circumstances under which he switches'.

(v) An introductory clause such as 'Remembering that advertisements pay for ITV programmes' may be dropped because it partly restricts the respondent's formulation of a reply and seems to clutter his thinking.

(vi) A shift worker who is asked for how many days of the week he usually watches TV, may find it easier to think simply in terms of the period when he is on day shift and so refers the question to that period only (without making this clear to the interviewer).

2 When a respondent is unsure of all the facts of the matter about which he is questioned:

(a) he may limit himself to that aspect of the matter about which he feels competent to reply;

(b) he may change the question to allow him to give a conditional or an evasive or a qualified reply.

The following appear to be examples of one or the other of these processes.

(i) A question about the effects of television upon children is converted into one about 'children known to you personally', or 'children such as your own', or 'the local children', or 'your daughter(s) only'.

(ii) A question asking the respondent if he thinks television has some particular kind of effect upon young people becomes something like 'do you think that television might/might possibly/could have such and such an effect'. Or the respondent might add to it a qualification of the sort 'provided the young people concerned have been properly brought up'.

3 When a question is so wide as to permit a 'yes' to one aspect of the 'point' of reference and a 'no' to another aspect of it, the respondent may qualify the 'point' of reference so that it refers to only ONE such section of the people/things concerned.

The following appear to be examples of this type of process:

(i) Respondents were asked about the appropriateness, for children, of television programmes seen by children. For some respondents, 'programme' became 'children's hour programmes', for others 'adult programmes' and for others again 'adult programmes such as plays' and for still others 'adult programmes such as plays with sex and violence in them'.

(ii) In another question about the effects of TV on children, the term 'children' was in one case qualified into 'children who are brought up properly', in another case into 'nervous' children, and in others into 'your own children'.

4 When a question seems to include conflicting questions, the respondent is likely to settle for one of them (without this necessarily being evident to the interviewer).

The following appears to be an example of such a process. Respondents were asked if they thought 'any programmes had a bad effect ... by teaching slang'. Some respondents thought that television did teach slang but that this was not a 'bad effect'. In this situation they answered either the question about slang or the question about bad effects.

> *Hypothesis 2: If a broad term or concept is used, there will be a strong tendency for respondents to interpret it less broadly*

Where a question designer uses a broad concept (e.g. 'programmes') without some limiting qualification (e.g. adult programmes presenting crime or violence) his purpose is usually to set respondents thinking in terms of the total 'area' defined by that broad concept. When this is attempted, however, there operates a strong tendency, on the part of respondents, to narrow that broad concept in some way. A number of different factors appear to enter into this narrowing process.

1 The respondent will tend to limit his interpretation of the broad concept to those aspects of it which relate specially to his own background or to his personal situation.

2 The respondent will tend to limit his interpretation of the broader issue to aspect(s) of it with which he has had personal experience of some kind.

3 The respondent will tend to limit his interpretation of the broader term to aspects of it with which he is preoccupied, or

374

that he wants specially to talk about, or about which he is emotionally aroused.

4 The respondent may desire to eliminate from consideration that aspect of the broader issue which could show him up in a 'poor light'—and so he tends to avoid consideration of that particular aspect of it.

The following appear to be examples of one or another of these four narrowing processes.

(i) Suppose that a respondent is asked to compare TV programmes of the present day with those of a few years ago. If his viewing experience has been largely in terms of ITV programmes, he may well make the comparison in terms of ITV programmes only. If, to take another possibility, he had only just started to receive ITV programmes, he might make the comparison in terms of BBC programmes alone (BBC being the only service which he could receive throughout the period of the comparison). Or, if a respondent is interested mainly in TV plays, the comparison may be made only in terms of the output of plays.

(ii) If the respondent has strong feelings about TV advertisements that interrupt his programmes, then a question about TV advertisements in general may well be narrowed down to one about TV advertisements that break into programmes.

(iii) If a respondent is asked about the amount of viewing he does, he may leave out of consideration his viewing of programmes not selected by himself.

(iv) If respondents are asked about the effects of television on young people, and if they are familiar with the viewing behaviour of only special sections of the population of young people, they may well answer the question solely in terms of those young people.

The narrowing of a broad term can also take place through the defining or limiting functions of (i) certain words in the question, (ii) the question as a whole. This influence of some words or of the question as a whole may be as intended by the question designer or it may be something that was not intended at all.

5 Narrowing, as intended, by context or by qualifying words. A very simple example of intended narrowing is the reference 'bad effects', where the word 'bad' defines the class of effect that is intended. When respondents are asked if TV has bad effects ... by setting ... poor moral standards, the term 'poor' moral standards further defines the sort of effect that is being referred to. Definition of this sort is, in fact,

a vital element in good question design.

6 The narrowing of concepts, in unintended ways, by certain words in the question and by the question as a whole (see also Hypothesis 6 dealing with the influence of context and of control words).

(i) One example of defective narrowing seems to have been the use of the term 'news' to qualify the word programmes. In many cases, a commonly evoked meaning of 'news' served to narrow the term 'programmes' into 'bulletins'.

(ii) Instances of unintended narrowing occurred with the question: 'Do you think that television programmes seen by children are appropriate for them?' On the basis of the phrase 'seen by children' some respondents wrongly interpreted the question to refer only to programmes designed for children.

(iii) In the question 'Is TV advertising time used properly?', the word 'time' was interpreted by nearly half the respondents concerned as 'timing'; this in turn led some of them to limit their thinking to advertisements that interrupt programmes (these being the ones most connected, in their minds, with 'poor timing' of advertisements).

Where the broad concept is not controlled/defined by context or by control words, two things may happen

7 The narrowing of a broad concept may take a great many different forms where the term concerned has to it many different aspects or facets and where no one of those aspects is dominantly in vogue. Thus the term 'properly' (in the context of the question 'Is television advertising time used properly?') was interpreted in terms of 'advertiser benefits', or of 'power to get viewer attention' or of 'service to viewers' or of 'the total amount of time given to advertisements', and so on.

8 The narrowing by respondents may be considerable, so that only some single narrow aspect of the original broad concept is considered by any one respondent.

It is fairly clear, on the evidence of this inquiry, that if a broad term were intended to be kept broad, then very special steps would have to be taken to maintain its breadth. However, since many people will not even be aware of some of the aspects of the broad issue which the question designer had in mind, it would probably be necessary to work, instead, through the various relevant elements of that broad concept. In other words, it is not only very difficult to keep a broad term meaningfully broad when the respondent goes to work upon the question, but the value of so endeavouring is suspect.

Often, however, a broad term is used mainly as the first step in defining some more specific aspect of it about which the question designer wants information. Where he may go wrong, however, is in his efforts to define or to qualify it as intended. Often his definition of that particular aspect of the broader concept to which he wants to refer is unintentionally too broad or unintentionally too unspecific. It may even be misleading. Accordingly, what is really necessary is a much more rigorous defining/controlling/qualifying process—a process which really needs to be pre-tested if the designer is to be sure that the respondent is, in fact, focusing upon that aspect of the broad issue to which a reaction is wanted. The essence of good question design is successful definition of this kind.

Hypothesis 3: Under certain circumstances a term or concept may be widened

Whereas a broad term, particularly an imprecise one, is likely to be narrowed to fit respondent's personal background or to serve his needs for self expression, a fairly narrow term may be widened. The widening of fairly narrow terms was much less in evidence in this inquiry than was the narrowing of fairly broad terms, though quite possibly this was a function of the relative distribution of narrow and of broad terms in the questions tested: the broad terms were predominant in number. Widening appears to have taken place under the following conditions:

1   Where the respondent feels he is too restricted by some very narrow concept or where respondent feels that he is saying too little by dwelling upon only one specific point of detail.

2   Where a reference splits off a single aspect of a broader matter about which respondent feels strongly (with the result that the single aspect may be widened into that broader matter itself.

3   Where a wide setting to a question leads the respondent to expect a wider concept than the one offered.

4   Where the setting of a narrow term is wide (leading the respondent to widen the narrow term 'to match').

5   Where a similar sounding, and familiar, concept is a wider one than the 'less familiar' one actually involved in the question.

Some examples will serve to illustrate the above hypothesised processes.

   (i) The question 'Amongst the programmes you watch at weekends, which one do you find the most interesting?' may leave a respondent wanting to widen the term 'weekend' (to any day of the week) because his favourite programme occurs on a weekday.

(ii) If a respondent is asked only about cartoon advertisements, but has a lot that he wants to say about TV advertising in general, he may well extend the narrow limits of the question to cover advertising in general.

(iii) In one of the test questions, respondents were asked: 'When the advertisements come on between two programmes, what do you usually do when you stay in the room with the television?' If a particular respondent feels it hard to split off his 'between programme' behaviour from his 'within programme' behaviour, he may widen the reference in order to talk about TV advertisements generally; similarly, if his main stimulus to 'avoidance behaviour' occurs when advertisements come within programmes or if 'within programme' advertising is what annoys him. Then again, a respondent may automatically convert the somewhat unusual specification of 'between programme' advertising into the more familiar and expected concept of 'advertising generally'. Another respondent, in dealing with that same question, may widen the question to deal with his behaviour irrespective of whether it occurs in the TV room or outside of it.

(iv) In one question, respondents were asked if children suffer ill effects from watching programmes with violence in them. The term 'violence', presented in the wider setting of 'ill effects', appears thereby to have been widened by some respondents to include matters such as bad language, rudeness.

Just as with the narrowing of broad terms, the only effective remedy to the unintended widening of narrow terms lies in the rigorous (and preferably pre-tested) use of qualifications, of control words, and of controlling context.

Hypothesis 4. Part of a question may be overlooked under certain conditions as set out below

Single words, grouped words or even whole phrases may be overlooked by some respondents under one or more of the following conditions.

1   When, at first impression, an element of the question seems to be superfluous (and so is discarded)

2   When other parts of the question seem to make some particular part of it superfluous

3   Where the respondent feels able to start answering the question before all of it is read out to him (e.g. where a qualifying clause is tacked on at the end of the question or where a question seems to be completely stated before this is in fact so).

4   Where two long alternatives are offered as answers at the end of a question (in which case, the second of them may be overlooked because the respondent thinks that he has heard enough to answer the question).

5   Where a qualifying clause postulates a condition that is unusual or imposes some odd qualification upon a familiar concept.

6   Where the wording of the question is such that ordinary mishearing is facilitated (e.g. 'impartial' becomes 'partial').

The following appear to be examples of one or another of the above processes.

(i)   In the question 'When the advertisements come on between two television programmes on a weekday evening, do you usually watch them?', a respondent may at first sight have regarded the term 'weekday' as an unnecessary specification and so have dropped it. Similarly for the opening phrase of Question 19, I, namely 'Remembering that advertisements pay for ITV programmes'.

(ii)   In the following question, the qualifying clause (in italics) is tacked on at the end of a question which respondent could have started to answer without reference to the qualification: 'How many days of the week do you usually watch television? *I mean weekdays and Saturdays and Sundays, of course, and daytime viewing as well as evening viewing*'. The same process could well have occurred for Question 5, III, which is closely similar in form to Question 19, I. Similarly for Question 4, IV.

(iii)   The overlooking process may well have been in marked operation in the following question, in which the qualifying clause is in italics: 'Do you think that children suffer any ill effects from watching programmes with violence in them, *other than ordinary Westerns?*' Up to half the respondents tested on this question failed to take note of that 'tacked on' restriction. The same kind of process may well have been involved with respect to the restrictive 'tail piece' to Question 3PD, IV: 'How many people are there in your household? Do not include yourself'. Similarly for the restrictive clause at the end of Question 21, II: 'When the advertisements come on, what do you usually do when you stay in the room with the television?'

(iv)   It is possible, however, that the dropping of some of the 'tail pieces' referred to in (iii) above arose partly (or even largely) from such clauses seeming to conflict with the rest of the question (e.g. 'ordinary Westerns' may have struck some respondents as the major source of violence on television) or as being contrary to respondent's understanding of the term (e.g. a request for size of household ordinarily includes the respondent himself).

> *Hypothesis 5(a): A respondent may distort a question to fit his own situation or position or experience*

This hypothesis may overlap Hypothesis 3, which dealt with the broadening of a narrow concept. In this case, however, the emphasis is upon distortion (which may or may not involve widening).

Distortion of the hypothesized kind may take one or another of the following forms.

1 The respondent may convert the question so that it fits or applies to his own case; this process will more probably occur when the term most likely to distorted is itself imprecise.

2 The respondent may leave out some part of the question which tends to exclude his own case.

The following seem to be examples of this type of process.

(i) In Question 10, III, the question was in terms of what the respondent usually did. Where a respondent has no usual form of behaviour, but only behaviour which varies quite a lot, he may convert 'usually' into 'sometimes' and so be able to reply to the question.

(ii) In Question 8, IV, respondents were asked about their use of weekly printed programmes. Some respondents, who used only the programmes printed in the daily papers, converted this reference to 'daily printed programmes'.

(iii) In one of the questions (9,I), the respondent was asked if, when he turned on his TV set, he went on viewing till the end of the evening or just watched one or two programmes. Two respondents qualified the first of the two offered answers with, respectively: 'except for breaks'; 'provided you are not interrupted'. For that same question, several respondents modified 'till the end of the evening' into 'till the end of *your* evening' (e.g. till your bedtime at 10.00 pm).

(iv) In response to the question about regular use of weekly printed programmes, the term weekly was dropped by several respondents who then answered 'Yes' with respect to programme lists in daily papers.

(v) Where a question asks about 'regular' behaviour of some kind, the term 'regular' may be dropped or overlooked with the result that the respondent qualifies for an affirmative answer on the basis of possibly *irregular* behaviour of the kind specified.

Hypothesis 5(b): A respondent may distort a question because he wants to create an opportunity to express an opinion, perhaps strongly held

Just as for Hypothesis 5(a), this one overlaps Hypothesis 3 to some extent, but differs from it in that it deals with distortion, i.e. irrespective of whether or not such distortion takes the form of a widening of terms.

Distortions of the hypothesised kind appear to operate in one or more of the following ways.

1   The respondent may want to say something beyond the strict limits of the question asked and so may, in effect, answer a question different from that put to him. The desire to reply beyond the actual question may arise from a preoccupation which the respondent brought to the interviewing situation or it may be specially triggered off by the question itself.

2   The respondent wanting to talk out in this way may do so by changing some of the elements of the question, or he may do it by adding to the original question.

3   The respondent may want to answer a question appreciably different from that actually asked, or even a different question altogether.

The following seem to be examples of these several suggested processes.

(i)   A respondent asked about what he likes in TV programmes may also offer some details of what he dislikes (i.e. in effect, 'What do you like?' is converted into 'what do you like *and what do you dislike?*').

(ii)   The question 'What are the things you dislike about programmes on television?' became, for some, questions such as 'Are you generally satisfied with ...?'; 'What do you do when programmes you dislike appear?'; 'What do you dislike, and give your reasons?'.

(iii)   The introduction: 'Remembering that advertisements pay for ITV programmes ... ' became, for one respondent, 'Remembering that advertisements break into programmes ... '.

(iv)   To the question 'Is television advertising time being used properly?', one respondent added 'and does the manner of presentation spoil programmes for you?'. Others interpreted this question solely in terms of the usefulness, to viewers, of advertising.

Hypothesis 5(c): A respondent may distort the question so as not to admit anything that puts him in a 'poor light'

The following appeared to be examples of such a process.

(i) A respondent who is asked if he went on viewing till the end of the evening (or watched just one or two programmes), may accept the first of the two alternatives after modifying it into the form: 'go on viewing provided you are interested in what you see'. Or it may be rejected after conversion into the form 'go on viewing indiscriminately'.

(ii) Questions of the kind 'How many days of the week do you watch TV' may be qualified by an addition of the sort: 'excluding days when you don't view much'.

Hypothesis 6(a): The general context or setting of a term in a question may wrongly influence the way that term is interpreted ('context' being the question and/or the questionnaire within which the term is set)

This process appears to operate in one or more of the following ways.

1 A term's context (i.e. the question as a whole/or the questionnaire) may distort its interpretation.

2 A term's context may wrongly narrow or wrongly widen it's interpretation.

3 An ambiguous or unstable context may lead to variable interpretation of a word.

4 An unstable word is especially open to influence by context.

5 Context may convert a neutral word into a qualifying term.

The following appear to be examples of one or another of these kinds of processes.

(i) In a question about the impartiality or otherwise of news programmes in their treatment of political matters, a respondent may be led, because the question refers to political matters, to interpret news programmes as political programmes (e.g. party political broadcasts, political interviews).

(ii) A question about the number of people in a respondent's household was presented in the context of a question about television: quite possibly as a result of this, some respondents limited their counts to viewing personnel (e.g. people who watch television/people old enough to watch television/people who sit down in this house to watch television.

(iii) In a question about advertising, the reference 'time' became 'timing' (of advertisements).

(iv) The reference 'television advertising' introduced into a questionnaire directly concerned with TV programmes may for some become 'television'.

(v) The word 'slang' may become 'crime' or 'violence' or 'bad way of life' when presented in questions about the possible 'bad effects of television programmes'.

> *Hypothesis 6(b): Specific words or clauses which are meant to define or qualify a wider term, may lead to the misinterpretation of that wider term*

This process seems to operate in one or another of the following ways.

1 A term in a question may wrongly be assumed to qualify or define some wider concept, leading to an unintended de-limiting of that wider term.

2 A term which is intended to define or qualify or de-limit a wider reference may itself be vague and variable in meaning and lead to varying interpretations of that wider reference.

3 A term which is intended to define or qualify or de-limit may be misleading and so produce some particular de-limitation of an unintended kind.

The following appear to be examples of one or another of these processes.

(i) The term 'programme' sometimes becomes 'children's programmes' when respondents are asked if TV programmes seen by children (are appropriate for them).

(ii) The term 'television' may become 'TV and radio' when respondent wrongly assumes that it's somewhat odd qualification 'news programmes' means 'news bulletins'.

(iii) In the question about 'any programmes having a bad effect by setting poor moral standards', a limited interpretation or 'morals' (e.g. sex morality only) can wrongly limit the sort of 'bad effect' considered.

(iv) In Question 15, II, the use of the word 'children', taken in combination with the word 'violence', may well have led to the widening of the word 'programmes' to include—Westerns—in spite of Westerns being specifically ruled out by a qualifying clause.

383

Hypothesis 7: A respondent may answer to what he regards as the 'spirit' or 'sense' of the question, rather than to its actual words, and so perhaps misinterpret the question

In this type of process, the respondent feels that he knows what it is that the interviewer is trying to get at and so answers that interpretation of the question. This interpretation may be a fairly 'free' one. The following appear to be examples of this kind of process.

(i) To the question 'How many times do you usually switch from one station to the other?', a respondent may judge that the interviewer really wants to know if the respondent sticks to just the one station or tries the other as well, and fits his answer to that question.

(ii) When respondent is asked if he goes on viewing till the end of the evening or watches just one or two programmes, he may assume that he is being asked if he views indiscriminately or selectively and so chooses the answer 'one or two' as indicating that he views selectively (even if he does in fact watch appreciably more than 'one or two').

(iii) To the question 'How many days of the week do you usually watch television?' a respondent who feels that the interviewer wants to know about what happens under fairly settled conditions, may refer the question back to a period when his viewing was settled (e.g. when your wife was alive/counting only weeks when you are home each night).

Hypothesis 8: A question may be wrongly interpreted if it has in it difficult words or words which mean different things to different people

This type of failure may arise in one or another of the following ways.

1 A respondent may have an incorrect idea as to the meaning of a key word in the question and so answer a question based on an incorrect interpretation of that word.

2 The respondent may realise he does not know the meaning of a key word, but may try to guess it from its context or from its sound.

3 Some words have different (but perhaps permissible) meanings for different people, with the result that one question is variably interpreted.

4 A word which is not understood may sound like another (familiar) word and be converted to that (familiar) word.

384

The following appear to be examples of such processes.

(i) The word 'usually' was interpreted by some as 'taking an average'.

(ii) The word 'proportion' was simply not understood by some respondents.

(iii) The word 'cartoon' in the context of 'cartoon advertisements' was narrowly interpreted as: (advertisements) presented through animated drawings; humorous advertisements; deliberately silly advertisements.

(iv) 'Slang' can mean: Cockney type language; Americanisms; swearing; etc.

(v) 'Weekday' can become for some, Monday through to (and including) Saturday.

✗ (iv) 'Slang' may be interpreted as: Cockney type language; Americanisms; swearing; etc.

(vii) 'Household' may mean 'all in the house' or 'all in the immediate family unit living in the house', or 'all in the immediate family even if some are not living there now', etc.

(viii) The term 'impartial' may be changed into 'partial' through conversion to a familiar sounding word when impartial is not understood.

(ix) For some respondents, 'news programmes' became 'the news'.

> *Hypothesis 9(a): A word or part of a word may not be heard properly and so lead to erroneous interpretation of the question in which it occurs.*

This source of difficulty may lead to misinterpretations of different kinds, for example:

1 The respondent's failure to hear a word or part of a word may leave the respondent with a question which, though different, is quite sensible sounding (e g only the first half of the word 'weekend' is heard). In the reference 'television advertising', the word 'advertising' may not be heard; in the reference 'weekday evening', ondly 'weekday' may be heard. The word 'impartial' is heard as 'partial'. The word 'not' goes unheard (e.g. 'do not include yourself' may become 'include yourself').

2 A word or part of a word may go unheard but be replaced by a word or part of a word which makes sense out of the question:

excluding may thus become including; a failure to hear 'other than' in the clause 'other than ordinary Westerns' (Q.15, II) may lead to the conversion of that phrase into something like 'including ordinary Westerns'.

3 A word may be misheard (e.g. 'one' is heard as 'one's').

> *Hypothesis 9(b): A respondent may, because he misses part of a question, reconstruct the question from those parts of it which he has heard*

It appears that some respondents may miss whole phrases in a question or perhaps key concepts. In this situation, the question may make little or no sense, but a respondent may (either unwittingly or hopefully) re-assemble all or some of the perceived parts to make a sensible sounding question—to which will offer an answer. The evidence available is not in any way conclusive, but it does suggest that such a process occurs, at least occasionally, for a wide range of people and that it is rather more likely to occur as the number of its constituent elements or concepts increases.

> *Hypothesis 9(c): When a question has in it a lot of information carrying words, it is specially open to misinterpretation*

The misinterpretation of such questions appears to occur through:

1 The loss of one or more of the elements necessary for its proper grasp (see also Hypothesis 9(b)).

2 Interference, at the perceptual level, of one concept with another (e.g. as when the use of an explanatory phrase or of a 'hammering home' clause interferes with the consolidation of other parts of the question initially understood).

> *Hypothesis 10: The word 'you' is prone to be interpreted collectively (e.g. as 'you and others') where it refers to behaviour in which the respondent is involved with others*

This was a very common phenomenon. The evidence also suggests that

1 The television context (e.g. family viewing) may be especially conducive to producing a collective interpretation of 'you'.

2 A question about family or about behaviour in family settings may help produce collective interpretation of this term.

3 It may be specially difficult (in questions about viewing behaviour) for respondents to separate their own behaviour from

386

that of others. The possibility certainly exists that certain other terms may also be subject to collective interpretation.

Numerous examples of this phenomenon are set out on earlier pages where the interpretation of this particular term is dealt with at length.

Hypothesis 11: A respondent may add to a question in order to be able to enlarge or to qualify his answer

There appear to be many examples of this sort of process scattered throughout the content analysis of respondent interpretation of the various test questions (e.g. to the question 'How many days of the week do you usually watch television?' the respondent adds 'and on which ones?').

Hypothesis 12: Where a question is ambiguous, a respondent may select one of the two possible interpretations, without the interviewer necessarily being aware that this has happened.

Hypothesis 13: A qualifying clause may interfere with the consolidation of respondent's grasp of preceding elements of the question (see also Hypothesis 9(c))

Hypothesis 14: When some concept presented to a respondent seems odd, he may well normalise it (e.g. 'cartoon advertisements' may become 'cartoons' or 'cartoon programmes'; 'advertising time' may become 'the timing of advertisements')

Hypothesis 15: When a complex or thought demanding question is followed by a simple choice of answers (e.g. yes/no/?), the respondent is likely to give less care to his consideration of the detail of the question and so is less likely to interpret the question as intended.

Still at the speculative level, this situation may perhaps be contrasted with that in which the respondent has to formulate his own answer to the question and is led, by this requirement, to work over the detail of the question in order to formulate that reply—a process which is more likely to leave him with a correct interpretation than would more superficial attention to the detail of the question.

Two recommendations have been put forward on the basis of the results of this enquiry.

1 Steps should be taken to investigate further the 15 sets of hypotheses that are formulated in Chapter 8. This work should be undertaken as a means of extending knowledge about the nature and the causes of misunderstanding of survey questions and for the further development of guidelines for the question designer.

2 There should be regular use of direct question testing for detecting misunderstanding of survey questions.

Each of these recommendations is developed in this chapter.

For the long-term development of question design principles and guidelines

The results of this enquiry provide a major case for conducting research on a substantial basis into the understanding by survey respondents of the questions put to them by interviewers. This work, which should be wide-ranging in its coverage, should include investigation of the 15 hypotheses set out on pages 370–389 of this book and involving over 50 principles. The purpose of such work would be to develop further the guidelines system available to the question designer.

This would be a long-term project involving quite a lot of research on an occasional basis over a lengthy period of time. I think it should include collaboration from time to time between academic and business personnel. It would need to be sustained as a project by a funding agency which has established question design research as a problem with some degree of funding priority. Alternateively a research group concerned with research methodology might support a long-term programme of work of this kind.

If the steady development of question design technology does not get under way—and very little has happened in a long time—then question design is not going to develop towards being a reliable science and mistakes will continue to be made. From time to time these will be big mistakes.

Though I have stressed the need to test the foregoing hypotheses as an important step in forwarding the science of question design, I am not for a moment suggesting that we let go of existing guidelines in the meantime—even where these guidelines are largely provisional in character. Indeed, there is a good case—including the dictates of common sense—for the continuing use of provisional guidelines such as the following. This case consists of one or more of: the evidence of the present enquiry; published research findings; common sense or common experience.

AVOID:

- loading up the question with a lot of different or defining terms;

- offering long alternatives (as possible answers to a question);

- the use of words that are not the usual working tools of the respondent;

- the use of words that mean something different if partly misheard;

- giving the respondent a difficult task to perform;

- giving the respondent a task that calls for a major memory effort;

- offering alternatives that could *both* be true.

BEWARE:

- the strong tendency of respondents to answer questions about their behaviour in terms of what they *usually* do—as distinct from what they did in fact do;

- the use of a qualifying clause, especially at the end of a question;

- the tendency of respondents to start answering a question as soon as they have heard enough to start formulating a reply;

- the very strong tendency of respondents to *narrow down* broad concepts, especially vague ones, in some selective and personally appropriate way;

- a tendency in some respondents to broaden a narrow concept;

- the tendency of respondents to apply their own special qualifications to the question without letting the interviewer

389

know that this is being done;

- the often strong influence of the question's context upon the interpretation of specific terms in that question;
- the distortion of the meaning of a wide range of terms of the sort frequently used in survey questions (e.g. you, regularly, proportion, usually).

The reader will find these guidelines useful for his own formulation of survey questions. No doubt he will add to this list as he reads further and gains experience in question design. He may well develop further provisional guidelines from an intensive reading of the results set out in this report or from his own analysis of the actual interpretations which are given in full in the Appendix. *But in the long term it is most important that we understand the principles and the processes that underlie such guidelines and that the guidelines themselves be subject to challenge through research. It is for this reason that I have recommended the investigation of the 15 sets of hypotheses specified in Chapter 8.*

Testing questions to detect sources of misinterpretation by respondents

The thoughtful and skilled use of the available guidelines will reduce the degree to which respondents misunderstand survey questions. Unfortunately, however, the guidelines system available to the question designer is by no means complete as yet. Moreover, many question designers make relatively little use of what *is* available.

In the circumstances, at least occasional direct testing of one's questions is essential. There is simply no way in which standard piloting can be used reliably to reveal the many misunderstandings of respondents, many of them unsuspected by the respondent himself and not visible to the piloting interviewer. Certainly question testing in the wake of standard piloting strongly supports such a recommendation.

To meet the requirements of safe practice in question design, a short form of question testing has been developed and is presented here. As a procedure, it is based closely on the methods used in the present enquiry, but it has been shortened to make it economically practical to use as a general tool of question design. It has been used, modified and re-used and in its present form it is suitable for general use as a practical question-testing procedure.

The question-testing method: in brief

The question-testing procedure begins with what appears to be a standard pilot interview. However, immediately that interview has been completed, the interviewer switches over to her question-testing role, explaining that her purpose is to test her questions. She will have been selected and trained for this class of work and there may be as many as four such people working at the one time on a range of questions.

A single question-testing interviewer usually tests the same 3—4 questions through each of her respondents. For each of the questions to be tested, she works through two stages of testing.

1 She reminds the respondent of the question to be tested and she does this by reading it out again. She also reads back the answer the respondent gave to that question. She asks the respondent to explain how she arrived at or worked out that answer. She probes extensively for all aspects of the way in which the respondent arrived at her answer.

2 She next delivers a set of specific check questions designed by headquarters staff to find out how each concept in the original question was interpreted.

She then repeats this two-stage operation for each of the other 2—3 questions that she has to test.

The question testing method: in detail

1 Question testing interviewers are ordinarily drawn from the ranks of the existing interviewers. Whatever the source, they should be people who are bright, flexible and who have something of a detective mentality, along with an empathetic and pleasant way of dealing with people. They must be trained to carry out question testing and this must include training them to probe. With the right person, a week of intensive training will be sufficient in the first place, but short re-training sessions are necessary from time to time.

2 In the usual question-testing situation, each question-testing interviewer will be given some 3—4 questions to test and she will do this in the context of the questionnaire in which they normally occur.

3 The question-testing interviewer starts by delivering the whole questionnaire just as she might do in a piloting interview, taking special note of her own experiences and/or any perceived respondent difficulties in relation to the, say four, questions that subsequently she will be testing. Once this is done, she tells the respondent that she would like to continue for a further 20 minutes and that she would be happy to pay for that extra time (saying how much). She explains that the extension of the interviewer is to find out if her questions are of the sort that people readily understand. If this request is made with charm and confidence, the great

391

majority of respondents will agree. Immediate continuation is what should be vigorously sought.

4 When agreement has been secured, the question-testing interviewer explains again that her purpose is to test the *questions* and *not* to test the respondent. She stresses this and then proceeds as follows with the several stages of the question-testing procedure. She gets the respondent's agreement to let her use a tape recorder.

SHE SAYS:

One of the questions I asked you was ..... (ASK RESPONDENT THE QUESTION AND PAUSE) and you answered ..... (REPEAT THE ORIGINAL ANSWER GIVEN). Is that *exactly* what you answered?

Now I want you to think back to when you were answering that question in the interview and tell me *exactly* how you arrived at that answer. Take your time about it.

> THE QUESTION-TESTING INTERVIEWER IS
> REQUIRED TO PROBE FULLY AND TO CLARIFY
> ANY VAGUE ASPECTS OF THE REPLY NOW GIVEN.
> SHE TAPE-RECORDS THE FULL REPLY AND
> MAKES BRIEF NOTES AS NECESSARY
>
> IF THE QUESTION DOES NOT STIMULATE A FULL
> REPLY, SHE USES ONE OR MORE OF THE FOLLOW-
> ING APPROACHES:

What led you to answer ..... (REPEAT ANSWER)
What went on in your mind when you were asked that question?

You must have worked out your answer *somehow*. How did you reach your answer of ..... (REPEAT THE ANSWER GIVEN).

Throughout this process, the question-testing interviewer has to be alert, ready to re-align the respondent if she is missing the point, ready to try again with a fresh question-stimulus if the respondent has still not got the idea of what is wanted. The question-testing interviewer should remain alert to the likelihood that a respondent will tell her what she understands NOW and must be ready to re-mind the respondent that *it is her understanding and thinking at the time the questionnaire was first delivered that is wanted.*

It is quite possible that something the interviewer observed at the time of her delivery of the questionnaire seems relevant to her first stage of questioning and in that event the interviewer may use this observation as a challenging or interrogating device. But the

392

interviewer must nonetheless remain neutral, must not suggest or otherwise prompt and must make full use of her probing tactics.

5 When this has been done, the question-testing interviewer moves into the second stage of her testing procedures. She has a number of quite specific 'check questions' to ask, these dealing with the respondent's understanding of each concept in the question that is to be tested. These 'check questions' will have been carefully de-signed at headquarters and the intensive interviewer must deliver them as specified. Their purpose is to find out how a particular term or concept was understood by the respondent.

6 The construction of these check questions by headquarters question designers will have been carried out on the lines illustra-ted in the following example.

7 Let the question to be tested be 'How many people are there in your household?'

The first step of the check question designer is to formulate, in precise language, the particular information that is needed, for example:

(a) Did the respondent understand that a *precise* count was wanted, or did he think he was being asked for *'about* how many'?

(b) Did the respondent include himself or herself in the count?

(c) To what period does the respondent think the question referred? Right now? Round about now? Over the last 12 months? Or what?

(d) How did the respondent interpret the term 'household'?

(e) Did the respondent think he was required to exclude at least some kinds of persons (e.g. baby; family members who have moved away permanently; lodgers who do not eat with the family (though they share bathroom facilities with the family); parents-in-law liv-ing with the family).

For each of these statements of what the question designer wants to know about the interpretation of the question, a check question or several check questions must be formulated. These check questions might take the following form:

(i) When you answered that question, were you giving me a *rough* count or an *exact* count?

(ii) When you answered that question, did you include yourself in the count?

(iii) When you told me how many people there are in your house-hold, what period were you referring to? Right now? A week ago?

Or what? What was the period your count actually referred to?

(iv) When you answered that question, what exactly did you think I meant by 'household'? (Probe for a full definition. If you get an evasive or a vague reply, clarify it).

(v) If a man was saying how many people there were in his household, should he include these people in his count?

His baby son? Yes/No

A lodger who does not eat with the rest of the family? Yes/No

A daughter who has now moved permanently away? Yes/No

A family member who is on holiday for a month? Yes/No

A student son who lives in a college most of the year but comes home during holidays? Yes/No

A father-in-law who eats and mixes with the family. Yes/No

8 These are the questions which would in this instance be passed to the question-testing interviewer to deliver in the second stage of her test of the question about household size. The question-testing interviewer would deliver them, entering the responses on her questionnaire but fully tape-recording the exchange.

9 If the question-testing interviewer has any remaining puzzles or hunches about the respondent's understanding of the question (from the Stage 1 or the Stage 2 procedures) she may deal with them now, under free interviewing conditions.

10 Once this has been done, the question-testing interviewer moves on to her next test question, going through the same two-stage procedure.

11 The several question-testing interviewers will between them straddle all the questions that are to be tested. But it is good policy to see that any one question-testing interviewer deals with the same small number of test questions in each of her interviews.

12 At the end of her interviewing day, the question-testing interviewer must write down for each respondent and each question what the respondent's interpretation of the question was, e.g:

(a) Apart from yourself, how many people are in permanent residence here within the premises that you call your home?

(b) Exactly how many people including yourself live in this house and have in general been sharing eating facilities here over recent months?

(c) Excluding any lodgers but including yourself, how many people currently live here as one family unit?

394

(d)   How many adults, excluding yourself, share this address with you?

(e)   Excluding yourself, what is the usual size of your family unit living here?

(f)   How many people are there in your flat who watch television, including yourself?

When there is doubt or ambiguity, the question-testing interviewer must make a record of this. She must in any case pass a tape-recording of each interview back to headquarters along with her report on the respondent's understanding of the question tested.

Recruiting and training the question testers

If a research organisation has its own force of a hundred or so interviewers, it is very likely that suitable individuals for training as question testers will be found within that force. Certainly there is no case for assuming that they must be clinical psychologists or other specialists. The vital characteristic is intellectual brightness associated with a detective mentality. It is necessary in addition that the candidates for training in question testing be sufficiently flexible regarding dress and personal manners to be acceptable to any social class; that they be empathetic without being naive; that they be conscientious. Physical and mental durability is also important.

In building up a small force of question testers, it is desirable to work through a selection-training arrangement, starting the training with perhaps twice as many candidates as are needed and using the training process to identify the better of them. A week of practical training is usually sufficient to sort out the promising people from the others. Training must include the techniques of probing and this must be fully integrated into the techniques of question testing itself. Training is *continued* both through the correction of interviewer performance as revealed by study of the tape recordings and through special training sessions periodically imposed on the interviewers.

Whereas the bulk of question testing must be done by these specially trained interviewers, it is essential that the young or new research officer should do some of it in his or her early period of employment as a researcher. That will bring home to him the realities of respondent misunderstanding of questions (along with much else as well). Furthermore, the question designer, however mature he is in that role, should from time to time take his own questions into the field for testing on the lines suggested. That can be a painful but enlightening experience.

10 Seeing the results and recommendations in proper perspective

The results presented in this book must be seen in proper perspective. Above all, we must guard against pessimistic conclusions about the value of research findings based upon questions asked in survey interviews. To this end, the following points must be kept in mind.

1 On some occasions, the misinterpretation of part of a question may in fact make no difference to the answer given. Thus what one 'usually' does may be the same as what one did on the particular evening asked about; the respondent's hearing of only the first of two alternatives may mean that the first alternative suited his position exactly; the substituting of 'you and your husband' for 'you' may make little difference if the respondent and her husband normally do their viewing together.

2 Then again, respondent error, arising out of misinterpretations of a question are unlikely to be all in the one direction—error in one direction may be partly cancelled out by error in the opposite direction.

3 Many of the points of failure detected in the 29 test questions occur very commonly indeed in questionnaires generally; nonetheless, the principles governing the formulation of most of the test questions seem likely to have rendered the latter somewhat more difficult than, say, a sample of questions drawn entirely at random.

4 Some research organisations are already using testing techniques of the kind recommended in the previous section, and additional ones too.

These considerations must be kept in mind in evaluating the findings. Moreover a good and experienced question designer will avoid the usual pitfalls. Nonetheless, there is no escaping the finding that misunderstandings of survey questions occurred in this enquiry at a major level. Accordingly there seems to be no alternative to the application, on a systematic basis, of genuine question-testing procedures. The question designer who uses the question-testing method will discover his failures and be in a position to do something about them. With each new testing operation undertaken he adds to his knowledge about question design and increasingly becomes the competent craftsman.

But what about the person who would simply dismiss the findings on

396

the grounds that most of the questions tested had difficulties built into them? Well, the following points must be carefully noted.

1 The inbuilt difficulties were of a kind that occur quite often in the day-to-day question design work of members of the social and the commercial research professions.

2 A great many of the instances of misunderstanding appear to have been quite independent of the inbuilt difficulties.

3 Five of the questions did not have difficulties specially built into them and they were subject to misunderstanding in much the same way as the 24 with built-in difficulties.

4 The testing of ordinary survey questions in the way advocated in Chapter 9 usually brings out evidence of misunderstanding at a substantial level.

There is no escaping the fact that question misunderstanding is a constant threat and that standard piloting of the questionnaire is no guarantee of safety. Direct question testing is essential.

There is of course the plea that the economics of survey research do not allow question testing. One often hears this view expressed along with a similar type of claim to the effect that the economics of survey research do not allow the rigorous training of interviewers. I have no sympathy for that sort of view. The economics of survey research will in that case have to be revised and I would expect the professional research organisation to put a major effort into making the testing of questions a necessary feature of both social and business investigations. The relatively low cost of doing this should be built into the estimated cost of the work. And above all, it is essential that the client who receives estimates for research he wants done should check to see that the testing of questions is provided for in that estimate.

The technology of social and business research based upon the survey interview questionnaire has come a long way in the past four decades. But that technology is still in a state of development. It still has a long way to go if it is to give us information that we can rely upon as being valid. Genuine question testing and a growing knowledge of the principles and processes of question misunderstanding are both overdue as additions to such a technology.

References

1 Belson, W. A., *Studies in Readership,* Business Publications Limited, London, 1962.
2 Cantril, H. and Fried, E., 'The meaning of questions' in Cantril, H. et al, *Gauging Public Opinion,* Princeton University Press, Princeton, 1944.
3 Campbell, A., 'Polling, open interviewing, and the problem of interpretation', *Journal of Social Issues,* Vol.2, No.4, 1946.
4 Terris, F., 'Are poll questions too difficult?', *Public Opinion Quarterly,* Vol.13, No.2, 1949.
5 Chall, J. S., *Readability: an Appraisal of Research and Application,* Ohio State University, Columbus, Ohio, 1958.
6 Nuckols, R. C., 'Verbi!', *International Journal of Opinion and Attitude Research,* Vol.3, No.4, 1949.
7 Nuckols, R. C., 'A note on pre-testing public opinion questions', *Journal of Applied Psychology,* Vol.37, No.2, 1953.
8 Klare, G. R., 'Understandability and indefinite answers to public opinion questions', *International Journal of Opinion and Attitude Research,* Vol.4, No.1, 1950.
9 Vernon, P. E., *An Investigation into the Intelligibility of Educational Broadcasts,* LR/50/2328, BBC, London, 1950.
10 Belson, W. A., *An Enquiry into the Comprehensibility of 'Topic for Tonight',* LR/52/1080, BBC, London, 1952.
11 Mass Observation, *The Language of Leadership,* Mass Observation, London, 1947.
12 Belson, W. A., *Facts and Figures: Knowledge of Words, Concepts and Events,* LR/54/498, BBC, London, 1954.
13 Gordon, W. D., 'Double Interview', in *New Developments in Research,* Market Research Society with the Oakwood Press, London, 1963.

PART II

APPENDIX

The appendix to this report
is presented here through the
sheets of microfiche inside
the back cover.